Your All-in-One Resource

On the CD that accompanies this book, you'll find additional resources to extend your learning.

The reference library includes the following fully searchable titles:

- *Microsoft Computer Dictionary*, 5th ed.
- *First Look 2007 Microsoft Office System* by Katherine Murray
- Windows Vista Product Guide

Also provided are a sample chapter and poster from *Look Both Ways: Help Protect Your Family on the Internet* by Linda Criddle

The CD interface has a new look. You can use the tabs for an assortment of tasks:

- Check for book updates (if you have Internet access)
- Install the book's practice file
- Go online for product support or CD support
- Send us feedback

The following screen shot gives you a glimpse of the new interface.

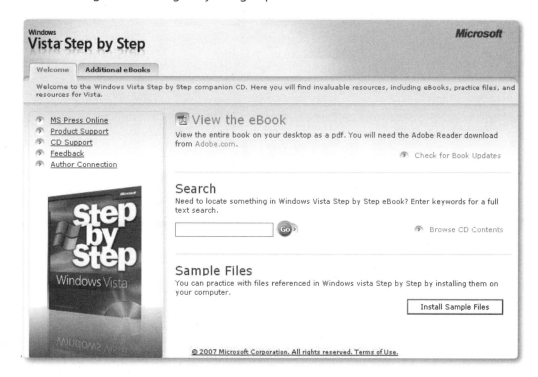

Microsoft®

Microsoft® Office Outlook® 2007 Step by Step

Joan Preppernau and Joyce Cox

PUBLISHED BY
Microsoft Press
A Division of Microsoft Corporation
One Microsoft Way
Redmond, Washington 98052-6399

Library of Congress Control Number: 2006937019

Printed and bound in the United States of America.

1 2 3 4 5 6 7 8 9   QWT   2 1 0 9 8 7

Distributed in Canada by H.B. Fenn and Company Ltd.

A CIP catalogue record for this book is available from the British Library.

Microsoft Press books are available through booksellers and distributors worldwide. For further information about international editions, contact your local Microsoft Corporation office or contact Microsoft Press International directly at fax (425) 936-7329. Visit our Web site at www.microsoft.com/mspress. Send comments to mspinput@microsoft.com.

Microsoft, Microsoft Press, Access, ActiveX, Aero, Calibri, Excel, Groove, Hotmail, InfoPath, Internet Explorer, OneNote, Outlook, PowerPoint, SharePoint, Visio, Windows, Windows Live, Windows Mobile, Windows Server, and Windows Vista are either registered trademarks or trademarks of Microsoft Corporation in the United States and/or other countries. Other product and company names mentioned herein may be the trademarks of their respective owners.

The example companies, organizations, products, domain names, e-mail addresses, logos, people, places, and events depicted herein are fictitious. No association with any real company, organization, product, domain name, e-mail address, logo, person, place, or event is intended or should be inferred.

This book expresses the author's views and opinions. The information contained in this book is provided without any express, statutory, or implied warranties. Neither the authors, Microsoft Corporation, nor its resellers, or distributors will be held liable for any damages caused or alleged to be caused either directly or indirectly by this book.

Acquisitions Editor: Juliana Aldous Atkinson
Project Editor: Sandra Haynes

Body Part No. X12-64023

Contents

About the Authors ix

Introducing Outlook 2007 xi

    What's New in Outlook 2007 xii

    Let's Get Started! xiv

Information for Readers Running Windows XP xv

    Managing the Practice Files xv

    Using the Start Menu xvi

    Navigating Dialog Boxes xvii

The Microsoft Business Certification Program xix

    Selecting a Certification Path xx

    Becoming a Microsoft Certified Application Specialist .xxi

    Taking a Microsoft Business Certification Exam xxi

    For More Information xxii

Features and Conventions of This Book xxiii

Using the Book's CD xxv

    What's on the CD? xxv

    Minimum System Requirements xxvi

    Installing the Practice Files xxviii

    Using the Practice Files xxviii

    Removing and Uninstalling the Practice Files xxix

Getting Help xxxi

    Getting Help with This Book and Its Companion CD xxxi

    Getting Help with Microsoft Office Outlook 2007 xxxi

    More Information xxxv

Quick Reference xxxvii

What do you think of this book? We want to hear from you!

Microsoft is interested in hearing your feedback so we can continually improve our books and learning resources for you. To participate in a brief online survey, please visit:

www.microsoft.com/learning/booksurvey/

1   Getting Started with Outlook 2007   **1**

    Sidebar: Different Types of E-Mail Accounts..............................2

    Connecting to Your Primary E-Mail Account 3

    Troubleshooting the Startup Wizard 7

    Connecting to Additional E-Mail Accounts.............................9

    Creating Additional Outlook Profiles 12

        Sidebar: Outlook with Business Contact Manager.....................13

    Personalizing Your Outlook Workspace 17

    Exploring the Advanced Toolbar.....................................25

    Key Points 27

2   Managing Contact Information   **29**

    Working in the Contact Window 30

        Sidebar: Importing SharePoint Contacts Lists.......................31

    Saving and Updating Contact Information............................37

        Sidebar: Quickly Communicating with Contacts 44

    Organizing Contacts by Using Color Categories 44

    Creating a Distribution List 46

    Personalizing an Electronic Business Card...........................49

    Creating an Additional Address Book 52

        Sidebar: Sharing Address Books 53

        Sidebar: Exporting Address Books 56

    Displaying Different Views of Contact Information....................56

    Quickly Locating Contact Information...............................62

    Printing Contact Information.......................................65

        Sidebar: Creating a OneNote Page Linked to a Contact Record...........71

    Key Points 71

3   Sending E-Mail Messages   **73**

    Working in the Message Window.....................................74

        Sidebar: Outlook Message Formats 80

    Creating and Sending Messages.....................................81

    Attaching Files to Messages 87

        Sidebar: Resending and Recalling Messages.........................88

        Sidebar: Sending Contact Information..............................91

    Creating and Formatting Business Graphics.........................92

        Sidebar: Changing Message Settings and Delivery Options 98

Personalizing the Appearance of Messages 100
Adding Signatures to Messages Automatically 106
Key Points 111

4   Handling E-Mail Messages   113

Viewing Messages and Message Attachments. 114
    Sidebar: Marking Messages as Read. 116
Replying to and Forwarding Messages 121
    Sidebar: Deleting Messages. 125
Working with New Mail Notifications 126
Creating a Task or an Appointment from a Message 130
Printing Messages 136
Key Points 141

5   Managing Your Inbox   143

Quickly Locating Messages 144
Arranging Messages in Different Ways 148
    Sidebar: Using Search Folders 160
Organizing Messages by Using Color Categories 161
Organizing Messages in Folders. 165
    Sidebar: Creating a OneNote Page from an E-Mail Message 168
Archiving Messages. 169
Key Points 173

6   Managing Appointments, Events, and Meetings   175

Working in the Calendar Item Windows 176
Scheduling and Changing Appointments 182
Scheduling and Changing Events 186
Scheduling, Updating, and Canceling Meetings 188
    Sidebar: Using the Exchange Server 2007 Smart Scheduling Feature 189
Responding to Meeting Requests. 192
    Sidebar: Creating a Meeting Workspace 193
Key Points 195

7   Managing Your Calendar   197

Displaying Different Views of a Calendar 198
    Sidebar: Adding and Removing Local Holidays 203
Defining Your Available Time 204

Configuring Outlook for Multiple Time Zones. 206
Printing a Calendar 207
    Sidebar: Saving Calendar Information as a Web Page 212
Sending Calendar Information in an E-Mail Message. 213
    Sidebar: Creating a OneNote Page Linked to an Appointment,
    an Event, or a Meeting 216
Linking to an Internet Calendar 216
Working with Multiple Calendars. 218
    Sidebar: Delegating Control of Your Calendar 220
Key Points 221

8   Tracking Tasks   **223**
Working in the Task Window. 224
Displaying Different Views of Tasks 229
    Sidebar: Finding and Organizing Tasks 231
Creating and Updating Tasks. 231
Managing Task Assignments 238
Removing Tasks from Your Task List. 240
    Sidebar: Tracking and Updating Tasks Created in OneNote 243
Key Points 243

9   Gathering Information   **245**
Subscribing to RSS Feeds 246
Participating in Newsgroups 250
Recording Information by Using Notes 251
Linking Notes to Contacts 254
    Sidebar: Recording Information in the Journal. 256
    Sidebar: Saving a Note as a File. 257
Sharing Notes. 257
Key Points 259

10   Collaborating with Other People   **261**
Sharing Your Folders with Other People 262
Accessing Other People's Folders. 266
Creating a Document Workspace from Outlook 269
    Sidebar: Creating Group Schedules 271
Working Offline with Document Library Contents 272
Connecting to a SharePoint Calendar 274

Key Points 275

11   Working Away from Your Office   277

Connecting Outlook to Your Server from a Remote Location. 278

Sidebar: Connecting Through OWA. 283

Working with Outlook Items While Offline. 283

Sidebar: Viewing Contacts While Offline. 286

Automatically Responding to Messages 287

Key Points 295

12   Customizing and Configuring Outlook   297

Making Favorite Outlook Commands Easily Accessible 298

Personalizing Your Office and Outlook Settings 301

Sidebar: Creating Outlook Forms 305

Sidebar: Adding and Removing Toolbar Commands. 306

Creating Rules to Process Messages. 307

Storing E-Mail Messages on Your Computer 314

Securing Your E-Mail. 317

Sidebar: Protecting Your Privacy. 322

Blocking Unwanted Messages. 323

Specifying Advanced E-Mail Options. 327

Key Points 329

Glossary **333**

Index. **339**

What do you think of this book? We want to hear from you!

Microsoft is interested in hearing your feedback so we can continually improve our books and learning resources for you. To participate in a brief online survey, please visit:

www.microsoft.com/learning/booksurvey/

About the Authors

Joan Preppernau

Joan is the author of more than a dozen books about Windows and Office, including the popular *Microsoft Windows XP Step by Step*, and a contributor to the development of the Microsoft certification exams for the 2007 Office system and Windows Vista. Having learned about computers literally at her father's knee, Joan's wide-ranging experiences in various facets of the computer industry contribute to her enthusiasm for producing interesting, useful, and reader-friendly training materials. Joan is the President of Online Training Solutions, Inc. (OTSI) and an avid telecommuter. The power of the Internet and an obsession with technology have made it possible for Joan to live and work in New Zealand, Sweden, Denmark, and various locations in the U.S. during the past 15 years. Having finally discovered the delights of a daily dose of sunshine, Joan has recently settled in San Diego, California, with her husband Barry and their daughter Trinity.

Joyce Cox

Joyce has 25 years' experience in the development of training materials about technical subjects for non-technical audiences, and is the author of dozens of books about Office and Windows technologies. She is the Vice President of Online Training Solutions, Inc. (OTSI). She was President of and principal author for Online Press, where she developed the *Quick Course* series of computer training books for beginning and intermediate adult learners. She was also the first managing editor of Microsoft Press, an editor for Sybex, and an editor for the University of California. Joyce and her husband Ted live in downtown Bellevue, Washington, and escape as often as they can to their tiny, offline cabin in the Cascade foothills.

The Team

Without the support of the hard-working members of the OTSI publishing team, this book would not exist. Susie Bayers and Marlene Lambert guided the editorial process, and Robert (RJ) Cadranell guided the production process. Jaime Odell copyedited the book, and Jan Bednarczuk created its index. Lisa Van Every laid out the book using Adobe InDesign, and Jeanne Craver processed the graphics. Another important member of our team, Microsoft Press Series Editor Sandra Haynes, provided invaluable support throughout the writing and production processes.

Online Training Solutions, Inc. (OTSI)

OTSI specializes in the design, creation, and production of Office and Windows training products for information workers and home computer users. For more information about OTSI, visit

www.otsi.com

Introducing Outlook 2007

Bill Gates's dream of "a computer on every desktop" is becoming more and more of a reality—many people today work (and play) on computers both in the office and at home. For people who spend much of the day at a computer and are dependent on electronic messages as a means of communicating with colleagues, clients, friends, and family members, Microsoft Office Outlook 2007 offers an ideal solution. Outlook 2007 integrates e-mail, address books, calendars, task lists, note pads, and more into one place, and more importantly, makes this information immediately available to you when you need it. From one window, you can work with e-mail messages, find contact information, view upcoming appointments, and track tasks. From one place, you can quickly search your messages (and message attachments) and organize your work more easily and in a more intuitive way. You can use Outlook to:

- Send, receive, organize, and archive e-mail messages.
- Send documents, spreadsheets, graphics, and other files as message attachments, and preview attachments you receive from other people.
- Schedule events, appointments, and meetings, invite attendees, and reserve conference rooms, projectors, and other managed resources.
- View upcoming appointments and tasks, and receive reminders for them.
- Store contact information in a transferable format that easily interacts with your e-mail system.
- Track tasks for yourself or for someone else, and schedule time to complete your tasks.
- Store random bits of information as notes.
- Share schedule information with other people, inside and outside your organization.
- Track the interactions you have with other people.
- Organize and easily locate information in messages, attachments, calendars, contacts, and tasks.
- Filter out annoying junk mail.
- Have information from favorite Web sites delivered directly to you.

What's New in Outlook 2007

The basic concepts of Outlook remain the same in the 2007 release as in earlier versions, with a few additions. The biggest improvement in this version is the way that the various functions and tools have been linked and organized, making it much easier to use all the tools from one place. The biggest change in this version is in the way tools and commands are available in the Outlook item windows. Instead of the traditional menus and toolbars which are still present in the program window), commands in the message, contact, appointment, and other item windows are organized in groups by function. The groups are organized on tabs by process, and all the tabs are organized on the "Ribbon" that is part of the user interface of several programs in the 2007 Microsoft Office system.

The new command structure might take some getting used to, but if you use other Office programs, you'll find that you can come up to speed pretty quickly.

If you're upgrading to Outlook 2007 from a previous version, you're probably more interested in the differences between the old and new versions and how they will affect you than you are in the basic functionality of Outlook. We don't identify new features with a special margin icon (as we did in previous versions of this book). We do, however, list them here. The following sections list new features introduced in Outlook 2007 and Outlook 2003. Throughout this book, we include special discussions about features that are new in Outlook 2007, including the benefits of the feature, how to use it, and any potential problems you might encounter.

> **Tip** Included in the back of this book is a four-color poster provided for your reference. This convenient guide points out some of the best new features of the redesigned Office user interface and includes tips to get you started. You will learn about these features and many more while working through this book.

If You Are Upgrading from Outlook 2003

If you have been using Outlook 2003, you might not expect to see many improvements in Outlook 2007, but you will soon realize that this is not just an incremental upgrade to what seemed like a pretty comprehensive set of features and tools. Outlook 2007 includes a long list of new and improved features, including the following:

- **Redesigned user interface.** Compose, format, and act upon information in a more accessible, intuitive way.

- **To-Do Bar.** View your appointments and tasks for the day.

- **Instant Search.** Search for keywords, dates, or other criteria in your e-mail messages, calendar, contact records, or task list.

- **Calendar functionalities.** Create and publish Internet calendars, and e-mail calendar snapshots.

- **Share information in one interface.** Interact with Microsoft Windows SharePoint Services to share and manage information.

- **Color Categories.** Easily personalize and add categories to e-mail, calendar items, contacts, or tasks.

- **View your Really Simple Syndication (RSS) feeds.** Catch up on the latest news or blogs right from within Outlook.

- **Attachment Preview.** Preview your attachments directly in the Reading Pane.

If You Are Upgrading from Outlook 2002

In addition to the features listed in the previous section, if you're upgrading from Outlook 2002 (part of the Microsoft Office XP system), you'll want to take note of the following new features that were introduced in Outlook 2003:

- **Navigation Pane.** Quickly access your mail, calendar, contacts, tasks, and other Outlook items.

- **Reading Pane.** Open attachments without opening the item.

- **Desktop Alerts.** Read and respond to an e-mail message without closing other applications.

- **Shared Attachments.** Post attachments for group input.

- **Arrangements.** View your messages in any of 13 predefined views.

- **Quick Flags.** Quickly mark messages for follow-up.

- **Unique signature per account.** Assign a different signature to each Outlook account.

- **Arrange by Conversation.** View your messages in a new way.

- **Search Folders.** Collect and automatically update related information in virtual folders.

- **Rules.** Create and organize rules in an easier way.

- **Calendar View.** View your Calendar and the Date Navigator in a new, streamlined format.

- **Side-by-side calendars.** View multiple calendars at the same time.

- **Contact Picture.** Add a picture to an Address Book entry.

- **View SharePoint Team Services contacts.** See a list of contacts with whom you can share information.

- **RPC over HTTP.** Connect directly to your Microsoft Exchange Server from Outlook over the Internet.

- **Cached Exchange Mode.** Store a local copy of your mailbox on your computer.

- **Go menu.** Quickly switch between panes in the Navigation Pane.

- **New Data File Type (.pst).** Create a Personal Folders file.

- **Expand Distribution Lists in an e-mail message.** Display the individual names of Distribution List members to edit the recipients of a message.

- **Information Rights Management.** Create messages with restricted permission to prevent messages from being forwarded, printed, copied, or edited by unauthorized people.

- **Enhanced privacy features.** Block or allow external Web content such as pictures or sounds to display in e-mail messages, and prevent Web beacons from validating your e-mail address to junk mail senders.

Let's Get Started!

With this version, Outlook has truly come into its own as a full-fledged information management system, making it easier than ever to efficiently handle communications, schedules, and tasks all in one convenient location. We look forward to showing you around Microsoft Office Outlook 2007 and sharing with you our enthusiasm for this truly useful product.

Information for Readers Running Windows XP

The graphics and the operating system–related instructions in this book reflect the Windows Vista user interface. However, Windows Vista is not required; you can also use a computer running Microsoft Windows XP.

Most of the differences you will encounter when working through the exercises in this book on a computer running Windows XP center around appearance rather than functionality. For example, the Windows Vista Start button is round rather than rectangular and is not labeled with the word *Start*; window frames and window-management buttons look different; and if your system supports Windows Aero, the window frames might be transparent.

In this section, we provide steps for navigating to or through menus and dialog boxes in Windows XP that differ from those provided in the exercises in this book. For the most part, these differences are small enough that you will have no difficulty in completing the exercises.

Managing the Practice Files

The instructions given in the "Using the Book's CD" section are specific to Windows Vista. The only differences when installing, using, uninstalling, and removing the practice files supplied on the companion CD are the default installation location and the uninstall process.

On a computer running Windows Vista, the default installation location of the practice files is *Documents\MSP\SBS_Outlook2007*. On a computer running Windows XP, the default installation location is *My Documents\MSP\SBS_Outlook2007*. If your computer is running Windows XP, whenever an exercise tells you to navigate to your *Documents* folder, you should instead go to your *My Documents* folder.

To uninstall the practice files from a computer running Windows XP:

1. On the Windows taskbar, click the **Start** button, and then click **Control Panel**.

2. In **Control Panel**, click (or in Classic view, double-click) **Add or Remove Programs**.

3. In the **Add or Remove Programs** window, click **Microsoft Office Outlook 2007 Step by Step**, and then click **Remove**.

4. In the **Add or Remove Programs** message box asking you to confirm the deletion, click **Yes**.

> **Important** If you need help installing or uninstalling the practice files, please see the "Getting Help" section later in this book. Microsoft Product Support Services does not provide support for this book or its companion CD.

Using the Start Menu

To start Outlook 2007 on a computer running Windows XP:

→ Click the **Start** button, point to **All Programs**, click **Microsoft Office**, and then click **Microsoft Office Outlook 2007**.

Folders on the Windows Vista Start menu expand vertically. Folders on the Windows XP Start menu expand horizontally. You will notice this variation between the images shown in this book and your Start menu.

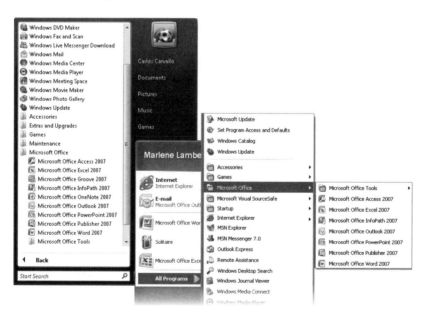

Navigating Dialog Boxes

On a computer running Windows XP, some of the dialog boxes you will work with in the exercises not only look different from the graphics shown in this book but also work differently. These dialog boxes are primarily those that act as an interface between Outlook and the operating system, including any dialog box in which you navigate to a specific location. For example, here are the Insert File dialog boxes from Outlook 2007 running on Windows Vista and Windows XP and some examples of ways to navigate in them.

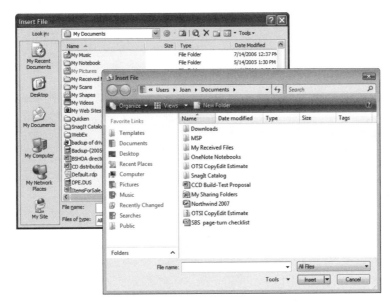

To navigate to the *Chapter01* folder in Windows Vista:

→ In the **Favorite Links** pane, click **Documents**. Then in the folder content pane, double-click **MSP**, **SBS_Outlook2007**, and double-click **Chapter01**.

To move back to the *SBS_Outlook2007* folder in Windows Vista:

Back

→ In the upper-left corner of the dialog box, click the **Back** button.

To navigate to the *Chapter01* folder in Windows XP:

→ On the **Places** bar, click **My Documents**. Then in the folder content pane, double-click **MSP**, double-click **SBS_Outlook2007**, and then double-click **Chapter01**.

To move back to the *SBS_Outlook2007* folder in Windows XP:

Up One Level

→ On the toolbar, click the **Up One Level** button.

The Microsoft Business Certification Program

Desktop computing proficiency is becoming increasingly important in today's business world. As a result, when screening, hiring, and training employees, more employers are relying on the objectivity and consistency of technology certification to ensure the competence of their workforce. As an employee or job seeker, you can use technology certification to prove that you already have the skills you need to succeed, saving current and future employers the trouble and expense of training you.

The Microsoft Business Certification program is designed to assist employees in validating their Windows Vista skills and 2007 Microsoft Office program skills. There are two paths to certification:

- A Microsoft Certified Application Specialist (MCAS) is an individual who has demonstrated worldwide skill standards for Windows Vista or the 2007 Microsoft Office suite through a certification exam in Windows Vista or in one or more of the 2007 Microsoft Office programs, including Microsoft Office Word 2007, Microsoft Office Excel 2007, Microsoft Office PowerPoint 2007, Microsoft Office Outlook 2007, and Microsoft Office Access 2007.

- A Microsoft Certified Application Professional (MCAP) is an individual who has taken his or her knowledge of the 2007 Microsoft Office suite and of Microsoft SharePoint products and technologies to the next level and has demonstrated through a certification exam that he or she can use the collaborative power of the Office suite to accomplish job functions such as Budget Analysis and Forecasting, or Content Management and Collaboration.

After attaining certification, you can include the MCAS or MCAP logo with the appropriate certification designator on your business cards and other personal promotional materials. This logo attests to the fact that you are proficient in the applications or cross-application skills necessary to achieve the certification.

Selecting a Certification Path

When selecting the Microsoft Business Certification path that you would like to pursue, you should assess the following:

- The program and program version(s) with which you are familiar
- The length of time you have used the program
- Whether you have had formal or informal training in the use of that program

Candidates for MCAS-level certification are expected to successfully complete a wide range of standard business tasks, such as formatting a document or spreadsheet. Successful candidates generally have six or more months of experience with Windows Vista or the specific Office the program, including either formal, instructor-led training or self-study using MCAS-approved books, guides, or interactive computer-based materials.

Candidates for MCAP-level certification are expected to successfully complete more complex, business-oriented tasks utilizing advanced functionality with the combined 2007 Microsoft Office suite of products. Successful candidates generally have between six months and one or more years of experience with the programs, including formal, instructor-led training or self-study using MCAP-approved materials.

Becoming a Microsoft Certified Application Specialist—Microsoft Office Outlook 2007

Every MCAS and MCAP certification exam is developed from a set of exam skill standards that are derived from studies of how Windows Vista and the 2007 Office programs are used in the workplace. Because these skill standards dictate the scope of each exam, they provide you with critical information on how to prepare for certification.

To become certified as a Microsoft Certified Application Specialist for Microsoft Office Outlook 2007, you must demonstrate proficiency in these five areas:

- **Managing messaging.** You must demonstrate the ability to create, send, reply to, and forward e-mail messages; create automatic signatures and reply messages; attach files to messages; preview, save, and open attachments; set message sensitivity, importance, security, and delivery options; and view messages in different ways.

- **Managing scheduling.** You must demonstrate the ability to create one-time and recurring appointments, meetings, and events, from scratch and from e-mail messages and tasks; schedule meetings and update, cancel, and respond to meeting requests; customize your work week, time zones, and holidays; share and publish your calendar; and view other calendars.

- **Managing tasks.** You must demonstrate the ability to create and modify one-time and recurring tasks from scratch and from messages; set the status, priority, and percent completion of a task and mark it as complete or private; and assign tasks to others and respond to tasks assigned by others.

- **Managing contacts and personal contact information.** You must demonstrate the ability to create and modify contacts from scratch or from messages, electronic business cards, and contact records; create and send an electronic business card, and use it as a signature; create and modify distribution lists; and create or import a secondary address book.

- **Organizing information.** You must demonstrate the ability to categorize and sort messages, appointments, meetings, contacts, and tasks by color; create and manage data files; create and populate mail folders; manage deleted, sent, and junk messages; locate specific messages, appointments, tasks, or contacts; create, modify, and remove rules to manage messages; customize the Outlook environment; and configure Office Outlook 2007 to be accessible over the Internet.

Taking a Microsoft Business Certification Exam

The MCAS and MCAP certification exams for Windows Vista and the 2007 Office programs are performance-based and require you to complete business-related tasks using an interactive simulation (a digital model) of the Windows Vista operating system or one or more programs in the Office suite.

Test-Taking Tips

- Follow all instructions provided in each question completely and accurately.

- Enter requested information as it appears in the instructions, but without duplicating the formatting unless you are specifically instructed to do otherwise. For example, the text and values you are asked to enter might appear in the instructions in bold and underlined (for example, **text**), but you should enter the information without applying these formats.

- Close all dialog boxes before proceeding to the next exam question unless you are specifically instructed otherwise.

- Don't close task panes before proceeding to the next exam question unless you are specifically instructed to do otherwise.

- If you are asked to print a document, spreadsheet, chart, report, or slide, perform the task, but be aware that nothing will actually be printed.

- Don't worry about extra keystrokes or mouse clicks. Your work is scored based on its result, not on the method you use to achieve that result (unless a specific method is indicated in the instructions), and not on the time you take to complete the question.

- If your computer becomes unstable during the exam (for example, if the exam does not respond or the mouse no longer functions) or if a power outage occurs, contact a testing center administrator immediately. The administrator will restart the computer and return the exam to the point where the interruption occurred with your score intact.

Certification

At the conclusion of the exam, you will receive a score report, which you can print with the assistance of the testing center administrator. If your score meets or exceeds the passing standard (the minimum required score), you will be mailed a printed certificate within approximately 14 days.

For More Information

To learn more about the Microsoft Certified Application Specialist exams and courseware, visit

http://www.microsoft.com/learning/mcp/mcas/

To learn more about the Microsoft Certified Application Professional exams and courseware, visit

http://www.microsoft.com/learning/mcp/mcap/

Features and Conventions of This Book

This book has been designed to lead you step by step through all the tasks you are most likely to want to perform in Microsoft Office Outlook 2007. If you start at the beginning and work your way through all the exercises, you will gain enough proficiency to be able to manage all types of information through Outlook. However, each topic is self contained. If you have worked with a previous version of Outlook, or if you completed all the exercises and later need help remembering how to perform a procedure, the following features of this book will help you locate specific information:

- **Detailed table of contents.** A listing of the topics and sidebars within each chapter.

- **Chapter thumb tabs.** Easily locate the beginning of the chapter you want.

- **Topic-specific running heads.** Within a chapter, quickly locate the topic you want by looking at the running head of odd-numbered pages.

- **Quick Reference.** General instructions for each procedure covered in specific detail elsewhere in the book. Refresh your memory about a task while working with your own documents.

- **Detailed index.** Look up specific tasks and features and general concepts in the index, which has been carefully crafted with the reader in mind.

- **Companion CD.** Contains the practice files needed for the step-by-step exercises, as well as a fully searchable electronic version of this book and other useful resources.

- **Full-color poster.** This handy reference guide introduces you to the basic features of the 2007 Microsoft Office system user interface, which you will learn more about in this book.

In addition, we provide a glossary of terms for those times when you need to look up the meaning of a word or the definition of a concept.

You can save time when you use this book by understanding how the *Step by Step* series shows special instructions, keys to press, buttons to click, and so on.

Convention	Meaning
(CD icon)	This icon at the end of a chapter introduction indicates information about the practice files provided on the companion CD for use in the chapter.
USE	This paragraph preceding a step-by-step exercise indicates the practice files that you will use when working through the exercise.
BE SURE TO	This paragraph preceding or following an exercise indicates any requirements you should attend to before beginning the exercise or actions you should take to restore your system after completing the exercise.
OPEN	This paragraph preceding a step-by-step exercise indicates files that you should open before beginning the exercise.
CLOSE	This paragraph following a step-by-step exercise provides instructions for closing open files or programs before moving on to another topic.
1 **2**	Blue numbered steps guide you through step-by-step exercises and Quick Reference versions of procedures.
1 2	Black numbered steps guide you through procedures in sidebars and expository text.
→	An arrow indicates a procedure that has only one step.
See Also	These paragraphs direct you to more information about a given topic in this book or elsewhere.
Troubleshooting	These paragraphs explain how to fix a common problem that might prevent you from continuing with an exercise.
Tip	These paragraphs provide a helpful hint or shortcut that makes working through a task easier, or information about other available options.
Important	These paragraphs point out information that you need to know to complete a procedure.
(Save button icon) Save	The first time you are told to click a button in an exercise, a picture of the button appears in the left margin. If the name of the button does not appear on the button itself, the name appears under the picture.
Enter	In step-by-step exercises, keys you must press appear as they would on a keyboard.
Ctrl + Home	A plus sign (+) between two key names means that you must hold down the first key while you press the second key. For example, "press Ctrl + Home" means "hold down the Ctrl key while you press the Home key."
Program interface elements	In steps, the names of program elements, such as buttons, commands, and dialog boxes, are shown in black bold characters.
User input	Anything you are supposed to type appears in blue bold characters.
Glossary terms	Terms that are explained in the glossary at the end of the book are shown in blue italic characters.

Using the Book's CD

The companion CD included with this book contains the practice files you'll use as you work through the book's exercises, as well as other electronic resources that will help you learn how to use Microsoft Office Outlook 2007.

What's on the CD?

The companion CD contains any practice files necessary to complete the exercises. In this book, you will create most of the practice files yourself while working through the initial exercises. This ensures that the practice files work with your system—for example, that e-mail messages are sent between real e-mail accounts.

The following table lists the practice files supplied on the book's CD.

Chapter	Files
Chapter 1: Getting Started with Outlook 2007	None
Chapter 2: Managing Contact Information	05_FourthCoffee.png
Chapter 3: Sending E-Mail Messages	03_Attaching.docx 03_Attaching.pptx
Chapter 4: Handling E-Mail Messages	None
Chapter 5: Managing Your Inbox	None
Chapter 6: Managing Appointments, Events, and Meetings	None
Chapter 7: Managing Your Calendar	None
Chapter 8: Tracking Tasks	None
Chapter 9: Gathering Information	None
Chapter 10: Collaborating with Other People	None
Chapter 11: Working Away from Your Office	None
Chapter 12: Customizing and Configuring Outlook	None

In addition to the practice files, the CD contains some exciting resources that will really enhance your ability to get the most out of using this book and Outlook 2007, including the following:

- *Microsoft Office Outlook 2007 Step by Step* in eBook format
- *Microsoft Computer Dictionary*, 5th ed. eBook
- *First Look 2007 Microsoft Office System* (Katherine Murray, 2006)
- Sample chapter and poster from *Look Both Ways: Help Protect Your Family on the Internet* (Linda Criddle, 2007)

> **Important** The companion CD for this book does not contain the Outlook 2007 software. You should purchase and install that program before using this book.

Minimum System Requirements

2007 Microsoft Office System

The 2007 Microsoft Office system includes the following programs:

- Microsoft Office Access 2007
- Microsoft Office Communicator 2007
- Microsoft Office Excel 2007
- Microsoft Office Groove 2007
- Microsoft Office InfoPath 2007
- Microsoft Office OneNote 2007
- Microsoft Office Outlook 2007
- Microsoft Office Outlook 2007 with Business Contact Manager
- Microsoft Office PowerPoint 2007
- Microsoft Office Publisher 2007
- Microsoft Office Word 2007

No single edition of the 2007 Office system installs all of the above programs. Specialty programs available separately include Microsoft Office Project 2007, Microsoft Office SharePoint Designer 2007, and Microsoft Office Visio 2007.

To install and run these programs, your computer needs to meet the following minimum requirements:

- 500 megahertz (MHz) processor
- 256 megabytes (MB) RAM
- CD or DVD drive
- 2 gigabytes (GB) available hard disk space; a portion of this disk space will be freed if you select the option to delete the installation files

> **Tip** Hard disk requirements will vary depending on configuration; custom installation choices might require more or less hard disk space.

- Monitor with 800×600 screen resolution; 1024×768 or higher recommended
- Keyboard and mouse or compatible pointing device
- Internet connection, 128 kilobits per second (Kbps) or greater, for download and activation of products, accessing Microsoft Office Online and online Help topics, and any other Internet-dependent processes
- Windows Vista or later, Microsoft Windows XP with Service Pack 2 (SP2), or Microsoft Windows Server 2003 or later
- Windows Internet Explorer 7 or Microsoft Internet Explorer 6 with service packs

The 2007 Microsoft Office suites, including Office Basic 2007, Office Home & Student 2007, Office Standard 2007, Office Small Business 2007, Office Professional 2007, Office Ultimate 2007, Office Professional Plus 2007, and Office Enterprise 2007, all have similar requirements.

Step-by-Step Exercises

In addition to the hardware, software, and connections required to run the 2007 Microsoft Office system, you will need the following to successfully complete the exercises in this book:

- Outlook 2007, PowerPoint 2007, and Word 2007
- Access to a printer
- 1 MB of available hard disk space for the practice files

Installing the Practice Files

You need to install the practice files in the correct location on your hard disk drive before you can use them in the exercises. Follow these steps:

1. Remove the companion CD from the envelope at the back of the book, and insert it into the CD drive of your computer.

   The Step By Step Companion CD License Terms appear. Follow the on-screen directions. To use the practice files, you must accept the terms of the license agreement. After you accept the license agreement, a menu screen appears.

   > **Important** If the menu screen does not appear, click the Start button, and then click Computer. Display the Folders list in the Navigation Pane, click the icon for your CD drive, and then in the right pane, double-click the StartCD executable file.

2. Click **Install Practice Files**.

3. Click **Next** on the first screen, and then click **Next** to accept the terms of the license agreement on the next screen.

4. If you want to install the practice files to a location other than the default folder (*Documents\MSP\SBS_Outlook2007*), click the **Change** button, select the new drive and path, and then click **OK**.

   > **Important** If you install the practice files to a location other than the default, you will need to substitute that path within the exercises.

5. Click **Next** on the **Choose Destination Location** screen, and then click **Install** on the **Ready to Install the Program** screen to install the selected practice files.

6. After the practice files have been installed, click **Finish**.

7. Close the **Step by Step Companion CD** window, remove the companion CD from the CD drive, and return it to the envelope at the back of the book.

Using the Practice Files

When you install the practice files from the companion CD that accompanies this book, the files are stored on your hard disk in chapter-specific subfolders under *Documents\MSP\SBS_Outlook2007*. Each exercise is preceded by a paragraph that lists the files needed for that exercise and explains any preparations needed before you start working through the exercise. Here are examples:

> **USE** the *Andrea Dunker* and *John Emory* contact records you created earlier in this chapter.
>
> **BE SURE TO** display the Contacts module before beginning this exercise.

You can browse to the practice files in Windows Explorer by following these steps:

Start

1. On the Windows taskbar, click the **Start** button, and then click **Documents**.

2. In your **Documents** folder, double-click **MSP**, double-click **SBS_Outlook2007**, and then double-click a specific chapter folder.

You can browse to the practice files from an Outlook 2007 dialog box by following these steps:

1. On the **Favorite Links** pane in the dialog box, click **Documents**.

2. In your **Documents** folder, double-click **MSP**, double-click **SBS_Outlook2007**, and then double-click the specified chapter folder.

Removing and Uninstalling the Practice Files

After you finish working through this book, delete the practice messages, appointments, contacts, and other Outlook items you created while working through the exercises, and then uninstall the practice files that were installed from the companion CD. Follow these steps:

Start

1. On the Windows taskbar, click the **Start** button, and then click **Control Panel**.

2. In **Control Panel**, under **Programs**, click the **Uninstall a program** task.

3. In the **Programs and Features** window, click **Microsoft Office Outlook 2007 Step by Step**, and then on the toolbar at the top of the window, click the **Uninstall** button.

4. If the **Programs and Features** message box asking you to confirm the deletion appears, click **Yes**.

See Also If you need additional help installing or uninstalling the practice files, see "Getting Help" later in this book.

> **Important** Microsoft Product Support Services does not provide support for this book or its companion CD.

Getting Help

Every effort has been made to ensure the accuracy of this book and the contents of its companion CD. If you do run into problems, please contact the sources listed below for assistance.

Getting Help with This Book and Its Companion CD

If your question or issue concerns the content of this book or its companion CD, please first search the online Microsoft Press Knowledge Base, which provides support information for known errors in or corrections to this book, at the following Web site:

www.microsoft.com/mspress/support/search.asp

If you do not find your answer at the online Knowledge Base, send your comments or questions to Microsoft Press Technical Support at:

mspinput@microsoft.com

Getting Help with Microsoft Office Outlook 2007

If your question is about Microsoft Office Outlook 2007, and not about the content of this Microsoft Press book, your first recourse is the Outlook Help system. This system is a combination of help tools and files stored on your computer when you installed the 2007 Microsoft Office system and, if your computer is connected to the Internet, information available from Microsoft Office Online.

To find out about an item on the screen, you can display a *ScreenTip*. For example, to display a ScreenTip for a button, point to the button without clicking it. The ScreenTip gives the button's name and, in most cases, a description of what it does when you click it.

In the Outlook program window, you can click the Microsoft Office Outlook Help button (a question mark in a blue circle) to display the Outlook Help window with information related to the functions of that dialog box.

When you have a question about using Outlook, you can type it in the Type A Question For Help box at the right end of the program window's menu bar. Then press Enter to display a list of Help topics from which you can select the one that most closely relates to your question.

If you want to practice getting help, you can work through this exercise, which demonstrates two ways of locating information.

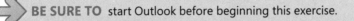

BE SURE TO start Outlook before beginning this exercise.

1. At the right end of the menu bar, click the **Type a question for help** box.

2. Type How do I get help?, and then press the ⎡Enter⎤ key.

   A list of topics that relate to your question appears in the Search Results task pane. If you have an active Internet connection, this list includes current content from Microsoft Office Online, so your results might vary from those shown here.

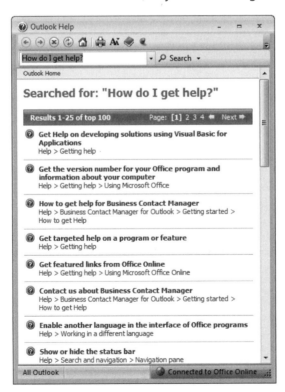

You can click any of the listed topics to get more information or instructions.

3. In the **Search Results** task pane, scroll the results list, and then click a topic that interests you.

   The Outlook Help window opens, displaying information about that topic.

Maximize

4. At the right end of the **Outlook Help** window's title bar, click the **Maximize** button, and then in the topic pane, click **Show All**.

   The topic content expands to provide in-depth information about getting help while you work.

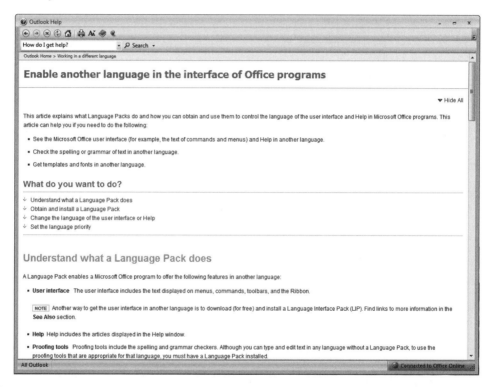

Close

5. At the right end of the Outlook Help window's title bar, click the **Close** button.

6. To access the Help system in a different way, on the **Help** menu, click **Microsoft Office Outlook Help**.

   Outlook Help opens, displaying a basic topic list from which you can browse to information.

Show Table of Contents

7. On the Outlook Help window's toolbar, click the **Table of Contents** button.

The Table Of Contents pane opens, displaying the same list in a tree structure that you can expand.

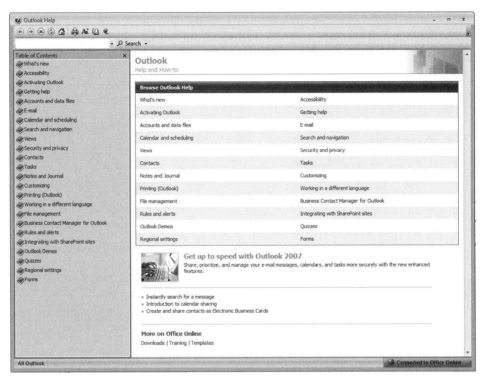

8. In the **Table of Contents** pane, click **E-mail**, click **Creating messages**, and then click **Save a message**.

   Outlook Help displays the Save A Message topic.

9. Experiment on your own with finding information in Outlook Help.

 CLOSE the Outlook Help window when you finish.

More Information

If your question is about Microsoft Office Outlook 2007 or another Microsoft software product and you cannot find the answer in the product's Help system, please search the appropriate product solution center or the Microsoft Knowledge Base at:

support.microsoft.com

In the United States, Microsoft software product support issues not covered by the Microsoft Knowledge Base are addressed by Microsoft Product Support Services. Location-specific software support options are available from:

support.microsoft.com/gp/selfoverview/

Quick Reference

1   Getting Started with Outlook 2007

To configure Outlook to connect to an e-mail account, page 3

1. On the **Start** menu, point to **All Programs**, click **Microsoft Office**, and then click **Microsoft Office Outlook 2007**.

2. On the welcome page of the **Outlook 2007 Startup** wizard, click **Next**.

3. On the **E-mail Upgrade Options** page, select the **Do not upgrade** option, and then click **Next**.

4. On the **E-mail Accounts** page, with the **Yes** option selected, click **Next**.

5. On the **Auto Account Setup** page, enter your name, e-mail address, and password in the corresponding text boxes, and then click **Next**.

To manually configure your Exchange Server account settings, page 8

1. On the **Start** menu, point to **All Programs**, click **Microsoft Office**, and then click **Microsoft Office Outlook 2007**.

2. On the welcome page of the **Outlook 2007 Startup** wizard, click **Next**.

3. On the **E-mail Upgrade Options** page, select the **Do not upgrade** option, and then click **Next**.

4. On the **E-mail Accounts** page, with the **Yes** option selected, click **Next**.

5. On the **Auto Account Setup** page select the **Manually configure server settings** check box, and then click **Next**.

6. On the **Choose E-mail Service** page, select the **Microsoft Exchange Server** option, and then click **Next**.

7. On the **Microsoft Exchange Settings** page, enter the name or address of your Exchange Server and your user name, and then click the **Check Name** button. If the **Connect to** dialog box appears, enter your logon information, and then click **OK**.

8. After your name is underlined, click **Next**, and then on the final page of the wizard, click **Finish**.

To connect to an additional e-mail account, page 10

1. On the **Tools** menu, click **Account Settings**.

2. On the **E-mail** tab of the **Account Settings** dialog box, click the **New** button.

3. On the **Choose E-mail Service** page of the **Add New E-mail Account** wizard, with the **Microsoft Exchange Server, POP3, IMAP, or HTTP** option selected, click **Next**.

4. On the **Auto Account Setup** page, enter the account display name, the e-mail address, and the password of the account you want to add to your profile. Then click **Next**.

5. Click **Finish** to complete the account setup.

To create an additional Outlook profile, page 14

1. Exit Outlook if it is running.

2. Display **Control Panel** in **Classic View**, and then double-click the **Mail** icon. In the **User Account Control** dialog box, if you're logged on as an administrator, click **Continue**. Otherwise, enter an administrator password, and then click **OK**.

3. In the **Mail Setup** dialog box, click the **Show Profiles** button.

4. In the **Mail** dialog box, click the **Add** button.

5. In the **Profile Name** box, type a name to identify the new profile, and then click **OK**.

6. On the **Choose E-mail Service** page, with the **Microsoft Exchange Server, POP3, or IMAP** option selected, click **Next**.

7. On the **Auto Account Setup** page, enter the name, e-mail address, and password in the corresponding text boxes, and then click **Next**.

8. After Outlook connects to the e-mail account, click **Finish**.

To configure Outlook to prompt for a profile when starting, page 14

1. Display **Control Panel** in **Classic View**, and then double-click the **Mail** icon. In the **User Account Control** dialog box, if you're logged on as an administrator, click **Continue**. Otherwise, enter an administrator password, and then click **OK**.

2. In the **Mail Setup** dialog box, click **Show Profiles**.

3. In the **Mail** dialog box, select the **Prompt for a profile to be used** option, and then click **OK**.

2 Managing Contact Information

To import information from a SharePoint Contacts List to your Outlook contacts folder, page 31

1. Display the SharePoint site in your Web browser, and then display the SharePoint Contacts List you want to import.

2. On the **Actions** menu, click **Link to Outlook**.

3. In the **Microsoft Office Outlook** message box asking whether you want to connect the SharePoint Contacts List to Outlook, click **Yes**.

To create a contact record, page 40

1. With the **Contacts** pane displayed, on the Standard toolbar, click the **New Contact** button.

   2. Enter the new contact information, and then on the **Contact** tab, in the **Actions** group, click the **Save & Close** button.

To edit a contact record, page 42

   1. In the **Contacts** pane, double-click the contact record to open it, and then edit or add information to the record.

   2. On the **Contact** tab, in the **Actions** group, click the **Save & Close** button.

To assign contact records to color categories, page 45

   1. In the **Contacts** pane, double-click the contact record you want to assign to a category.

   2. Do one of the following:

      ○ On the **Contact** tab, in the **Options** group, click the **Categorize** button, and click a category. Then in the **Actions** group, click the **Save & Close** button.

      ○ On the **Options** tab, click the **Categorize** button, and click **All Categories** to display the **Color Categories** dialog box. Then in the **Name** list, select any pertinent check boxes, and click **OK**.

To create a distribution list, page 47

   1. In the **New** list, click **Distribution List**.

   2. In the **Name** box, type a name for your list, and then in the **Members** group, click the **Select Members** button.

   3. If the **Select Members** dialog box is displaying an address book other than your Contacts list, in the **Address Book** list, under **Outlook Address Book**, click **Contacts**.

   4. In the **Name** list, click the names of the people you want to include, click the **Members** button, and then click **OK**.

   5. On the **Contact** tab, in the **Actions** group, click the **Save & Close** button.

To modify a business card, page 50

   1. In the **Contacts** pane, double-click the contact record to open it.

   2. On the **Contact** tab, in the **Options** group, click the **Business Card** button.

   3. In the **Card Design** area of the **Edit Business Card** dialog box, click **Background Color**.

   4. In the **Color** dialog box, click a color you like, and then click **OK**.

   5. To add or change an image, in the **Card Design** area, to the right of **Image**, click **Change**. Then browse to the folder containing the image, click the image, and click **OK**.

   6. In the **Image Area** box, type or select the image area size.

   7. In the **Image Align** list, click a type of alignment, and then click **OK**.

To share one or more address books with other people on your network, page 53

1. In the **Contacts** module **Navigation Pane**, under **My Contacts**, right-click the address book you want to share, and then click **Share**. Or if you want to share all your address books, in the **Navigation Pane**, click **Share My Contacts folder**.

2. In the **To** box of the **Sharing invitation** message, enter the names of people or distribution lists on your network with whom you want to share the address book.

3. If you are sharing your primary address book and want to request reciprocal permission, select the **Request permission to view recipient's Contacts folder** check box. If you are sharing a secondary address book and want to give the recipient full access, select the **Recipient can add, edit, and delete items in this contacts folder** check box.

4. Click **Send**.

To create a contacts folder, page 53

1. With the **Contacts** module displayed, in the **New Contact** list, click **Folder**.

2. In the **Name** box of the **Create New Folder** dialog box, type a name by which you want to identify the folder.

3. In the **Folder contains** list, click the type of folder you want to create.

4. In the **Select where to place the folder** list, click a location for the folder, and then click **OK**.

To export an address book, page 56

1. On the **File** menu, click **Import and Export**.

2. In the **Choose an action to perform** list, click **Export to a file**, and then click **Next**.

3. In the **Create a file of type** list, click **Personal Folder File (.pst)**, and then click **Next**.

4. In the **Select the folder to export from** list, click the contacts folder you want to export, and then click **Next**.

5. Click **Browse** to the right of the **Save exported file as** box. Then In the **Open Personal Folders** dialog box, select the location where you want to save the file.

6. Type the file name, click **OK**, and then click **Finish.**

To sort contact records, page 59

→ Click a column heading to sort the contact records in ascending order based on the column. Click the column heading again to reverse the sort.

To change how you view contact records, page 59

→ Select an option from the **Current View** list.

To locate a contact record by using Instant Search, page 63

→ At the top of the **Contacts** pane, click the **Search** box, and then type a search word.

→ To return to previous search results, at the right end of the **Search** box, click the **Show Instant Search Pane Menu** button, point to **Recent Searches**, and then select the search you want to use from the list.

To print a phone list, page 66

1. Select **Phone List** in the **Current View** list.

2. On the Standard toolbar, click the **Print** button. Then in the **Print range** area of the **Print** dialog box, ensure that the **All rows** option is selected, and click **OK**.

To print an address card for a contact, page 68

1. Select **Address Cards** in the **Current View** list.

2. In the **Contacts** pane, click the contact record for which you want to print a card.

3. On the Standard toolbar, click the **Print** button.

4. In the **Print** dialog box, scroll the **Print style** list and click **Card Style**.

5. Under **Print range**, select the **Only selected items** option, and then click **OK**.

To print address cards for multiple contacts, page 70

1. In the **Contacts** pane, click a contact record to select it.

2. Hold down the Ctrl key, and then click other contact records to add them to the selection.

3. On the Standard toolbar, click the **Print** button.

4. In the **Print style** list, be sure that **Card Style** is selected. Then in the **Print range** area, select the **Only selected items** option, and click **OK**.

To link one or more contact records to Microsoft Office OneNote, page 71

→ In the **Contacts** pane, select the contact record (or records) you want to link. Then on the Standard toolbar, click the **Open or create linked contact notes in OneNote** button.

3   Sending E-Mail Messages

To check addresses, page 82

→ If a message recipient's address is in your address book, type the person's name and either wait for Outlook to validate the name or press Ctrl+K to immediately validate it.

To have Outlook search additional address books, page 82

1. On the **Tools** menu, click **Address Book**. Then in the **Address Book** window, on the **Tools** menu, click **Options**.

2. In the **Addressing** dialog box, click **Add**.

3. In the **Add Address List** dialog box, click the address list you want to add, click **Add**, and then click **Close**.

4. In the **Addressing** dialog box, click **OK**, and then in the **Address Book** window, click the **Close** button.

To send a courtesy copy of a message, page 82

→ In the message window, enter an e-mail address in the **Cc** or **Bcc** box.

To display the Bcc field in an outgoing message, page 82

→ In the message window, on the **Options** tab, in the **Fields** group, click the **Show Bcc** button.

To compose and send a new e-mail message, page 83

1. On the Standard toolbar, click the **New Mail Message** button.

2. In the **To** box of the message window, type an e-mail address.

3. In the **Subject** box, enter the main idea of your message.

4. In the message content area, type the body of the message.

5. When you finish, click **Send**.

To recall a message, page 88

1. In the **Sent Items** folder, open the message you want to recall.

2. On the **Message** tab, in the **Actions** group, click the **Other Actions** button, and then click **Recall This Message**.

3. Select the option to delete unread copies of the message or to replace them with a new message, and then click **OK**.

To attach a file to an e-mail message, page 89

1. Display the message window.

2. On the **Message** tab, in the **Include** group, click the **Attach File** button (not the arrow under the button).

3. Browse to the file you want to attach, click it, and then click **Insert**.

To send a business card, page 91

1. Display the message window.

2. On the **Message** tab, in the **Include** group, click the **Insert Business Card** button, and then in the list, click **Other Business Cards**.

3. In the **Insert Business Card** dialog box, select the card or cards you want to send, and then click **OK**.

To create a SmartArt diagram within an e-mail message, page 92

1. Click to place the insertion point in the message content area.

2. On the **Insert** tab, in the **Illustrations** group, click the **SmartArt** button.

3. In the **SmartArt** gallery, click the diagram you want to create, and then click **OK**.

To format the text of an e-mail message, page 102

→ In the message content area, select the text you want to format. Then do one of the following:

  ○ Click formatting buttons on the **Mini toolbar**.

  ○ Click formatting buttons in the **Basic Text** group on the **Message** tab.

To apply a different theme to an outgoing e-mail message, page 104

1. In the message window, on the **Options** tab, in the **Themes** group, click the **Themes** button.

2. In the **Themes** gallery, click the theme you want.

To create a signature and insert it in all the new messages, page 107

1. On the **Tools** menu, click **Options**. On the **Mail Format** tab of the **Options** dialog box, click **Signatures**.

2. On the **E-mail Signature** tab of the **Signatures and Stationery** dialog box, click **New**.

3. In the **New Signature** dialog box, type a name for the signature, and then click **OK**.

4. In the signature content area, type a salutation, such as Regards, and a comma. Press the Enter key once or twice, and then type your name.

5. Add any other information you want to include, such as a telephone number, legal disclaimer, or link to your organization's Web site, and format the text and paragraphs the way you want them to appear in messages.

6. In the **Choose default signature** area of the **Signatures and Stationery** dialog box, in the **New messages** list, click the name you gave your signature. Then click **OK** twice.

4 Handling E-Mail Messages

To mark messages as read after previewing them in the Reading Pane, page 116

1. On the **Tools** menu, click **Options**. On the **Other** tab of the **Options** dialog box, in the **Outlook Panes** area, click **Reading Pane**.

2. In the **Reading Pane** dialog box, select the check box corresponding to the way you want Outlook to handle messages viewed in the Reading Pane, and then click **OK** twice.

To manually mark an e-mail message as read or unread, page 116

→ Right-click the message, and then click **Mark As Read** or **Mark As Unread**.

To preview and open a message attachment, page 118

1. In the **Reading Pane**, point to the **Message** button below the message header, and then point to the attachment to preview its name, type, and size.

2. Click the attachment, and then click the **Preview file** button.

3. In the **Reading Pane**, double-click the attachment. If Outlook prompts you to confirm that you want to open the file, click the **Open** button.

To reply to or forward messages, page 123

→ In the message window, on the **Message** tab, in the **Respond** group, click the **Reply**, **Reply to All**, or **Forward** button.

To instruct Outlook to close original messages after you respond to them, page 123

1. On the **Tools** menu, click **Options**. On the **Preferences** tab, of the **Options** dialog box, click **E-mail Options**.

2. In the **E-mail Options** dialog box, select the **Close original message on reply or forward** check box, and then click **OK** twice.

To customize your desktop alert settings, page 127

1. On the **Tools** menu, click **Options**. On the **Preferences** tab of the **Options** dialog box, click **E-mail Options**.

2. In the **E-mail Options** dialog box, click **Advanced E-mail Options**.

3. In the **Advanced E-mail Options** dialog box, click **Desktop Alert Settings**.

4. In the **Desktop Alert Settings** dialog box, set the duration and transparency as you want, previewing your changes as necessary. When you finish, click **OK** in each of the open dialog boxes.

To customize where you want desktop alerts to appear, page 129

1. On the **Tools** menu, click **Options**. On the **Preferences** tab of the **Options** dialog box, click **E-mail Options**.

2. In the **E-mail Options** dialog box, click **Advanced E-mail Options**.

3. In the **Advanced E-mail Options** dialog box, click **Desktop Alert Settings**.

4. Click **Preview**, drag the sample desktop alert to where you want it to appear on the screen, and then click **OK**.

To turn off desktop alerts, page 129

1. On the **Tools** menu, click **Options**. On the **Preferences** tab of the **Options** dialog box, click **E-mail Options**.

2. In the **E-mail Options** dialog box, click **Advanced E-mail Options**.

3. In the **Advanced E-mail Options** dialog box, clear the **Display a New Mail Desktop Alert** check box, and then click **OK**.

To quickly access the Desktop Alert Settings dialog box, page 129

→ When a desktop alert appears on your screen, click the **Options** button in the alert, and then click **Desktop Alert Settings**.

To mark a message as read through its desktop alert, page 130

→ When a desktop alert appears on your screen, point to it to keep it active, click its **Options** button, and then click **Mark as Read**.

To delete a message through its desktop alert, page 130

→ When the desktop alert appears on your screen, point to it, and then click its **Delete Item** button.

To specify a task due date other than the default when you flag a message, page 131

→ In the Inbox, right-click the flag in the message header, and then click the due date.

Or

1. Right-click the flag, and then click **Set Quick Click**.

2. In the **Set Quick Click** dialog box, click the due date you want, and then click **OK**.

To create a task from an e-mail message, page 132

→ In the Inbox, click the transparent flag at the right end of the message header.

To create an appointment based on a message, page 134

→ Drag the message from your Inbox, and drop it on the **Calendar** button at the bottom of the Navigation Pane.

To convert an appointment to an event, page 135

→ Open the appointment, and then select the **All day event** check box.

To convert an appointment to a meeting, page 135

1. Open the appointment.

2. On the **Appointment** tab, in the **Actions** group, click **Invite Attendees**.

3. In the **To** box that appears, type the e-mail addresses of the people you want to invite. Then click **Send**.

To set up a message for printing, page 136

1. In the message window, click the **Microsoft Office Button**, point to the **Print** arrow, and then click **Print Preview**.

2. In the **Print Preview** window, click the **Page Setup** button.

3. In the **Page Setup: Memo Style** dialog box, click the **Paper** tab to view and change the available options.

4. Click the **Header/Footer** tab, and then type the text you want to appear in the header and footer of the message.

5. To print the message, click **Print**.

5   Managing Your Inbox

To use Instant Search to locate a specific message, page 145

● In the **Search** box at the top of the Inbox, type a word contained in the message.

● To refine the search, click the **Expand the Query Builder** button to the right of the **Search** box, and supply additional information.

● To expand the search to include all the folders in your mailbox, at the bottom of the Search Results pane, click **Try searching again in All Mail Items**.

● To remove the search filter and view all messages, click the **Clear Search** button.

To change the display, arrangement, sort order, and grouping of messages, page 154

● On the **View** menu, point to **Arrange By**, and then click the command you want; or

● Click the column heading on which you want to sort messages. Click it again to reverse the order.

To expand or collapse groups, page 155

→ On the **View** menu, point to **Expand/Collapse Groups**, and then click the collapse or expand view you want.

To filter the Inbox content, page 155

→ On the **View** menu, point to **Current View**, and then click the view you want. Click **Messages** on the **Current View** list to remove the filter.

To add and remove fields, page 156

1. On the **View** menu, point to **Current View**, and then click **Customize Current View**.

2. In the **Customize View** dialog box, click the **Fields** button.

3. To add fields, in the **Available fields** list of the **Show Fields** dialog box, click the fields you want to add, and then click **Add**.

4. To remove fields in any list view, drag the column heading downward, and release the mouse button when a large black X appears over the heading.

To change the order of columns in any view, page 158

→ Drag the column headings to the locations you prefer.

To restore the default Inbox settings, page 159

1. On the **View** menu, point to **Current View**, and then click **Define Views**.

2. In the **Custom View Organizer** dialog box, click **Reset**. In the **Microsoft Office Outlook** message box asking whether you want to reset the current view to its original settings, click **OK**.

3. Reset any customized views you want by clicking the view name and then clicking **Reset**. When you finish, click the **Messages** view, and then click **Apply View**.

To create a custom Search Folder, page 160

1. In the **Navigation Pane**, right-click the **Search Folders** folder, and then click **New Search Folder**.

2. In the **New Search Folder** dialog box, scroll the **Select a Search Folder** list to see the available options, select the option you want, and then click **OK**.

To make changes to the contents of an existing Search Folder, page 160

→ Right-click the folder, and then click **Customize this Search Folder**.

To display the default color categories, page 162

→ In the Inbox, click a message you want to categorize, and then on the Standard toolbar, click the **Categorize** button.

To rename categories, page 162

1. On the Standard toolbar, click the **Categorize** button, and in the **Category** list, click **All Categories**.

2. In the **Color Categories** dialog box, click the category (not the check box), and then click **Rename**.

3. Type the name you want, and then press ⌗Enter⌗.

To change the color associated with a category, page 163

1. On the Standard toolbar, click the **Categorize** button, and in the **Category** list, click **All Categories**.

2. In the **Color Categories** dialog box, click the category you want.

3. In the **Color** palette, click the icon of the color you want.

To create categories, page 163

1. On the Standard toolbar, click the **Categorize** button, and in the **Category** list, click **All Categories**.

2. In the **Color Categories** dialog box, click **New**.

3. In the **Name** box of the **Add New Category** dialog box, type the name you want to give the category. Then if you want, assign a color and a shortcut key.

To sort the Inbox contents by category, page 164

1. At the top of the Inbox, click the **Arranged By** bar, and then click **Categories**.
2. To the right of the **Arranged By** bar, click the command you want.

To create a folder, page 166

1. On the Standard toolbar, in the **New** list, click **Folder**.
2. In the **Name** box of the **Create New Folder** dialog box, type the folder name, and then click **OK**.

To move messages to a folder, page 167

→ Drag the message to the desired folder in the **Navigation Pane**.

Or

1. Right-click the message, and then click **Move to Folder**.
2. In the **Move Items** dialog box, in the **Move the selected items to the folder** list, click the folder where you want to move the message, and then click **OK**.

To send the content of an e-mail message to OneNote, page 168

→ Select the message, and then on the Standard toolbar, click the **Send selected e-mail to OneNote** button.

To set the default automatic archive options, page 169

1. On the **Tools** menu, click **Options**. On the **Other** tab of the **Options** dialog box, click **AutoArchive**.
2. Make the changes you want to your AutoArchive settings, then click **OK** in each of the open dialog boxes.

To manually archive a folder, page 172

1. Click the folder you want to archive. Then on the **File** menu, click **Archive**.
2. In the **Archive** dialog box, select the **Archive this folder and all subfolders** option, and then click **OK**.

To set the archive options for an individual folder, page 172

1. Right-click the folder in the **Navigation Pane**, and then click **Properties**.
2. On the **AutoArchive** tab of the **Properties** dialog box, set the archive options you want, and then click **OK**.

6   Managing Appointments, Events, and Meetings

To schedule an appointment, page 183

1. In the Calendar, display the date on which you want to schedule an appointment.

2. Click the desired time slot, type information about the appointment, and then press Enter.

3. To change the end time for the appointment, drag the bottom border of the time slot down to the bottom of the end time.

To reschedule an appointment, page 183

→ Drag the appointment to a different time slot on the calendar.

To make an appointment recurring, page 185

1. Open the appointment. Then on the **Appointment** tab, in the **Options** group, click the **Recurrence** button.

2. In the **Recurrence pattern** area of the **Appointment Recurrence** dialog box, select the option that corresponds to the desired recurrence, and then click **OK**.

3. On the **Recurring Appointment** tab, in the **Actions** group, click the **Save & Close** button.

To schedule an event, page 187

1. In the **Date Navigator**, click the date on which you want to schedule an event, and then in the **Calendar** pane, click the blank space below the day header and above the time slots.

2. Type the name of the event, and then press Enter.

To make an event recurring, page 187

1. Double-click the event, and then on the **Event** tab, in the **Options** group, click the **Recurrence** button.

2. In the **Recurrence pattern** area of the **Appointment Recurrence** dialog box, select the option that corresponds to the recurrence you want, and then click **OK**.

3. On the **Recurring Event** tab, in the **Actions** group, click the **Save & Close** button.

To create and send a meeting request, page 190

1. In the **Date Navigator**, click the date on which you want the meeting to occur.

2. On the Standard toolbar, in the **New Appointment** list, click **Meeting Request**.

3. In the **To** box, type the e-mail addresses of the meeting attendees; in the **Subject** box, type the name of the meeting; and in the **Location** box, indicate where the meeting will take place.

4. On the **Meeting** tab, in the **Show** group, click the **Scheduling** button. Then set the meeting time, and click **Send**.

To manually respond to a meeting request, page 194

1. In the **Date Navigator**, double-click the scheduled meeting.

2. In the meeting request window, in the **Reading Pane**, click **Accept**, **Tentative**, or **Decline**.

3. Choose whether to send a standard response, a personalized response, or no response at all.

To propose a new time for a meeting, page 194

1. In the **Reading Pane** of the meeting request window, click **Propose New Time**.

2. In the schedule area of the **Propose New Time** dialog box, set the proposed meeting start and end times, and then click **Propose Time**.

3. In the meeting response window that opens, enter a message to the meeting organizer, and then click **Send**.

To instruct Outlook to automatically respond to meeting requests, page 195

1. On the **Tools** menu, click **Options**. On the **Preferences** tab of the **Options** dialog box, click **Calendar Options**.

2. In the **Calendar Options** dialog box, click **Resource Scheduling**.

3. In the **Resource Scheduling** dialog box, select the **Automatically accept meeting requests and process cancellations** check box.

4. Select the **Automatically decline conflicting meeting requests** and/or the **Automatically decline recurring meeting requests** check boxes if you want Outlook to do this.

5. Click **OK** in each of the open dialog boxes.

7   Managing Your Calendar

To add the holidays of other countries to your calendar, page 203

1. On the **Tools** menu, click **Options**. On the **Preferences** tab of the **Options** dialog box, click **Calendar Options**.

2. In the **Calendar Options** dialog box, click **Add Holidays**.

3. In the **Add Holidays to Calendar** dialog box, select the check boxes of the countries whose holidays you want to add, and then click **OK** in each open dialog box.

To remove holidays from your calendar, page 203

1. In Calendar view, on the **View** menu, point to **Current View**, and then click **All Appointments**.

2. On the **View** menu, point to **Current View**, and click **Customize Current View**. Then in the **Customize View** dialog box, click **Group By**.

3. In the **Group By** dialog box, clear the **Automatically group according to arrangement** check box if it is selected. Then in the **Group items by** list, click **Location**.

4. Ensure that all the **Then by** lists display **(none)**, and then click **OK** in each of the open dialog boxes.

5. In the **Calendar** pane, collapse the displayed groups or scroll the pane until the **Location** group of the holidays you want to remove is visible. Then do the following:

   ○ To remove a specific holiday, click it, and then press `Del`.

   ○ To remove all the holidays of the displayed country, click the **Location** group header, and then press `Tab`. If a **Microsoft Office Outlook** message box warns you that this action will apply to all items in the selected group, click **OK**.

To change your work week, page 204

1. Display your calendar in **Week** view, and at the top of the **Calendar** pane, select the **Show work week** option.

2. On the **Tools** menu, click **Options**. On the **Preferences** tab of the **Options** dialog box, click **Calendar Options**.

3. In the **Calendar work week** area of the **Calendar Options** dialog box, select or clear the check boxes of the days of the week.

4. Set the start and end times, and then click **OK** in the open dialog boxes.

To change the time zone, page 206

1. On the **Tools** menu, click **Options**. On the **Preferences** tab of the **Options** dialog box, click **Calendar Options**.

2. In the **Calendar Options** dialog box, click **Time Zone**.

3. In the **Time zone** list, click the time zone you want. Then click **OK** in each of the open dialog boxes.

To simultaneously display two time zones in your Calendar, page 206

1. On the **Tools** menu, click **Options**. On the **Preferences** tab of the **Options** dialog box, click **Calendar Options**.

2. In the **Calendar Options** dialog box, click **Time Zone**.

3. In the **Time Zone** dialog box, select the **Show an additional time zone** check box. Then in the second **Time zone** list, click the additional time zone you want to display.

4. Type a label for each time zone in its corresponding **Label** box, and then click **OK** in each of the open dialog boxes.

To preview and print your calendar, page 208

1. On the **View** menu, click **Day**.

2. On the Standard toolbar, click the **Print** button. Then in the **Print** dialog box, click **Preview**.

3. On the **Print Preview** toolbar, click the **Print** button to redisplay the **Print** dialog box.

4. In the **Print style** list, click the style of printing you want.

5. In the **Print range** area, set the first and last dates you want to print, and then click **OK**.

To save calendar information as a Web page, page 212

1. Display your calendar, and then on the **File** menu, click **Save as Web Page**.

2. In the **Save as Web Page** dialog box, enter the start and end dates for which you want to publish calendar information.

3. In the **Options** area, select whether to include appointment details or a background graphic.

4. In the **Save as** area, append a file name (the extension is unnecessary) at the end of the path shown in the **File name** box. If you want, change the title that will be displayed on the Web page and the location where Outlook saves it.

5. With the **Open saved web page in browser** check box selected, click **Save**.

To embed information about your schedule in an e-mail message, page 214

1. Display your calendar, and then in the **Navigation Pane**, under **Other Calendars**, click **Send a Calendar via E-mail**.

2. In the **Send a Calendar via E-mail** dialog box, in the **Date Range** list, click the command you want.

3. In the **Detail** list, click the option you want.

4. Click **Advanced**, set any options you want, and then click **OK**.

To link one or more calendar entries to OneNote, page 216

→ Select the calendar item (or items) you want to link. Then on the Standard toolbar, click the **Open or create linked notes in OneNote** button.

To link to an Internet calendar, page 217

1. In the **Calendar** module **Navigation Pane**, scroll the **All Calendar Items** list to the **Other Calendars** section, and then click **Search Calendars Online**.

2. On the **Internet Calendars** page, scroll to the **Subscribe to a Free Internet Calendar** section, and then click the Internet calendar you want.

3. If an **Internet Explorer Security** message box prompts you to allow Outlook to open Web content, click the **Allow** button.

4. In the **Microsoft Office Outlook** message box asking whether you want to add the calendar to Outlook and subscribe to updates, click **Yes**.

To view multiple calendars side by side and as a composite, page 219

1. In either the **My Calendars** or **Other Calendars** list in the **Navigation Pane**, select the check box for at least one other calendar.

2. On the title bar tab of a secondary calendar, click the **View in Overlay Mode** button.

3. Click either **Calendar** tab to display that calendar on top of the other calendar.

4. On either of the overlaid calendars, click the **View in Side-By-Side Mode** button to return to the standard display.

To delegate control of your calendar so that meeting requests can be created and responded to on your behalf, page 220

1. On the **Tools** menu, click **Options**. On the **Delegates** tab of the **Options** dialog box, click **Add**.

2. In the **Add Users** dialog box, click the person you want to delegate control to, click **Add**, and then click **OK**.

3. In the **Delegate Permissions** dialog box, in the **Calendar** list, click the level of permission you want to delegate.

4. Select the **Automatically send a message to delegate summarizing these permissions** check box, and then click **OK** in each of the open dialog boxes.

8 Tracking Tasks

To create a folder that can contain tasks, page 231

1. On the Standard toolbar, in the **New** list, click **Folder**.

2. In the **Create New Folder** dialog box, enter the name and select the location of the folder.

3. In the **Folder contains** list, click **Task Items**, and then click **OK**.

To create a task, page 234

→ On the **To-Do Bar**, click the **Type a new task** box, type a description of your task, and then press `Enter`.

To update a task, page 234

● To assign a completion time, in the **To-Do Bar Task List**, right-click the flag following the task, and then click the timeframe you want.

● To assign the task to a category, right-click the **Category** bar following the task, and then click the category you want.

● To change the task text, double-click the task in the **Tasks** pane, and in the content pane, type the new text. Then save and close the task.

● To change the status, double-click the task in the **Tasks** pane, and in the **Status** list, click the option that applies to the task. Then in the **% Complete** box, change the completion percentage of the task, and save and close the task.

To delegate a task to another Outlook user, page 238

1. On the **To-Do Bar**, double-click the task you want to delegate.

2. In the task window, on the **Task** tab, in the **Manage Task** group, click the **Assign Task** button.

3. In the **To** box that appears, type the e-mail address of the person you want to assign the task to.

4. If you want Outlook to display a reminder for the task, in the **Options** group, click the **Follow Up** button.

5. Click **Send**. If a message box appears to notify you that the task reminder has been turned off, click **OK**.

To update the status of tasks assigned to you by other people, page 240

- To change the percentage of the project you estimate as complete, open the task, and then in the **% Complete** list, type or select (by clicking the arrows) the percentage.

- To manually change the task status, open the task, and then in the **Status** list, click the status you want.

To send a status report about a task, page 240

1. In the **Tasks** pane, double-click the task, and then on the **Task** tab, in the **Manage Task** group, click the **Send Status Report** button.

2. Address the message to the people you want to send the report to, and click **Send**.

To mark a task as complete, page 241

→ In the **Tasks** pane, double-click the task, and then on the **Task** tab, in the **Manage Task** group, click the **Mark Complete** button.

To stop a reminder from appearing, page 242

1. In the **To-Do Bar Task List**, right-click the task, point to **Follow Up**, and then click **Add Reminder**.

2. Clear the **Reminder** check box, and then click **OK**.

To delete a task, page 243

→ In the **To-Do Bar Task list**, click the task, and then press Del.

9 Gathering Information

To subscribe to an RSS feed, page 247

1. In the **Navigation Pane**, under your primary mailbox, click the **RSS Subscriptions** folder.

2. Scroll the **Outlook Syndicated Content (RSS) Directory** page to the **Partner Feeds** section.

3. Click one of the feed links.

4. In the **Microsoft Office Outlook** message box asking whether to add the RSS feed to Outlook, click **Yes**.

To remove an RSS feed, page 249

1. On the **Tools** menu, click **Account Settings**.

2. In the **Account Settings** dialog box, click the **RSS Feeds** tab.

3. In the **Feed Name** list, click the name of the feed you want to remove.

4. Click **Remove**. Then in the **Microsoft Office Outlook** message box asking whether to remove the RSS feed from Outlook, click **Yes**.

To change the default note color, size, or font, page 252

1. On the **Tools** menu, click **Options**. On the **Preferences** tab of the **Options** dialog box, click **Note Options**.

2. Change the settings you want, and then click **OK** twice.

To create a note, page 252

→ In the **Notes** pane, on the Standard toolbar, click the **New Note** button. Then type the note titles, press ⌐Enter⌐, type the note text, and click the **Close** button.

To link a note to a contact, page 254

1. Open a note in the **Notes** pane, click the **Note** icon in its upper-left corner, and then click **Contacts**.

2. In the **Contacts for Note** dialog box, click **Contacts**.

3. In the **Select Contacts** dialog box, with **Contacts** selected in the **Look in** list, click the contact you want to link to in the **Items** list. Then click **OK**.

4. In the **Contacts for Note** dialog box, click **Close**. Then close the note.

To access a note from a contact record, page 255

1. In the **Contacts** pane, open the contact record. Then on the **Contact** tab, in the **Show** group, click the **Activities** button.

2. In the **Show** list, click **Notes**.

To display the Journal, page 256

→ On the **Go** menu, click **Journal**.

To add the Journal button to the Navigation Pane, page 256

1. In the lower-right corner of the **Navigation Pane**, click the **Configure buttons** button.

2. Point to **Add or Remove Buttons**, and then click **Journal**.

To record activities automatically, page 256

1. On the **Tools** menu, click **Options**. On the **Preferences** tab of the **Options** dialog box, click **Journal Options**.

2. In the **Journal Options** dialog box, in the **Automatically record these items** box, select the check boxes for the activities you want to record.

3. In the **For these contacts** box, select the check boxes for the contacts whose items you want to record.

4. In the **Also record files from** box, select the check boxes for the programs whose files you want to record, and then click **OK** in the open dialog boxes.

To forward a note, page 257

1. Right-click a note in the **Notes** pane, and then click **Forward**.

2. In the **To** box, type the e-mail address of the person you want to send the note to, and then click **Send**.

To save a note as a file, page 257

1. Open the note, click its **Note** icon, and then click **Save As**.

2. In the **Save As** dialog box, browse to the folder where you want to save the file.

3. In the **Save as type** list, click the file type you want to create.

4. In the **File name** box, change the file name if you want it to be something other than the current note title, and then click **Save**.

To open a received note, page 258

1. In your **Inbox**, click the message with the note attached to it.

2. In the **Reading Pane**, right-click the attached note, and then click **Open**.

10   Collaborating with Other People

To allow another person on your Exchange Server network to access a folder, page 263

1. In the **Navigation Pane**, right-click the folder, and then click **Change Sharing Permissions**.

2. On the **Permissions** tab of the **Properties** dialog box, click **Add**.

3. In the **Add Users** dialog box, double-click the name of the person with whom you want to share this folder, and then click **OK**.

4. With the person's name selected on the **Permissions** tab, in the **Permission Level** list, click the level you want.

5. In the **Properties** dialog box, click **Apply**.

To create a document workspace from a message, page 269

1. In a new message window, enter the addresses of the people you want to invite to the document workspace and a subject.

2. On the **Message** tab, in the **Include** group, click the **Attach File** button. Then in the **Insert File** dialog box, browse to and select the file(s) you want to share through a document library, and click **Insert**.

3. Click the **Include** Dialog Box Launcher. Then under **Send attachments as** in the **Attachment Options** task pane, select the **Shared attachments** option.

4. In the **Create Document Workspace at** box, enter the address of your collaboration site, and then press the ⌨Tab⌨ key.

5. Send the message invitation that appears in the content area.

To create a group schedule, page 271

1. Display your calendar, and then on the **Actions** menu, click **View Group Schedules**.

2. In the **Group Schedules** dialog box, click **New**. In the **Create New Group Schedule** dialog box, type a name for the schedule, and then click **OK**.

3. In the scheduling window, add members to the group by clicking in the **Group Members** list and then typing a name or an e-mail alias, or by clicking **Add Others** and then selecting group members from your address book.

To get a local copy of document library contents, page 272

1. On your organization's collaboration site, display the document library.

2. On the **Actions** menu, click **Connect to Outlook**. If an **Internet Explorer Security** alert appears, click **Allow**.

3. In the **Microsoft Office Outlook** message box asking you to confirm that you want to connect the SharePoint document library to Outlook, click **Yes**. If a **Connect** dialog box appears, prompting you for your site credentials, enter your user name and password, and then click **OK**.

4. To preview downloaded items, click them; to open a read-only version, double-click it.

11 Working Away from Your Office

To configure Outlook to connect to an Exchange account by using Outlook Anywhere, page 279

1. On the **Tools** menu, click **Account Settings**.

2. On the **E-mail** tab of the **Account Settings** dialog box, in the **Name** list, click your **Microsoft Exchange** account, and then click **Change**.

3. In the **Change E-mail Account** dialog box, click **More Settings**.

4. In the **Microsoft Exchange** dialog box, click the **Connection** tab.

5. In the **Outlook Anywhere** area, select the **Connect to Microsoft Exchange using HTTP** check box.

6. Click the **Exchange Proxy Settings** button that becomes active.

7. In the **Microsoft Exchange Proxy Settings** dialog box, in the **Connection settings** area, in the **https://** box, type your organization's Exchange proxy address.

8. Click **OK** in the **Microsoft Exchange Proxy Settings** dialog box and the **Microsoft Exchange** dialog box. Then in the message box that appears, click **OK** to acknowledge that the change will not take effect until you restart Outlook.

9. In the **Change E-mail Account** dialog box, click **Next**, and then click **Finish**.

10. Close the **Account Settings** dialog box, and then quit and restart Outlook.

11. In the **Connect to** dialog box, enter your user name and password, and click **OK**.

To set up a VPN connection from a computer running Windows Vista, page 281

1. In the right pane of the **Start** menu, click **Connect To**.

2. In the **Connect to a Network** dialog box, click **Set up a connection or network**.

3. Scroll the **Choose a connection option** list, click **Connect to a workplace**, and then click **Next**.

4. Under **Do you want to use a connection that you already have?**, select **No, create a new connection**, and then click **Next**.

5. Under **How do you want to connect?**, click **Use my Internet connection (VPN)** option.

6. Under **Type the Internet address to connect to**, type the Internet address you want to connect to in the **Internet address** box. In the **Destination name** box, type a name for the VPN connection, select any options that you want, and then click **Next**.

7. Under **Type your user name and password**, type your user name and password (the domain name is optional), and then click **Connect**.

To set up a VPN connection from a computer running Windows XP, page 282

1. On the **Start** menu, if the **Connect To** menu appears on the right side, click **Connect To**, and then click **Show all connections**. Otherwise, open **Control Panel** in **Classic** view, and then click **Network Connections**.

2. In the **Network Connections** window, on the **Network Tasks** menu, click **Create a new connection**.

3. On the first page of the **New Connection** wizard, click **Next**.

4. On the **Network Connection Type** page, select the **Connect to the network at my workplace** option, and then click **Next**.

5. On the **Network Connection** page, select the **Virtual Private Network connection** option, and then click **Next**.

6. In the **Company Name** box, type a name by which you will identify the connection. Then click **Next**.

7. If the wizard displays the **Public Network** page, select the **Do not dial the initial connection** option to indicate that you will always connect to the Internet before starting the VPN connection. Then click **Next**.

8. On the **VPN Server Selection** page, type the URL of your organization's VPN server in the **Host name** box, and then click **Next**.

9. If your system includes a SmartCard reader, the wizard displays the **Smart Cards** page. If you don't need to use your SmartCard to log in to this particular connection, select the **Do not use my smart card** option, and then click **Next**.

10. On the **Connection Availability** page, select the **My use only** option, and then click **Next**.

11. On the **Completing** page, click **Finish**.

12. In the **User name** box of the **Connect** dialog box, type your domain\username, and in the **Password** box, type your domain password.

13. Select the **Save this user name** check box and the **Me only** or **Everyone** option. Then click **Connect**.

To make the contents of a folder available for offline use, page 285

→ In the **Navigation Pane**, click the folder. Then on the **Tools** menu, point to **Send/Receive**, point to **Send/Receive Settings**, and then click **Make This Folder Available Offline**.

To manually update your offline address book, page 286

1. On the **Tools** menu, point to **Send/Receive**, and then click **Download Address Book**.

2. In the **Offline Address Book** dialog box, with the **Download changes since last Send/Receive** check box selected, select the **Full Details** option, and then click **OK**.

To configure Outlook to automatically reply to incoming messages, page 288

1. On the **Tools** menu, click **Out of Office Assistant**.

2. In the **Out Of Office Assistant** dialog box, select the **I am currently Out of the Office** option.

3. In the **AutoReply only once to each sender with the following text** box, type the text of the auto-reply message you want to send, click **OK**, and then click the notification to close it.

To set up a rule to auto-forward messages to another e-mail address, page 289

1. On the status bar, click **Out of Office**. Then on the **Out of Office** menu, click **Out of Office Assistant**.

2. In the **Out of Office Assistant** dialog box, click **Add Rule**. Then in the **Edit Rule** dialog box, click **Advanced**.

3. In the **Received** area, specify the start date, end date, or any date range you want.

4. To set the importance of the message, select the **Importance** check box, select the option you want in the **Importance** list, and then click **OK**.

5. In the **Edit Rule** dialog box, under **Perform these actions**, select the **Forward** check box. Then in the **To** box, type the e-mail address to which you want to forward messages.

6. In the **Method** list, click the forwarding option you want. Then click **OK**.

To turn off Out Of Office auto-reply messages, page 291

→ Click the **Out of Office** icon on the status bar, and then click **Turn off Out of Office auto-replies**.

To automatically reply to messages during a future time period (applies only to Exchange Server 2007 accounts), page 292

1. On the **Tools** menu, click **Out Of Office Assistant**.

2. In the **Out of Office Assistant** dialog box, select the **Send Out of Office auto-replies** option.

3. Select the **Only send during this time range** check box. Then set the **Start time** and **End time** settings as you want.

4. On the **Inside My Organization** tab, in the message box, type the text of the message you want to send, and then click **OK**.

To send a different auto-reply message to people outside your organization (applies only to Exchange Server 2007 accounts), page 294

1. Display the **Out Of Office Assistant** dialog box, and click the **Outside My Organization** tab.

2. Select the **Anyone outside my organization** option.

3. In the message box, type the text of the message you want to send to people outside your organization, and then click **OK**.

12 Customizing and Configuring Outlook

To add a button to the Quick Access Toolbar, page 299

1. At the right end of the **Quick Access Toolbar**, click the **Customize Quick Access Toolbar** button, and then click **More Commands**.

2. In the **Editor Options** window, on the **Customize** page, in the **Choose commands from** list, click the tab from which you want to choose a command.

3. In the tab's command list, click a command you want to add to the toolbar, and then click **Add**.

4. Click the **Move Up** and **Move Down** buttons to position the command where you want on the toolbar, and then at the bottom of the **Customize** page, click **OK**.

To customize Outlook, page 301

1. Click the **Microsoft Office Button**, and then in the lower-right corner of the **Office** menu, click **Editor Options**.

2. In the **Editor Options** window, in the page list in the left pane, click the page you want, make your changes, and then click **OK** to save your changes.

To add a button to a toolbar, page 306

1. Click the **Toolbar Options** button at the right end of any toolbar, point to **Add or Remove Buttons**, and then click **Customize**.

2. In the **Customize** dialog box, click the **Commands** tab. In the **Categories** list, click the category containing the command you want to add.

3. In the **Commands** list, locate the command you want to add. Then drag the command from the list to the position where you want it to appear on the toolbar.

To rearrange the commands on a toolbar, page 306

1. Click the **Toolbar Options** button, point to **Add or Remove Buttons**, and then click **Customize**.

2. In the **Customize** dialog box, on the **Commands** tab, click **Rearrange Commands**.

3. In the **Rearrange Commands** dialog box, under **Choose a menu or toolbar to rearrange**, select the **Toolbar** option. Then in the **Toolbar** list, select the toolbar or menu bar you want to rearrange.

4. In the **Controls** list, click the command you want to reposition, click **Move Up** or **Move Down** as many times as necessary to position the command where you want it, and then click **Close**.

To remove a custom button from a toolbar, page 307

1. Click the **Toolbar Options** button, point to **Add or Remove Buttons**, and then click **Customize**.

2. In the **Customize** dialog box, on the **Commands** tab, click **Rearrange Commands**.

3. In the **Rearrange Commands** dialog box, under **Choose a menu or toolbar to rearrange**, select the **Toolbar** option, and then in the list, click the toolbar containing the button you want to remove.

4. In the **Controls** list, click the button you want to remove. Click **Delete**, and then click **Close**.

To reset a toolbar to its default state, page 307

→ Click the **Toolbar Options** button, point to **Add or Remove Buttons**, and then click **Customize**. Then in the **Customize** dialog box, on the **Toolbars** tab, click the toolbar you want to restore to its default settings, and then click **Reset**.

To create a rule to process incoming messages that meet specific criteria, page 308

1. On the **Tools** menu, click **Rules and Alerts**. Then in the **Rules and Alerts** window, on the **E-mail Rules** tab, click **New Rule**.

2. In the **Rules** wizard, in the **Select a template** list, under **Start from a blank rule**, click **Check messages when they arrive**, and then click **Next**.

3. In the **Select condition(s)** list, select the conditions you want to apply to your new rule.

4. In the **Edit the rule description** box, click the underlined term **specific words**.

5. In the **Search Text** dialog box, in the **Specify words or phrases to search for in the subject** box, type the words you want to search for, click **Add**, and click **OK**. Then in the **Rules** wizard, click **Next**.

6. Scroll the **Select action(s)** list to review and select the actions Outlook can perform on incoming items meeting the criteria you specify, and click **OK**. Then in the **Rules** wizard, click **Next**.

7. Select any exceptions you want to set for your rule, and then click **Next**.

8. Select the **Run this rule now on messages already in "Inbox"** check box, and then click **Finish**. Then in the **Rules and Alerts** dialog box, click **OK**.

To create a Personal Folders file, page 314

1. On the **File** menu, point to **New**, and then click **Outlook Data File**.

2. If you run Microsoft Outlook 2002 or an earlier version on a different computer and you might want to open this Personal Folders file in that version, click **Outlook 97-2002 Personal Folders File** in the **New Outlook Data File** dialog box. Otherwise, select **Office Outlook Personal Folders File**, and then click **OK**.

3. In the **Create or Open Outlook Data File** dialog box, in the **Favorite Links** list, click the type of link you want.

4. In the **File name** box, type the name of your personal folder file, and then click **OK**.

5. In the **Create Microsoft Personal Folders** dialog box, replace the suggested name with a new name or accept it, and click **OK**.

To move messages or folders to your Personal Folders file, page 316

1. In the **Navigation Pane**, expand the Inbox to display its folder list.

2. Drag the messages or folders from your Inbox to your personal folder.

To copy messages and folders to your Personal Folders file, page 316

1. In the **Navigation Pane**, expand the Inbox to display its folder list.

2. Hold down the right mouse button, and drag the messages or folders from your Inbox to your personal folder. When you release the mouse button, click **Copy**.

To open and close data files from within Outlook, page 316

1. On the **File** menu, point to **Open**, and then click **Outlook Data File**.

2. In the **Open Outlook Data File** dialog box, browse to the location of your data file, and then double-click it.

To digitally sign all outgoing messages, page 317

1. On the **Tools** menu, click **Trust Center**, and in the page list, click **E-mail Security**. Then on the **E-mail Security** page, select the **Add digital signature to outgoing messages** check box.

2. If all your message recipients don't have Secure Multipurpose Internet Mail Extensions (S/MIME) security, select the **Send clear text signed message when sending signed messages** check box, and then click **OK**.

To obtain a digital ID to sign or encrypt documents and messages, page 318

1. On the **Tools** menu, click **Trust Center**, and then in the page list, click **E-mail Security**.

2. On the **E-mail Security** page, click **Get a Digital ID**.

3. On the **Microsoft Office Marketplace** Web page, click the link at the end of a provider's description to display the provider's Web site.

4. Follow the instructions on the Web site to register for a digital ID.

To export or import a digital ID, page 319

1. On the **Tools** menu, click **Trust Center**, and then in the page list, click **E-mail Security**.

2. On the **E-mail Security** page, click **Import/Export**.

3. In the **Import/Export Digital ID** dialog box, select whether you want to import or export your digital ID, fill in the information, and then click **OK**.

To digitally sign an individual e-mail message, page 319

→ On the **Message** tab, in the **Options** group, click the **Digitally Sign Message** button.

To encrypt all outgoing messages, page 320

1. On the **Tools** menu, click **Trust Center**, and then in the page list, click **E-mail Security**.

2. On the **E-mail Security** page, select the **Encrypt contents and attachments for outgoing messages** check box.

3. To receive verification that a message recipient received an encrypted message in its encrypted format, select the **Request S/MIME receipt for all S/MIME signed messages** check box, and then click **OK**.

To encrypt an individual message, page 320

→ On the **Message** tab, in the **Options** group, click the **Encrypt Message Contents and Attachments** button.

To receive all messages in plain text format, page 321

1. On the **Tools** menu, click **Trust Center**, and then in the page list, click **E-mail Security**.

2. On the **E-mail Security** page, select the **Read all standard mail in plain text** check box, and then click **OK**.

To prevent message recipients from forwarding, printing, or copying a message, page 322

→ With a message open, on the **Message** tab, in the **Options** group, in the **Permissions** list, click **Do Not Forward**.

To view the blocked content in an individual e-mail message, page 322

→ In the message header, click the **InfoBar**, and then click **Download Pictures**.

To change the way Outlook handles external content:, page 323

1. On the **Tools** menu, click **Trust Center**, and then in the page list, click **Automatic Download**.

2. Select the check boxes for the options you want, and then click **OK**.

To apply spam filtering options provided by the Junk E-Mail Filter, page 324

1. On the **Actions** menu, point to **Junk E-mail**, and then click **Junk E-mail Options**.

2. In the **Junk E-mail Options** dialog box, on the **Options** tab, select a level of protection.

3. If you want Outlook to automatically delete suspected junk e-mail, select the **Permanently delete suspected Junk E-mail instead of moving it to the Junk E-mail folder** check box.

4. Click the **Safe Senders** tab, add any e-mail addresses you want included in the Safe Senders List, or specify that e-mail received from a particular domain is safe.

5. Click the **Safe Recipients** tab, and add any addresses or domains to your Safe Recipients List.

6. Click the **Blocked Senders** tab, and add any addresses or domains to the Blocked Senders List.

7. Click the **International** tab, and set options to block messages from country-specific domains or messages containing specific language text encoding, and then click **OK**.

To save message drafts more frequently, page 327

1. On the **Tools** menu, click **Options**. On the **Preferences** tab of the **Options** dialog box, click **E-mail Options**. Then in the **E-mail Options** dialog box, click **Advanced E-mail Options**.

2. In the **Save messages** area of the **Advanced E-mail Options** dialog box, select the **AutoSave items every** check box, and enter a number in the **minutes** box. Then click **OK** in each of the open dialog boxes.

To specify what happens when a message arrives, page 329

1. On the **Tools** menu, click **Options**. On the **Preferences** tab of the **Options** dialog box, click **E-mail Options**. Then in the **E-mail Options** dialog box, click **Advanced E-mail Options**.

2. In the **Advanced E-mail Options** dialog box, in the **When new items arrive in my Inbox** area, select the options for how you want to be notified when a new message arrives. Then click **OK** in each of the open dialog boxes.

To set options for sending messages, page 329

1. On the **Tools** menu, click **Options**. On the **Preferences** tab of the **Options** dialog box, click **E-mail Options**. Then in the **E-mail Options** dialog box, click **Advanced E-mail Options**.

2. In the **Advanced E-mail Options** dialog box, in the **When sending a message** area, set the options you want to apply to the messages you send. Then click **OK** in each of the open dialog boxes.

Chapter at a Glance

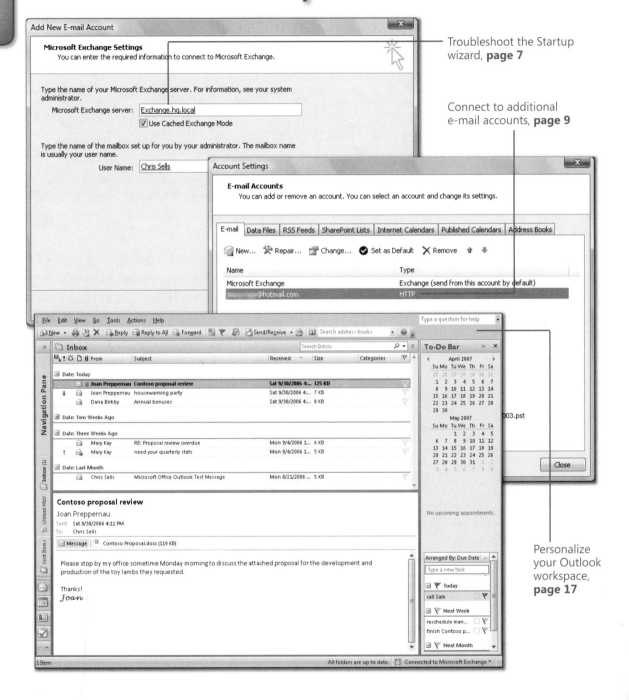

Troubleshoot the Startup wizard, **page 7**

Connect to additional e-mail accounts, **page 9**

Personalize your Outlook workspace, **page 17**

1 Getting Started with Outlook 2007

In this chapter, you will learn to:

✔ Connect to your primary e-mail account.

✔ Troubleshoot the Startup wizard.

✔ Connect to additional e-mail accounts.

✔ Create additional Outlook profiles.

✔ Personalize your Outlook workspace.

✔ Explore the Advanced toolbar.

Before you can begin using Outlook, you need to configure it to connect to your e-mail server, and thereby create your e-mail profile. Your profile consists of information about your e-mail account such as the user name, display name, server name, password, and where your Outlook data is stored. You can connect to more than one e-mail account, to manage all your e-mail communications through Outlook.

The Outlook user interface is organized in a manner intended to enable most people to easily view, locate, and link to information. You might find, though, that it is not perfectly suited for the way that you work on a day-to-day basis. Or perhaps you'd just like to try a different layout. There are many ways in which you can personalize the way Outlook appears and functions.

In this chapter, you will configure Outlook to connect to different types of e-mail accounts. You will also create additional Outlook profiles and personalize your Outlook workspace layout to suit your needs.

See Also Do you need only a quick refresher on the topics in this chapter? See the Quick Reference entries on pages xxxvii–lxv.

> **Important** No practice files are required to complete the exercises in this chapter. For more information about practice files, see "Using the Book's CD" on page xxv.

Troubleshooting Graphics and operating system–related instructions in this book reflect the Windows Vista user interface. If your computer is running Microsoft Windows XP and you experience trouble following the instructions as written, please refer to the "Information for Readers Running Windows XP" section at the beginning of this book.

Different Types of E-Mail Accounts

Outlook 2007 supports the following types of e-mail accounts:

- **Exchange Server.** If your organization runs Microsoft Exchange Server, you can send mail within or outside of your organization's network. Messages are usually stored on the e-mail server, but you can alternatively store them elsewhere (for example, on your computer or on a network share). By default, Outlook creates a local copy of your mailbox on your computer and synchronizes with the server when you're connected, so you can easily work offline if necessary.

- **Post Office Protocol 3** (*POP3*). When connected to a POP3 account, Outlook downloads (copies) messages from your e-mail server to your computer. You can choose to remove the messages from the server or to leave them there for a specified amount of time. If you access your e-mail account from multiple computers, you will probably want to leave messages on the server to ensure that they're available to you.

- **Internet Message Access Protocol** (*IMAP*). When connected to an IMAP account, Outlook stores copies of messages on your computer, but leaves the originals on the e-mail server. You read and manage messages locally, and Outlook synchronizes with the server when connected.

- **Hypertext Transfer Protocol** (*HTTP*). Messages sent through an HTTP account (such as a Hotmail account), are in the form of Web pages that Outlook copies from your HTTP mail server and displays within the message window.

You can add multiple POP3, IMAP, and HTTP accounts (but only one Exchange Server account) to your Outlook profile.

Connecting to Your Primary E-Mail Account

The automatic setup functionality provided by the Outlook 2007 Startup wizard is a significant improvement over previous versions of Outlook, which required that you provide much more information. It might not work under all circumstances, but it generally does a very good job. In most cases, the only information you need is your e-mail address and password.

See Also If the Outlook automatic setup functionality doesn't work for you, see "Troubleshooting the Startup Wizard" later in this chapter.

In this exercise, you will start Outlook and configure it to connect to a Microsoft Exchange Server account. Although we demonstrate connecting to an Exchange Server account, you can follow the same basic process to connect to another type of e-mail server. There are no practice files for this exercise.

BE SURE TO have your e-mail address and password available before beginning this exercise. If connecting to an Exchange Server account, you must be connected to your network. If you are working off-network, you might first need to establish a virtual private network (VPN) connection.

See Also For information about establishing a VPN connection, see "Connecting Outlook to Your Server from a Remote Location" in Chapter 11, "Working Away from Your Office."

Start

1. On the taskbar, click the **Start** button.

2. On the **Start** menu, point to **All Programs**, click **Microsoft Office**, and then click **Microsoft Office Outlook 2007**.

> **Tip** If the E-mail link at the top of the Start menu specifies Microsoft Office Outlook as your default e-mail program, you can click that link instead.

Outlook 2007 starts. If Outlook hasn't yet been configured to connect to an e-mail account, the Outlook 2007 Startup wizard starts.

> **Tip** What you see on your screen might not match the graphics in this book exactly. The screens in this book were captured on a monitor set to a resolution of 1024×768 pixels, with the Windows taskbar hidden to increase the display space.

See Also If Outlook is already configured to connect to an e-mail account and you would like to configure a second account, see "Connecting to Additional E-Mail Accounts" later in this chapter.

3. On the welcome page, click **Next**.

If you have an e-mail account set up in another e-mail program on this computer, Outlook offers the option of importing account information from that account.

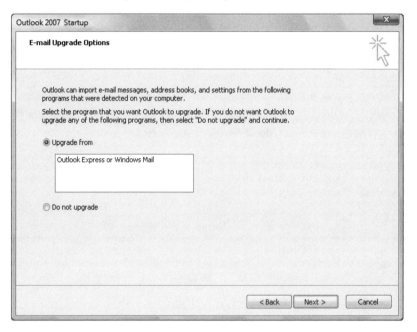

For the purposes of this exercise, we will not select that option, but you might find it convenient to do so when setting up your own account.

4. On the **E-mail Upgrade Options** page, select the **Do not upgrade** option, and then click **Next** to display the E-mail Accounts page.

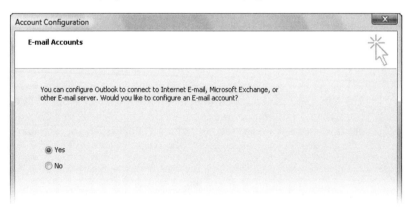

5. With the **Yes** option selected, click **Next**.

6. On the **Auto Account Setup** page, enter your name, e-mail address, and password in the corresponding text boxes.

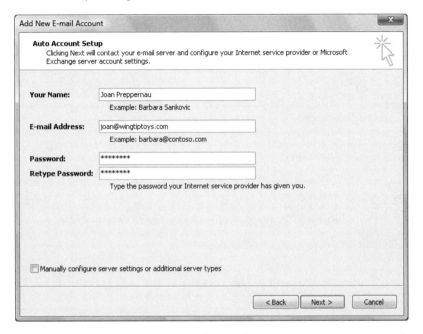

Notice the option here to manually configure your server settings. If you have trouble configuring Outlook by using the automatic setup tool, you can make manual changes by selecting this check box and then clicking Next.

See Also For information about manually setting up Outlook, see "Troubleshooting the Startup Wizard" later in this chapter.

7. On the **Auto Account Setup** page, click **Next**.

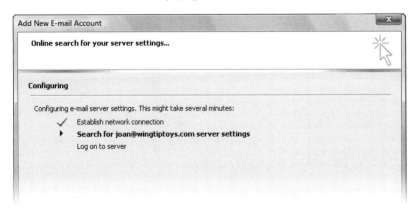

Provided it doesn't encounter any connection or security issues, Outlook uses the minimal information you provided to connect to your e-mail server and create your Outlook profile.

> **Tip** If this is the first time you have started a 2007 Microsoft Office system program, Office prompts you to enter your full name and initials. The programs in the 2007 Office system use this information when tracking changes, responding to messages, and so on. Next, Office prompts you to select the type of information you want to share over the Internet, and finally, offers the option of signing up for automatic program updates from the Microsoft Update service. None of these options place you at risk, and all can be quite useful.

The first time you start Outlook, it asks whether you want to combine and synchronize RSS feeds in Outlook and Microsoft Internet Explorer.

8. Unless you have a reason not to do so, in the **Microsoft Office Outlook** message box asking whether to combine the RSS Feed lists, click **Yes**.

Outlook displays your Inbox.

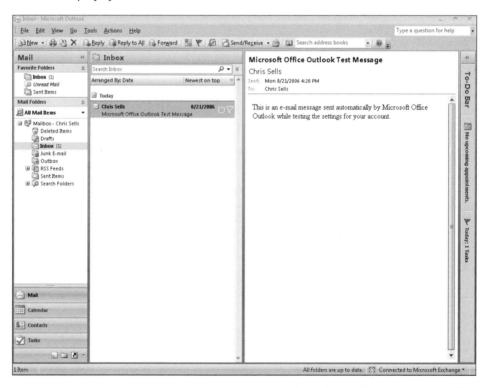

A test message from Outlook appears at the top of the Inbox. Your other e-mail messages will appear below the test message.

Troubleshooting the Startup Wizard

You are most likely to encounter problems with the automatic setup feature when configuring Outlook to connect to an Exchange Server account from a remote location (not directly connected to your domain). Here are some common error messages and problems you could encounter:

- **Server certificate does not match site.** If Outlook encounters any security issues— for example, if the mail server's digital certificate does not match the name of your domain—Outlook notifies you of this problem and lets you choose whether to proceed.

  If a Security Alert message box appears, you can click the View Certificate button to see the digital certificate of the remote server and verify that you know and trust the company that issued the certificate. If you want, you can install the certificate on your computer by clicking the Install Certificate button and following the steps in the Certificate Import wizard. When you are confident of the validity of the certificate, in the Security Alert message box, click Yes.

  See Also For more information about digital certificates, see "Securing Your E-Mail" in Chapter 12, "Customizing and Configuring Outlook."

- **Encrypted connection not available.** Outlook first tries to establish an encrypted connection with the server. If this attempt is not successful, Outlook notifies you of this problem and asks whether you want to try to establish an unencrypted connection.

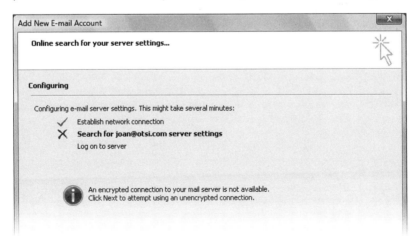

If you select this option, Outlook will most likely configure your Exchange Server account as an IMAP or POP3 account instead of as an Exchange Server account. This configuration will result in a loss of functionality—for example, the To-Do Bar will not display your calendar and task information.

If you encounter either of these errors when connecting to your Exchange Server account, verify that your computer is connected to your network domain (locally or over a VPN connection, if you're not connecting by using HTTP) and using the correct internal server address method. For example, if your e-mail address is *jane@adatum.com*, you might address your e-mail server as *mail.adatum.com* or by an internal address such as *ADATUMExchange.adatum.local*.

See Also For information about connecting to Microsoft Exchange by using HTTP, see "Connecting Outlook to Your Server from a Remote Location" in Chapter 11, "Working Away from Your Office."

To successfully troubleshoot your connection issues, you will most likely need to manually configure your server settings. This process is similar to that of configuring an account in Outlook 2003.

1. Display the **Auto Account Setup** page of the **Outlook 2007 Startup** wizard.

2. Select the **Manually configure server settings** check box, and then click **Next** to display the Choose E-mail Service page.

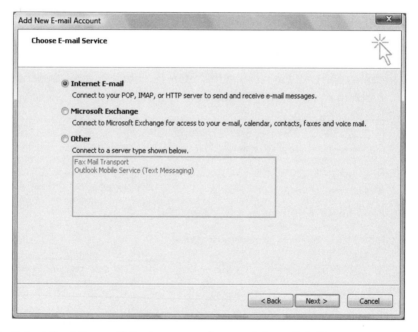

3. Select the **Microsoft Exchange** option, and then click **Next**.

4. On the **Microsoft Exchange Settings** page, enter the name or address of your Exchange Server and your user name, and then click the **Check Name** button.

5. If you didn't provide your password on the Auto Account Setup page, Outlook prompts you for it now. If the **Connect to** dialog box appears, enter your logon information, and then click **OK**.

   If you are connected to your network and the user name you enter matches the information on the server, the wizard replaces your user name with your display name (as recorded in your organization's Global Address List) and underlines it. (This is known as *resolving* the address.)

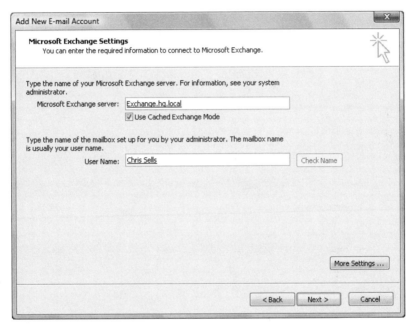

6. After your name appears underlined, click **Next**, and then on the final page of the wizard, click **Finish**.

Connecting to Additional E-Mail Accounts

You can add e-mail accounts to the your primary Outlook profile. For example, if you want to check your work and personal e-mail accounts from the same Outlook profile, or if you monitor another e-mail alias, such as a support alias. Your profile may include only one Exchange Server account, but it may contain multiple HTTP, IMAP, and POP3 accounts.

> **Tip** If your profile includes multiple e-mail accounts, you can select the account you want to use each time you send an e-mail message. In the message header, click the Account button, and then in the list, click the account from which you want to send the message. The Account button is visible only when multiple accounts are configured within a profile.

See Also For information about connecting to a second Exchange Server account, see "Creating Additional Outlook Profiles" later in this chapter.

In this exercise, you will add an HTTP, IMAP, or POP3 e-mail account to your Outlook profile. There are no practice files for this exercise.

> **BE SURE TO** have the logon information for your HTTP, IMAP, or POP3 account available before beginning this exercise.

1. On the **Tools** menu, click **Account Settings**.

   The Account Settings dialog box opens.

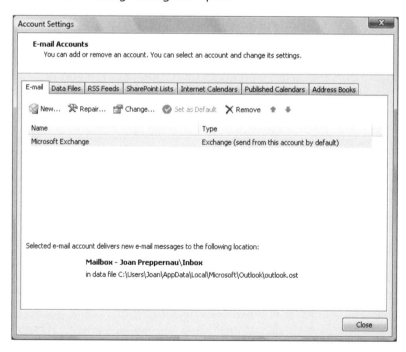

2. On the **E-mail** tab, click **New**.

   The Add New E-mail Account wizard starts.

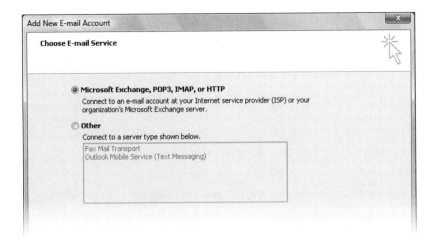

Although Microsoft Exchange is shown as an option, you can't configure more than one Exchange Server account per profile.

3. On the **Choose E-mail Service** page, with the **Microsoft Exchange, POP3, IMAP, or HTTP** option selected, click **Next**.

4. On the **Auto Account Setup** page, enter the display name, e-mail address, and password of the account you want to add to your profile. Then click **Next**.

   Outlook establishes a network connection and searches for the server settings. After locating the server and validating your user name and password, Outlook displays a confirmation message.

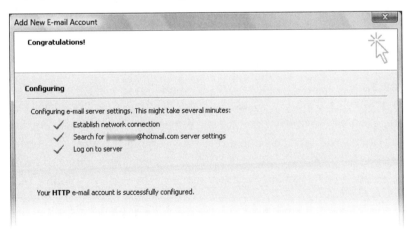

5. Click **Finish** to complete the account setup.

The new account appears on the E-mail tab of the Account Settings dialog box and in the All Mail Folders list.

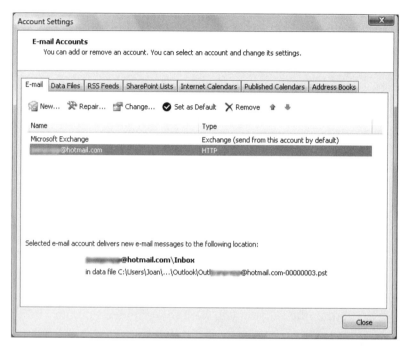

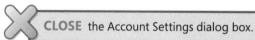

CLOSE the Account Settings dialog box.

Creating Additional Outlook Profiles

In the same way that multiple users of a computer running Windows Vista or Windows XP can have individual user profiles, you can have more than one e-mail profile on your computer. Each profile can include multiple e-mail accounts, but only one Exchange account. Most people will have only one e-mail profile, but if you want to connect to multiple Exchange accounts—for example, if you have e-mail accounts with two companies that you access from the same computer—you can do so only through a second e-mail profile.

E-mail profiles are stored in the Windows registry. You create additional profiles from Windows, rather than from Outlook.

If you have multiple e-mail profiles, you can instruct Outlook to log on to one by default or to prompt you to select a profile each time it starts. If you're planning to regularly access more than one profile, the latter is the easiest solution.

> **Tip** You can't switch between profiles while Outlook is running. If you don't select the option to have Outlook prompt you for a profile, you can change the default profile from the Windows Control Panel.

In this exercise, you will create a second Outlook profile and configure Outlook so that you can choose which profile to log on to each time you start Outlook. There are no practice files for this exercise.

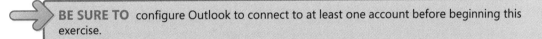

BE SURE TO configure Outlook to connect to at least one account before beginning this exercise.

1. Exit Outlook if it is running.

2. On the **Start** menu, click **Control Panel**.

3. If your computer is running Windows Vista, type Mail in the **Search** box, and then double-click the **Mail** icon in the search results. Otherwise, click **Classic View** in the left pane, and then double-click the **Mail** icon in the individual icon view.

4. In the **User Account Control** dialog box, if you're running as an administrator, click **Continue**. Otherwise, enter an administrator password, and then click **OK**.

> **Troubleshooting** The Mail icon appears only after you have completed the initial Outlook account configuration.

The Mail Setup dialog box opens. You can set up e-mail accounts and data files from this dialog box or from Outlook.

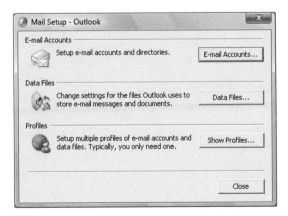

5. In the **Mail Setup** dialog box, click **Show Profiles**.

The Mail dialog box opens, listing the mail profiles set up on your computer under your user account profile. Other people's mail profiles are not visible to you.

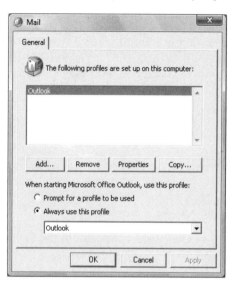

Outlook created the *Outlook* profile the first time you configured Outlook to connect to an e-mail account.

6. In the **Mail** dialog box, click **Add**.

The New Profile dialog box opens.

7. In the **Profile Name** box, type a name to identify your second profile.

> **Tip** You cannot change the name of a profile after you create it. If you want to work under a different profile name you must create a new profile.

You should make this name obvious—for example, the name of the company or e-mail account the profile applies to.

8. Click **OK**.

The Add New E-mail Account wizard starts.

9. If the **Choose E-mail Service** page appears, select the **Internet E-mail or Microsoft Exchange** option, and then click **Next**.

10. On the **Auto Account Setup** page, enter the display name, e-mail address, and password of the e-mail account you want to associate with the new profile in the corresponding text boxes, and then click **Next**.

11. After Outlook connects to the e-mail account, click **Finish**.

> **Troubleshooting** If Outlook isn't able to successfully connect to your account, see "Troubleshooting the Startup Wizard" earlier in this chapter.

The new profile appears in the Mail dialog box.

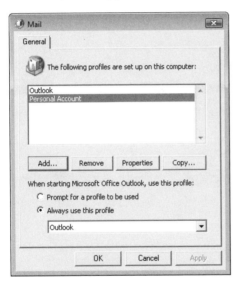

12. In the **Mail** dialog box, select the **Prompt for a profile to be used** option, and click **OK**.

13. Start Outlook.

The Choose Profile dialog box opens.

14. Click the **Profile Name** arrow, and in the list, click the profile you want to connect to.

If you want to stop this box from appearing in the future, you can click Options, and then select the Set As Default Profile check box. You can select an alternate default profile or have Outlook prompt you by returning to the Mail dialog box in Control Panel.

 BE SURE TO adjust your settings in the Mail dialog box before continuing, if you want to change the Outlook profile options.

Personalizing Your Outlook Workspace

The Outlook program window includes six areas or elements in which you work with Outlook or with your Outlook items (e-mail messages, contact records, calendar entries, tasks, or notes).

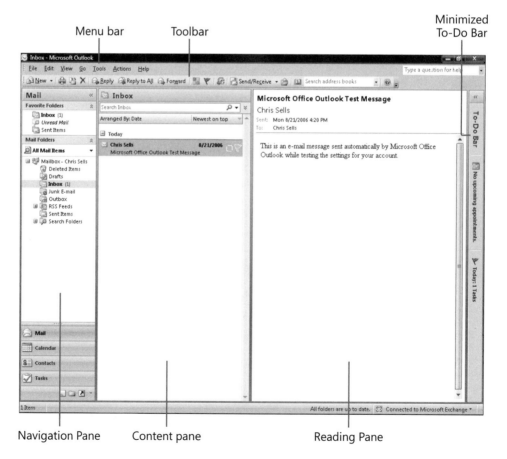

You might find that this is an ideal arrangement for the way you work. But if you're viewing the program window on a low-resolution screen, don't need all the available tools, or would like more space for the main work area, you can easily change the appearance and layout of the workspace in the following ways:

- **Menu bar.** When working in the Outlook program window, you can access commands from the menus displayed here. You can't hide the menu bar, but you can move it, docking it on any side of the program window or floating it anywhere on your screen.

- **Toolbars.** The buttons on the Standard toolbar, which is shown by default, represent frequently used commands in the File, Edit, and Actions categories. You can also display the Advanced toolbar and the Web toolbar. To display or hide a toolbar, right-click anywhere on the menu bar or toolbar area, and then click the name of the toolbar.

  See Also For information about the Advanced toolbar, see "Exploring the Advanced Toolbar" later in this chapter.

- **Navigation Pane.** This view pane appears on the left side of the Outlook window. Its contents change depending on the module you're viewing—it might display the module organizational structure, view options, links to external content or Help topics, and so on. You can tailor the Navigation Pane to suit your preferences:

  - You can minimize or expand the Navigation Pane by clicking the left- or right-facing chevrons at the top of the pane.

  - You can change the width of the Navigation Pane by dragging the vertical frame divider to its right.

  - You can change the number and size of the module buttons.

    To display more buttons at the bottom of the Navigation Pane, drag the handle above the module buttons to increase the available space, or click the Configure Buttons button in the lower-right corner of the Navigation Pane, and then click Show More Buttons. To display buttons in a small format or allocate more space to the Navigation Pane folders and options, drag the handle to decrease the available space, or click the Configure Buttons button and then click Show Fewer Buttons.

- **Module content pane.** This view pane appears in the center of the window, and displays the content of the selected module—your e-mail messages, calendar, contacts, and so on. You can display and organize content in this pane in many ways. These options are covered in this book as part of the individual module discussions.

- **Reading Pane.** When displayed, you can preview a selected message, appointment, attached document, and so on in this view pane. You can display the pane to the right of or below the content pane, or close it entirely.

See Also For information about previewing messages and message attachments in the Reading Pane, see "Viewing Messages and Message Attachments" in Chapter 4, "Handling E-Mail Messages."

- **To-Do Bar.** On the right side of the Outlook window, this view pane displays a monthly calendar, your upcoming appointments, and your task list. You can hide or display the pane, change the number of calendar months and appointments shown, and arrange the task list in different ways. You can change the size of the module content pane by minimizing or maximizing the To-Do Bar—the minimized pane bar displays your next appointment and the number of active and completed tasks due today.

    See Also For information about working with tasks on the To-Do Bar, see "Displaying Different Views of Tasks" in Chapter 8, "Tracking Tasks."

All of these window elements are available from every Outlook module, but the Reading Pane and To-Do Bar are not always displayed by default. The following table indicates whether they appear by default in each module.

Module	Reading Pane	To-Do Bar
Mail	Yes	Yes
Calendar	No	No
Contacts	No	Yes
Tasks	Yes	Yes
Notes	No	Yes

> **Tip** We refer to each of the above as modules. You might also think of them as folders, because each is represented in the Navigation Pane as a folder.

You can display or hide any of the workspace elements (other than the menu bar, which can't be changed) from the View menu. Your Outlook environment preferences are preserved from session to session. When you start Outlook, the Navigation Pane, To-Do Bar, and Calendar will appear the same way they did when you last exited.

When you first start Outlook, the Mail module appears and displays your Inbox. The Navigation Pane displays the folder structure of your mailbox (e-mail account). When connecting to any type of e-mail account, these four folders are visible:

- **Deleted Items.** Outlook items that you delete from other folders are held in this folder, and not deleted permanently until you empty the folder.

    See Also For information about deleting and restoring items, see the sidebar "Deleting Messages" in Chapter 4, "Handling E-Mail Messages."

- **Inbox.** Outlook delivers new messages to this folder.

- **Junk E-mail.** Outlook delivers messages held by the spam filter to this folder.
- **Sent Items.** When you send a message, Outlook stores a copy of it in this folder.

In Exchange account mailboxes, these four folders are also visible:

- **Drafts.** Outlook stores temporary copies of in-progress messages in this folder.

  See Also For information about creating and working with drafts, see "Creating and Sending Messages" in Chapter 3, "Sending E-Mail Messages."

- **Outbox.** Outlook holds outgoing messages in this folder while establishing a connection to your mail server.
- **RSS Feeds.** Web site information feeds you subscribe to are available from this folder. When you first start Outlook, you might find information feeds recommended by Microsoft here.
- **Search Folders.** These virtual folders track messages matching specific search criteria.

When you click the Folder List button at the bottom of the Navigation Pane, these six folders appear in Exchange Server mailboxes:

- **Calendar.** Displays the Outlook Calendar module.
- **Contacts.** Displays the Outlook Contacts module.
- **Journal.** Displays the Outlook Journal.
- **Notes.** Displays the Outlook Notes module.
- **Sync Issues.** Tracks conflicts and communication failures on your mail server or in your mailbox.
- **Tasks.** Displays the Outlook Tasks module.

You can display any of the modules—Mail, Calendar, Contacts, Tasks, or Notes—by clicking the corresponding button at the bottom of the Navigation Pane, by clicking the module name on the Go menu, or by holding down the Ctrl key and then pressing the function key representing the module you want to display:

Module	Keyboard shortcut
Mail	Ctrl+1
Calendar	Ctrl+2
Contacts	Ctrl+3
Tasks	Ctrl+4
Notes	Ctrl+5

The Navigation Pane contents differ depending on the displayed module. We discuss each module's Navigation Pane in the related chapters of this book.

In this exercise, you will change the space allocated to the module content pane, change the content displayed on the To-Do Bar, and learn how to move the menu bar and move or hide the toolbars. There are no practice files for this exercise.

BE SURE TO start Outlook and display the Inbox before beginning this exercise.

Minimize the
Navigation Pane

1. At the top of the **Navigation Pane**, click the **Minimize the Navigation Pane** button.

   The Navigation Pane contracts to display only a vertical bar on the left side of the program window. In the Mail module, buttons on the minimized Navigation Pane give you one-click access to the folders included in your Favorite Folders list.

2. Click the **Navigation Pane** bar at the top of the pane.

   Outlook displays your Favorite Folders and Mail Folders in a slide-out window.

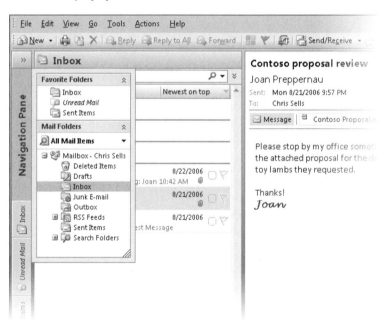

3. Click away from the slide-out window to collapse it.

4. At the top of the **To-Do Bar**, click the **Expand the To-Do Bar** button.

Expand the
To-Do Bar

   The To-Do Bar expands to display the calendars of the current and next months, your next four appointments, and your task list.

> **Tip** You can remove the To-Do Bar from the program window by clicking the Close button in the upper-right corner of the expanded To-Do Bar. To redisplay the To-Do Bar after closing it, point to To-Do Bar on the View menu, and then click Normal or Minimized.

5. On the **View** menu, point to **To-Do Bar**, and then click **Options**.

The To-Do Bar Options dialog box opens.

6. Change the **Date Navigator** setting to display 2 months and the **Appointments** setting to display 4 appointments. Then click **OK**.

7. On the **View** menu, point to **Reading Pane**, and then click **Bottom**.

The Reading Pane moves from the side of the content pane to the bottom.

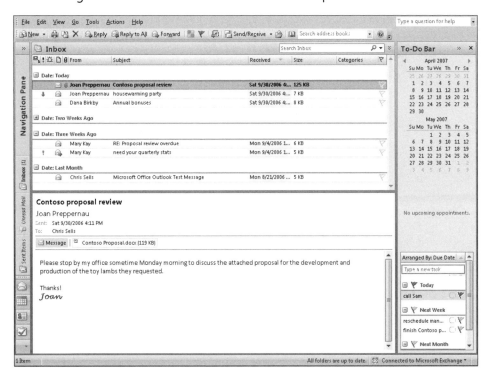

8. On the **View** menu, point to **Reading Pane**, and then click **Off** to close the Reading Pane entirely.

9. At the top of the Outlook window, point to the move handle (the vertical line of four dots) to the left of the **File** menu.

   The mouse pointer changes to a four-headed arrow.

10. Drag the menu bar to the right side of the Outlook program window. (Release the menu bar when it changes to a vertical orientation.)

    The menu names rotate to follow the window edge, but clicking any menu name displays the menu at the normal angle. You can use the same drag-and-drop technique to move any of the displayed toolbars.

11. Drag the menu bar by the move handle to the content pane.

    The menu bar becomes a *floating toolbar*.

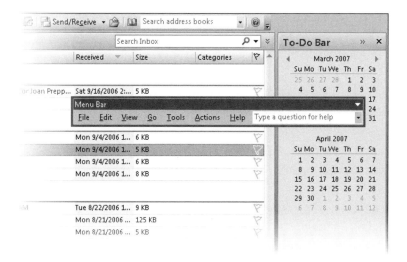

> **Tip** When the Outlook window is not maximized, you can place a floating toolbar inside or outside of the program window.

12. Right-click the floating menu bar or the toolbar area at the top of the Outlook window.

On the toolbar shortcut menu, you can select the toolbars you want to display.

13. Using the techniques discussed in this topic, rearrange the Outlook window elements to your liking.

> **Troubleshooting** Changes you implement might make your Outlook window appear different from those shown in this book. We depict the Outlook window with the menu bar and Standard toolbar at the top of the window, the Navigation Pane and To-Do Bar maximized, and the Reading Pane displayed on the right side of the window.

Exploring the Advanced Toolbar

The Outlook program window has three toolbars: the Standard toolbar, the Advanced toolbar, and the Web toolbar. Even people who use Outlook on a daily basis might find that they have never displayed the Advanced toolbar or used any of the commands available on it.

> **Tip** You can access Internet resources and interact with Internet Explorer from the Web toolbar. Because the Web toolbar functionality is not specific to Outlook, we don't discuss it in this book.

We don't make use of the Advanced toolbar in this book, but you can experiment with it on your own—you might find it very useful to have its commands available to you. To display the Advanced toolbar, right-click the menu bar or toolbar and then click Advanced.

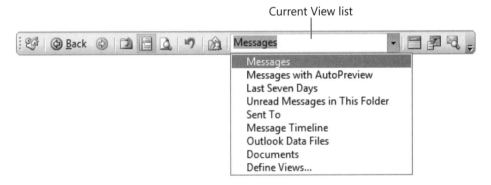

In the Mail module, the features and commands available from the Advanced toolbar include:

● **Outlook Today.** The Outlook Today page, which in a previous version of Outlook appeared by default when you started the program, presents information from your Calendar and Tasks list along with a count of the unread messages in your Inbox and all the messages in your Drafts folder and Outbox. If you would like to see this overview page when you start Outlook, display the Outlook Today page, click the Customize Outlook Today button, select the When Starting, Go Directly To Outlook Today check box, and then click Save Changes. On the Customize Outlook Today page, you can also configure what is shown in the message, calendar, and tasks areas, and choose between five page layouts and themes.

● **Back, Forward, and Up One Level.** You can quickly move between folders by using these commands.

- **Reading Pane.** Toggles the display of the Reading Pane on the right side of the window.

- **Print Preview.** Previews the currently selected item as it would be printed using the default settings.

- **Undo.** Reverts your most recent change. For example, if you delete an e-mail message and then click the Undo button, the message moves back to the original folder.

- **Rules and Alerts.** Opens the Rules And Alerts dialog box, where you can create and manage rules for incoming e-mail and RSS feeds, and alerts.

- **Current View list.** This drop-down list includes all available views of the current folder.

- **Group By Box.** Toggles the display of a box in the content pane header from which you can choose how Outlook groups the displayed content.

- **Field Chooser.** Toggles the display of the Field Chooser window, from which you can specify the item fields you want to display in the content pane, by dragging fields between the Field Chooser window and the content pane header.

- **AutoPreview.** Toggles the display of the first three lines of message text within the content pane. AutoPreview is specific to the folder in which you select it, so you can choose to display extra message text in only certain folders.

In the Calendar module, the Advanced toolbar includes:

- **Plan a Meeting.** Opens the Plan A Meeting dialog box in which you can view prospective attendees' schedules. This is similar to the Scheduling page of a meeting window. After you enter information in the Plan A Meeting dialog box, Outlook displays a meeting window in which you can enter the meeting subject and location before sending invitations.

In the Contacts module, the Advanced toolbar includes:

- **New Meeting Request to Contact.** Opens a meeting window addressed to the currently selected contact(s).

- **New Task for Contact.** Opens a task window assigned to the currently selected contact.

- **Explore Web Page.** Displays the Web page listed in the currently selected contact record in your default Internet browser.

When you display the Advanced toolbar it is available (in its different forms) from any module.

Outlook with Business Contact Manager

Microsoft Office Outlook 2007 with Business Contact Manager integrates complete small business contact-management capabilities into Outlook so that you can easily manage prospect and customer information and track sales and marketing activities all in one place. You can use the Business Contact Manager tools to:

- **Organize your customer information in one place.** Track your prospects, leads, and customers from initial contact through closing and after the sale.

- **Manage sales leads and opportunities.** Monitor opportunities by type, sales stage, projected amount of sale, and probability of closing, and then easily re-assign leads.

- **Review important sales metrics.** Use the summaries in the new central information dashboard to help you make decisions and prioritize tasks.

- **Distribute personalized marketing communications.** Create filtered mailing lists, and then use the improved mail merge integration functionality with Microsoft Office Publisher, Microsoft Office Word, or HTML to personalize print and e-mail marketing materials.

- **Track marketing campaign activities.** Evaluate the success of your campaign so that you can target your marketing budget more effectively in the future.

- **Centralize project information.** Organize project information and follow up on project-related tasks, including activities, e-mail messages, meetings, notes, and attachments.

When using Outlook with Business Contact Manager you can easily access all of your customer communications history in one place within the familiar Outlook environment. The Business Contact Manager toolbar at the top of the Outlook window contains commands for managing Accounts, Business Contacts, Opportunities, Business Projects, Project Tasks, and Marketing Campaigns. The Business Contact Manager home page, or dashboard, is your central point for managing your company's important business contact and opportunity information.

Outlook 2007 with Business Contact Manager is available in the Microsoft Office Professional 2007 and Microsoft Office Small Business 2007 product suites, or through volume licensing programs. For more information about Outlook 2007 with Business Contact Manager, visit

www.microsoft.com/office/outlook/contactmanager/prodinfo/

Key Points

- You can configure Outlook 2007 to connect to most e-mail accounts automatically. You need to provide only your e-mail address and account password.

- You can configure multiple e-mail accounts within one Outlook profile, but you can have only one Exchange account per profile. To connect to multiple Exchange accounts from the same computer, you must log on to each through its own profile.

- You can rearrange the Outlook window to suit your working preferences. Any of the Outlook view panes—the Navigation Pane, To-Do Bar, and Reading Pane—as well as the Advanced toolbar can be displayed in any Outlook module. Outlook preserves changes to the default arrangement from session to session.

Chapter at a Glance

Personalize an electronic business card, **page 49**

Quickly locate contact information, **page 62**

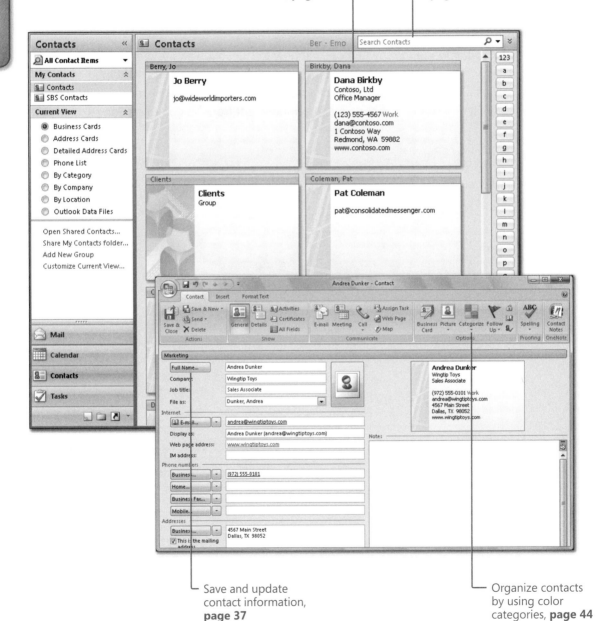

Save and update contact information, **page 37**

Organize contacts by using color categories, **page 44**

2 Managing Contact Information

In this chapter, you will learn to:

✔ Work in the contact window.

✔ Save and update contact information.

✔ Organize contacts by using color categories.

✔ Create an address book and a distribution list.

✔ Personalize an electronic business card.

✔ Display different views of contact information.

✔ Locate and print contact information.

Having immediate access to current, accurate contact information for the people you need to interact with—by e-mail, telephone, mail, or otherwise—is important for timely and effective communication. You can easily build and maintain a detailed contact list, or address book, in the Microsoft Office Outlook 2007 *Contacts module*. From your address book, you can look up information, generate messages, and share contact information with other people. You can also keep track of your interactions with a person whose contact information is stored in Outlook.

> **Tip** Throughout this chapter, as well as this book, we frequently refer to people whose contact information you have stored in Outlook as *contacts*.

In this chapter, you will investigate the command structure in the Outlook contact window, create contact records, and organize your contacts by using color categories. You will create a distribution list and an address book, and personalize your own electronic business card. Next, you will display different views of contact information and filter and find contacts by using the new Instant Search feature. Then you will print a contact record and an address list.

See Also Do you need only a quick refresher on the topics in this chapter? See the Quick Reference entries on pages xxxvii–lxv.

Important Before you can use the practice files in this chapter, you need to install them from the book's companion CD to their default location. See "Using the Book's CD" on page xxv for more information.

Troubleshooting Graphics and operating system–related instructions in this book reflect the Windows Vista user interface. If your computer is running Microsoft Windows XP and you experience trouble following the instructions as written, please refer to the "Information for Readers Running Windows XP" section at the beginning of this book.

Working in the Contact Window

Outlook displays *contact records* in the Contacts module. When you create or open a contact record, it opens in a *contact window*. The contact window has its own set of commands separate from those in the Outlook program window. You can create, insert, and format information in a contact record by using the contact window commands.

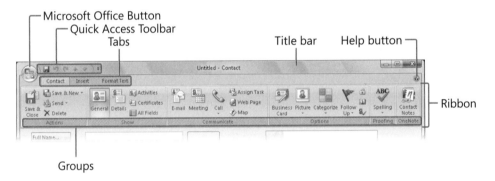

The new Outlook item window interface is designed to more closely reflect the way people generally work within the item windows. In a contact window, the interface includes the following elements:

- Commands related to managing contact records (such as creating, saving, and printing) are available from the menu that appears when you click the *Microsoft Office Button*. This menu, which we refer to throughout this book as the *Office menu*, takes the place of the File menu that appeared in previous versions of Outlook in the message, appointment, contact, and other form windows. The File menu still appears in the standard Outlook program window.

- Some commands are represented by buttons on the *Quick Access Toolbar* to the right of the Microsoft Office Button. By default, the contact window Quick Access Toolbar displays the Save, Undo, Redo, Print, Previous Item, and Next Item buttons. The Save and Print commands are available on the Office menu, but the other commands are not available on either the Office menu or the Ribbon; they are available only from the Quick Access Toolbar. You can add commands to the Quick Access Toolbar so that they are available regardless of which tab is currently active in the message window.

> **Important** Adding a command to the Quick Access Toolbar in an Outlook contact window does not add it to the Quick Access Toolbar of any other Outlook item window or any other 2007 Microsoft Office system program window.

- The *title bar* displays the contact's name. At the right end of the title bar are the three familiar buttons that have the same function in all Windows programs. You can temporarily hide the Word window by clicking the Minimize button, adjust the size of the window by clicking the Restore Down/Maximize button, and close the active document or quit Word by clicking the Close button.

Importing SharePoint Contacts Lists

If your organization uses Microsoft SharePoint products and technologies, you might have access to a SharePoint site containing, among other things, contact information for employees, project team members, or other groups of people. You can import the information stored in a SharePoint Contacts List into Outlook. Follow these steps:

1. Display the SharePoint site in your Web browser and then display the SharePoint Contacts List you want to import into Outlook.

2. On the **Actions** menu, click **Connect to Outlook**.

   If it isn't already running, Outlook starts.

3. In the **Microsoft Office Outlook** message box asking whether you want to connect the SharePoint Contacts List to Outlook, click **Yes**.

   If you don't already have one, Outlook creates a folder named SharePoint Lists within your profile and creates a contacts folder containing the information from the SharePoint Contacts List. Then Outlook displays your Contacts pane. The new contacts folder is available in the Other Contacts list.

● Below the title bar is the *Ribbon*, a new feature in many of the programs in the Office system. In Outlook 2007, the Ribbon appears in the message, contact, appointment, meeting, event, and task windows. (The Outlook program window displays a menu bar and toolbars.) Commands are presented on the Ribbon rather than on the more-traditional menus or toolbars so that you can work most efficiently within the window. The Ribbon is organized into task-specific *tabs*, which are further divided into feature- or task-specific *groups* of commands.

See Also For information about the Ribbon in the Outlook message window, see "Working in the Message Window" in Chapter 3, "Sending E-Mail Messages." For information about the Ribbon in the appointment, meeting, and event windows, see "Working in the Calendar Item Windows" in Chapter 6, "Managing Appointments, Events, and Meetings." For information about the Ribbon in the task window, see "Working in the Task Window" in Chapter 8, "Tracking Tasks."

● The buttons in each group change size depending on the width of the program window. They might be large, small, or wide, and might be labeled with the button name, icon, or both. Pointing to any button displays the button name in a *ScreenTip* that sometimes also describes the button's function.

Some buttons have arrows, but not all arrows function the same way. If you point to a button that has the arrow incorporated into the button body, clicking the button will display a list of options for you to choose from. If the arrow is separate from the button body, clicking the arrow will display a list of options and clicking the button will perform the currently selected action.

● Related but less common commands are not represented in a group as buttons. Instead they are available from a dialog box, which you can display by clicking the *Dialog Box Launcher* at the right end of the group title bar.

● The **Microsoft Office Outlook Help** button appears at the right end of the Ribbon.

The goal of the redesigned environment is to make working within an item window more intuitive. Commands for tasks you perform often are no longer hidden on menus and in dialog boxes, and features that you might not have discovered before are now plainly visible.

See Also For information about customizing the commands shown on the Quick Access Toolbar, see "Making Favorite Outlook Commands Easily Accessible" in Chapter 12, "Customizing and Configuring Outlook." For information about repositioning the Quick Access Toolbar and hiding the Ribbon tabs, see "Working in the Message Window" in Chapter 3, "Sending E-Mail Messages."

In this exercise, you will take a tour of the available menu, tabs, and groups in an Outlook 2007 contact window. There are no practice files for this exercise.

> ➤ **BE SURE TO** start Outlook before beginning this exercise.

Contacts

1. In the **Navigation Pane**, click the **Contacts** button.

The Contacts module opens. The content pane, which in the Contacts module is the **Contacts pane**, displays your main address book, with any contact records it contains displayed as business cards.

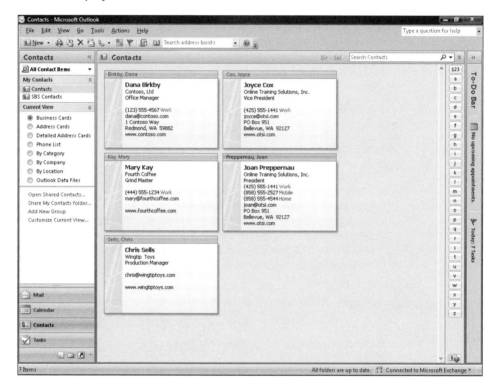

> **Troubleshooting** If the contact records in your Contacts module aren't presented like those shown here, click the Business Cards option in the Current View list in the Navigation Pane.

New Contact

2. On the Standard toolbar, click the **New Contact** button.

> **Tip** If you want to work in two modules at the same time, you can open a module in a second instance of Outlook by right-clicking the module button in the Navigation Pane, and then clicking Open In New Window.

A new contact window opens.

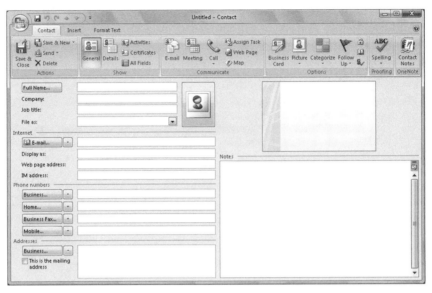

> **Important** Depending on your screen resolution and the size of the contact window, you might see more or fewer buttons in each of the groups, the buttons you see might be represented by larger or smaller icons than those shown, or the group might be represented by a button that you click to display the group's commands. Experiment with the size of the contact window to understand the effect on the appearance of the tabs.

Microsoft Office
Button

3. Click in the Notes area to activate the buttons on the Ribbon. Then in the upper-left corner of the message window, click the **Microsoft Office Button** to display the menu.

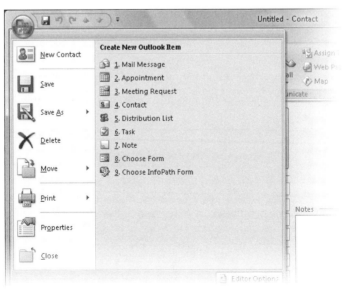

Notice that although you are working in the contact window, you can create any type of Outlook item from the Office menu. We'll talk more about the commands available from the Office menu in other chapters of this book.

4. Click away from the Office menu to close it.

In the contact window, the Ribbon includes three tabs:

- Contact
- Insert
- Format Text

> **Tip** Depending on what programs are installed on your computer, tabs and groups other than those described here might also appear on the Ribbon. For example, if Microsoft Outlook with Business Contact Manager is installed on your computer, you will have a Business Tools tab. If you have add-ins installed that interface with Outlook or with the Office system, you might also have an Add-Ins tab.

The Contact tab is active by default. Buttons representing commands related to creating contact records are organized on this tab in five groups:

- Actions
- Show
- Communicate
- Options
- Proofing

You can create a basic contact record by using only the commands available on this tab.

> **Tip** Only the buttons for the commands that can be performed on the currently selected message element are active.

5. Click the **Insert** tab.

Buttons representing commands related to inserting additional content in a contact record are organized on this tab in six groups:

- Include
- Tables
- Illustrations
- Links
- Text
- Symbols

6. Click the **Format Text** tab.

Buttons representing commands related to formatting the text within the Notes field are organized on this tab in six groups:

- Clipboard
- Font
- Paragraph
- Styles
- Zoom
- Editing

> **Tip** Some groups have a small button in the lower-right corner called the *Dialog Box Launcher*; clicking this button opens a task pane or dialog box related to the group of buttons.

Dialog Box
Launcher

7. On the **Format Text** tab, in the **Clipboard** group, click the **Dialog Box Launcher**.

The Clipboard task pane opens.

> **Tip** In this book, when we give instructions to implement a command we tell you on what tab and in which group the command button appears. When directing you to use multiple command buttons on the same tab, we might omit the tab name to avoid needless repetition.

8. In the **Font** group, click the **Dialog Box Launcher**.

The Font dialog box opens.

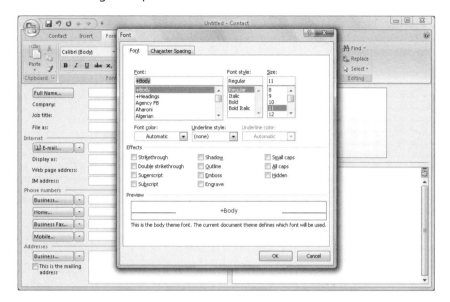

You can access certain settings not available from the Font group, such as Underline Style, Underline Color, and the many font effects, from this dialog box.

 CLOSE the Font dialog box, the Clipboard task pane, and the contact window.

Saving and Updating Contact Information

Outlook stores contact information from different sources in separate address lists:

- *Global Address List (GAL).* If you're using Outlook to connect to a Microsoft Exchange Server account, your organization's contact information is stored in the GAL. The GAL might include names, job titles, e-mail addresses, office locations, telephone numbers, and other contact information. It can also include organizational information (each person's manager and direct subordinates) and group membership information (the distribution lists and aliases each person belongs to). The GAL is administered as part of Exchange Server. Outlook users can view the GAL but not change its contents.

- *Outlook Address Books.* The Contacts address book automatically created by Outlook is your main address book. This address book does not appear in the folder structure within the Navigation Pane—you display it by clicking the Contacts button.

You can create additional address books; for example, you might want to keep contact information for family and friends in an address book separate from client contact information, or maintain an address book for team members attached to a specific project. Each address book is a folder that contains contact items; in other words, a *contacts folder*. Contacts folders appear in the Navigation Pane along with other folders you create, and you can organize them in the same manner—for example, at the same level as your Inbox or within a project folder. All contacts folders are available from the My Contacts list in the Navigation Pane of the Contacts module.

See Also For information about creating contact folders, see "Creating an Additional Address Book" later in this chapter.

● *Mobile Address Book*. A Mobile Address Book containing all the contacts in your main address book for whom you have mobile phone numbers listed is created automatically if you have an Outlook Mobile Service account

See Also A discussion of Outlook Mobile Service is beyond the scope of this book. For information about Outlook Mobile Service and Mobile Address Books, refer to *Microsoft Office Outlook 2007 Inside Out* by Jim Boyce (Microsoft Press, 2007).

You can view all your address lists and address books in the Contacts module, or you can display a simple list from the Address Book window that opens when you click the Address Book button on the Standard toolbar. In the Address Book list, click the name of the Outlook address book or address list you want to display.

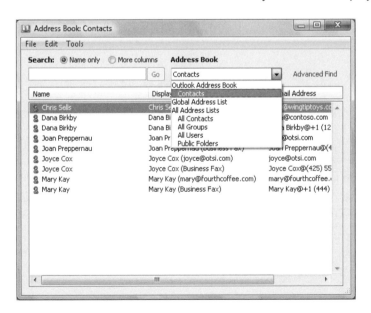

When you send an e-mail message to a person whose contact information is stored in one of your address books, you can quickly address the message to that person by typing his or her name into the To, Cc, or Bcc box, or by clicking the adjacent button to open the Address Book window and then selecting the intended recipient's name.

For each person whose information you record in an address book, you can store the following types of general information:

● Name, company name, and job title

● Business, home, and alternate addresses

● Business, home, mobile, pager, and other telephone numbers

● Business, home, and alternate fax numbers

● Web page address (*URL*), instant messaging (*IM*) address, and up to three e-mail addresses

● Photo or other identifying image

● General notes, which can include text and illustrations such as photos, clip art images, SmartArt diagrams, charts, and shapes

You can also store personal and organization-specific details for each contact:

● Professional information, including department, office location, profession, maager's name and assistant's name

● Personal information, including nickname, spouse or partner's name, birthday, anniversary, and the title (such as Miss, Mrs., or Ms.) and suffix (such as Jr. or Sr.) to use in correspondence

You can create a contact record containing only one piece of information (for example, a name or company name), or as much information as you want to include. You can quickly create contact records for several people who work for the same company by cloning the company information from an existing record to a new one. And of course, you can add to or change the information stored in a contact record at any time.

The order in which Outlook displays contact records is controlled by the *File As* setting. By default, Outlook files contacts by last name (Last, First order). If you prefer, you can change the File As order for new contacts to any of the following:

● First Last

● Company

● Last, First (Company)

● Company (Last, First)

To set the File As order, click Options on the Tools menu, and then in the Options dialog box, click the Contact Options button. You can change the File As order for an individual contact by selecting the order you want in the File As list in the contact record.

In this exercise, you will create and then edit a contact record. There are no practice files for this exercise.

> **BE SURE TO** display the Contacts module before beginning this exercise.

New Contact

1. On the Standard toolbar, click the **New Contact** button.

   A new contact window opens.

   See Also For information about the toolbars available in Outlook, see "Personalizing Your Outlook Workspace" and "Exploring the Advanced Toolbar" in Chapter 1, "Getting Started with Outlook 2007."

2. In the **Full Name** box, type John Emory, and then press the ⌨Tab key.

   Outlook transfers the name to the File As box and displays it in the default order (Last, First).

3. In the **Company** box, type Wingtip Toys.

4. In the **Job title** box, type Assembly Plant Manager.

5. In the **Internet** area, type john@wingtiptoys.com in the **E-mail** box, and press ⌨Tab.

   The Display As box shows the contact's name and e-mail address as they will appear in the headers of e-mail messages you send and receive. You can change the display name, for example by removing the e-mail address or by adding a designator of *Work* or *Home*.

6. In the **Web page address** box, type www.wingtiptoys.com.

   Outlook automatically formats the text as a hyperlink.

7. In the **Phone numbers** area, type 9725550101 in the **Business** box, and press ⌨Tab.

   > **Troubleshooting** The first time you enter a phone number for a contact, The Location Information dialog box opens, prompting you to enter your own country, area code, and any necessary dialing information such as a carrier code. Outlook sets up dialing rules based on the information you enter. You *must* enter at least your country and area code in the dialog box and then click OK; you can't close the dialog box without entering the requested information.

   Outlook formats the series of numbers you entered as a telephone number.

8. In the **Addresses** area, click in the text box, type 4567 Main Street, press the ⌨Enter key, and then type Dallas, TX 98052.

> **Tip** When you finish entering information in the Addresses area, Outlook verifies that the address conforms to a standard pattern. If Outlook detects irregularities in the address you enter, the Check Address dialog box opens, prompting you to enter the street address, city, state or province, postal code, and country in separate fields from which it reassembles the address. The intention of this feature is to verify that you have the information necessary to send mail to the contact. If you often create contact records with foreign addresses that don't conform to the pattern Outlook is looking for, you might find this annoying. If you determine that the information in the Check Address dialog box is correct, you can click Cancel to close the dialog box without making changes.

9. Click the **Business** arrow, and then in the list, click **Home**.

   The button label changes to indicate that you are displaying John's home address information.

10. In the text box, type 111 Magnolia Lane, press Enter , and then type Flower Mound, TX 98053.

> **Tip** If you record multiple addresses for a contact and want to specify one as the default mailing address, display that address and then select the This Is The Mailing Address check box.

11. On the **Contact** tab, in the **Actions** group, click the **Save & Close** button.

   The contact window closes.

The Contacts pane now includes the new contact record for John Emory.

New contact record

12. In the Contacts pane, double-click the contact record for **John Emory**.

 13. On the **Contact** tab, in the **Show** group, click the **Details** button.

Outlook displays the Details page of the contact record.

> **Tip** You can assign follow-up flags to contact entries, and link contact entries to e-mail messages, appointments, tasks, and other Outlook items. You can view all items linked to a contact on the Activities page of the contact record.

14. In the **Spouse/Partner** box, type Barbara.

15. Click the **Birthday** arrow, scroll the calendar to **July**, and then click **31**.

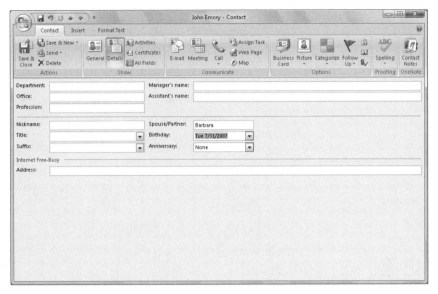

16. In the **Actions** group, click the **Save & New** arrow, and then in the list, click **New Contact from Same Company**.

Outlook creates a new contact record, already containing the company's name, URL, phone number, and address.

17. In the **Full Name** box, type Andrea Dunker, and in the **Job title** box, type Sales Associate.

18. In the **E-mail** box, type andrea@wingtiptoys.com.

19. Save and close the open contact records.

20. Use the techniques described in this exercise to create contact records for the following people:

Full name	E-mail address
Greg Guzik	greg@wideworldimporters.com
Jo Berry	jo@wideworldimporters.com
Andy Ruth	andy@wideworldimporters.com

You will use these contact records in later exercises.

CLOSE each of the open contact records to return to the Contacts pane.

BE SURE TO retain the contact records for use in a later exercise.

Quickly Communicating with Contacts

Contact records aren't useful only for storing information; you can also initiate a number of actions that are specific to the selected contact.

Here are some of the actions you can perform from within a contact record by using the commands in the Communicate group on the Contact tab:

● You can create an e-mail message addressed to the contact by clicking the E-mail button.

● You can create a meeting request that includes the contact by clicking the Meeting button.

● If you have Internet telephone capabilities, you can place a call to the contact by clicking the Call arrow, and then in the list, clicking the telephone number you would like to dial.

● You can create a task assigned to the contact by clicking the Assign Task button.

● You can display the contact's Web site by clicking the Web Page button.

● You can display a map of the contact's address by clicking the Map button.

If you have OneNote 2007 installed, you can create a OneNote note linked to the contact record. On the Contact tab, in the OneNote group, click the Contact Notes button.

Organizing Contacts by Using Color Categories

You can organize contacts in related groups by assigning them to *categories*. For example, you might assign contact records for customers to a Customers category. You can sort and filter Outlook items by category.

Whereas previous versions of Outlook used simple named categories, Outlook 2007 uses *color categories* in which category names are linked to colors to provide a quick visual representation of information. You can change the name or color of any category, and create new categories. Twenty-five colors are available, but if that's not sufficient, you can assign the same color to multiple categories. When you assign a contact to a category, the category color appears at the top of the contact record.

See Also For more information about color categories, see "Organizing Messages by Using Color Categories" in Chapter 5, "Managing Your Inbox." For information about grouping contact records by color categories, see "Displaying Different Views of Contact Information" later in this chapter.

In this exercise, you will assign contacts to color categories and rename a category.

> **USE** the *Andrea Dunker* and *John Emory* contact records you created earlier in this chapter.
> **BE SURE TO** display the Contacts module before beginning this exercise.

1. Double-click the contact record for **Andrea Dunker to open the contact window**.

2. On the **Contact** tab, in the **Options** group, click the **Categorize** button, and then in the list, click **Green Category**.

   Because this is the first time you've assigned an item to this category, the Rename Category dialog box opens.

3. With the current category name selected, type Marketing, and then click **Yes**.

> **Tip** You can assign shortcut keys to up to 11 categories.

A green category bar labeled *Marketing* appears across the top of the contact record.

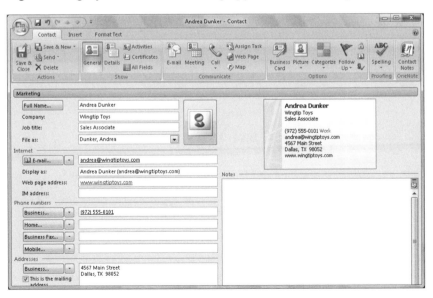

Save & Close

4. In the **Actions** group, click the **Save & Close** button.

5. Double-click the contact record for **John Emory**.

6. In the **Options** group, in the **Categorize** list, click **All Categories**.

   The Color Categories dialog box opens.

7. In the **Name** list, select the **Marketing** check box, select the **Purple Category** check box, and then click **Rename**.

   The Purple Category name is selected for editing.

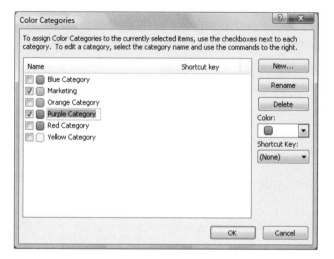

8. Type Personal to rename the category, and then click **OK**.

   Purple and green category bars at the top of the contact record indicate that John Emory is a member of the Personal and Marketing categories.

CLOSE the open contact record to return to the Contacts pane.

Creating a Distribution List

In an address book, you can create a contact record containing a variety of contact information for an individual person, or a distribution list containing the e-mail addresses of multiple people. You can add people to a distribution list by selecting them from an address book or by manually entering e-mail addresses.

When you send a message to a distribution list, each member of the distribution list receives a copy of the message. This is a useful tool if you frequently send messages to specific groups of people such as employees working in the marketing department, clients located in a particular region, or players on a sports team.

If you want to send a message to most, but not all, members of a distribution list, you can remove people from the recipient list for a specific message at the time you send it.

In this exercise, you will create a distribution list and add new contacts to your address book.

USE the *John Emory* contact record you created earlier in this chapter.
BE SURE TO display the Contacts module before beginning this exercise.

New Contact

1. On the Standard toolbar, click the **New Contact** arrow, and then in the list, click **Distribution List**.

   A distribution list window opens.

Select
Members

2. In the **Name** box, type Clients, and then on the **Distribution List** tab, in the **Members** group, click the **Select Members** button.

   The Select Members dialog box opens. If your organization has a Global Address List, Outlook displays its contents.

3. If your address book isn't already displayed, click the **Address Book** arrow, and then in the list, under **Outlook Address Book**, click **Contacts**.

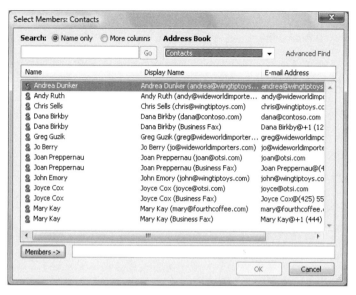

4. In the **Name** list, click **John Emory**. Click the **Members** button, and then click **OK**.

> **Tip** You can add multiple names to a distribution list by double-clicking each name to insert it in the Members box and then clicking OK, or by holding down the Ctrl key while selecting multiple names, clicking the Members button, and then clicking OK.

The Clients distribution list now includes John Emory.

5. In the **Members** group, click the **Add New** button.

6. In the **Add New Members** dialog box, type **Pat Coleman** in the **Display name** box, and then type **pat@consolidatedmessenger.com** in the **E-mail address** box.

7. Select the **Add to Contacts** check box to add Pat to your address book as well as to the distribution list.

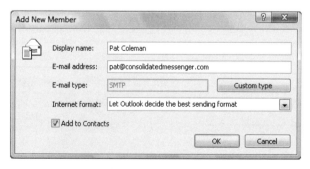

8. In the **Add New Member** dialog box, click **OK**.

The distribution list now includes John Emory and Pat Coleman.

9. Repeat steps 5 through 8 to add the following people to the Clients distribution list and to your address book:

Display name	E-mail address
Holly Dickson	holly@consolidatedmessenger.com
Max Stevens	max@consolidatedmessenger.com
Linda Mitchell	linda@lucernepublishing.com
Jill Shrader	jill@lucernepublishing.com

Each new distribution list member appears in the distribution list in alphabetical order.

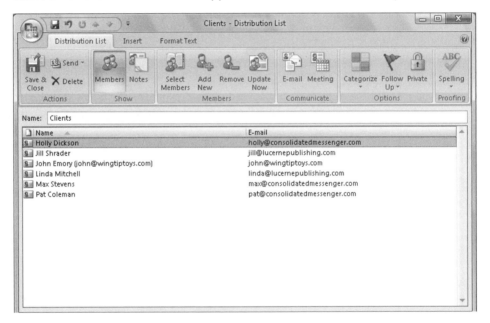

BE SURE TO retain the distribution list for use in a later exercise.

CLOSE the Clients distribution list window, saving your changes when prompted to do so.

Personalizing an Electronic Business Card

A new feature in Outlook 2007 is the presentation of contact record information in the form of a graphic that resembles a business card. When you enter a person's contact information in a contact record, basic information including the person's name, company, and job title; work, mobile, and home telephone numbers; and e-mail, postal, Web page, and instant messaging addresses appear in the business card shown in the upper-right corner of the contact window. (Only the first ten lines of information fit on the card.) If the contact record includes an image, the image appears on the left side. You can change the types of information that appear, rearrange the information fields, format the text and background, and add, change, or remove images such as a logo or photograph.

Creating a business card for yourself provides you with an attractive way of presenting your contact information to people you correspond with in e-mail. You can attach your business card to an outgoing e-mail message or include it as part (or all) of your e-mail signature. The recipient of your business card can easily create a contact record for you by saving the business card to his or her Outlook address book.

See Also   For information about e-mail signatures, see "Adding Signatures to Messages Automatically" in Chapter 3, "Sending E-Mail Messages."

In this exercise, you will modify the business card associated with your contact record.

> **USE** the *05_FourthCoffee* image. This practice file is available in the *Chapter02* subfolder under *SBS_Outlook2007*.
>
> **BE SURE TO** display the Contacts module in Business Cards view before beginning this exercise.

1. If you haven't already done so, create a contact record for yourself. Include your name, company, job title, business and mobile phone numbers, fax number, and one or more e-mail addresses.

   As you enter your information, it appears in the generic business card displayed in the upper-right corner of the contact window.

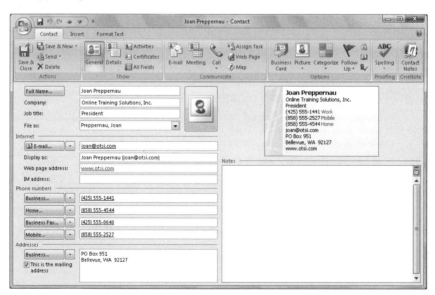

**Business
Card**

2. On the **Contact** tab, in the **Options** group, click the **Business Card** button.

The Edit Business Card dialog box opens.

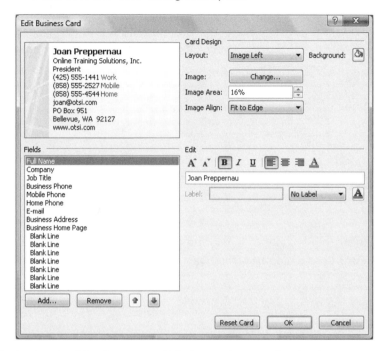

Background
Color

3. In the **Card Design** area, click the **Background Color** button.

You can select from the basic colors or define a custom background color.

4. In the **Color** dialog box, click a color you like, and then click **OK**.

The card preview reflects the new background color.

5. In the **Card Design** area, click **Change**.

The Add Card Picture dialog box opens, displaying the contents of your Pictures folder. You can add a business logo, your photograph, or any other identifying image you would like to appear on your business card.

6. Browse to your *Documents\SBS_Outlook2007\Chapter02* folder, click the *05_FourthCoffee* image, and then click **OK**.

The Fourth Coffee company logo appears on the left side of your business card.

7. In the **Image Area** box, type or select (by clicking the arrows) **30%**.

8. Click the **Image Align** button, and then in the list, click **Center Left**.

The enlarged logo moves to the vertical center of the business card.

> **Tip** You can add or remove fields from the business card, format the text, and add labels, by using the commands in the Fields and Edit areas.

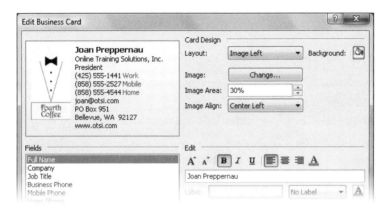

9. Make any other changes to your business card that you want, and then in the **Edit Business Card** dialog box, click **OK**.

> **Tip** You can undo all your changes by clicking the Reset Card button at the bottom of the dialog box.

The contact window displays your customized business card. Any changes you make to your contact information will be immediately reflected in your business card.

10. In the **Actions** group, click the **Save & Close** button.

The Contacts pane displays your personalized business card.

CLOSE the contact window, saving your changes when prompted to do so.

Creating an Additional Address Book

Although you can certainly track all your contacts—business or personal—within the Contacts module, and locate specific contacts or groups of contacts by categorizing, sorting, and filtering, you might find it useful to create a separate address book containing contact records for only a specific group of people. For example, you might want to have an address book containing only club members, neighborhood contacts, parents and teachers from your child's school, or sports teammates. You create this additional address book by creating a folder designated as containing contact items (a *contacts folder*). As with other folders, you can share the contacts folder with other Outlook users on your network, or export it for distribution to other people.

> ## Sharing Address Books
>
> To share one or more address books with other people on your network:
>
> 1. In the Contacts module **Navigation Pane**, in the **My Contacts** list, right-click the address book you want to share, and then click **Share** (for example, **Share "SBS Contacts"**). Or if you want to share all your address books, click the **Share My Contacts folder** link at the bottom of the pane.
>
>   Outlook creates a Sharing Invitation message containing information about the selected address book.
>
> 2. In the **To** box, enter the names of people or distribution lists on your network with whom you want to share the address book.
>
>   Your sharing options vary depending on the address book you are sharing. If you are sharing your primary address book, you can request reciprocal permission by selecting the Request Permission To View Recipient's Contacts Folder check box. If you are sharing a secondary address book, you can give the recipient full access by selecting the Recipient Can Add, Edit, And Delete Items In This Contacts Folder check box.
>
> 3. In the message header, click **Send**.
>
> 4. In the **Microsoft Office Outlook** message box asking you to confirm that you want to share the selected contacts folder(s), click **Yes**.

In this exercise, you will create a contacts folder. There are no practice files for this exercise.

> **BE SURE TO** display the Contacts module before beginning this exercise.

New Contact

1. Click the **New Contact** arrow, and then in the list, click **Folder**.

   The Create New Folder dialog box opens.

2. In the **Name** box, type SBS Contacts.

   > **Important** The name of this folder begins with *SBS* so that you can easily differentiate it from other folders in your mailbox.

3. Click the **Folder contains** arrow, and note the types of folders you can create.

Because you are creating this folder from within the Contacts module, Contact Items is selected by default. However, you can create any type of folder from within any module.

4. In the **Folder contains** list, click **Contact Items**.

5. In the **Select where to place the folder** list, click **Mailbox** (or your account name, depending on your installation) to place the folder at the same level as your Inbox.

6. In the **Create New Folder** dialog box, click **OK**.

The SBS Contacts address book appears in the My Contacts list at the top of the Contacts module Navigation Pane.

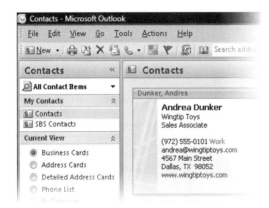

Mail

7. In the **Navigation Pane**, click the **Mail** button to display your Inbox.

The SBS Contacts folder is not visible in the Mail Folders area of the Navigation Pane, which currently displays the All Mail Items list.

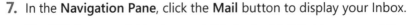

Folder List

8. At the bottom of the **Navigation Pane**, click the **Folder List** button.

The Folder List Navigation Pane, displaying all Outlook items rather than only mail items, replaces the Mail Navigation Pane. The SBS Contacts folder appears above your Sent Items folder.

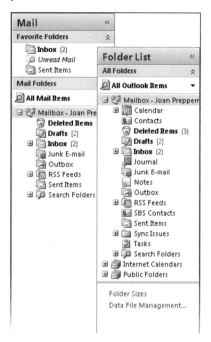

A contact card icon next to the folder name indicates that the folder is designed to hold contact items.

9. In the **All Outlook Items** list, click the **SBS Contacts** folder.

Outlook displays the currently empty SBS Contacts address book. The same functionality available to you within your main address book is available within this custom address book.

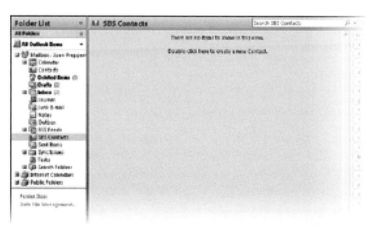

10. In the **Navigation Pane**, click the **Contacts** button.

    The Contact module opens, still displaying the SBS Contacts address book.

11. In the **My Contacts** list, click **Contacts** to display your main address book.

Exporting Address Books

To export an address book for distribution to Outlook users outside of your network:

1. In the Outlook program window, on the **File** menu, click **Import and Export**.

   The Import And Export wizard starts.

2. In the **Choose an action to perform** list, click **Export to a file**, and click **Next**.

3. In the **Create a file of type** list, click **Personal Folder File (.pst)**, and click **Next**.

4. In the **Select the folder to export from** list, click the contacts folder you want to export, and then click **Next**.

5. Click the **Browse** button to the right of the **Save exported file as** box. Then in the **Open Personal Folders** dialog box, select the location where you want to save the file, type the file name, and click **OK**.

6. On the wizard's last page, click **Finish**.

7. In the **Create Microsoft Personal Folders** dialog box, you can rename the file or enter a password to restrict access to the file's contents. Make any changes you want, and then click **OK**.

   Outlook exports the selected address book to a file that you can send to other Outlook users, who can import and display it.

The process of exporting an address book for use outside of Outlook is identical to that described above, except that in step 3, you select the type of file you want to create. You can create a comma-separated file, tab-separated file, Microsoft Office Access database, or Microsoft Office Excel workbook.

Displaying Different Views of Contact Information

You can view an address book in many different formats; each view presents differing information from your contact records either as cards or in a list.

- **Business Cards view** displays the business card associated with each contact record—either the default card created by Outlook, or a custom card if you have one. Business cards are displayed in alphabetical order by first or last name, depending on the File As selection.

- **Address Cards view** displays contact information as truncated business cards, with only the contact's name and e-mail address visible. Address cards are displayed in alphabetical order by the File As field.

- **Detailed Address Cards view** displays contact information in a format similar to that of Address Cards view but includes more information, such as job title and company name.

- **Phone List view** displays a columnar list including each contact's name, company, and contact numbers.

Other list views include:

- By Category
- By Company
- By Location

In these views, contact records are grouped by the selected field. You can expand and collapse the groups, or select and take action on an entire group of contacts.

You can search and filter your contact records in any view by using the Instant Search feature. You can sort contact records by any displayed column in a list view by clicking the column header, and you can display or hide any column.

> **Tip** You can change the fields displayed in each view; the way records are grouped, sorted, and filtered; the display font; the size of business cards; and other settings to suit your preferences. To personalize a view, point to Current View on the View menu, and then click Customize Current View.

In this exercise, you will sort contact records and look at some of the ways you can view contact records.

> **USE** the contact records you created earlier in this chapter.
> **BE SURE TO** display the Contacts module before beginning this exercise.

1. In the **Navigation Pane**, look at the **Current View** list. If the **Business Cards** option isn't already selected, select it now.

   In Outlook 2007, this is the default Contacts module view, displaying the standard business cards for each contact (as well as any personalized business cards you have saved), organized alphabetically by last name.

By clicking the buttons on the alphabet bar that appears on the right side of the Contacts pane in Business Cards view, Address Cards view, and Detailed Address Cards view, you can quickly jump to contact records beginning with that letter.

Language Settings button

> **Tip** You can display an additional alphabet in the alphabet bar. Options include Arabic, Cyrillic, Greek, Thai, and Vietnamese—other alphabets might be available depending on the version of Outlook and any language packs you have installed. To get started, click the Language Settings button at the bottom of the alphabet bar.

2. In the **Current View** list, select the **Address Cards** option.

> **Tip** The view options are also available as a drop-down list on the Advanced toolbar.

Outlook displays your contact records on smaller cards similar to the Business Cards, but without the additional formatting and sized to fit the available primary contact information, including name, telephone and fax numbers, and postal and e-mail addresses. (Detailed Address Cards view displays all the information available in the contact record, including the Notes field.)

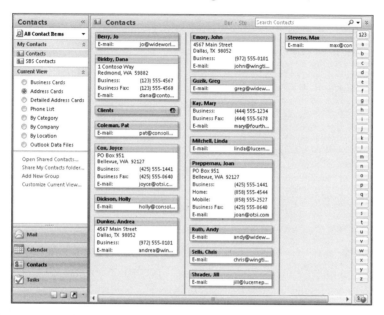

3. In the **Current View** list, select the **Phone List** option.

   Outlook displays your contact records in a grid of columns and rows organized in ascending order based on the File As column. If you have a lot of information recorded for each of your contacts, you will probably find that this view displays more contact information on one screen than any other.

4. Click the **Full Name** column heading.

   Outlook sorts the contact records in ascending order based on the Full Name field, as indicated by the upward-pointing sort arrow to the right of the column heading. You can reverse the sort order by clicking the active heading again.

Sort order indicator

5. Click the **Company** column heading.

   Outlook sorts the contact records in ascending order based on the Company field. You can enter information into contact records from this view.

   > **Tip** You can add a contact to your address book in any list view by clicking the box under the Full Name header (labeled Click Here To Add A New Contact) and entering the contact's information.

6. In the **Greg Guzik** record, click the **Company** cell, type Wide World Importers, and then press the ⌷Enter⌷ key.

   Outlook automatically reorganizes the list so Greg Guzik's record is alphabetized by the company name you entered.

7. Repeat Step 6 for the **Jo Berry** and **Andy Ruth** records.

8. In the **Navigation Pane**, in the **Current View** list, select the **By Category** option.

   Outlook displays the contact records in a grid grouped by category and sorted by the File As field.

> **Tip** You can collapse or expand a group of contacts by clicking the – (Collapse) button or the + (Expand) button to the left of the group header, or you can collapse or expand all groups by clicking Expand/Collapse Groups on the View menu and then clicking Collapse All Groups or Expand All Groups.

Collapse

9. Click the **Collapse** button to the left of the **Categories: none** header.

Only the categorized contacts are visible.

Collapsed group

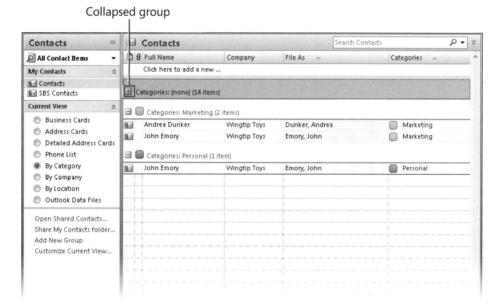

Notice that Andrea Dunker appears in the Marketing group, and John Emory appears in the Marketing group as well as the Personal group. When you sort contacts, messages, or other Outlook items by category, items assigned to multiple categories appear in both lists.

10. In the **Current View** list, select the **By Company** option.

Outlook displays the contact records in a grid that is sorted and grouped by the Company field.

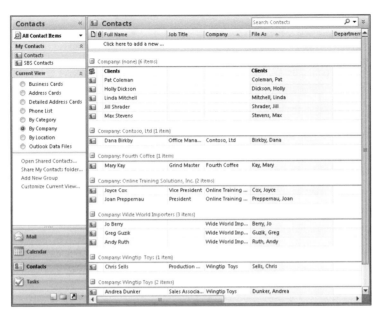

11. In the **Pat Coleman**, **Holly Dickson**, and **Max Stevens** records, type Consolidated Messenger in the **Company** field. In the **Linda Mitchell** and **Jill Shrader** records, type Lucerne Publishing in the **Company** field.

    As you change each record, Outlook reorganizes the display, creating new groups if necessary.

12. In the **Current View** list, select the **Business Cards** option.

    Outlook returns to the default view of your contact records.

Quickly Locating Contact Information

You can use the new Instant Search feature available in many of the programs in the 2007 Office system to immediately find a specific contact record or to filter records based on their content. Instant Search is available in any view of an address book, and all the other Outlook modules as well. We'll touch on this feature several times throughout this book, but because this is the first time we've discussed it, we'll go into more depth in this chapter.

In this exercise, you will locate a contact record by using Instant Search.

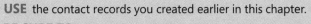

> **USE** the contact records you created earlier in this chapter.
> **BE SURE TO** display the Contacts module before beginning this exercise.

1. At the top of the **Contacts** pane, click to position the insertion point in the **Search** box.

   When not in use, this box contains the words *Search Contacts*.

2. Type the letter j.

   Outlook filters the list to display only those contact records containing the letter *j*.

3. Switch to **Phone List** view.

   In any view other than Business Cards view, the search term is highlighted in the results in yellow.

4. In the Search box, after the letter *j*, type the letter o.

   Outlook filters the list to display only contact records containing *jo*.

5. Type hn.

   Outlook displays only the contact record for John Emory. The filter will remain in place even if you select another view of the address book.

Show Instant
Search Pane
Menu

6. At the right end of the **Search** box, click the **Show Instant Search Pane Menu** button, and then point to **Recent Searches**.

You can quickly return to previous search results by clicking the search term in this box.

7. On the Instant Search pane menu, click **Search Options**.

The Search Options dialog box opens.

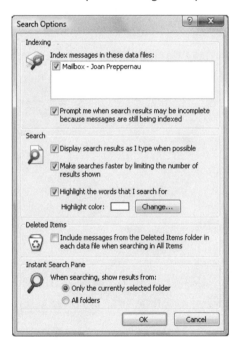

From this dialog box, you can set the default search scope and the highlight color for located search terms.

8. In the **Search Options** dialog box, click **Cancel**.

Clear Search

9. At the right end of the **Search** box, click the **Clear Search** button.

Outlook displays the entire contents of your Contacts module.

Printing Contact Information

You can print your Outlook address book or individual contact records, either on paper or to an electronic file (such as a PDF or XPS file), from any address book view. Depending on the view, Outlook offers a variety of print styles, such as the following:

Style	Description	Available in these views
Card Style	Contact information displayed alphabetically in two columns. Letter graphics appear at the top of each page and the beginning of each letter group	Address Cards, Business Cards, Detailed Address Cards
Medium Booklet Style	Contact information displayed alphabetically in one column. Formatted to print four numbered pages per sheet. Letter graphics appear at the top of each page and the beginning of each letter group, and a contact index at the side of each page indicates the position of that pages entries in the alphabet. Print double-sided if possible.	Address Cards, Business Cards, Detailed Address Cards
Memo Style	Contact information displayed under a memo-like header containing your name. One record per sheet.	Address Cards, Business Cards, Detailed Address Cards
Phone Directory Style	Contact names and telephone numbers displayed in two columns. Letter graphics appear at the top of each page and the beginning of each letter group.	Address Cards, Business Cards, Detailed Address Cards
Small Booklet Style	Contact information displayed alphabetically in one column. Formatted to print eight numbered pages per sheet. Letter graphics appear at the top of each page and the beginning of each letter group, and a contact index at the side of each page indicates the position of that pages entries in the alphabet. Print double-sided if possible.	Address Cards, Business Cards, Detailed Address Cards
Table Style	Contact information displayed in a grid. Field names appear at the top of each page.	By Category, By Company, By Location, Phone List

You can customize the layout of most of the default print styles, and save custom print styles.

In this exercise, you will print a contact list and individual address cards.

> **Important** Your computer must be connected to a local or network printer to complete this exercise. If you don't have a printer installed, you can install one at this time or follow the alternate instruction in Step 15.

USE the contact records you created earlier in this chapter.

BE SURE TO display the Contacts module in Phone List view before beginning this exercise.

Print

1. On the Standard toolbar, click the **Print** button.

   The Print dialog box opens.

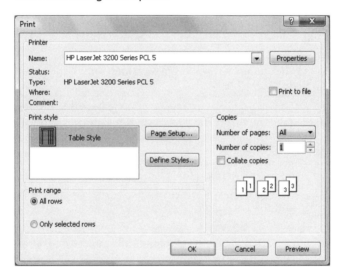

> **Tip** Your Print dialog box might look slightly different than the one shown here, depending on your operating system and printer.

Only one print style (Table Style) is available in the Print Style box.

2. With the **All rows** option selected in the **Print range** area, click **Preview**.

> **Tip** The Print Preview button is also available from the Advanced toolbar.

The Print Preview window opens, displaying the contact list in Table Style. The current page and total number of pages are shown at the left end of the status bar.

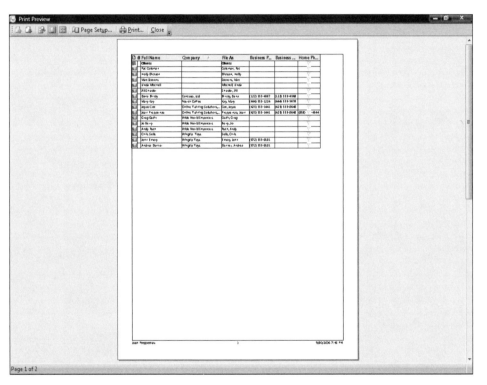

3. Click below the vertical scroll bar to display Page 2.

The last few columns of the phone list appear on the second page.

4. On the **Print Preview** window toolbar, click **Page Setup**.

The Page Setup: Table Style dialog box opens.

Look at the settings available from each of the dialog box tabs. For this print style, you can change only the fonts, paper size, page orientation and margins, header and footer, and other basic settings.

5. Close the **Page Setup** dialog box and the **Print Preview** window.

6. In the **Navigation Pane**, in the **Current View** list, click **Address Cards**.

7. On the Standard toolbar, click the **Print** button.

   The Print dialog box opens, displaying more options than it did when printing from Phone List view.

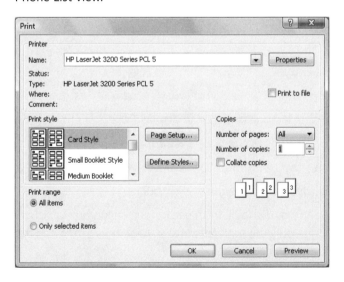

8. In the **Print style** list, click **Phone Directory Style**. Then click **Preview**.

The Print Preview window opens, showing the contact list as it will appear when printed in Phone Directory Style.

9. Click the center of the preview page to zoom in for a closer look at the information included in this style.

10. On the **Print Preview** window toolbar, click **Page Setup**.

The Page Setup: Phone Directory Style dialog box opens.

In addition to the basic settings, you can change the number of columns shown on a page and stipulate whether to display a contact index and letter graphics.

11. In the **Options** area, select the **Contact index on side** check box. Then click **Print Preview**.

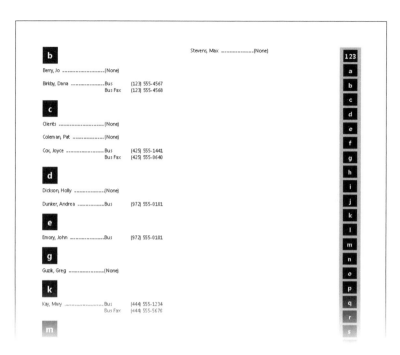

12. Close the **Print Preview** window.

13. In the **Contacts** pane, click the **Andrea Dunker** contact record to select it, press and hold the `Ctrl` key, and then click the **John Emory** contact record to add it to the selection.

14. On the Standard toolbar, click the **Print** button.

15. In the **Print style** list, click **Card Style**. In the **Print range** area, select the **Only selected items** option, and then click **OK**.

> **Troubleshooting** If you don't have a printer installed, click Preview instead of OK.

Outlook prints a page displaying only the selected contacts.

16. Experiment with the other ways in which you can print your contact records and your address book.

Creating a OneNote Page Linked to a Contact Record

If your 2007 Office system installation includes both Outlook and OneNote, you can send or link items you create in Outlook, such as e-mail messages, contact records, and meeting invitations, to your OneNote notebook. You can also link tasks from your OneNote notebook to Outlook so that they appear in your Outlook tasks list.

To link one or more contact records to OneNote:

1. Display your address book, and select the contact record (or records) you want to link.

2. On the Standard toolbar, click the **Contact Notes** button.

   OneNote starts (if it isn't already running) and creates a page in your Unfiled Notes section for each of the selected contact records. Each contact's page contains his or her business contact information and a link to open the original Outlook item from within OneNote.

You can move pages from the Unfiled Notes section to a notebook section by dragging or by right-clicking the page tab and then clicking Move Page To, Another Section, and the target notebook section.

Key Points

- You can create and access different types of address books including the Global Address List provided by your Exchange Server account, your main address book, and any custom address books that you create.

- You can share your stored contact information with other people on or off your network.

- Contact records can include names, e-mail and IM addresses, phone numbers, mailing addresses, birthdays, and other information.

- You can assign contact records and distribution lists to color-coded categories in order to more easily locate a group of records.

- You can print your address book or individual contact records in several formats.

Chapter at a Glance

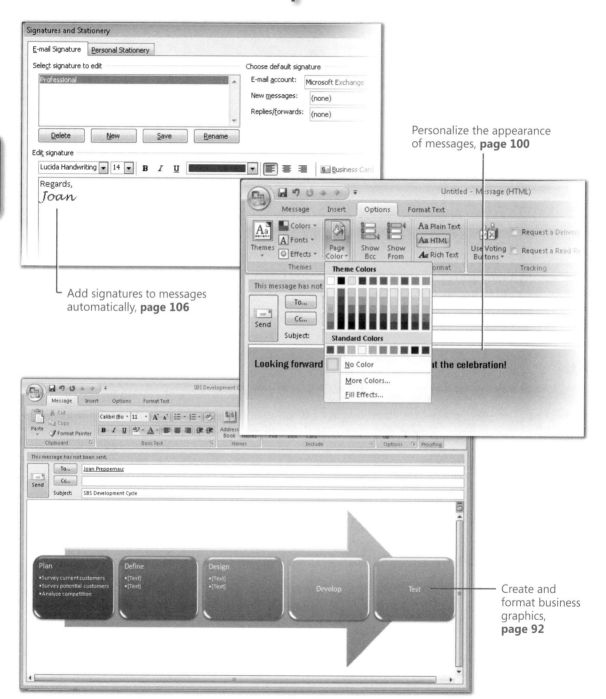

Personalize the appearance
of messages, **page 100**

Add signatures to messages
automatically, **page 106**

Create and
format business
graphics,
page 92

3 Sending E-Mail Messages

In this chapter, you will learn to:

✔ Work in the message window.

✔ Create and send messages.

✔ Attach files to messages.

✔ Create and format business graphics.

✔ Personalize the appearance of messages.

✔ Add signatures to messages automatically.

Although Microsoft Office Outlook 2007 includes useful components for managing your calendar, contacts, tasks, and notes, the primary reason most people use Outlook is to send and receive e-mail messages. Over the past decade, *e-mail* (short for *electronic mail*) has become an accepted and even required form of business communication. And of course, many people use e-mail to keep in touch with friends and family, either from work or from home. Outlook makes it easy to connect to multiple e-mail accounts, either on a business network or over the Internet, and provides all the tools you need to send, respond to, organize, filter, sort, find, and otherwise manage e-mail messages.

> **Tip** In this chapter and throughout this book, for expediency's sake, we might refer to e-mail messages simply as *messages*.

When sending messages from Outlook, you can:

- Include attachments such as documents, spreadsheets, or business graphics.
- Personalize your messages by using colors, fonts, backgrounds, electronic signatures, and electronic business cards.
- Set message options such as voting buttons, importance, sensitivity, and reminders.
- Request electronic receipts when a message is delivered to the recipient's mailbox or opened by the recipient.

In this chapter, you will look at elements of the item window interface in addition to those we discussed in Chapter 2, "Managing Contact Information." You will create and send messages, learn various ways of addressing messages to recipients, and practice sending messages with and without attachments. Then you will create and format a business graphic using the exciting new SmartArt feature provided in Outlook as well as in Microsoft Office PowerPoint 2007 and Microsoft Office Word 2007. Finally, you will experiment with the various ways you can personalize a message, including changing the font and background and adding a signature.

> **Important** You will use the messages you create in this chapter as practice files for exercises in later chapters of this book.

See Also Do you need only a quick refresher on the topics in this chapter? See the Quick Reference entries on pages xxxvii–lxv.

> **Important** Before you can use the practice files in this chapter, you need to install them from the book's companion CD to their default location. See "Using the Book's CD" on page xxv for more information.

> **Troubleshooting** Graphics and operating system–related instructions in this book reflect the Windows Vista user interface. If your computer is running Microsoft Windows XP and you experience trouble following the instructions as written, please refer to the "Information for Readers Running Windows XP" section at the beginning of this book.

Working in the Message Window

Outlook displays e-mail messages in the Mail module. When you create or respond to an e-mail message, it opens in a *message window*. The message window has its own set of commands separate from those in the Outlook program window. You can format and modify outgoing e-mail messages by using the message window commands.

Commands related to managing messages (such as saving, printing, securing, and sharing a message) are available from the Office menu.

See Also For more information about the elements of the Ribbon, see "Working in the Contact Window" in Chapter 2, "Managing Contact Information."

In this exercise, you will take a tour of the message item window elements that differ from the contact window elements discussed in Chapter 2, "Managing Contact Information." There are no practice files for this exercise.

> **BE SURE TO** start Outlook and display the Inbox before beginning this exercise.

New Mail
Message

1. On the Standard toolbar, click the **New Mail Message** button.

   An untitled message window opens.

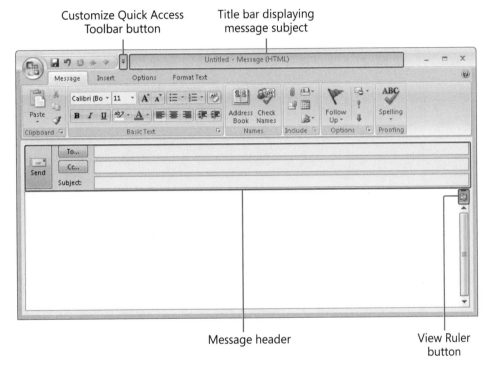

Customize Quick Access
Toolbar button

Title bar displaying
message subject

Message header

View Ruler
button

Important Depending on your screen resolution and the size of the message window that opens, you might see more or fewer buttons in each of the groups, or the buttons you see might be represented by larger or smaller icons than those shown in this book. Experiment with the size of the message window to understand the effect on the appearance of the command interface tabs.

2. In the upper-left corner of the message window, click the **Microsoft Office Button to display the menu**.

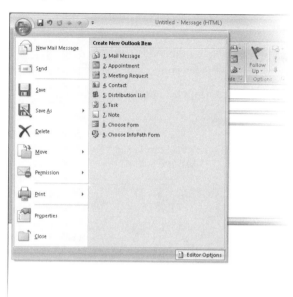

Notice that although you are working in the message window, you can create any type of Outlook item from the Office menu. We'll review the commands available from the Office menu in other chapters of this book.

See Also For more information about restricting recipients from forwarding, copying, or printing messages you send, see "Securing Your E-Mail" in Chapter 12, "Customizing and Configuring Outlook." For information about the Print commands, see "Printing Messages" in Chapter 4, "Handling E-Mail Messages." For information about the commands available in the Editor Options dialog box, see "Personalizing Your Office and Outlook Settings" in Chapter 12, "Customizing and Configuring Outlook."

3. Click away from the **Office** menu to close it.

4. Click the **Customize Quick Access Toolbar** button.

A menu of commonly used commands and customization options appears.

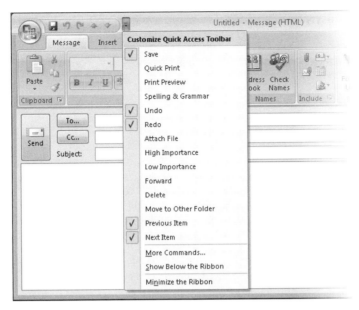

Clicking a command in the first menu section adds it to the Quick Access Toolbar.

See Also For information about customizing the commands shown on the Quick Access Toolbar, see "Making Favorite Outlook Commands Easily Accessible" in Chapter 12, "Customizing and Configuring Outlook."

5. On the **Customize Quick Access Toolbar** menu, click **Show Below the Ribbon**.

The Quick Access Toolbar moves to a position between the tabs and the *message header*. You might find this position useful if you place many additional commands on the Quick Access Toolbar and it crowds the text shown in the message title bar.

Alternate Quick Access
Toolbar location

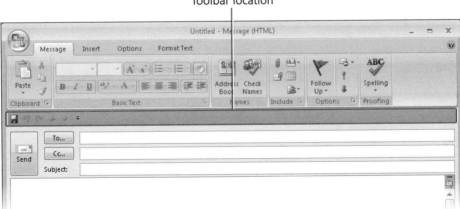

6. On the **Customize Quick Access Toolbar** menu, click **Show Above the Ribbon** to return the Quick Access Toolbar to its original location.

The message window commands are organized in groups on four tabs:

- Message
- Insert
- Options
- Format Text

> **Tip** Depending on what programs you have installed on your computer, tabs and groups other than those described here might also appear on the Ribbon.

The Message tab is active by default. Buttons representing commands related to creating messages are organized on this tab in six groups:

- Clipboard
- Basic Text
- Names
- Include
- Options
- Proofing

You can compose and send any standard e-mail message by using only the commands available on this tab.

7. Double-click the **Message** tab.

Double-clicking the active tab hides the Ribbon and provides more space for the message.

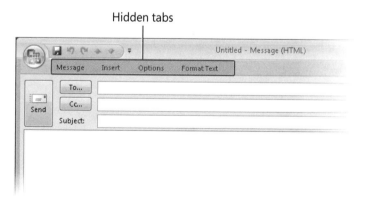

Hidden tabs

8. Click the **Insert** tab.

The Ribbon reappears, with the Insert tab active.

> **Tip** If you click away from the Ribbon (for example, in the content pane) the Ribbon hides again. This behavior is the default until you again double-click a tab.

Buttons representing commands related to items you can insert are organized on this tab in six groups:

- Include
- Tables
- Illustrations
- Links
- Text
- Symbols

9. Click the **Options** tab.

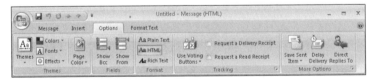

Buttons representing commands related to the format, appearance, and actions of messages are organized on this tab in five groups:

- Themes
- Fields
- Format
- Tracking
- More Options

10. Click the **Format Text** tab.

Command buttons related to the appearance of message content are organized on this tab in six groups:

- Clipboard
- Font
- Paragraph
- Styles
- Zoom
- Editing

Many of the commands on this tab also appear on the Message tab.

 CLOSE the message window.

Outlook Message Formats

Outlook can send and receive e-mail messages in three message formats:

- *Hypertext Markup Language (HTML)* supports paragraph styles (including numbered and bulleted lists), character styles (such as fonts, sizes, colors, weight), and backgrounds (such as colors and pictures). Most (but not all) e-mail programs support the HTML format—those that don't display HTML messages as Plain Text.

- *Rich Text Format (RTF)* supports more paragraph formatting options than HTML, including borders and shading, but is compatible with only Outlook and Microsoft Exchange Server. Outlook converts RTF messages to HTML when sending them outside of your Exchange network.

- *Plain Text* does not support the formatting features available in HTML and RTF messages, but is supported by all e-mail programs.

Creating and Sending Messages

Regardless of the type of e-mail account you have, as long as you have an Internet connection you can send e-mail messages to people within your organization and around the world. You can personalize your messages by using an individual font style or color, and by inserting your contact information in the form of an e-mail signature or business card. (You can apply other formatting, such as themes and page backgrounds, but these won't always appear to e-mail recipients as you intend them to, and they can make your communications appear less professional.) You can format the text of your message to make it more readable, by including headings, lists, or tables, and represent information graphically by including charts, pictures, clip art, and other types of graphics. You can attach files to your message and link to other information such as files or Web pages.

See Also For more information about formatting messages, see "Personalizing the Appearance of Messages" later in this chapter.

Addressing Messages

Addressing an e-mail message is as simple as typing the intended recipient's e-mail address into the To box. If you want to send a message to more than one person, indicate a different level of involvement for certain recipients, or include certain people without other recipients knowing, here are some tips.

By default, Outlook requires that you separate multiple e-mail addresses with semicolons. If you prefer, you can instruct Outlook to accept both semicolons and commas. To do this:

1. On the **Tools** menu, click **Options**.

2. In the **Options** dialog box, on the **Preferences** tab, click **E-mail Options**.

3. In the **E-mail Options** dialog box, click **Advanced E-mail Options**.

4. In the **When sending a message** area, select the **Allow comma as address separator** check box, and then click **OK** in each of the three open dialog boxes.

As you type a name or an e-mail address into the To, Cc, or Bcc box, Outlook displays matching addresses in a list below the box. Select a name or e-mail address from the list and then press Tab or Enter to insert the entire name or address in the box.

If your e-mail account is part of an Exchange Server network, you can send messages to another person on the same network by typing only his or her e-mail alias (for example, *joan*)—the at symbol (@) and domain name aren't required.

If a message recipient's address is in your address book, you can type the person's name and Outlook will look for the corresponding e-mail address. (You can either wait for Outlook to validate the name or press Ctrl+K to immediately validate the names and addresses in the address boxes.) By default, Outlook searches your Global Address List and main address book. To have Outlook also search other address books:

1. On the **Tools** menu, click **Address Book**.

2. In the **Address Book** window, on the **Tools** menu, click **Options**.

3. In the **Addressing** dialog box, click **Add**.

4. In the **Add Address List** dialog box, click the address list you want to add, click **Add**, and then click **Close**.

5. In the **Addressing** dialog box, click **OK**, and then close the **Address Book** window.

If the address book does not contain an entry for a name that you type in the To, Cc, or Bcc box of a new message, when you send the message, Outlook prompts you to select an address book entry or provide a full e-mail address.

Sending Courtesy Copies

To send a courtesy copy of a message to a person, enter his or her e-mail address in the Cc box. This is commonly referred to as "CCing" a person. You might CC someone to provide him or her with information but indicate that you don't require his or her involvement in the conversation. To send a message to a person without making it known to other recipients, enter the person's e-mail address in the Bcc box to send a "blind" courtesy copy (also known as "BCCing" a person). Outlook does not display the Bcc field by default. To display the Bcc field:

1. Display a message window.

2. On the **Options** tab, in the **Fields** group, click the **Show Bcc** button.

Addresses entered in the Bcc box can't be seen by other message recipients. They also aren't included in any replies to the original message.

Saving Message Drafts

Until you save or send a message, Outlook maintains a temporary copy of it in your Drafts folder. If you close Outlook (or if a problem causes Outlook to close or your computer to shut down) before you send the message, the *draft* retains most or all of your work. When the first draft of a message is saved (either automatically or manually), a banner appears in the message header with the notation "This message has not been sent."

You can save a message draft at any time by clicking the Save button on the Quick Access Toolbar in the message window, or by closing the message window and then clicking Yes in the Microsoft Office Outlook message box asking whether to keep the draft. (If you click No, Outlook deletes the draft.) To restart work on a draft message, display the Mail module, click the Drafts folder in the Navigation Pane, and then double-click the message you want to open.

> **Troubleshooting** Some users running Adobe Acrobat version 6 or 7 might experience problems when creating new messages or responding to messages in Outlook 2007. If you have Adobe Acrobat installed and experience these types of problems, try uninstalling the Adobe Outlook add-ins.

In this exercise, you will compose and send a new e-mail message. There are no practice files for this exercise.

BE SURE TO start Outlook and display the Inbox before beginning this exercise.

New Mail
Message

1. On the Standard toolbar, click the **New Mail Message** button.

A new message window opens.

Message header

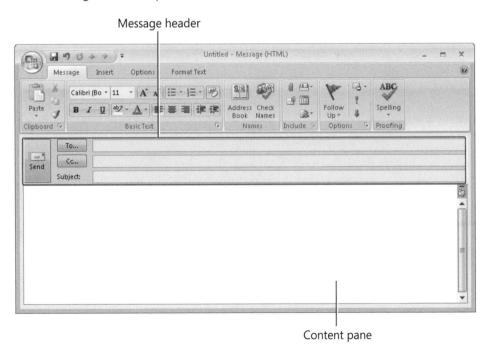

Content pane

> **Tip** By clicking the New Mail Message arrow, you can choose to create other types of Outlook items such as appointments, contacts, tasks, notes, or faxes, as well as organizational items such as folders and data files.

2. In the **To** box, type your own e-mail address.

3. In the **Subject** box, type SBS Tradeshow Schedule.

> **Important** The subject of this message begins with *SBS* so that you can easily differentiate it from other messages in your Inbox and Sent Items folders.

4. In the content pane, type The following people will be working at the tradeshow: and press the [Enter] key twice. Then type the following names, pressing [Enter] once after each of the first four names, and twice at the end: Anna, Barry, Carl, Denis, Emma.

Bullets

5. Select the list of names. Then on the **Message** tab, in the **Basic Text** group, click the **Bullets** button (not its arrow).

> **Tip** The Bullets button is also available in the Paragraph group on the Format Text tab.

Outlook converts the list of names to a simple bulleted list.

> **Tip** In this book, when we give instructions to implement a command, we tell you on what tab and in which group the command button appears. When directing you to use multiple command buttons on the same tab, we might omit the tab name to avoid needless repetition.

6. With the bulleted list still selected, in the **Basic Text** group, click the **Bullets** arrow.

Outlook has saved a
draft of this message

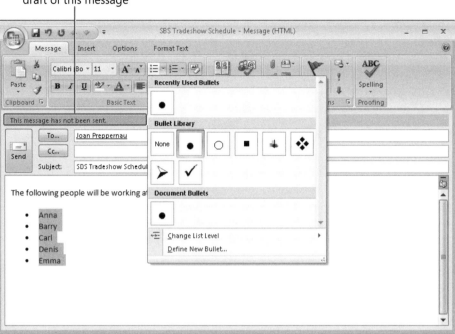

Notice the types of bullets available in the Bullet Library. You can change the list to use any of these bullets by clicking the bullet you want.

7. In the **Bullets** gallery, point to **Change List Level**.

You can demote (or promote) a list item to any of nine levels, differentiated by the bullet character and indent level.

8. Press Esc twice to close the **Bullets** gallery without making changes.

9. Press Ctrl + End to move the insertion point to the end of the message. Type Giveaways are: and then press Enter twice.

10. On the **Insert** tab, in the **Tables** group, click the **Table** button.

11. On the **Insert Table** menu, point to the third cell in the second row.

A preview of the table appears in the message window behind the Insert Table menu. This is a display of the new live preview functionality available in many parts of Outlook and other programs in the 2007 Microsoft Office system. You can use live preview to see the effect of an option before you actually select it.

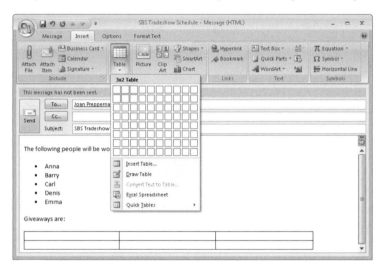

12. Click the selected cell to insert the table in the message.

The Table Tools contextual tabs, *Design* and *Layout*, appear on the Ribbon. Contextual tabs appear only when the element they control is active (selected). Contextual tabs are differentiated from standard tabs by color: the contextual group name is highlighted and the active tab is colored. Contextual groups are differentiated from each other by color.

13. Enter the following information in the table:

9:00-11:00	12:00-2:00	3:00-5:00
Mouse pads	T-shirts	Pens

Contextual tabs related to
managing the active table

Table selector

14. In the message header, click the **Send** button.

Outlook closes the message window and sends the message. When you receive the
message in your Inbox, leave it there for use in a later exercise.

Attaching Files to Messages

A convenient way to distribute a file (such as a Microsoft Office Word document,
Microsoft Office Excel spreadsheet, or Microsoft Office PowerPoint presentation) to
other people is by attaching the file to an e-mail message. The message recipient can
save the file to his or her hard disk, open the file from the message, or if he or she is
using Outlook 2007, preview the file in the Reading Pane.

Resending and Recalling Messages

If you want to send a new version of a message you've already sent, for example, a weekly status report, you can *resend* the message. Resending a message creates a new version of the message with none of the extra information that might be attached to a forwarded message. To resend a message:

1. From your **Sent Items** folder, open the message you want to resend.

2. On the **Message** tab, in the **Actions** group, click the **Other Actions** button, and then in the list, click **Resend This Message**.

Outlook creates a new message form identical to the original. You can change the message recipients, subject, attachments, or content if you want before sending it.

If, after sending a message, you realize that you shouldn't have sent it (for example, if the message contained an error or was sent to the wrong people), you can *recall* it by instructing Outlook to delete or replace any unread copies of the message. To recall a message:

1. From your **Sent Items** folder, open the message you want to recall.

2. On the **Message** tab, in the **Actions** group, click the **Other Actions** button, and then click **Recall This Message**.

3. In the **Recall This Message** dialog box, select the option to delete unread copies of the message or the option to replace unread copies with a new message, and then click **OK**.

Message recall is available only for Exchange Server accounts.

You can send a file as a regular attachment or—if your organization has a collaboration site built on Microsoft SharePoint products and technologies—as a *shared attachment*. When you send a shared attachment, Outlook creates a *document workspace* for the attached file and, rather than sending a copy of the file to each message recipient, sends an invitation to visit the workspace.

See Also For information about creating a shared workspace for a file attachment, see "Creating a Document Workspace from Outlook" in Chapter 10, "Collaborating with Other People."

In this exercise, you will send a Word document and a PowerPoint presentation as attachments to an e-mail message.

> **USE** the *03_Attaching* document and the *03_Attaching* presentation. These practice files are available in the *Chapter03* subfolder under *SBS_Outlook2007*.
>
> **BE SURE TO** start Outlook and display the Inbox before beginning this exercise.

New Mail
Message

1. On the Standard toolbar, click the **New Mail Message** button.

2. In the **To** box of the new message window, type your own e-mail address.

> **Tip** If you completed the previous exercise, Outlook will display your e-mail address in a list as you begin typing. You can insert the address by pressing the Down Arrow key to select it (if necessary) and then pressing Enter.

3. In the **Subject** box, type SBS First Draft.

4. In the content pane, type Here is some information for your review. Then press Enter to move to the next line.

Attach
File ▾

5. On the **Message** tab, in the **Include** group, click the **Attach File** button.

> **Tip** A larger version of the Attach File button is available in the Include group on the Insert tab.

The Insert File dialog box opens, displaying the contents of your Documents folder.

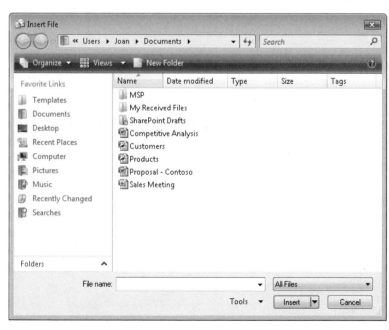

6. Browse to the *Documents\MSP\SBS_Outlook2007\Chapter03* folder, click the *03_Attaching* document, hold down the ⌨Ctrl key, click the *03_Attaching* presentation, and then click **Insert**.

> **Troubleshooting** By default, Windows does not display file extensions in Explorer windows or dialog boxes. You can usually differentiate file types by their icons—for example, the Word icon precedes the *03_Attaching* document name. However, the icon preceding a PowerPoint 2007 presentation is an image of the first slide in the presentation, and in the default Small Icons view, you will probably see only the slide background.
>
> You can display the file type by clicking Details on the Views list, or you can display larger icons by clicking Extra Large Icons, Large Icons, Medium Icons, or Tiles on the Views list. In these views, you can see that the PowerPoint icon appears in the lower-right corner of the icon image. If you want Windows to display file extensions, display a folder (such as your Documents folder) in Explorer, click Folder And Search Options on the Organize menu, and then on the View tab of the Folder Options dialog box, clear the Hide Extensions For Known File Types check box, and click Apply or OK.

The files appears in the Attach box in the message header.

7. In the message header, click the **Send** button.

Outlook closes the message window and sends the message. When you receive the message in your Inbox, leave it there for use in a later exercise.

Sending Contact Information

You can send your own or someone else's contact information from your address book to another Outlook user by attaching the contact's Outlook business card to an e-mail message. The recipient can then save the contact information in his or her own address book.

To send a business card:

1. In the message window, on the **Message** tab, in the **Include** group, click the **Insert Business Card** button, and then in the list, click **Other Business Cards**.

> **Tip** Business cards that you've previously sent appear in the Insert Business Card list. You can insert a card in the message by selecting it from the list.

2. In the **Insert Business Card** dialog box listing all your contacts, select the card or cards you want to send, and then click **OK**. If you have multiple address books, you can display a different address book in the dialog box by clicking it in the Look In list.

   To select multiple sequential cards, click the first card, hold down the Shift key, and then press the Up Arrow or Down Arrow key to select additional cards. To select multiple non-sequential cards, click the first card, hold down the Ctrl key, click the next card, and so on.

The message recipient can add the contact to his or her main address book by dragging the business card from the received message to the Contacts module or by opening the card from the message and then clicking the Save & Close button.

> **Tip** Readers of a previous edition of this book wrote to us asking how to create mail-merge e-mail messages from Outlook. This is actually a function of Word, rather than Outlook.
>
> For information about creating e-mail messages to multiple recipients by using mail-merge, refer to *Microsoft Office Word 2007 Step by Step* (ISBN 0-7356-2302-3) by Joyce Cox and Joan Preppernau (Microsoft Press, 2007).

Creating and Formatting Business Graphics

The saying that "a picture is worth a thousand words" is especially true in business communications, when you need to clearly explain facts or concepts, particularly to an increasingly global audience. Several programs in the 2007 Office system include a new feature called *SmartArt*. This tool is very useful for creating professional business graphics within documents, spreadsheets, presentations, and messages. You can easily create lists and diagrams depicting relationships, processes, cycles, hierarchies, and so on in your e-mail messages. When sending a message, Outlook converts any SmartArt graphics within the message to static graphics.

In this exercise, you will create a SmartArt diagram within an e-mail message. There are no practice files for this exercise.

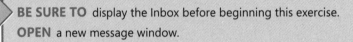

BE SURE TO display the Inbox before beginning this exercise.

OPEN a new message window.

1. Maximize the message window, and then click in the content pane.

 SmartArt

2. On the **Insert** tab, in the **Illustrations** group, click the **SmartArt** button.

   The Choose A SmartArt Graphic dialog box opens.

3. Scroll the center pane of the dialog box for an overview of the available SmartArt graphics. You can display the name of a graphic by pointing to it.

4. In the left pane, click **Process**, and then in the center pane, click the last icon in the top row (**Alternating Flow**).

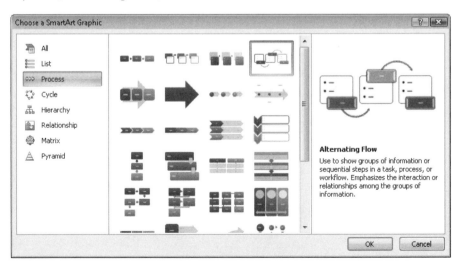

A preview of the selected SmartArt graphic appears in the right pane. This is a process diagram showing the details of a three-step process.

5. In the **Choose a Smart Art Graphic** dialog box, click **OK**.

Outlook inserts the selected process diagram in the content pane. It looks similar to the preview graphic, but without the colors and three-dimensional aspects. (You select formatting options later.) The SmartArt Tools contextual tabs, *Design* and *Format*, appear on the Ribbon.

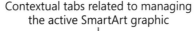

Contextual tabs related to managing the active SmartArt graphic

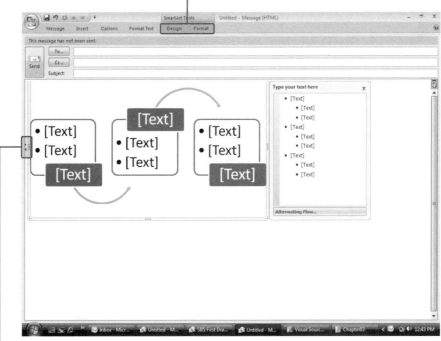

Text Pane tab

Tip You can display or hide the Text Pane for any SmartArt diagram by clicking the diagram and then clicking the Text Pane button in the Create Graphic group on the Design contextual tab, or by clicking the Text Pane tab on the left side of the diagram drawing area.

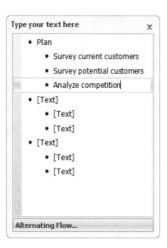

You can enter text in the Text Pane or directly in the diagram—selecting a diagram element or positioning the insertion point within the bulleted list also selects the corresponding element in the diagram or Text Pane. The diagram type appears at the bottom of the Text Pane; pointing to it displays a ScreenTip describing the purpose of the selected type of diagram.

6. In the **Text Pane**, click the **[Text]** placeholder to the right of the first bullet, and then type Plan.

As you type in the pane, the text appears in the diagram.

7. Click the **[Text]** placeholder to the right of the first second-level bullet, and type Survey current customers. Press the ⬇ key to move to the next second-level bullet, and then type Survey potential customers.

The font size in the diagram adjusts to fit the available space.

8. Press Enter to create another second-level bullet in the Text Pane and in the diagram, and then type Analyze competition.

9. In the diagram, click the second solid blue box to select the placeholder, and then type Define.

As you type, the text also appears in the second first-level bullet in the Text Pane.

10. In the third solid blue box, type Design.

11. On the **Design** contextual tab, in the **Create Graphic** group, click the **Add Shape** arrow (not the button), and then in the list, click **Add Shape After**.

An additional item appears at the right end of the diagram and in the Text Pane.

You can add shapes above, below, before, or after the selected shape, depending on the diagram layout.

12. In the new solid blue box, type **Develop**.

13. In the **Text Pane**, click at the end of the word *Develop*, and then press Enter .

A first-level bullet and additional shape appear.

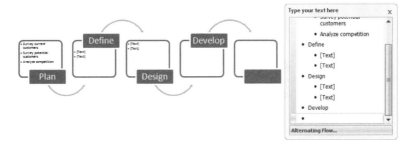

Close

14. Type Test, and then in the **Text Pane**, click the **Close** button.

At its current size, the text within the diagram is very difficult to read.

15. Point to the move handle on the right side of the diagram until the pointer becomes a double-headed arrow. Drag the move handle to the right to fill the message window.

More

16. In the **Layouts** group, click the **More** button.

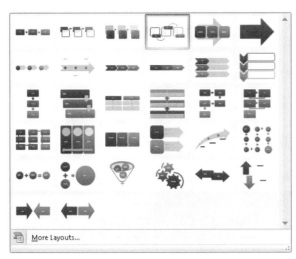

17. In the **Layouts** gallery, point to a few of the diagram layouts to display live previews. Then click the fifth icon in the first row (**Continuous Block Process**).

The process diagram layout changes but the contents remain the same.

18. In the **SmartArt Styles** group, click the **More** button.

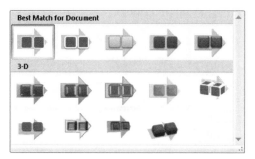

19. In the **SmartArt Styles** gallery, point to a few of the diagram styles to display live previews. Then under **3-D**, click the first icon (**Polished**).

20. In the **SmartArt Styles** group, click the **Change Colors** button.

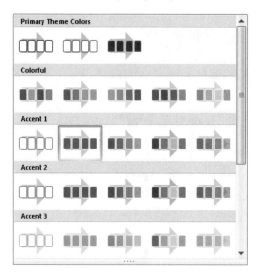

The color schemes displayed in the Colors gallery are variations of the current theme, and are organized in groups reflecting the six thematic accent colors. Changing the theme also changes the color schemes in the gallery.

21. Point to a few of the diagram styles to display live previews. Then under **Colorful**, click the second icon (**Colorful Range – Accent Colors 2 to 3**).

22. Enter your own e-mail address in the **To** box, and type SBS Development Cycle in the **Subject** box.

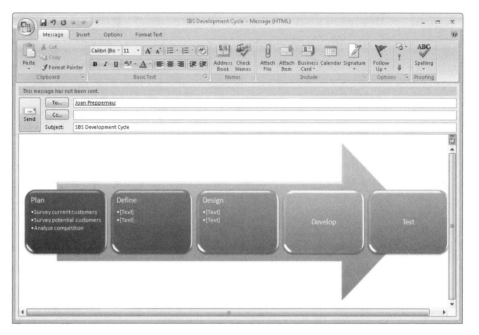

23. Send the message, and then display your Inbox.

24. When you receive the message, the diagram is visible in the Reading Pane. Open the message, and click the diagram.

The diagram is no longer an active SmartArt graphic; it has been converted to a static image. If you open the message from your Sent Items folder, you will find that the same is true of the diagram in that message.

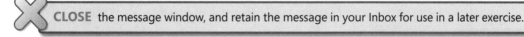

CLOSE the message window, and retain the message in your Inbox for use in a later exercise.

Changing Message Settings and Delivery Options

When sending a message, you can optionally include visual indicators of the importance, sensitivity, or subject category of a message or other Outlook item, restrict other people from changing or forwarding message content, provide a simple feedback mechanism in the form of voting buttons, and specify message delivery options to fit your needs.

Common message settings and delivery options include:

- **Importance.** You can indicate the urgency of a message by setting its *importance* to High or Low. A corresponding banner appears in the message header and, if the Importance field is included in the view, an importance icon appears in the Inbox or other message folder.

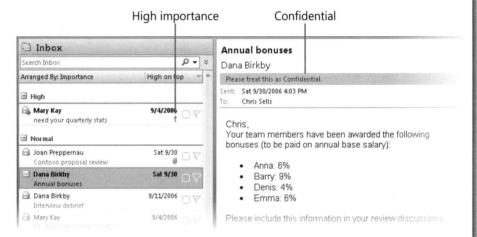

High importance   Confidential

You can easily sort and group messages based on importance by clicking Importance in the Arranged By list.

- **Sensitivity.** You can indicate that a message should be kept private by setting its *sensitivity* to Confidential, Personal, or Private). No indicator appears in the message folder, but a banner appears in the message header to indicate a sensitivity other than Normal. You can choose to include the sensitivity as one of the message attributes shown in the Inbox pane, but if you do, it replaces the message subject, which isn't very helpful.

- **Security.** If you have a digital ID, you can digitally sign the message; or you can encrypt the contents of the message.

  See Also For information about digital signatures, see "Securing Your E-Mail" in Chapter 12, "Customizing and Configuring Outlook."

- **Voting options.** If you and your message recipients have Exchange Server accounts, you can add *voting buttons* to your messages to enable recipients to quickly select from multiple-choice response options.

- **Tracking options.** You can track messages by requesting delivery receipts and read receipts. These receipts are messages automatically generated by the recipient's e-mail server when it delivers the message to the recipient and when the recipient reads the message.

- **Categories.** You can assign a message to a color category that will be visible to the recipient if he or she views the message in Outlook.

The most commonly used options are available in the Options group on the Message tab of the message window. You can access other options from the Message Options dialog box, which you open by clicking the Dialog Box Launcher in the lower-right corner of the Options group.

You can limit the actions other people can take with messages they receive from you by restricting the message permissions. For example, you can prevent recipients from forwarding or printing the message, copying the message content, or changing the content when they forward or reply to the message. (Restrictions apply also to message attachments.) Within a message window, permission options are available both on the Office menu and in the Options group on the Message tab.

See Also For more information about restricting recipients from forwarding, copying, or printing messages you send, see "Securing Your E-mail" in Chapter 12, "Customizing and Configuring Outlook."

Personalizing the Appearance of Messages

By default, the content of an Outlook message appears in black, 10-point Calibri (a very readable *sans serif* font that is new in this release of the Office system), arranged in left-aligned paragraphs on a white background. You can change the appearance of a message either by applying *local formatting* (text or paragraph attributes) or *global formatting* (a theme or style).

The local formatting options available in Outlook 2007 are largely the same as those available in Word and other programs in the 2007 Office system, and you might already be familiar with them from working with those programs. Here's a quick review of the types of formatting changes you can make:

- **Font, size, and color.** More than 220 fonts in a range of sizes and in a virtually unlimited selection of colors.
- **Font style.** Regular, bold, italic, or bold italic.
- **Underline style and color.** Plain, multiple, dotted, dashed, wavy, and many combinations thereof, in every color of the rainbow.
- **Effects.** Strikethrough, superscript, subscript, shadow, outline, emboss, engrave, small caps, all caps, or hidden.
- **Character spacing.** Scale, spacing, position, and kerning.
- **Paragraph attributes.** Alignment, indentation, and spacing.

The global formatting options are sets of local formatting that you can apply with a couple of clicks. You use a theme to apply a pre-selected combination of several formatting options to the entire message. In addition, the 2007 Office system introduces a handy new set of formatting options called *Quick Styles* that you can apply to individual elements of a message.

You are more likely to use Quick Styles when working in Word documents than in messages, but we'll give you an overview and you can investigate further on your own. Within a message window, Quick Styles are available in the Styles group on the Format Text tab. They include a number of standard styles for titles, headings, lists, quotes, emphasis, and so on. You can see a live preview of the effect of a style on your text by pointing to the style in the Quick Styles gallery.

You can change the appearance of all the styles in the Quick Styles gallery by selecting any of the 11 available style sets (or creating your own). Selecting a style set changes the appearance of all the text in the current document, as well as the appearance of the icons in the Quick Style gallery. You can select or preview a style set, color scheme, or font set by clicking the Change Styles button in the Styles group on the Format Text tab and then pointing to Style Set, Colors, or Fonts.

See Also For more information about Quick Styles, style sets, color schemes, and font sets, refer to *Microsoft Office Word 2007 Step by Step* (ISBN 0-7356-2302-3) by Joyce Cox and Joan Preppernau (Microsoft Press, 2007).

In this exercise, you will experiment with some of the formatting features that are new or improved in this version of Outlook while changing the font and background color of an e-mail message. Then you will apply a theme to the same message, overwriting the local formatting. There are no practice files for this exercise.

> **BE SURE TO** start Outlook and display the Inbox before beginning this exercise.
>
> **OPEN** a new message window.

1. In the content pane, type

   Looking forward to seeing you next week at the celebration!

2. Select the sentence you just typed by pointing to its left edge until the pointer
   becomes an arrow (pointing at the paragraph), and then clicking once.

   The *Mini toolbar* appears.

   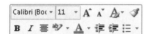

   This context-sensitive toolbar makes several common formatting options immediately available when you select a letter, word, or phrase by using the mouse. When
   the toolbar first appears, it is nearly transparent, and it disappears in a short time if
   you don't activate it by pointing to it.

Font

3. On the **Mini toolbar**, click the **Font** arrow.

> **Tip** If the Mini toolbar is not visible, you can find the Font box in the Basic Text
> group on the Message tab, and in the Font group on the Format Text tab.

Many more fonts are available in Outlook 2007 than in previous versions of Outlook. The name of each font appears in the list in that font, so you can easily select a font that appeals to you.

4. Scroll the **Font** list, noting the many available fonts, and then click **Franklin Gothic Medium**.

The font of the selected text changes.

Font Size

5. On the Mini toolbar or in the Font group on the Format Text tab, click the **Font Size** arrow, and in the list, click **12**.

The size of the selected text changes.

Font Color

6. Click once in the word *next*, without selecting any letters. Then on the **Format Text** tab, in the **Font** group, click the **Font Color** arrow.

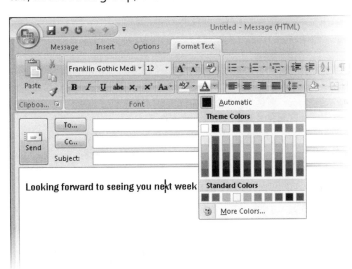

Outlook 2007 offers a new palette of theme colors (which change depending on the selected theme) and standard colors.

7. In the **Font Color** gallery, under **Standard Colors**, click the **Red** box.

The font color of the word *next* changes to red. Notice that the entire word changes even though you didn't select it. This is a new feature of Outlook 2007.

8. Double-click the word *next*, and on the **Mini toolbar** (or in the **Clipboard** group), click the **Format Painter** button. Then click once in the word *week*.

Format Painter

Outlook copies the formatting of the word *next* to the word *week*. By using the Format Painter, you can copy formatting from one item to any other item. To copy formatting to multiple items, double-click the Format Painter button to turn it on and then click it again to turn it off after you're finished applying the formatting.

9. On the **Options** tab, in the **Themes** group, click the **Page Color** button.

The Page Color gallery includes the same theme colors and standard colors as the Font Color gallery.

10. In the **Page Color** gallery, point to any color.

Outlook displays a live preview of the color in the message window.

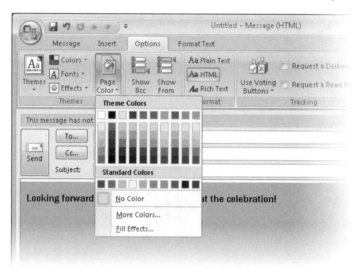

11. In the **Page Color** gallery, in the color gradient area, click the second shade down in the fifth column from the left (**Accent 1, Lighter 60%**).

The message background changes to the selected color.

12. In the **Themes** group, click the **Themes** button.

Outlook displays a gallery of themes. In each theme icon, the theme colors appear across the bottom, and the presentation background appears on the right.

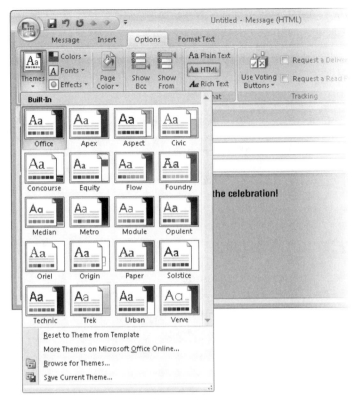

13. In the **Themes** gallery, click **Oriel**.

The message background and font change to those of the theme.

Notice that the colors displayed on the Colors button in the Themes group have changed.

14. In the **Themes** group, click the **Page Color** button. In the list, compare the new page background to the new set of colors displayed in the color gradient area. The page background color is still *Accent 1, Lighter 60%* (the shade you selected in Step 11).

> **Tip** The formatting changes you make in this exercise apply only to the active message, and will not be automatically applied to other messages.

15. Enter your own e-mail address in the **To** box; type SBS Festival Reminder in the **Subject** box, and then send the message.

When you receive the message in your Inbox, leave it there for use in a later exercise.

> **Tip** You can change the colors, fonts, and effects associated with a theme by clicking those buttons in the Themes group on the Options tab. You might want to experiment with different combinations on your own. However, Outlook offers such an extensive selection of themes that you will more than likely find that one of these ready-made combinations fits your needs.

Adding Signatures to Messages Automatically

When you create a paper-based message, you can add a signature at the end of the message by writing your name. When you create an Outlook message, you can add an *e-mail signature* at the end of the message by manually or automatically inserting a predefined block of text (with optional graphics). An e-mail signature provides consistent information to message recipients. You can include any text or graphics you want in your e-mail signature; you would commonly include your name and contact information, but depending on your own situation you might also include information such as your company name, job title, a legal disclaimer, a corporate or personal slogan, a photo, and so on. When using Outlook 2007, you can choose to include your electronic business card as part or all of your e-mail signature.

See Also For more information about electronic business cards, see "Personalizing an Electronic Business Card" in Chapter 2, Managing Contact Information."

You can create different signatures for use in different types of messages. For example, you might create a formal business signature for client correspondence, a casual business signature for interoffice correspondence, and a personal signature for messages sent from a secondary account. Or you might create a signature containing more information to send with original e-mail messages, and a signature containing less information to send with message replies. You can format the text of your e-mail signature in the same ways that you can format message text.

In this exercise, you will create an e-mail signature and then instruct Outlook to insert the signature in all the new messages you create. There are no practice files for this exercise.

> **BE SURE TO** start Outlook and display the Inbox before beginning this exercise.

1. On the **Tools** menu, click **Options**.

   The Options dialog box opens.

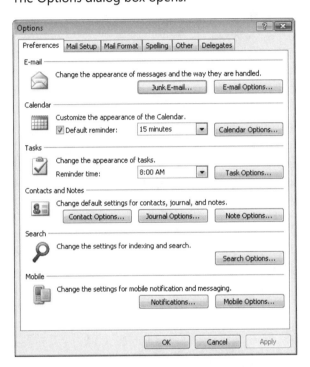

2. On the **Mail Format** tab, click **Signatures**.

   The Signatures And Stationery dialog box opens.

3. On the **E-mail Signature** tab, click **New**.

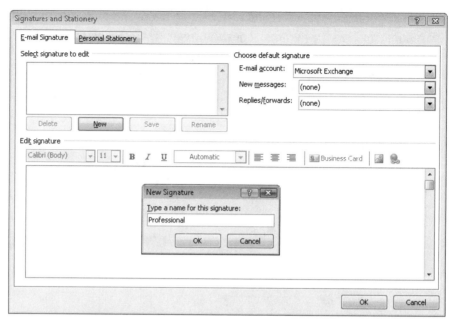

4. In the **New Signature** dialog box, type Professional as the name of your new e-mail signature, and then click **OK**.

   Outlook creates the *Professional* signature.

5. In the **Edit signature** area, type Regards followed by a comma, press the `Enter` key, and then type your name.

6. Select your name, click the **Font** arrow, and then in the list, click **Lucida Handwriting** (or any other font you like).

7. Click the **Font Size** arrow, and then in the list, click **14**.

8. Click the **Font Color** arrow, and then under **Standard Colors**, click the **Purple** box. Then click away from your name to see the results of your changes.

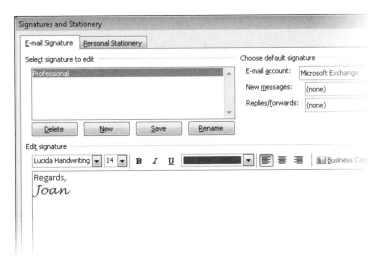

9. Apply any other types of formatting you want.

> **Tip** If you would like to include your electronic business card as part of your signature, click the Business Card button. Then in the Insert Business Card dialog box, locate and click your name, and click OK.

You can manually insert any signature you create in an e-mail message, but it is more common to instruct Outlook to automatically insert it for you.

10. In the **Choose default signature** area, click the **New messages** arrow, and then in the list, click **Professional**.

Outlook will now insert your signature into all new e-mail messages you send from this account, but not into replies or forwarded messages.

> **Tip** If you have more than one e-mail account set up in Outlook, you can instruct Outlook to insert a different signature in messages sent from each account. To do so, click the account in the E-mail Account list, click the signature you want to use with that account in the New Messages and/or Replies/Forwards list, and then click OK.

11. Make any other changes you want, and then click **OK** in the two open dialog boxes.

12. On the Standard toolbar, click the **New Mail Message** button.

A new message opens, with your e-mail signature in the content pane.

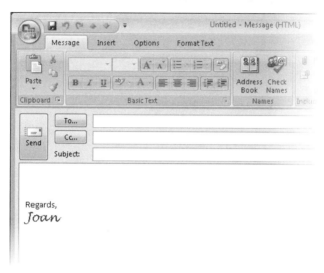

> **Tip** You can remove the automatically inserted signature from a message by select-ing and deleting it as you would any other text.

CLOSE the message window.

BE SURE TO reset the New Messages signature to <none> if you don't want to use the Professional signature you created in this exercise.

Key Points

- All the commands you need when creating a message in Outlook 2007 are available on the Ribbon at the top of the message window, grouped on tabs by function.

- You can easily create e-mail messages that include text, hyperlinks, and attachments.

- You can send messages in a variety of formats. Some message formats support more formatting options than others. Recipients using e-mail programs that don't support HTML or Rich Text Formatting will see the message in plain text.

- You can format the text and background of your messages, either by choosing individual formatting options and styles or by applying a theme.

- You can create professional business graphics by using the new SmartArt feature available in Outlook 2007, Word 2007, and PowerPoint 2007.

- You can automatically insert contact information in e-mail messages by using an electronic signature. You can create different signatures for different purposes and instruct Outlook to insert a specific signature depending on the e-mail account and message type.

Chapter at a Glance

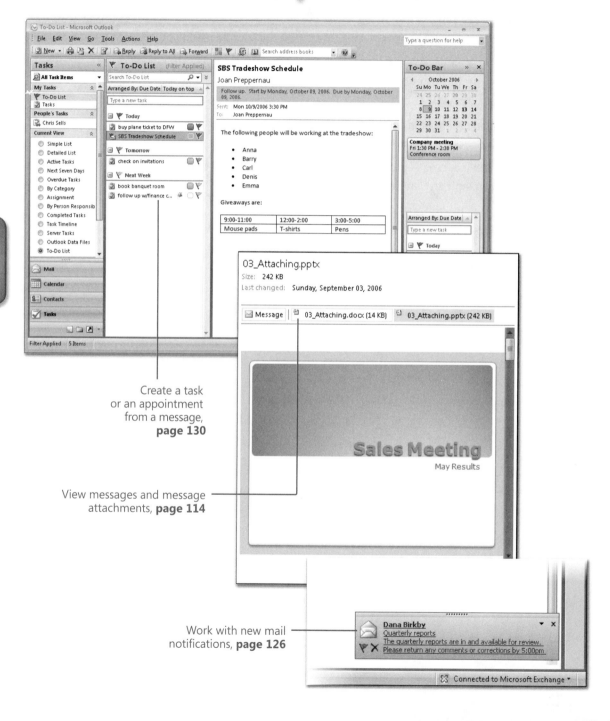

Create a task
or an appointment
from a message,
page 130

View messages and message
attachments, **page 114**

Work with new mail
notifications, **page 126**

4 Handling E-Mail Messages

In this chapter, you will learn to:

✔ View messages and message attachments.

✔ Reply to and forward messages.

✔ Work with new mail notifications.

✔ Create a task or an appointment from a message.

✔ Print messages.

Most new e-mail messages you receive appear in your Microsoft Office Outlook Inbox. (The exceptions to this are messages processed by any Outlook rules you or your administrator has set up, and messages diverted to the Junk E-mail folder due to suspicious content.)

After messages arrive in your Inbox, you can handle them in various ways. For example, you can:

- Read the message, either in the Reading Pane or in a message window.
- View any attachments, either in the Reading Pane or in the appropriate program, and save attachments to your hard drive.
- Respond to the message sender or to the message sender and all recipients.
- Forward the message to another person.
- Create an appointment or task based on the message.
- Categorize the message or file it in an Outlook folder for future electronic reference.
- Print the message for future "hard copy" reference.
- Delete the message.

When you are working online, you usually receive messages as soon as they are processed by your e-mail server. If you are working offline, you will need to connect to your server to download new messages. You can do this manually or set up Outlook to automatically check for new messages at regular intervals.

See Also For information about Outlook rules, see "Creating Rules to Process Messages" and for information about junk e-mail, see "Blocking Unwanted Messages," both in Chapter 12, "Customizing and Configuring Outlook."

In this chapter, you will experiment with receiving, viewing, responding to, or otherwise processing e-mail messages. You will preview and view messages and files attached to them. You will reply to and forward messages. Then you will work with incoming messages through New Mail notifications and learn to configure the notifications to display the way you want. You will also flag a message for follow-up so that it appears in the To-Do list, create an appointment from a message, and print a message.

See Also Do you need only a quick refresher on the topics in this chapter? See the Quick Reference entries on pages xxxvii–lxv.

> **Important** The exercises in this chapter require only practice files created in earlier chapters; none are supplied on the book's CD. For more information about practice files, see "Using the Book's CD" on page xxv.

> **Troubleshooting** Graphics and operating system–related instructions in this book reflect the Windows Vista user interface. If your computer is running Microsoft Windows XP and you experience trouble following the instructions as written, please refer to the "Information for Readers Running Windows XP" section at the beginning of this book.

Viewing Messages and Message Attachments

Each time you start Outlook and connect to your *e-mail server*, any new messages received since the last time you connected appear in your Inbox. Depending on your settings, Outlook downloads either the entire message to your computer or only the *message header*, which provides basic information about the message, such as:

- The item type (message, meeting request, task assignment, and so on)
- Who sent it
- When you received it
- The subject
- If you forwarded or replied to it
- If it contains attachments
- If it has been digitally signed or encrypted
- If it has been marked as being of high or low importance

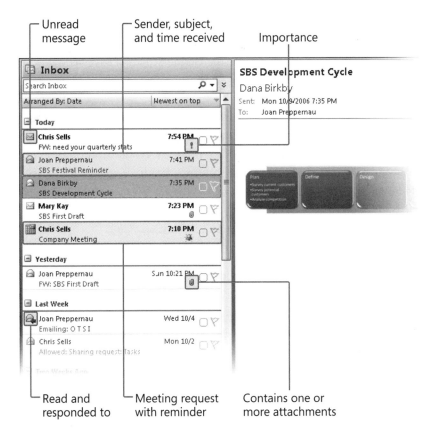

Messages that you haven't yet read are indicated by closed envelope icons and bold headers. You can view the text of a message in several ways:

● You can open a message in its own window by double-clicking its header in the message list.

● You can read a message without opening it by clicking its header in the message list to display the message in the Reading Pane.

● If you turn on the Single Key Reading Using Space Bar option, you can page through a message in the Reading Pane by pressing the Spacebar. When you reach the end of a message, the first page of the next message is displayed. This option is very convenient if you want to read through several consecutive messages in the Reading Pane, or if you find it easier to press the Spacebar than to scroll the Reading Pane by using the mouse. If you do not turn on this option, pressing the Spacebar while viewing a message does nothing, so there is no harm in turning it on even if you aren't sure you will use it.

> **Tip** To control whether you can page through messages by pressing the Spacebar, click Options on the Tools menu. On the Other tab of the Options dialog box, under Outlook Panes, click Reading Pane. Then in the Reading Pane dialog box, select or clear the Single Key Reading Using Space Bar check box, and click OK twice.

● You can display the first three lines of each message under the message header by using the AutoPreview feature. Scanning the first three lines of a message frequently gives you enough information to make basic decisions about how to manage it. The only drawback is that AutoPreview dedicates five lines to each message rather than the two lines of the default Messages view, so fewer messages are visible on your screen at one time.

Marking Messages as Read

When you open a message, Outlook indicates that you have read it, by changing the message icon from a closed envelope to an open envelope and changing the header font in the message list from bold to normal. You can also instruct Outlook to mark a message as read after you have previewed it in the Reading Pane for a certain length of time. To do so:

1. On the **Tools** menu, click **Options**.

2. On the **Other** tab of the **Options** dialog box, in the **Outlook Panes** area, click **Reading Pane**.

3. In the **Reading Pane** dialog box, select the check box corresponding to the way you want Outlook to handle messages you view in the Reading Pane.

   ● **Mark items as read when viewed in the Reading Pane**. Outlook will mark the item as read after it has been displayed in the Reading Pane for five seconds or the amount of time you specify.

   ● **Mark item as read when selection changes**. Outlook will mark the item as read when you select another item.

4. Click **OK** in the two open dialog boxes.

You can manually mark an item as read or unread by right-clicking the item and then clicking Mark As Read or Mark As Unread. (The context menu shows only the available option.)

You can view message attachments in several ways:

- You can open the attachment from an open message or from the Reading Pane.

- You can preview certain types of attachments (including Microsoft Office Excel spreadsheets, Microsoft Office PowerPoint slideshows, Microsoft Office Word documents, and Portable Document Format (PDF) files) directly in the Reading Pane without opening the attached file. This new feature of Outlook 2007 saves time and increases efficiency. If you install add-ins provided by companies other than Microsoft (called *third-party add-ins*), you can preview other types of files as well.

- You can save the attachment to your hard disk and open it from there. This strategy is recommended if you suspect an attachment might contain a virus, because you can scan the attachment for viruses before opening it (provided that you have a virus scanning program installed).

See Also For information about protecting your computer from viruses, refer to *Windows Vista Step by Step* (ISBN 0-7356-2269-8) by Joan Preppernau and Joyce Cox (Microsoft Press, 2007) or *Microsoft Windows XP Step by Step*, 2nd ed. (ISBN 0-7356-2114-1) by Online Training Solutions, Inc. (Microsoft Press, 2004).

In this exercise, you will preview and open a message and an attachment.

USE the *SBS First Draft* message you created in "Attaching Files to Messages" in Chapter 3, "Sending E-Mail Messages." If you did not complete that exercise, you can do so now, or you can use any message with an attachment in your Inbox.

BE SURE TO start Outlook and display your Inbox before beginning this exercise.

1. On the **View** menu, click **AutoPreview**.

> **Troubleshooting** If the AutoPreview icon on the View menu is shaded, this feature is already turned on.

The first three lines of each message appear in the Inbox below the message header.

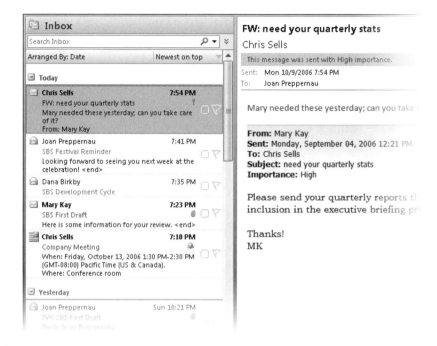

2. Locate the *SBS First Draft* message in your Inbox, and then click the message.

   Outlook displays the message in the Reading Pane. Note that the Reading Pane displays the message header and the names of any attached files.

3. In the **Reading Pane**, point to the **Message** button below the message header.

   Troubleshooting If you are working through this exercise with a message that does not have an attachment, you will not see a Message button.

   A ScreenTip displays the number of attachments.

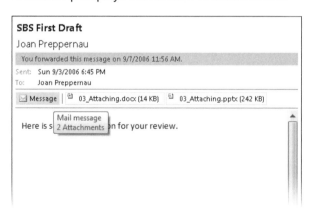

4. Point to the *03_Attaching.docx* attachment.

A ScreenTip displays the name, type, and size of the attached file.

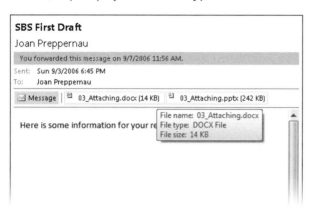

5. Click the *03_Attaching.docx* attachment once.

Outlook asks you to confirm that you want to preview the file. This security measure is designed to prevent viruses or other malicious content from running without your consent.

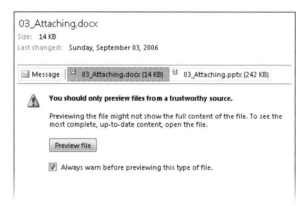

6. In the **Reading Pane**, click **Preview file**.

> **Tip** If you want Outlook to display previews of attachments without your explicit permission in the future, clear the Always Warn Before Previewing This Type Of File check box.

The fully formatted Word 2007 document appears in the Reading Pane. You can scroll through the entire document within this pane, without starting Word.

7. Click the *03_Attaching.pptx* attachment, and then click the **Preview file** button.

The title slide of this PowerPoint presentation appears in the Reading Pane. You can move among the presentation's slides by clicking the Previous Slide and Next Slide buttons in the lower-right corner of the pane.

Slide navigation buttons

8. In the **Reading Pane**, click the **Message** button.

The message text reappears in the Reading Pane. You can switch between the message and any attachments in this way.

9. In the **Reading Pane**, double-click the *03_Attaching.pptx* attachment, and then in the **Opening Mail Attachment** message box, click **Open**.

PowerPoint 2007 starts and opens the *03_Attaching* presentation.

See Also For an introduction to the features of PowerPoint 2007, refer to *Microsoft Office PowerPoint 2007 Step by Step* (ISBN 0-7356-2301-5), by Joyce Cox and Joan Preppernau (Microsoft Press, 2007).

10. Close the presentation to return to your Inbox.

11. In the message list, double-click the *SBS First Draft* message.

The message opens in its own window.

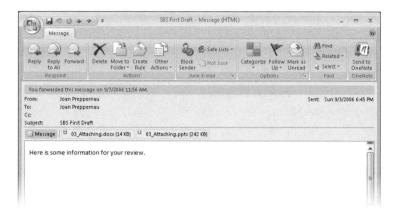

Note the message header and the attached file at the top. You can preview an attachment in the message window by clicking it once, and open an attachment by double-clicking it.

 CLOSE the SBS First Draft message window.

Replying to and Forwarding Messages

You can reply to or forward most e-mail messages that you receive by clicking the Reply, Reply To All, or Forward button either within the message window or on the Standard toolbar. When replying to a message, Outlook fills in the To and Cc boxes for you, addressing the response either to only the original message sender or to the message sender and all other people to whom the message was addressed or copied (recipients listed in the To and Cc boxes), depending on the reply option you choose. Outlook does not include recipients of blind courtesy copies (Bcc recipients) in message replies. You can add, change, and delete recipients from any reply before sending it.

To include all recipients of a message in your reply, click the Reply To All button. Outlook addresses your reply to the original message sender and any recipients listed in the To box of the original message, and sends a copy to any recipients listed in the Cc box of the original message.

Similarly, you can forward a received message to any e-mail address (regardless of whether the recipient uses Outlook) provided the message was not sent with restricted permissions. When forwarding a message, Outlook does not fill in the recipient boxes for you.

See Also For information about restricting recipients from copying, printing, or forwarding messages, see "Securing Your E-mail" in Chapter 12, "Customizing and Configuring Outlook."

When responding to an e-mail message, take care to use good e-mail etiquette. For example, don't forward messages containing large attachments to people with low-bandwidth connections who don't need the attachment. If your response is not pertinent to all the original recipients of a message, don't reply to the entire recipient list, especially if the message was addressed to a distribution list that might include hundreds of members.

> **Tip** You can prevent people who are using Outlook from automatically replying to all recipients of a message you send, by creating a custom message form with the Reply To All functionality disabled. For more information, see the article "Prevent e-mail message recipients from using Reply All or Forward" at
>
> *office.microsoft.com/en-us/assistance/HA011142241033.aspx*
>
> This method does not prevent recipients using Microsoft Windows Mail, Microsoft Outlook Express, or Microsoft Outlook Web Access from using the Reply To All function. And of course, the person responding to your message can always choose to manually address his or her response to all the original recipients.
>
> An easier way to prevent people from replying to multiple message recipients is to address the message to yourself and send blind courtesy copies to all other recipients. Then the recipient list will not be visible to anyone.

If the original message contains one or more attachments, be aware that replies do not include attachments, and forwarded messages do.

> **Tip** If a message contains voting buttons, you can respond by opening the message and clicking the button corresponding to the response you want to send. Or you can click the Infobar (labeled *Click Here To Vote*) in the Reading Pane and then click the option you want. You can choose to send a blank response containing your vote in the message header, or you can edit the response to include additional text.

See Also For information about responding to other Outlook items, see "Responding to Meeting Requests" in Chapter 6, "Managing Appointments, Events, and Meetings," and "Managing Task Assignments" in Chapter 8, "Tracking Tasks."

If you use an e-mail signature, you can specify a different signature to appear in replies and forwarded messages than in new messages. For example, you might want to include your full name and contact information in the signature that appears in new messages, but only your first name in the signature that appears in replies and forwarded messages.

See Also For more information about e-mail signatures, see "Adding Signatures to Messages Automatically" in Chapter 3, "Sending E-Mail Messages."

If you reply to or forward a received message from within the message window, the original message remains open after you send your response. You can instruct Outlook to close original messages after you respond to them—you will probably be finished working with the message at that point. To do so, click Options on the Tools menu. On the Preferences tab of the Options dialog box, click the E-mail Options button. In the E-mail Options dialog box, select the Close Original Message On Reply Or Forward check box, and then click OK in each of the two open dialog boxes.

In this exercise, you will reply to and forward messages.

USE the *SBS First Draft* message you created in "Attaching Files to Messages" in Chapter 3, "Sending E-Mail Messages." If you did not complete that exercise, you can do so now, or you can use any message in your Inbox.

BE SURE TO display your Outlook Inbox before beginning this exercise.

OPEN the *SBS First Draft* message.

1. Look at the header information at the top of the message window.

Note that this message includes two attachments, and the message window Ribbon displays only one tab (the Message tab), which contains all the commands you can use in a received message.

2. On the **Message** tab, in the **Respond** group, click the **Reply** button.

Outlook creates a reply message, already addressed to you (the original sender). If the message had been sent to any other people, the reply would not include them.

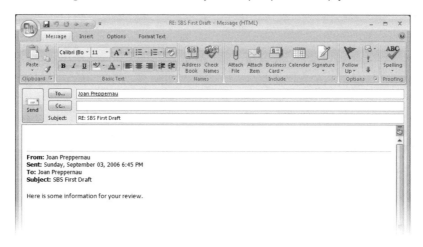

A prefix, *RE:*, appears at the beginning of the message subject to indicate that this is a response to an earlier message. Note that the response does not include the original attachments (and in fact there is no indication that the original message had any). The original message, including its header information, appears in the content pane separated from the new content by a horizontal line.

3. With the insertion point at the top of the content pane, type

   We'll need to get approval from the Marketing team before proceeding.

4. In the reply message header, click the **Send** button.

Send

   Outlook sends your reply. (If you are connected to your e-mail server, the reply will appear shortly in your Inbox.) The original message remains open on your screen.

5. In the original message, in the **Respond** group, click the **Forward** button.

Forward

   > **Troubleshooting** If the original message is closed, click the Forward button on the Standard toolbar.

Outlook creates a new version of the message that is not addressed to any recipient. The *FW:* prefix at the beginning of the message subject indicates that this is a forwarded message. The files that were attached to the original message appear in the Attached box. The message is otherwise identical to the earlier reply message.

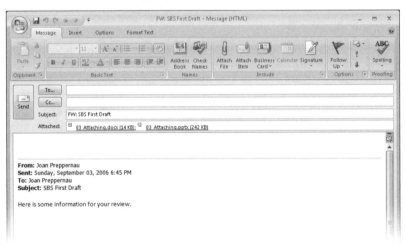

You address and send a forwarded message as you would any other.

6. With the insertion point at the top of the content pane, type

   Don't forget to review these!

7. Send the message, and then close the original message window.

Troubleshooting If you are not working online you will not receive the messages. Connect to your server to download the messages before continuing.

When the second message appears in your Inbox, compare the two messages. The forwarded message includes the original message attachments. Otherwise, other than the Subject prefixes and the text you entered, the messages are identical.

 CLOSE any open message windows.

Deleting Messages

When you delete a message, contact record, or any other item, Outlook temporarily moves it to the Deleted Items folder of your mailbox. You can open the folder from the Navigation Pane, view items that have been deleted but not purged, and restore items (undelete them) by moving them to other folders.

Outlook does not permanently delete items until you purge them from the Deleted Items folder, You can empty the entire Deleted Items folder manually or automatically, or permanently delete individual items from it.

To permanently delete an individual item:

1. In the **Navigation Pane**, click the **Deleted Items** folder to display its contents.
2. In the **Deleted Items** list, click the item (or select multiple items) you want to delete.
3. On the Standard toolbar, click the **Delete** button (or press the $\boxed{\text{Del}}$ key).
4. In the **Microsoft Office Outlook** message box asking you to confirm that you want to delete the selected item(s), click **Yes**.

To manually empty the Deleted Items folder:

→ In the **Navigation Pane**, right-click the **Deleted Items** folder, and then click **Empty "Deleted Items" Folder**.

To automatically empty the Deleted Items folder each time you exit Outlook:

1. On the **Tools** menu, click **Options**.
2. On the **Other** tab of the **Options** dialog box, select the **Empty the Deleted Items folder upon exiting** check box. Then click **OK**.

Working with New Mail Notifications

When new messages, meeting requests, or task delegations arrive in your Inbox, Outlook alerts you in several ways so that you can be aware of e-mail activity if you are working in another application or away from your computer:

- A New Mail Message icon appears in the notification area at the right end of the Microsoft Windows taskbar.

New Mail Message icon

- A semi-transparent *desktop alert* appears on your screen for a few seconds, displaying the name of the sender, the subject, and the first few words of the message (approximately 125 characters). From the desktop alert, you can open a message, mark it as read, flag it for action, respond to it, or delete it.

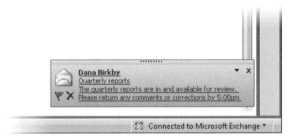

You can change the location, transparency, and length of time desktop alerts appear, or choose to not display them:

- You can position the alert inside or outside of the Outlook program window. For example, if you usually work with the Windows taskbar hidden, you might want to position the alert away from the taskbar to prevent you from accidentally displaying the taskbar each time you point to an alert.

- The alert can stay on screen for 3 to 30 seconds. The default is 7 seconds.

- The alert can be a solid color or up to 80% transparent. The default is 20% transparent. You might find that transparent alerts are less likely to interfere with your view of the work you're doing.

- If Outlook is minimized or another application window is active, a beep sounds. You can change the sound or turn it off.

- The mouse pointer briefly changes shape when you receive a message. You can turn off this feature.

You can customize and turn off these notifications.

In this exercise, you will customize your desktop alert settings and process messages through desktop alerts as you receive them. There are no practice files for this exercise.

> **BE SURE TO** display your Outlook Inbox before starting this exercise.

1. On the **Tools** menu, click **Options**.

   The Options dialog box opens.

   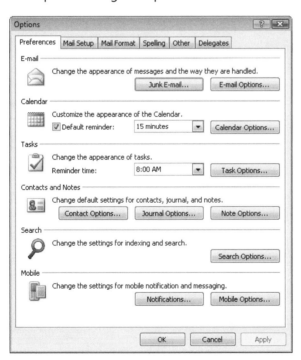

2. On the **Preferences** tab, click **E-mail Options**. Then in the **E-mail Options** dialog box, click **Advanced E-mail Options**.

3. In the **Advanced E-mail Options** dialog box, click **Desktop Alert Settings**.

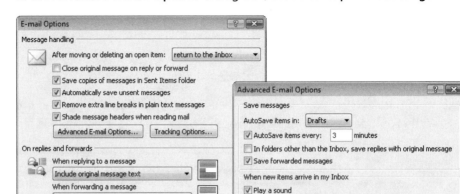

Tip To turn off desktop alerts, clear the Display A New Mail Desktop Alert check box.

4. Click the **Desktop Alert Settings** button.

The Desktop Alert Settings dialog box opens.

> **Tip** To quickly access the Desktop Alert Settings dialog box, when a desktop alert arrives, click the Options button in the alert, and then click Desktop Alert Settings. You can turn off desktop alerts by clicking the Options button and then clicking Disable New Mail Desktop Alert.

5. Drag the **How long should the Desktop Alert appear** slider to the left end of the slider bar to set it to *3 seconds*, and then click **Preview**.

   A semi-transparent sample desktop alert appears in the lower-right corner of your desktop and fades away after three seconds.

6. Click **Preview** again, and when the alert appears, point to it.

   The transparent alert becomes solid. As long as the mouse pointer is positioned over the alert, it remains visible.

7. Drag the sample desktop alert to the upper-right corner of your screen.

   Future desktop alerts will appear wherever you move the sample alert.

8. In the **Desktop Alert Settings** dialog box, drag the **How transparent should the Desktop Alert be** slider to the left end of the slider bar to set it to *0% transparent*, and then click **Preview**.

   The sample desktop alert appears in the upper-right corner of the screen, and darkens until it is opaque.

9. Move the desktop alert to the position you want it to appear in the future. Then experiment with the options in the **Desktop Alert Settings** dialog box, and set the duration and transparency as you want, previewing your changes as necessary.

10. When you're done, click **OK** in each of the four open dialog boxes.

New Mail
Message

11. On the Standard toolbar, click the **New Mail Message** button.

    A new message window opens.

12. Enter your e-mail address in the **To** box, and then in the **Subject** box, type SBS Alert Test 1.

> **Important** The subject of each message we have you send to yourself while working through the exercises in this book begins with *SBS* so that you can easily differentiate the practice files from other messages in your Inbox and Sent Items folders.

13. In the message body, type This is a test. Then send the message.

When the message arrives in your Inbox, a New Mail Message icon appears in the notification area at the right end of the Windows taskbar, and a desktop alert appears on your screen.

14. When the desktop alert appears, point to it to keep it active.

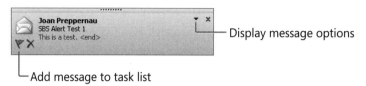

Display message options

Add message to task list

If you point to the text displayed in the alert, it appears underlined. You can click the underlined text to open the message in a message window.

Options

15. In the desktop alert, click the **Options** button, and then click **Mark as Read**.

The desktop alert closes, and the message in your Inbox is marked as read (whether on not the Inbox is visible).

16. On the Standard toolbar, click the **New Mail Message** arrow, and then in the list, click **Meeting Request**.

A new meeting request window opens.

17. In the **To** box, type your e-mail address; in the **Subject** box, type SBS Alert Test 2; and in the **Location** box, type my Inbox. Then send the meeting request.

18. If a **Reminder** window opens, click **Dismiss**.

See Also For more information about meeting requests, see "Scheduling, Updating, and Canceling Meetings" in Chapter 6, "Managing Appointments, Events, and Meetings."

Delete Item

19. When the desktop alert appears, point to it, and then click the **Delete Item** button.

Close alert

Delete message

The message moves from your Inbox to the Deleted Items folder, and the desktop alert closes.

Creating a Task or an Appointment from a Message

Frequently you need to take some type of action based on the information you receive from another person in an e-mail message. Among other actions, you might need to add an item to your task list or calendar.

Outlook 2007 makes it incredibly simple to add a task to your task list from an e-mail message. In Outlook 2003, you could flag messages for follow up, locate flagged messages within a folder by sorting it on flags, or within your entire mailbox by viewing the For Follow Up Search Folder. In Outlook 2007, flagging a message in any mail folder or flagging a contact record adds that item to your task list, which you can view from the To-Do Bar or the Tasks module.

See Also For more information about the To-Do Bar and the To-Do Bar Task List, see "Personalizing Your Outlook Workspace" in Chapter 1, "Getting Started with Outlook 2007." For information about creating and managing tasks, see Chapter 8, "Tracking Tasks."

Although creating a task by flagging a message is very useful, you should be aware of a few limitations. Flagging the message doesn't create a regular task; it simply adds the message to the task list. Because of this, you can't assign a flagged message to another Outlook user or track its status. You can mark it as complete by clicking its flag in either the message window, message list, or task list, or by selecting the message and then clicking the Follow Up button on the Standard toolbar: doing so removes the message from your task list and changes the flag to a check mark. The biggest drawback, however, is that you must retain the message—you can move it between mail folders, but deleting the message deletes the task as well.

> **Tip** Tasks created by simply clicking a message flag appear on your task list under the default due date header. You can change the default due date by right-clicking the flag and then clicking Set Quick Click. In the Set Quick Click dialog box, click the due date you want to appear by default (options are limited to Today, Tomorrow, This Week, Next Week, No Date, and Complete), and then click OK.
>
> You can specify a task due date other than the default when you flag the message, by right-clicking the flag and then clicking the due date: Today, Tomorrow, This Week, Next Week, No Date, or Custom (which allows you to set specific start and end dates).

Outlook also provides a convenient method of creating a Calendar items (an appointment, event, or meeting request) based on an e-mail message; you simply drag the message to the Calendar button in the Navigation Pane. When you release the mouse button, an appointment window opens, already populated with the message subject as the appointment subject, the message text in the content pane, and any message attachments attached to the appointment. The start and end times are set to the next half-hour increment following the current time. You can convert the appointment to an event or meeting in the same way that you would create an event or meeting from within the Calendar module. You can retain any or all of the information within the message as part of the Calendar item so that you (and other participants, when creating a meeting request) have the information on hand when you need it. After creating the Calendar item, you can delete the actual message from your Inbox.

See Also For information about creating and managing Outlook Calendar items, see Chapter 6, "Managing Appointments, Events, and Meetings."

In this exercise, you will create a task and then an appointment from an e-mail message.

USE the *SBS Tradeshow Schedule* message you created in "Creating and Sending Messages" in Chapter 3, "Sending E-Mail Messages." If you did not complete that exercise, you can do so now, or you can use any message in your Inbox.

BE SURE TO display your Outlook Inbox and the To-Do Bar before beginning this exercise.

Inactive Message flag

1. In the message list, scroll to the *SBS Tradeshow Schedule* message, and then click the transparent flag in the right margin of the message header.

   The flag becomes red, and a task named *SBS Tradeshow Schedule* appears under the Today header on your To-Do Bar task list.

2. In the **To-Do Bar Task List**, point to the *SBS Tradeshow Schedule* task.

A ScreenTip appears displaying the start date, reminder time, due date, the folder in which the message appears, and any categories assigned to the message.

3. Double-click the *SBS Tradeshow Schedule* task.

The flagged message opens in a message window. The message header indicates that you need to follow up on this message. The start and due dates given are tomorrow's date.

Task information

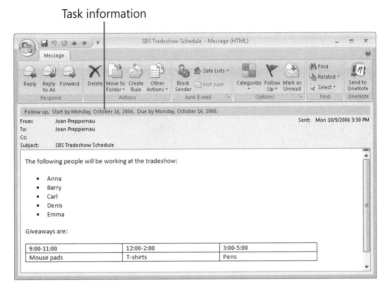

4. Close the message window.

5. In the **Navigation Pane**, click the **Tasks** button to display the Tasks module.

Your active tasks appear in the To-Do List. The icon preceding each item in the list indicates whether it is a standard task, e-mail message, contact, and so on. Message icons match those shown in the Inbox, indicating whether the message is read or unread and whether you've replied to or forwarded the message.

6. In the **To-Do List**, click the *SBS Tradeshow Schedule* task to display its details in the Reading Pane.

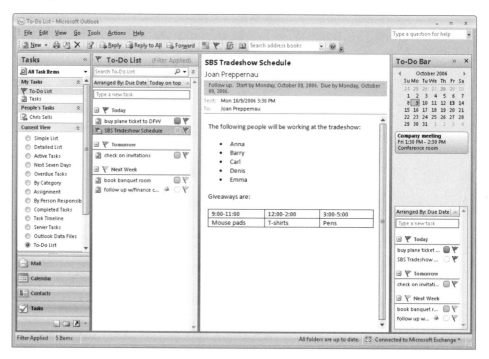

For the purposes of this exercise, assume that you flagged this message for follow-up because you need to organize a meeting with colleagues to discuss its contents.

7. Drag the message from the **To-Do List** to the **Calendar** button in the Navigation Pane, but don't release the mouse button.

As you hold the dragged message over the Calendar button, the Navigation Pane changes to display the Calendar module information instead of the Mail module information.

8. Drop the message on the **Calendar** button to create an appointment based on the message.

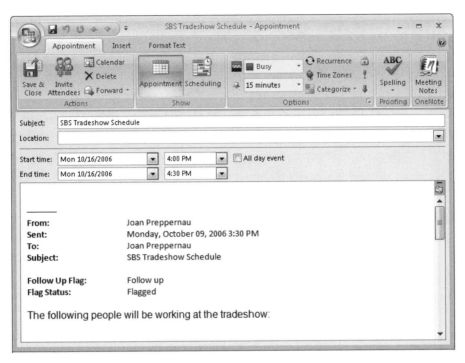

You can convert the appointment to an event by selecting the All Day Event check box, or convert it to a meeting by inviting other people to attend. You can edit the information in the content pane without affecting the content of the original message, and you can move or delete the original message without affecting the appointment.

9. In the appointment window, click the **Save & Close** button to save the appointment to your calendar.

10. When the appointment reminder window appears (15 minutes prior to the start time of the appointment) click **Dismiss**.

See Also For information about appointment reminders, see "Scheduling and Changing Appointments" in Chapter 6, "Managing Appointments, Events, and Meetings."

Printing Messages

You can print an e-mail message, for example, if you want to take a hard copy of it to a meeting for reference, or if you keep a physical file of important messages or kudos. You can print the message exactly as it appears in your Inbox, or embellish it with page headers and footers. Outlook prints the message as shown on-screen, including font and paragraph formats.

In this exercise, you will preview a message as it will appear when printed, add a page header, and then print the message.

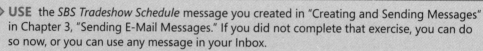

USE the *SBS Tradeshow Schedule* message you created in "Creating and Sending Messages" in Chapter 3, "Sending E-Mail Messages." If you did not complete that exercise, you can do so now, or you can use any message in your Inbox.

BE SURE TO install a printer before beginning this exercise.

OPEN the *SBS Tradeshow Schedule* message.

Microsoft Office
Button

1. In the message window, click the **Microsoft Office Button**, and then point to **Print**.

> **Tip** Unlike previous versions of Outlook, the Print and Print Preview commands are not available from the message window toolbar (or in this case, the Ribbon).

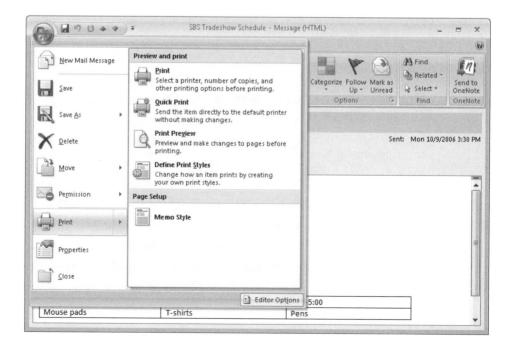

The right pane displays these preview, print, and page setup options:

- Print opens the Print dialog box, where you can make changes to the default printing options before printing.

- Quick Print prints the open or selected message with the default printing options, without first displaying the Print dialog box.

- Print Preview displays the message as it will appear when printed. You can change the page setup options before printing the message.

- Define Print Styles allows you to make changes to an existing *print style* (the way the message is presented on the printed page) or create a new one. The default print style is Memo style, which prints your name, the message header information, and then the message content.

2. Click the **Print** button (not its arrow).

The Print dialog box opens, displaying your default printer settings, which you can change before printing just as you would when printing from any Office program. Clicking OK prints the message with the default settings.

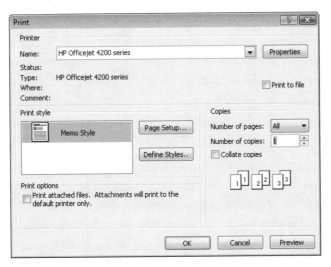

3. In the **Print** dialog box, click **Preview**.

The Print Preview window opens, displaying the message as it will appear when printed.

> **Tip** You can also display the Print Preview window by pointing to Print on the Office menu and then clicking Print Preview.

Actual Size

4. On the Print Preview window toolbar, click the **Actual Size** button to display the message at 100% magnification.

> **Tip** When previewing a message that will be longer than one page when printed with the current settings, you can click the Multiple Pages button to preview all pages of the message at the same time. This can be useful when, for example, you want to check page breaks or scan a document for a particular element.

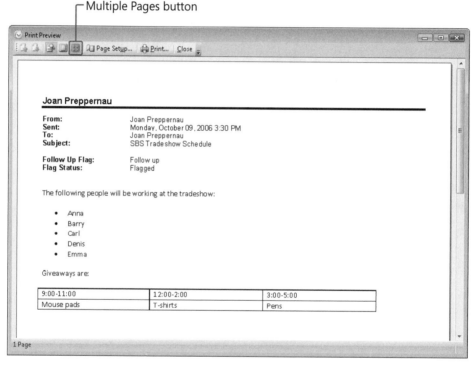

Multiple Pages button

5. In the **Print Preview** window, click the **Page Setup** button.

The Page Setup: Memo Style dialog box opens. You can change the font, paper size, page margins, header, and footer from this dialog box.

> **Tip** You can also display the Page Setup dialog box by pointing to Print on the Office menu and then clicking the print style you want under Page Setup.

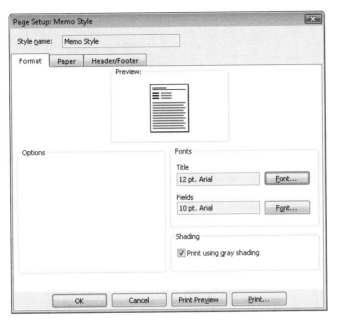

6. In the **Page Setup: Memo Style** dialog box, click the **Paper** tab to see the available options.

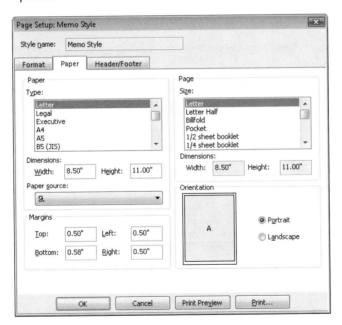

In addition to choosing the paper size, you can select the number of pages that print on each sheet of paper and set the page margins and the orientation.

7. Click the **Header/Footer** tab.

8. In the **Header** area, type For Your Information in the center box, and then click the **Font** button. In the **Font** dialog box, under **Size**, click **16**, and then click **OK**.

User Name

9. In the **Footer** section, select the default text (the page number) that appears in the center box. Then in the **AutoText** box, click the **User Name** button.

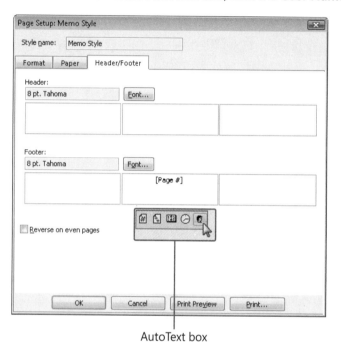

AutoText box

Outlook will print the specified text at the top of the page and your name (or user name, if different) at the bottom.

10. In the **Page Setup** dialog box, click **Print**, and then in the **Print** dialog box, click **OK**.

> **Troubleshooting** If the Save As dialog box opens, you do not have a printer installed. Click the Start button, click Printers And Faxes, and then under Printer Tasks, click Add A Printer. Follow the wizard's instructions to install a local or network printer.

Outlook prints the message, including your custom header and footer.

BE SURE TO remove the custom header and footer from the Memo print style if you don't want to retain them.

CLOSE the SBS Tradeshow Schedule message.

Key Points

- By default, messages you receive appear in your Inbox. Outlook alerts you to new messages in several ways, all of which are customizable.
- You can see the first few lines of each message in AutoPreview, open a message in its own window, or preview messages in the Reading Pane.
- You can preview message attachments in the Reading Pane.
- You can reply to the message sender only or to the sender and all other recipients. You can also forward a message and its attachments to other people.
- You can create tasks or calendar items from received e-mail messages.
- You can print a message when you need a paper copy of its information.

Chapter at a Glance

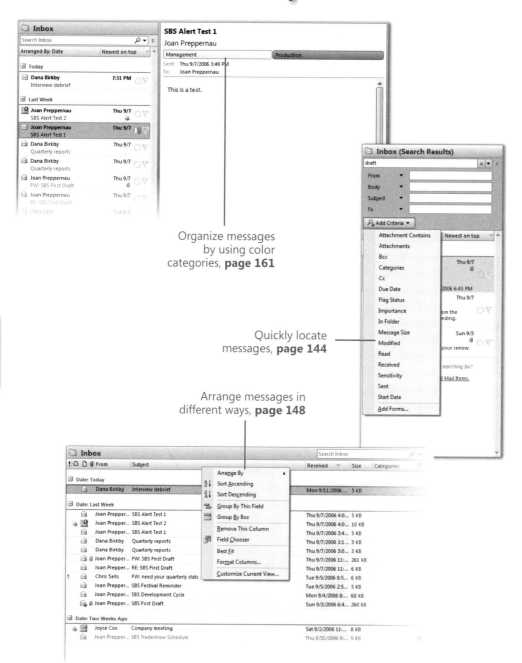

Organize messages by using color categories, **page 161**

Quickly locate messages, **page 144**

Arrange messages in different ways, **page 148**

5 Managing Your Inbox

In this chapter, you will learn to:

✔ Quickly locate messages.

✔ Arrange messages in different ways.

✔ Organize messages by using color categories.

✔ Organize messages in folders.

✔ Archive messages.

So far in this book, we've discussed the basic mechanics of sending and receiving messages, and the Outlook components used for those purposes. Now we'll tackle the task that heavy e-mail users spend a lot of time on—managing the messages you receive. This is where Microsoft Office Outlook 2007 really stands apart from its competitors.

In addition to providing ways to organize messages in subfolders within the Inbox and to archive messages, Outlook 2007 includes a number of new features that simplify the process of managing messages and other Outlook items. The greatest of these is the new Instant Search capability, which filters messages as you type the keywords you want to search for, highlighting the search terms within each message. Another useful tool is Color Categories, which combines the named categories available in earlier versions of Outlook with colored labels to provide quick visual recognition and search capabilities.

In this chapter, you will filter and find messages by using Instant Search, display the messages in your Inbox in a variety of arrangements, and use Search Folders. Then you will organize messages by assigning color categories and by organizing them in folders within the Inbox. Finally, you will look at the default archive settings and manually archive an e-mail folder.

See Also Do you need only a quick refresher on the topics in this chapter? See the Quick Reference entries on pages xxxvii–lxv.

> **Important** The exercises in this chapter require only practice files created in earlier chapters; none are supplied on the book's CD. For more information about practice files, see "Using the Book's CD" on page xxv.

> **Troubleshooting** Graphics and operating system–related instructions in this book reflect the Windows Vista user interface. If your computer is running Microsoft Windows XP and you experience trouble following the instructions as written, please refer to the "Information for Readers Running Windows XP" section at the beginning of this book.

Quickly Locating Messages

We discussed using the Instant Search feature to locate contact records in Chapter 2, "Managing Contact Information." Although you can use Instant Search in the Calendar, Contacts, and Tasks modules, you will most often use it to locate messages in your Inbox and other mail folders. You can search a particular mail folder or search all mail folders.

See Also For information about mail folders, see "Organizing Messages in Folders" later in this chapter.

As you define the criteria for a search, Outlook filters out all messages that don't match, making it easy to find exactly what you're looking for. And here's the neat thing: Outlook searches not only the content of the e-mail message header and the message itself, but also the content of message attachments. So if the search term you're looking for is in a Microsoft Office Word document attached to a message, the message will be included in the search results.

> **Tip** You can't instantly filter content in a Public Folder (if your organization uses these) but you can enter the search criteria and then click the Search button to get the same results as you would in your Inbox.

Instant Search is based on the same technology that drives the search functionality in Windows Vista. With this very powerful search engine, you can find any file on your computer containing a specified search term—whether in a file or folder name, in document or spreadsheet content, in an e-mail message within Outlook, in a message attachment, in a picture, music, or video file, and so on. As a matter of fact, if you prefer to do so, you can conduct all of your Outlook searches from the Windows Vista Start menu.

See Also For information about Windows Vista search features, refer to *Windows Vista Step by Step* (ISBN 0-7356-2269-8) by Joan Preppernau and Joyce Cox (Microsoft Press, 2007).

If the search term you enter produces more than 200 results, the Search Results pane displays this information bar:

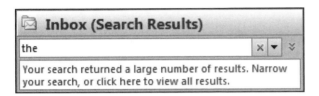

You can display all the results for the current search term by clicking the message bar, or you can narrow the results by expanding the search term or by specifying other search criteria, such as the sender, the recipient (whether the message was addressed or only copied to you), whether the message contains attachments, and so on.

In this exercise, you will use the Instant Search feature to locate a specific message in your Inbox. There are no practice files for this exercise.

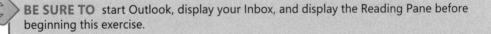

BE SURE TO start Outlook, display your Inbox, and display the Reading Pane before beginning this exercise.

1. In the **Search Inbox** box in the Inbox header, type one or more words likely to appear in messages in your Inbox. For example, if you completed the exercises in previous chapters of this book, you could enter alert, draft or development.

As you type, Outlook filters the contents of your Inbox to display only those items containing the characters, word, or words you enter, and highlights the search term in the displayed messages.

Search term

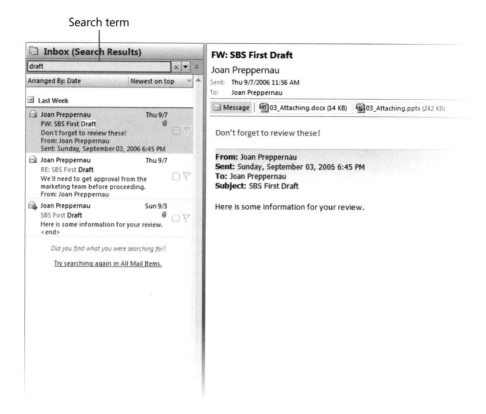

In the lower-left corner of the program window, the status bar displays the number of messages included in the search results. The search results include only messages contained in the Inbox folder and not in any of its subfolders or any other mailbox folders.

Expand the
Query Builder

2. To the right of the **Search Inbox** box, click the **Expand the Query Builder** button.

The search pane expands to include text boxes in which you can specify the sender, a term that appears in the message body, a term that appears in the message subject, or a primary recipient of the message.

3. In the expanded **Search Results** pane, click **Add Criteria** to display a list of additional criteria.

Selecting a field from this list adds the field to the search criteria section.

Alternatively, you can click the arrow to the right of any of the default criteria and select a different field.

4. In the **Add Criteria** list, click **Attachments** to add that field to the search pane.

5. Click the **Attachments** arrow, and then in the list, click **Yes**.

Notice that your search criteria are also described in the search term box.

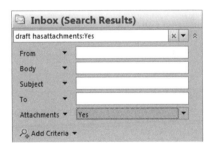

Outlook instantly updates the search results to display only the messages in your Inbox that contain the search term and one or more attachments.

6. To expand the search to include all the folders in your mailbox, at the end of the list of results shown in the Search Results pane, click **Try searching again in All Mail Items**.

   Outlook displays the expanded search results grouped by the folder in which they appear. You can open, delete, and process a message from the Search Results pane as you would from any other. If, however, you change a message so that it no longer fits the search criteria—for example, if you search for flagged messages and then mark the message task as complete, the message no longer appears in the Search Results pane. (It does still appear in whatever folder it is in.)

Clear Search

7. Experiment with locating information by specifying criteria. When you finish, click the **Clear Search** button to remove the filter and redisplay the Inbox message list.

Arranging Messages in Different Ways

As the number of messages in your Inbox increases, it can be challenging to prioritize them. You can customize how you view, arrange, sort, and group messages in Outlook to help you quickly determine which are the most important, decide which can be deleted, and locate any that need an immediate response. You can view only certain groups of messages, such as messages received in the last seven days, unread messages, or messages sent to a certain person or distribution list. You can also view a timeline of all your received messages. Outlook 2007 offers eight predefined *views*, and you can customize any of these to fit your needs.

Category views	List views	Other views
Messages	Messages with AutoPreview	Message Timeline
Sent To	Last Seven Days	
Outlook Data Files	Unread Messages in This Folder	
Documents		

In category views, the Inbox header includes only the arrangement and sort order, the Reading Pane is visible by default, and the message header information is grouped on multiple lines. In list views, information appears in columns; the Reading Pane is not displayed by default, but you can display it if you want. To experiment with different views, point to Current View on the View menu, and then click the view option you want.

> **Tip** For one-click access to the various views available in the Mail module, on the View menu, point to Navigation Pane, and then click Current View Pane. (If a check mark appears before the command, this feature is already in use.) You can then switch views by selecting the view option you want from the list.
>
> The Current View pane is displayed by default in the Contacts, Tasks, and Notes modules but not in the Mail and Calendar modules.

See Also For more information about viewing messages in the Reading Pane or by using the AutoPreview feature, see "Viewing Messages and Message Attachments" in Chapter 4, "Handling E-Mail Messages."

You can also group messages by the contents of any field—by the sender of the message, for example, or by the subject. You can arrange messages by conversation.

By default, Outlook displays messages in the order you receive them, with the newest messages at the top of your Inbox. Messages received during the current week are grouped by day. Earlier messages are grouped by week or by longer periods. You can easily change the order in which messages and other items (such as meeting requests and task assignments) appear in the Inbox or any other mail folder. You can arrange items by:

● **Attachments.** Messages are grouped by whether they have attachments, and secondarily by date received.

● **Category.** Messages are arranged by the category to which they are assigned. Messages without a category appear first. Messages assigned to multiple categories appear in each of those category groups.

● **Conversation.** This grouped view is similar to sorting messages by subject except that each series of related messages is grouped together, and messages within the group appear in a *threaded* conversation order. This arrangement is particularly useful when you want to find a response to a specific version of a message in a multi-person *e-mail trail*. In conversations with multiple messages, Outlook displays only unread or flagged messages, indicating additional messages by a small arrow to the left of the conversation title. Click the arrow to display all the messages in the conversation.

● **Date.** Messages are arranged by date of receipt in order from newest to oldest. Outlook groups messages received on each of the past four days, each of the previous four weeks, the previous month, and those more than one month old.

- **E-mail Account.** Messages are grouped by the e-mail account to which they were sent. This is useful if you receive messages for more than one e-mail account in your Inbox (for example, if you receive messages sent to your POP3 account within your Microsoft Exchange Server mailbox).

- **Importance.** Messages are grouped by priority: High (indicated by a red exclamation point), Normal (the default), or Low (indicated by a blue arrow).

- **Recipient (To).** Messages are grouped alphabetically by the primary recipients (the addresses or names on the To line). The group name exactly reflects the order in which addresses appear on the To line. Therefore, a message addressed to *Bart Duncan; Lukas Keller* will not be grouped with a message addressed to *Lukas Keller; Bart Duncan.*

- **Sender (From).** Messages appear in alphabetical order by the message sender's display name. If you receive messages from a person who uses two different e-mail accounts, or who sends messages from two different e-mail clients (for example, from Outlook and from Microsoft Windows Mail), the messages will not necessarily be grouped together.

- **Size.** Messages are grouped by the size of the message, including any attachment. Groups include Huge (1–5 MB), Very Large (500 KB–1 MB), Large (100–500 KB), Medium (25–100 KB), Small (10-25 KB), and Tiny (less than 10 KB). This feature is useful if you work for an organization that limits the size of your Inbox, because you can easily locate large messages and delete them or move them to a personal folder.

- **Start date or due date.** Unflagged messages and messages without specific schedules appear first. Messages that you've added to your task list with specific start or due dates are grouped by date.

- **Subject.** Messages are arranged alphabetically by their subject lines and secondarily by date. This is similar to arranging by conversation except that the messages aren't threaded.

- **Type.** Items in your Inbox (or other folder) are grouped by the type of item; for example, messages, encrypted messages, message receipts, meeting requests and meeting request responses, tasks, Microsoft InfoPath forms, and server notifications.

When viewing messages in a category view, the Arranged By bar in the Inbox header indicates how the messages are arranged and in what order. Clicking the order indicator reverses the order; for example, from Newest On Top to Oldest On Top. Regardless of what order you choose, group headers divide the messages into groups that you can collapse or expand.

Arrangement ⌐ Groups   ⌐ Order

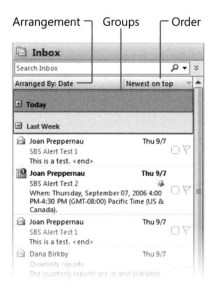

To experiment with the *arrangement* options, on the View menu, point to Arrange By, and then click the arrangement option you want.

Regardless of the view and arrangement you choose, you can sort messages by any visible field simply by clicking its column heading (and reverse the sort order by clicking the column heading a second time). You can change the displayed fields from the Show Fields dialog box, which you display by pointing to Arrange By on the View menu, and then clicking Custom.

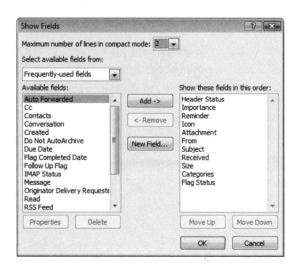

Outlook displays the selected fields in the order shown in the right column. If displaying all the fields requires more space than is available, only some of the fields will be visible. If necessary, you can change the number of lines shown to accommodate more fields. However, it is likely that one of the standard views will fit your needs.

In a list view, you can control the message arrangement, sorting, grouping, visible fields, and other settings from the context menu that appears when you right-click any column header.

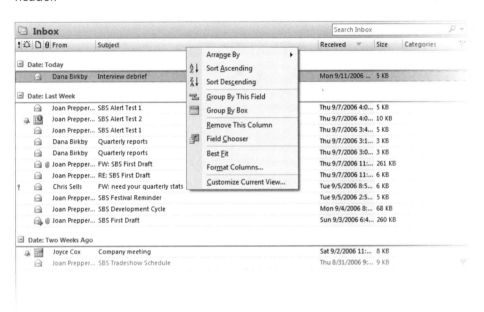

In this exercise, you will change the display, arrangement, sort order, and grouping of messages in your Inbox. Then you will filter the Inbox content, add and remove fields, and change the appearance of the Inbox. Finally, you will restore the default settings. There are no practice files for this exercise.

BE SURE TO start Outlook and display the Inbox in Messages view before beginning this exercise.

1. If there are no unread messages in your Inbox, right-click a message, and then click **Mark as Unread**.

The message header will change to bold, and its icon will change from an open envelope to a closed envelope.

> **Tip** Unread items are distinguished from read items by their bold type and closed-envelope icons.

2. On the **View** menu, point to **Navigation Pane**, and then if a check mark doesn't appear to the left of it, click **Current View Pane**.

The basic view options appear at the bottom of the Navigation Pane.

3. On the **View** menu, if the icon to the left of it is not shaded, click **AutoPreview**.

The first three lines of each unread message appear in the Inbox below the message header.

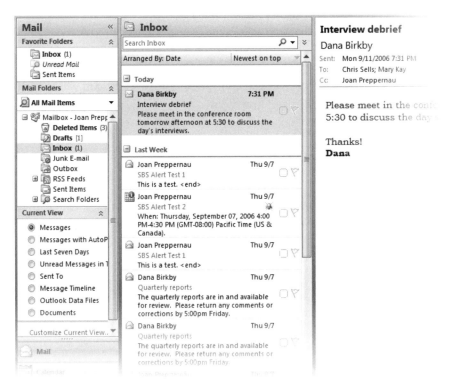

4. On the **View** menu, point to **Arrange By**, and then click **From**.

   Outlook rearranges and groups the messages in your Inbox alphabetically by sender.

5. In the Inbox header, click **A on Top**.

   Outlook reverses the order of the messages.

6. In the Inbox header, click the **Arranged By** bar, and then click **Subject**.

   Outlook groups the messages by subject.

7. On the **View** menu, point to **Expand/Collapse Groups**, and then click **Collapse All Groups**.

Notice that the number of unread items in each group (if there are any) is indicated in parentheses following the conversation subject.

You can use this method to expand or collapse all groups. You can expand or collapse individual groups by clicking the Expand (+) or Collapse (-) button to the left of the group name. You can collapse the group containing the currently selected item by pressing the Left Arrow key and expand a selected group by pressing the Right Arrow key.

8. In the **Current View** pane, select the **Unread Messages in This Folder** option.

Outlook filters the Inbox to display only unread messages.

The Inbox header and the status bar indicate that a filter has been applied. (If you have no unread messages in your Inbox, it will appear to be empty.)

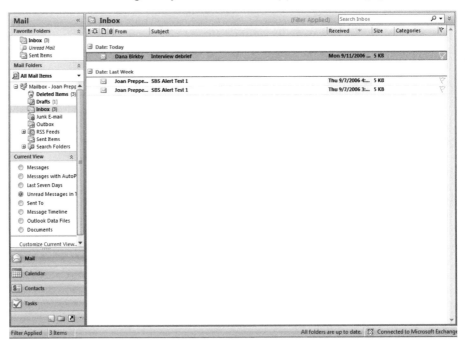

9. In the **Current View** pane, select the **Messages with AutoPreview** option.

    Outlook removes the filter and displays a list view of the messages, with the first lines of each unread message visible.

10. Experiment with the available arrangement, sorting, and grouping options if you want. Then on the **View** menu, point to **Current View**, and click **Customize Current View**.

> **Tip** If the Reset Current View button at the bottom of the Customize View dialog box is active, your view is currently customized and you can reset the view to its default settings by clicking the button.

11. In the **Customize View** dialog box, click **Fields**.

The Show Fields dialog box (shown earlier) opens.

12. In the **Available fields** list, click **Sensitivity**, and then click **Add**.

The Sensitivity field moves to the bottom of the list of columns to be shown in this view.

13. In the **Show these fields in this order** list, drag **Sensitivity** to appear below **Importance**.

While you drag the field, red arrows indicate where it will appear when you release the mouse button.

14. In the **Show Fields** dialog box, click **OK**.

> **Tip** To change the order of columns in any list view, simply drag the column headings to the locations you prefer. While you are dragging a column heading, red arrows indicate where the column will appear when you release the mouse button.

15. In the **Customize View** dialog box, click **Other Settings**.

The Other Settings dialog box opens.

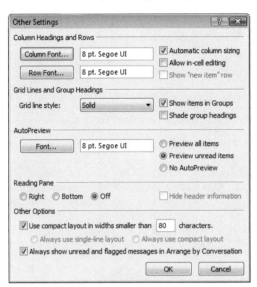

16. Under **Grid Lines and Group Headings**, click the **Grid line style** arrow, and then in the list, click **Small dots**. Then click **OK** in each of the two open dialog boxes to return to the Inbox, which displays the new view settings.

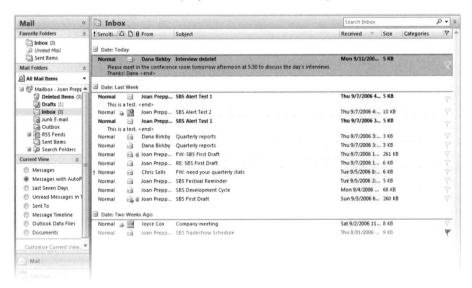

17. Drag the **Sensitivity** column heading downward into the message list, and release the mouse button when a large black X appears over the heading.

Outlook removes the Sensitivity column from the view.

18. On the **View** menu, point to **Current View**, and then click **Define Views**.

The Custom View Organizer dialog box opens, with the current view selected.

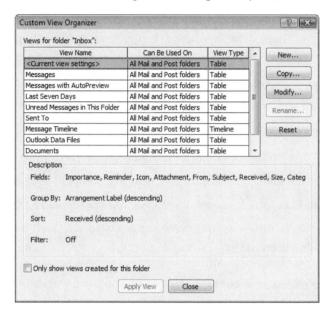

19. In the **Custom View Organizer** dialog box, click the **Reset** button. In the **Microsoft Office Outlook** message box asking whether you want to reset the current view to its original settings, click **OK**.

20. In the **View Name** list, click each view in turn.

If the view settings have been changed from the default, the Reset button becomes active.

21. Repeat Step 19 to reset any customized views you want. When you finish, click the **Messages** view, and then click **Apply View**.

The Inbox is restored to its default view.

BE SURE TO restore the default view settings before continuing, if you want them to match those shown in the rest of this book.

Using Search Folders

A Search Folder is a *virtual folder* that displays all the messages in your mailbox that match a specific set of search criteria, no matter which folders the messages are actually stored in. When you create a Search Folder, it becomes part of your mailbox and is kept up to date. The Search Folder module is located in the All Mail Items list under your top-level mailbox, at the same level as the Inbox.

Depending on the contents of your Inbox and your previous use of Outlook, you might have any of the following four folders within the Search Folders folder:

- The Categorized Mail folder displays messages assigned to a category.
- The For Follow Up folder displays messages flagged for future action.
- The Large Mail folder displays messages larger than 100 kilobytes (KB).
- The Unread Mail folder displays messages that are marked as unread.

The names of folders containing unread items are bold, followed by the number of unread items in parentheses. The names of folders containing items flagged for follow up are bold, followed by the number of flagged items in square brackets. The names of folders whose contents are not up to date are italic. To update a Search Folder, click the folder name.

Each message in your mailbox is stored in only one folder (such as your Inbox), but it might appear in many Search Folders. Changing or deleting a message in a Search Folder changes or deletes the message in the folder where it is stored.

If you want quick access to messages that fit a specific set of criteria, you can create a custom Search Folder. To do so:

1. In the **Navigation Pane**, expand the Search Folders folder to display the default Search Folders.

2. Right-click the **Search Folders** folder, and then click **New Search Folder**.

3. In the **New Search Folder** dialog box, select the type of Search Folder you want to create, and then click **OK**.

   You can choose from the standard options presented or click Custom to specify other search options.

You can make changes to the contents of an existing Search Folder by right-clicking the folder and then clicking Customize This Search Folder.

Organizing Messages by Using Color Categories

Assigning messages to categories can help you more easily locate information. Outlook 2007 introduces the Color Categories feature, which combine named categories with color bars to provide an immediate visual cue when viewing messages in your Inbox.

You can apply color categories to messages, calendar items, contacts, tasks, and notes. You can apply color categories several ways:

Categorize

- In any folder, you can select one or more items, click the Categorize button on the Standard toolbar, and then click the category you want.

> **Troubleshooting** The Categorize button might not appear on the toolbar until you select one or more items.

- In any folder, you can right-click a single item or a selection of multiple items, point to Categorize, and then click the category you want.

Category bar

- In any mail folder, you can right-click the Category bar that appears when the Reading Pane is displayed, and then click the category you want.

- If you frequently use a particular category, you can assign it as your Quick Click category. You can then apply the Quick Click category to a message by clicking its Category bar.

To quickly view the messages belonging to a category, you can group your messages by category or include the category as a search criterion in the Query Builder. On the To-Do Bar, you can arrange your flagged messages and tasks by category.

See Also For more information about color categories, see "Organizing Contacts by Using Color Categories" in Chapter 2, "Managing Contact Information."

> **Tip** To help you easily distinguish messages received from certain people, you can color-code message headers. For example, you might show all messages from your boss in red and all messages from the finance department in green. You can also choose to have messages that were sent only to you displayed in a different color than messages sent to multiple people or a distribution list. You apply color-coding on a per-folder basis. To experiment with color-coding, click Organize on the Tools menu, and then click the Using Colors tab.

In this exercise, you will display the default color categories, rename and create categories, change the color associated with a category, categorize a message, and sort the Inbox contents by category.

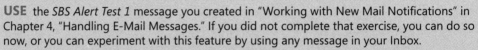

USE the *SBS Alert Test 1* message you created in "Working with New Mail Notifications" in Chapter 4, "Handling E-Mail Messages." If you did not complete that exercise, you can do so now, or you can experiment with this feature by using any message in your Inbox.

BE SURE TO start Outlook and display your Inbox in the default Messages view before beginning this exercise.

1. In the Inbox, click the *SBS Alert Test 1* message.

2. On the Standard toolbar, click the **Categorize** button.

Categorize

> **Troubleshooting** If the Categorize button is not visible or active, click any message in the Inbox to activate it.

The Category list displays the standard and currently assigned categories. Notice that you can remove all categorizations from a message by clicking Clear All Categories.

3. In the **Category** list, click **All Categories**.

The Color Categories dialog box opens, displaying the current color-to-category assignments. You can rename any of the standard color categories or create new color categories.

4. In the **Color Categories** dialog box, click the **Blue Category** name (not the check box), and then click **Rename**. With the category name selected for editing, type Management, and then press Enter .

> **Tip** If you haven't renamed a color category, Outlook gives you the option of renaming the category the first time you use it.

The category name changes.

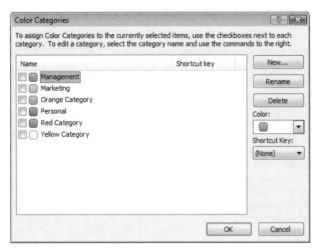

5. With the **Management** category still selected, click the **Color** arrow, and then in the color palette, click the **Yellow** square.

   The color associated with the Management category changes from Blue to Yellow.

6. In the **Color Categories** dialog box, click **New**.

   The Add New Category dialog box opens.

7. In the **Name** box, type Marketing. Click the **Color** arrow, and then in the color palette, click the **Red** square. Then click the **Shortcut Key** arrow.

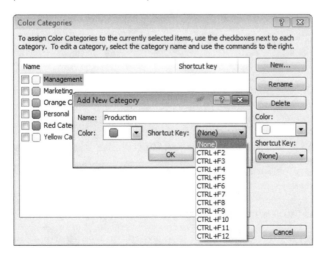

You can assign keyboard shortcuts to up to 11 color categories. You might want to implement this feature if you frequently use multiple categories.

8. In the **Shortcut Key** list, click **None**. Then in the **Add New Category** dialog box, click **OK**.

The new category appears at the bottom of the Color Categories list. Its check box is selected, indicating that it has been assigned to the currently selected message.

9. In the **Color Categories** dialog box, click **OK**.

In the message list, a red square appears in the Category bar of the selected message, and in the Reading Pane, a red bar with the category name *Production* appears at the top of the message.

10. In the message list, right-click the **Category** bar of the *SBS Alert Test 1* message, and then in the list, click **Management**.

The Category bar changes to display both red and yellow icons, indicating that the message is assigned to two categories. You can assign a message to an unlimited number of categories, but only the three most recently assigned appear in the Category bar.

The Reading Pane displays two colored bars of equal size. Up to three categories can be displayed in one row; additional categories are displayed in additional rows.

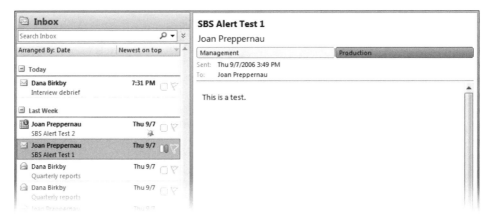

11. In the Inbox header, click the **Arranged By** bar, and then click **Categories**.

The messages are arranged by category, beginning with the uncategorized messages.

12. To the right of the **Arranged By** bar, click **A on top**.

The order reverses to display the categorized messages at the top of the list.

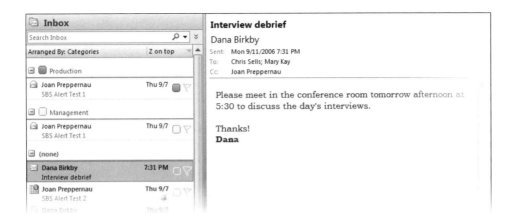

BE SURE TO sort the Inbox by date before continuing to the next exercise.

Organizing Messages in Folders

After you've read and responded to messages, you might want to keep some for future reference. You can certainly choose to retain them all in your Inbox if you want, but as the number of messages in your Inbox increases to the hundreds and then into the thousands, it might quickly become overwhelming. To keep your Inbox content low and avoid an accumulation of unrelated messages, you can organize messages into folders.

Popular personal-organization gurus advocate various folder structures as an important part of an organizational system. You can apply any of these physical folder structures to Outlook, or you can use any other structure that works for you. For example, you might create a folder for each project you're working on and store all messages regarding a particular project in its own folder. Or you might create a folder to store all messages from a particular person, such as your manager, no matter what they are about.

You can move messages to folders manually, or if your organization is running Exchange Server, you can have Outlook move them for you. You can automatically move messages to another folder by creating a rule; for example, you can instruct Outlook to automatically move all messages received from your manager to a separate folder. You can set up different rules that go into effect when you're away from the office.

See Also For information about automatically moving messages, see "Creating Rules to Process Messages" in Chapter 12, "Customizing and Configuring Outlook."

In this exercise, you will create a folder and then move messages to it.

USE the *RE: SBS First Draft* and *FW: SBS First Draft* messages you created in "Replying to and Forwarding Messages" in Chapter 4, "Handling E-Mail Messages." If you did not complete that exercise, you can do so now, or you can experiment with this feature by using any messages in your Inbox.

BE SURE TO start Outlook and display your Inbox in Messages view before beginning this exercise.

1. On the Standard toolbar, click the **New** arrow, and then in the list, click **Folder**.

   The Create New Folder dialog box opens.

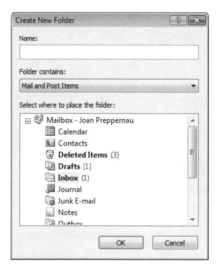

Troubleshooting If your default data file (the file where your messages are stored) is a personal folder on your hard disk, the first item in the Select Where To Place The Folder box is Personal Folders.

2. In the **Name** box, type SBS Practice Messages, and then click **OK**.

Important The name of this folder begins with *SBS* so that you can easily differentiate it from other folders in your mailbox.

Because you created this folder from the Inbox, Outlook creates the new folder as a subfolder of the Inbox, and formats it to contain mail items.

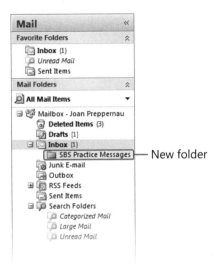 — New folder

3. In the **Navigation Pane**, locate the *RE: SBS First Draft* and *FW: SBS First Draft* messages.

4. Drag the *RE: SBS First Draft* message to the **SBS Practice Messages** folder in the Navigation Pane.

The message disappears from the Inbox.

5. Right-click the *FW: SBS First Draft* message, and then click **Move to Folder**.

The Move Items dialog box opens.

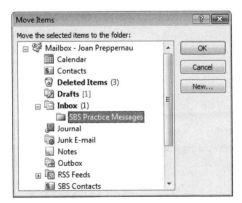

6. In the **Move the selected items to the folder** list, click **SBS Practice Messages** (if it isn't already selected). Then click **OK**.

The message disappears from the Inbox.

7. In the **Navigation Pane**, under the **Inbox** folder, click the **SBS Practice Messages** folder.

The two messages appear in the new folder.

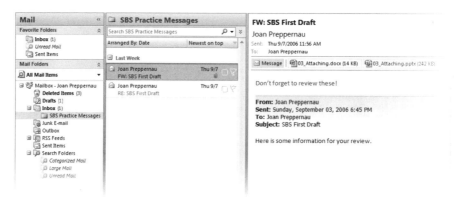

BE SURE TO move the messages back to your Inbox if you used your own messages rather than the practice messages.

See Also For information about sharing Outlook folders, see "Sharing Your Folders with Other People" in Chapter 10, "Collaborating with Other People."

Creating a OneNote Page from an E-Mail Message

If your 2007 Office system installation includes Microsoft Office OneNote, you can send or link items you create in Outlook, such as e-mail messages, contact records, and meeting invitations, to your OneNote notebook.

To send the content of an e-mail message to OneNote:

1. Display the Inbox, and then select the message (or messages) you want to send.

2. On the Standard toolbar, click the **Send to OneNote** button.

OneNote starts and, for each selected message, creates a page in your Unfiled Notes section. Each page contains the full text of the original message and links to any attachments.

You can move pages from the Unfiled Notes section to a notebook section by dragging it, or by right-clicking the page tab, and then clicking Move Page To, Another Section, and the target notebook section.

Archiving Messages

As messages accumulate in your Inbox and other message folders, you might need to consider other ways to store them in order to cut down on the amount of storage space you're using. For example, you might want to *archive* all messages received or sent before a certain date. Archiving messages in a separate Outlook message file helps you manage clutter and the size of your primary data file, while still allowing easy access to the archived messages from within Outlook.

By default Outlook automatically archives messages in all your folders at regular intervals to a location determined by your operating system—usually an Archive data file you can access from the Navigation Pane. You can change the default *AutoArchive* settings, such as the archive frequency and location, and you can specify unique archive settings for individual folders.

If you are working on an Exchange Server network, your archival options might be limited by retention policies set by your network administrator. For instance, your company might have a policy that you may retain items for no more than a certain number of days.

> **Tip** You can use the Mailbox Cleanup feature to see the size of your mailbox, find and delete old items or items that are larger than a certain size, manually archive your mail, empty your Deleted Items folder, and delete conflicting versions of items stored on your computer or on the server. To use this feature, click Mailbox Cleanup on the Tools menu.

In this exercise, you will learn how to set the default automatic archive options, how to manually archive a folder, and how to set the archive options for an individual folder. There are no practice files for this exercise.

> **BE SURE TO** start Outlook and display the Inbox before beginning this exercise.

1. On the **Tools** menu, click **Options**.

   The Options dialog box opens.

2. In the **Options** dialog box, click the **Other** tab.

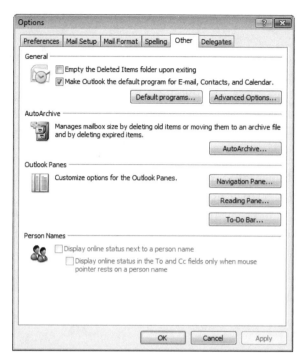

3. In the **AutoArchive** area, click **AutoArchive**.

   The AutoArchive dialog box opens.

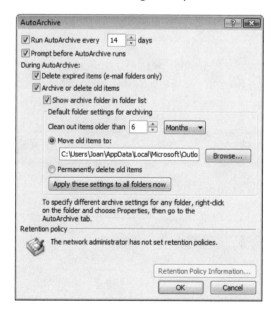

4. Review your AutoArchive settings—particularly note how often Outlook will start the archival process, the age at which items will be archived, and the location in the **Move old items to** box.

   If the Prompt Before AutoArchive Runs check box is selected, Outlook requests your approval each time it runs the AutoArchive process. If you decline, the process doesn't start again until the next scheduled time.

   Notice that you have the option to permanently delete old items. If you make changes to your AutoArchive settings or want to standardize settings across all folders, you can apply the changes to all the folders in your mailbox by clicking the Apply These Settings To All Folders Now button.

5. If you want to make changes to your AutoArchive settings, do so, and then click **OK** in each of the open dialog boxes. Otherwise, click **Cancel** in each of the dialog boxes to close them without initiating any changes.

6. With the Inbox active, on the **File** menu, point to **Folder**, and then click **Properties for "Inbox"**.

   The Inbox Properties dialog box opens.

7. Click the **AutoArchive** tab.

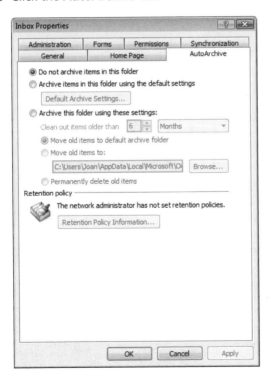

You can set the archive options for each folder individually from the AutoArchive tab of the folder's Properties dialog box.

- If you select the Archive Items In This Folder Using The Default Settings option, you can view and modify the default settings in the AutoArchive dialog box shown earlier by clicking the Default Archive Settings button.

- If you select the Archive This Folder Using These Settings option, you can specify a unique archival age and location for the items in this folder.

8. If you want to make changes to the Inbox AutoArchive settings, do so, and then click **OK**. Otherwise, click **Cancel** to close the dialog box without initiating any changes.

9. On the **File** menu, click **Archive**.

The Archive dialog box opens.

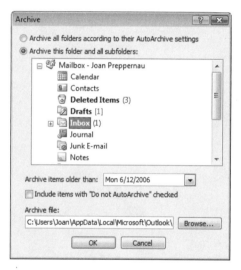

From this dialog box, you can manually start the archive process for your entire mailbox or for selected folders.

10. If you want to initiate the archive process for your mailbox now, select the **Archive all folders according to their AutoArchive settings** option, and then click **OK**. Otherwise, click **Cancel**.

If you click OK, Outlook displays the progress of the archive process on the status bar in the lower-right corner of the program window. You can cancel an archive process by clicking the Archiving button on the status bar and then in the list, clicking Cancel Archiving.

The first time Outlook archives messages, it creates an Archive Folders data file that you can access from the Navigation Pane. The data file contents are organized in the same folder structure as the original contents, and are stored in a separate file on your computer.

> **Tip** You can restore archived Outlook items from the Archive Folders data file to your mailbox by dragging or moving them to the mailbox folder.

 BE SURE TO review your AutoArchive settings and ensure they are set the way you want.

Key Points

- You can filter and locate messages in your mailbox by using the new Instant Search function. You can create virtual Search Folders that automatically update to display messages meeting certain criteria.
- You can group and sort messages by sender, time, subject, size, category, or any other field.
- You can assign color-coded categories to messages, tasks, appointments, and other Outlook items, and then group and sort items by color category. You can use the default Outlook categories or tailor them to fit your needs.
- You can create folders to organize your mail, and move items to folders manually or automatically.
- Outlook automatically archives old and expired items to a separate data file. You can specify the AutoArchive frequency, location, and other settings on a global and per-folder basis.

Chapter at a Glance

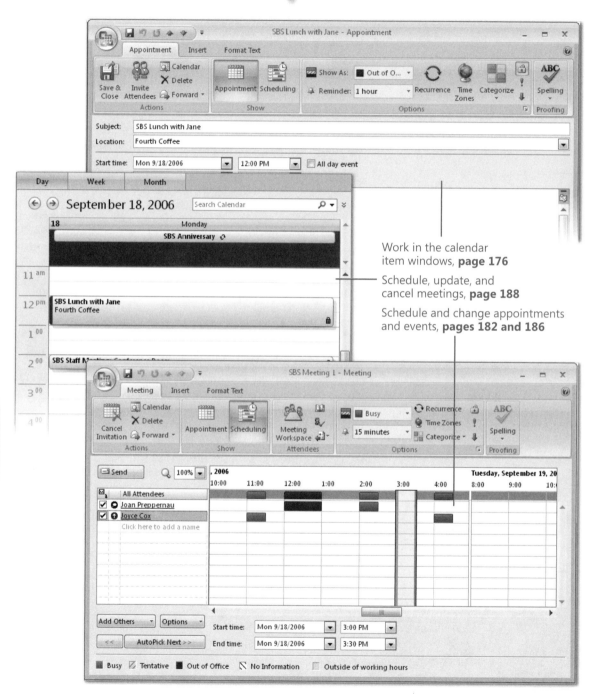

Work in the calendar item windows, **page 176**

Schedule, update, and cancel meetings, **page 188**

Schedule and change appointments and events, **pages 182 and 186**

6 Managing Appointments, Events, and Meetings

In this chapter, you will learn to:

✔ Work in the calendar item windows.

✔ Schedule and change appointments and events.

✔ Schedule, update, and cancel meetings.

✔ Respond to meeting requests.

You might find that your Microsoft Office Outlook Calendar runs your life—but that isn't necessarily a bad thing! Using the Calendar effectively can help you to stay organized, on task, and on time. You can schedule and track appointments, meetings, and events. Because Outlook 2007 maps your scheduled tasks to your calendar, you can look at your calendar in Day view or Week view to see the tasks that need to be completed that day or that week, and you can track your progress by marking tasks as complete when you finish them.

In this chapter, you will record different types of information in your Outlook calendar, scheduling an appointment and an event on your own calendar and then scheduling a meeting with another person. You will learn methods of determining meeting times during which other people are available. Then you will learn about responding to, updating, and canceling meeting requests.

See Also Do you need only a quick refresher on the topics in this chapter? See the Quick Reference entries on pages xxxvii–lxv.

> **Important** No practice files are required to complete the exercises in this chapter. For more information about practice files, see "Using the Book's CD" on page xxv.

Working in the Calendar Item Windows

We refer to the window in which you create or respond to an appointment as the *appointment window*, to a meeting as the *meeting window*, and to an event as the *event window*; collectively we refer to these windows as the *calendar item windows*. Like the contact and message windows, the calendar item windows contain their own commands, arranged on the new Office Ribbon instead of on menus and toolbars.

See Also For more information about the user interface for Outlook 2007 item windows, see "Working in the Contact Window" in Chapter 2, "Managing Contact Information."

In this exercise, you will take a tour of the calendar item window elements that differ from the contact and message window elements discussed in earlier chapters, and you'll learn about the differences between the types of calendar items. There are no practice files for this exercise.

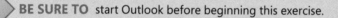

BE SURE TO start Outlook before beginning this exercise.

Calendar

1. In the **Navigation Pane**, click the **Calendar** button to display the Calendar module.

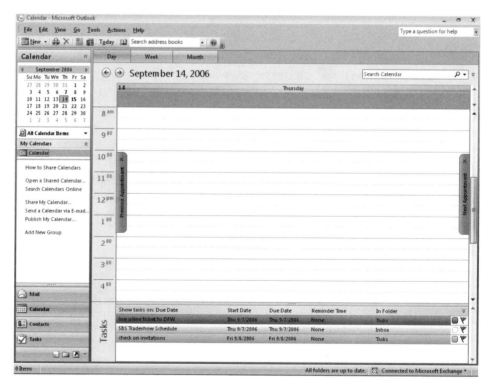

Troubleshooting Graphics and operating system–related instructions in this book reflect the Windows Vista user interface. If your computer is running Microsoft Windows XP and you experience trouble following the instructions as written, please refer to the "Information for Readers Running Windows XP" section at the beginning of this book.

New
Appointment

2. On the Standard toolbar, click the **New Appointment** button.

An untitled appointment window opens.

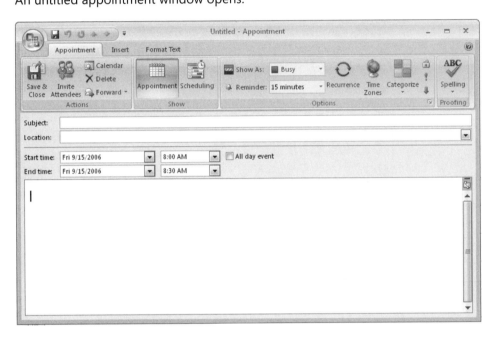

Important Depending on your screen resolution and the size of the appointment window that opens, you might see more or fewer buttons in each of the groups, or the buttons you see might be represented by larger or smaller icons than those shown in this book. Experiment with the size of the appointment window to understand the effect on the appearance of the Ribbon.

See Also For more information about the tabs and groups on the Ribbon, see "Working in the Contact Window" in Chapter 2, "Managing Contact Information."

Microsoft Office
Button

3. In the upper-left corner of the window, click the **Microsoft Office Button**.

Commands related to managing appointments (such as creating, saving, deleting, and printing) are available from the Office menu that appears.

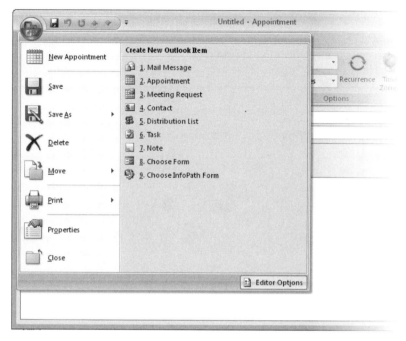

See Also For information about the Print commands, see "Printing Messages" in Chapter 4, "Handling E-Mail Messages." For information about the commands available in the Editor Options window, see "Personalizing Your Office and Outlook Settings" in Chapter 12, "Customizing and Configuring Outlook."

4. Click away from the Office menu to close it.

    The appointment window commands are organized in groups on three tabs:

    ● Appointment

    ● Insert

    ● Format Text

    > **Tip** Depending on what programs you have installed on your computer, tabs and groups other than those described here might also appear on the Ribbon. For example, if Microsoft Office OneNote is installed on your computer, a OneNote group appears on the Appointment tab.

    The Appointment tab is active by default. Buttons representing commands related to creating appointments are organized on this tab in four groups:

    ● Actions

    ● Show

    ● Options

    ● Proofing

You can create a simple appointment by using only the commands available on this tab.

5. Click the **Insert** tab.

Buttons representing commands related to items you can insert are organized on this tab in six groups:

- Include
- Tables
- Illustrations
- Links
- Text
- Symbols

6. Click the **Format Text** tab.

Buttons representing commands related to the appearance of message content are organized on this tab in six groups:

- Clipboard
- Font
- Paragraph
- Styles
- Zoom
- Editing

7. On the **Appointment** tab, in the **Options** group, click the **Time Zones** button.

A new field displaying the time zone for each of the start and end times appears. With this useful Outlook 2007 feature, you can schedule an appointment that crosses time zones—for example, a flight from Los Angeles to New York.

See Also For more information about configuring Outlook for different time zones, see "Configuring Outlook for Multiple Time Zones" in Chapter 7, "Managing Your Calendar."

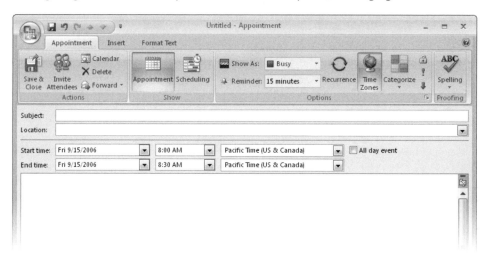

8. In the **Start time** area, select the **All day event** check box.

The window changes from an appointment window to an event window. The contents of the Format Text and Insert tabs don't change, but an Event tab replaces the Appointment tab.

9. Click the **Event** tab.

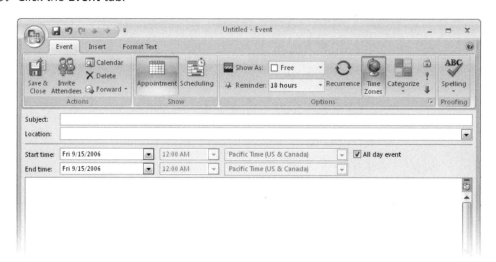

The Event tab contents are nearly identical to the Appointment tab contents—the only change is that on the Event tab, in the Options group, by default your time is shown as Free rather than Busy, and the reminder is set to display 18 hours prior to the event rather than 15 minutes.

10. In the **Start time** area, clear the **All day event** check box to change the event to an appointment.

Invite Attendees

11. In the **Actions** group, click the **Invite Attendees** button.

The window changes from an appointment window to a meeting window. The contents of the Format Text and Insert tabs don't change, but a Meeting tab that includes one additional group, Attendees, replaces the Appointment tab:

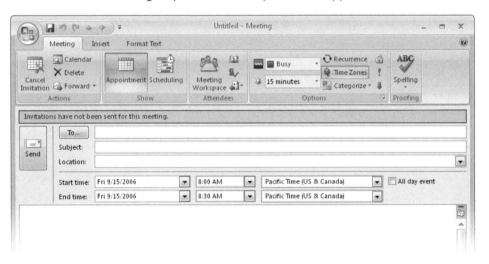

> **Tip** You can invite people to an event in the same way you do to a meeting, by clicking the Invite Attendees button from within an event window.

The meeting window header includes a To field in addition to the standard Subject and Location fields. You can invite attendees by entering them in the To field or by clicking the Scheduling button in the Show group.

BE SURE TO click the Time Zones button to hide the time zone settings, if you don't want to display them.

CLOSE the meeting window without saving your changes.

Scheduling and Changing Appointments

Appointments are blocks of time you schedule for only yourself (as opposed to meetings, to which you invite other people). If an appointment recurs at specific intervals, such as every Tuesday and Thursday, every other week or every month, you can set it up in your Outlook calendar as a *recurring* appointment; doing so creates multiple instances of the appointment in your calendar at the time interval you specify. Recurring appointments are linked. When making changes to recurring appointments, you can choose to update all occurrences or only an individual occurrence of the appointment.

When creating an appointment, you can show your time on the calendar as Free, Tentative, Busy, or Out Of Office. This information is available to other people on your network, and also when you send your schedule information to other people in an e-mail message or share your calendar. You can include information such as driving directions or Web site links in the Notes field, and attach related files so that they are easily available to you at the time of the appointment.

See Also For information about sending your schedule information via e-mail, see "Sending Calendar Information in an E-Mail Message" in Chapter 7, "Managing Your Calendar." For information about sharing your calendar, see "Sharing Your Folders with Other People" in Chapter 10, "Collaborating with Other People."

When Outlook is running, it displays a *reminder* message 15 minutes before the appointment start time—you can change the reminder time or turn it off completely if you want to. If you synchronize your Outlook installation with a mobile device such as a BlackBerry or a mobile phone running Microsoft Windows Mobile, you can also receive reminders on your device. This is very convenient when you are away from your computer.

See Also For information about creating an appointment from an e-mail message, see "Creating a Task or an Appointment from a Message" in Chapter 4, "Handling E-Mail Messages." For information about assigning appointments to categories, see "Organizing Messages by Using Color Categories" in Chapter 5, "Managing Your Inbox."

In this exercise, you will schedule an appointment and a recurring appointment. There are no practice files for this exercise.

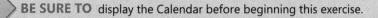

BE SURE TO display the Calendar before beginning this exercise.

> **Troubleshooting** The default Calendar display is Day view. If your calendar does not look like the one shown in this exercise, click the Day button on the Standard toolbar.

1. In the **Navigation Pane**, in the **Date Navigator**, click tomorrow's date.

> **Tip** The Date Navigator displays six weeks at a time, including the selected month. The days of the selected month are black; days of the previous and next months are gray, but you can still select them in the Date Navigator.

Outlook displays tomorrow's schedule.

2. In the Calendar pane, point to the **1:00 P.M.** time slot (or, if you already have an appointment scheduled at 1:00 P.M., to another time when you have 30 minutes available).

Click To Add Appointment appears in the time slot.

3. Click once to activate the time slot.

In this mode, you can enter basic appointment details directly in the Calendar pane.

4. Type SBS Lunch with Jane, and then press Enter.

> **Important** The subject of each appointment, meeting, or event we have you create while working through the exercises in this book begins with *SBS* so that you can easily differentiate the practice files from other items on your calendar.

Outlook creates a half-hour appointment beginning at 1:00 P.M.

5. Drag the appointment from the 1:00 P.M. time slot to the **12:00 P.M.** time slot (or, if you already have an appointment scheduled at noon, to another time when you have an hour available).

Outlook changes the appointment start time.

6. Point to the bottom border of the appointment, and when the pointer becomes a double-headed arrow, drag down so that the appointment ends at **1:00 P.M.**

You can add more details to the appointment and vary from the default settings from within the appointment window.

7. Double-click the **SBS Lunch with Jane** appointment.

The appointment window opens. The subject, start time, and end time are set according to the information you entered in the Calendar pane.

8. In the **Location** box, type Fourth Coffee.

9. On the **Appointment** tab, in the **Options** group, click the **Show As** arrow, and then in the list, click **Out of Office**.

10. In the **Options** group, click the **Reminder** arrow, and then in the list, click **1 hour**.

Private

11. In the **Options** group, click the **Private** button.

Marking an appointment, event, or meeting as Private hides the details from anyone you share your calendar with.

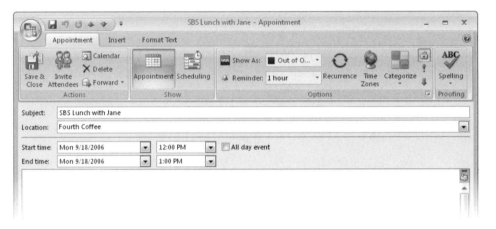

12. In the **Actions** group, click the **Save & Close** button.

Save & Close

Outlook adds a purple stripe at the left side of the appointment to indicate you will be out of the office, and displays the location. The lock icon in the lower-right corner indicates that the appointment has been marked as private.

13. Double-click the **2:00 P.M.** time slot.

Outlook opens an appointment window with the appointment start time set to 2:00 P.M. and the end time set 30 minutes later.

14. In the **Subject** box, type SBS Staff Meeting. Then in the **Location** box, type Conference Room.

Recurrence

15. On the **Appointment** tab, in the **Options** group, click the **Recurrence** button.

The Appointment Recurrence dialog box opens.

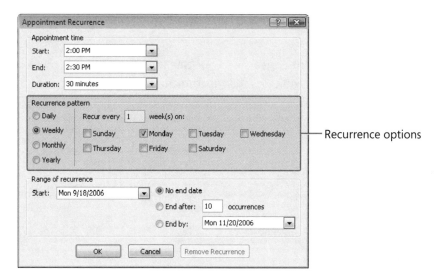

Recurrence options

The default appointment recurrence is weekly on the currently selected day of the week. You can set the appointment to recur until further notice, or to end after a certain number of occurrences or by a certain date.

16. In the **Range of recurrence** area, select the **End after** option, and then in the box, replace *10* with *2*.

17. To create a 30-minute appointment beginning at 2:00 P.M. on the selected day of the week, this week and next week only, click **OK**.

The appointment window title bar changes to reflect that this is now a recurring appointment, the Appointment tab changes to a Recurring Appointment tab, and the frequency (labeled *Recurrence*) appears in the header.

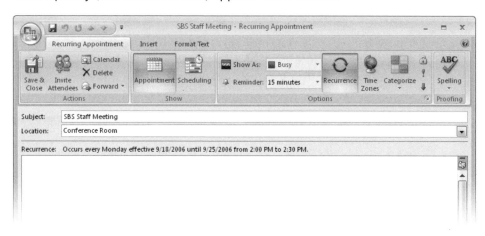

18. On the **Recurring Appointment** tab, in the **Actions** group, click the **Save & Close** button.

The appointment appears on your calendar. The circling arrow icon at the right end of the time slot indicates the recurrence.

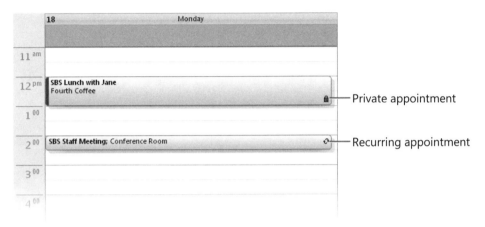

19. In the **Date Navigator**, click the day of the appointment in each of the next two weeks, to verify that the appointment appears on your calendar the next week, but not the following week.

See Also   For information about creating a OneNote page linked to an appointment, see the sidebar "Creating a OneNote Page Linked to an Appointment, an Event, or a Meeting" in Chapter 7, "Managing Your Calendar."

Scheduling and Changing Events

Events are day-long blocks of time that you schedule on your Outlook calendar—for example, a birthday, a payroll day, or anything else occurring on a particular day but not at a specific time. In all other respects, events are identical to appointments, in that you can specify a location, indicate recurrence, indicate your availability, invite attendees, and attach additional information to the event item.

You can create an event when viewing your calendar in Day view, Week view, or Month view.

See Also   For information about creating an event from an e-mail message, see "Creating a Task or an Appointment from a Message" in Chapter 4, "Handling E-Mail Messages."

In this exercise, you will schedule an event and convert it to a recurring event. There are no practice files for this exercise.

BE SURE TO display the Calendar in Day view before beginning this exercise.

1. In the **Date Navigator**, click tomorrow's date.

2. In the Calendar pane, point to the blank space below the day header and above the delineated time slots.

   Click To Add Event appears in the space.

3. Click once to activate the event slot.

   In this mode, you can enter basic event details directly in the Calendar pane.

4. Type SBS Anniversary, and then press ⌑Enter⌑.

   Outlook creates a one-day event. You can add more details to the event and vary from the default settings from within the event window.

5. Double-click the **SBS Anniversary** event.

   The event window opens. The subject and date are set according to the information you entered in the Calendar pane.

 6. On the **Event** tab, in the **Options** group, click the **Recurrence** button.

   The Appointment Recurrence dialog box shown earlier in this chapter opens. The default recurrence for events is the same as for appointments—weekly on the currently selected day of the week.

7. In the **Recurrence pattern** area, select the **Yearly** option.

   You can schedule an annual event to recur on a specific date or on a selected (first, second, third, fourth, or last) day of the month.

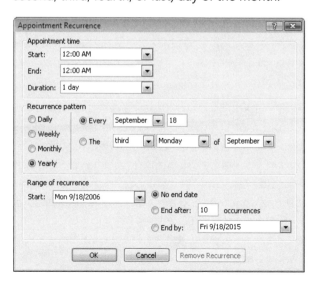

8. To create a recurring annual appointment on the same date each year, click **OK**.

   The event window title bar changes to reflect that this is now a recurring event, the Event tab changes to a Recurring Event tab, and the frequency appears in the header.

9. On the **Recurring Event** tab, in the **Actions** group, click the **Save & Close** button.

Save & Close

   The event appears at the top of the Calendar pane. The circling arrow icon at the right end indicates the recurrence.

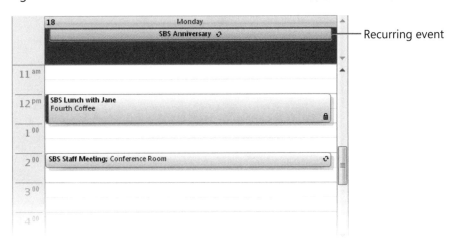
Recurring event

Scheduling, Updating, and Canceling Meetings

Scheduling meetings through Outlook is significantly simpler than scheduling meetings manually, particularly when you are coordinating the schedules of several people. A primary difficulty when scheduling a meeting is finding a time that works for everyone. Outlook displays the individual and collective schedules of people within your own organization, and of people outside of your organization who have published their availability to the Internet.

You can send a meeting invitation (referred to as a *meeting request*) to any person who has an e-mail account (even to people who don't use Outlook). You can inform non-critical attendees of the meeting by marking their attendance as Optional. You can invite entire groups of people by using an e-mail alias or distribution list. The meeting request can include text and Web links, as well as file attachments. This is a convenient way of ensuring that meeting attendees have specific information available to them. Outlook automatically tracks responses from attendees and those responsible for scheduling the resources you requested, so you always have an up-to-date report of how many people will be attending your meeting.

Using the Exchange Server 2007 Smart Scheduling Feature

If your organization is running Exchange Server 2007, Outlook simplifies even further the process of selecting a suitable meeting time by presenting you with a list of meeting times of any duration you specify, and indicating for each time the number of required and optional attendees who are available.

The Scheduling Assistant page is similar to the Scheduling page displayed when organizing a meeting on an Exchange Server 2003 network.

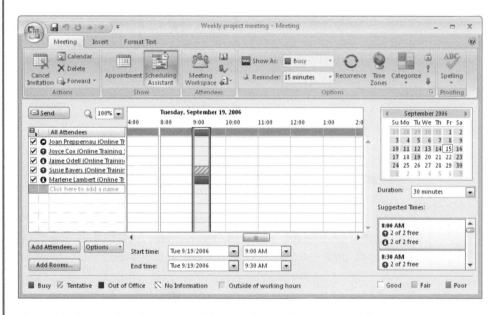

The calendar on the right side of the window indicates the collective availability of the group by color. Dates that occur in the past and non-working days are shaded; scheduling suggestions are not provided for those days.

- Days when all attendees are available are white (Good)

- Days when most attendees are available are light blue (Fair)

- Days when most attendees are not available are medium blue (Poor)

In the Suggested Times list, Outlook displays attendee availability for appointments of the length specified in the Duration list. The availability of required attendees is shown separately from that of optional attendees and resources.

Selecting a date in the calendar displays the suggested meeting times for that day. Clicking a meeting time in the Suggested Times list updates the meeting request.

If your organization is running Microsoft Exchange Server and the Exchange Server directory includes shared resources such as conference rooms or presentation equipment, you can request these resources by inviting them to the meeting. Resource requests may be automatically approved, or an individual may be assigned the responsibility of approving each resource request.

You might find it necessary to change the date, time, or location of a meeting—for example, because of a schedule conflict. You can change any information in a meeting request at any time, including adding or deleting invited attendees, or canceling the meeting. After you make changes, Outlook sends an updated meeting request to the invited attendees to keep them informed. If the only change you make is to the attendee list, Outlook gives you the option of sending an update only to the affected attendees.

See Also For information about creating a meeting request from an e-mail message, see "Creating a Task or an Appointment from a Message" in Chapter 4, "Handling E-Mail Messages."

In this exercise, you will create and send a meeting request. There are no practice files for this exercise.

> **BE SURE TO** display the Calendar and inform a co-worker or friend that you are going to practice inviting him or her to a meeting.

1. In the **Date Navigator**, click tomorrow's date. Then in the Calendar pane, click the **3:00 P.M.** time slot (or if you have a conflicting appointment, click a time when you have 30 minutes available).

New
Appointment

2. On the Standard toolbar, click the **New Appointment** arrow, and then in the list, click **Meeting Request**.

   An untitled meeting window opens.

   > **Troubleshooting** If the active selection in the Calendar pane is an event, Outlook will create an Invited Event request instead; if this happens, clear the All Day Event check box to convert the Invited Event to a Meeting.

3. In the **To** box, type the e-mail address of someone within your organization, or if you aren't working on an Exchange Server network, type any e-mail address, for example, adam@contoso.com.

4. In the **Subject** box, type SBS Meeting 1.

5. In the **Location** box, type Test – please accept to indicate to the person you are inviting that the meeting request is for testing purposes only.

Scheduling

6. On the **Meeting** tab, in the **Show** group, click the **Scheduling** button.

The All Attendees list on the Scheduling page includes you and the e-mail address (or if the person is in your address book, the associated name) you entered in the To box. The black icon next to your name indicates that you are the meeting organizer. The red icon next to the sole attendee's name indicates that he or she is a required attendee. You can click an attendee's icon to switch between Required Attendee and Optional Attendee status, or to indicate a resource rather than a person.

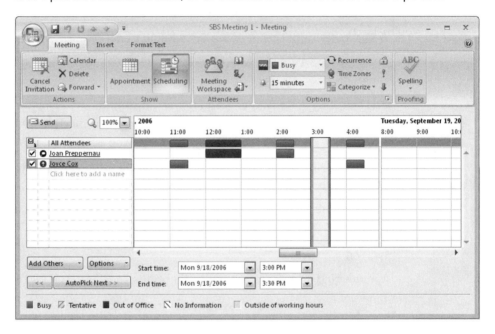

> **Tip** You can enter additional attendees in the To box on the Appointment page or in the All Attendees list on the Scheduling page. If you prefer, you can organize a meeting directly from a Scheduling page-like interface by clicking Plan A Meeting on the Actions menu.

Outlook indicates the suggested meeting time with green (start time) and red (end time) vertical bars. If free/busy information is available for meeting invitees, their time is shown as white (Available), blue (Busy), or purple (Out of Office). Tentative bookings are indicated by light-blue diagonal stripes. If no information is available (either because Outlook can't connect to a person's calendar or because the proposed meeting is further out than the scheduling information stored on the server), Outlook indicates this by gray diagonal stripes. The gray row at the top of the schedule indicates the collective schedule of all the invitees.

> **Tip** To send an e-mail message to everyone you've invited to a meeting, first open the meeting window, and then on the Meeting tab, in the Attendees group, click the Message To Attendees button.

You can change the time and duration of the meeting to work with the displayed schedules by selecting from the lists at the bottom of the Scheduling page, by dragging the green and red vertical bars in the schedule area, or by clicking the time you want in the schedule area.

7. In the lower-right corner of the **Scheduling** page, click the **AutoPick Next** button.

   The green Start Time and red End Time lines move to the next available half-hour time slot.

   You can change the Show As and Reminder settings, create recurrences, assign color categories, and make any other changes you want. The availability specified in the Show As list will apply to all attendees who accept your meeting request.

8. After you select the meeting time you want, click the **Appointment** button in the **Show** group.

   The Appointment page is displayed.

9. Verify the meeting details, and then click the **Send** button in the meeting request header.

   The meeting appears in your calendar on the specified date and in the specified time slot.

Responding to Meeting Requests

When you receive a meeting request from another Outlook user, the meeting appears on your calendar with your time scheduled, but shown as Tentative. Until you respond to the meeting request, the organizer doesn't know whether you plan to attend. You can respond in one of four ways:

● You can accept the request. Outlook deletes the meeting request and shows your time scheduled on your calendar as the meeting organizer indicated in the meeting request.

● You can tentatively accept a request, indicating that you might be able to attend the meeting but are undecided. Outlook deletes the meeting request and shows your time on your calendar as tentatively scheduled.

- You can propose a new meeting time. Outlook sends your request to the meeting organizer for confirmation and shows the original time on your calendar as tentatively scheduled.

- You can decline the request. Outlook deletes the meeting request and removes the meeting from your calendar.

Creating a Meeting Workspace

If your organization has a collaboration site built with Microsoft SharePoint products and technologies, such as a team site, on which you have permission to create document libraries, you can create a *meeting workspace* (a shared site for planning a meeting and tracking related tasks and results) at the same time that you schedule the meeting. You can also create a meeting workspace for a meeting that you previously scheduled; after you change the meeting request to include the meeting workspace information, Outlook sends an updated request containing the information to all attendees.

To create a meeting workspace in a new or existing meeting request:

1. In the meeting window, on the **Meeting** tab, in the **Attendees** group, click the **Meeting Workspace** button.

2. In the **Meeting Workspace** pane that opens on the right side of the meeting window, click the **Select a location** arrow, and then in the list, click the SharePoint site where you want to create the meeting workspace. (If this is the first time you've used the Meeting Workspace pane, you might first need to click **Change settings**.) If you haven't previously set up a meeting workspace or document library on the SharePoint site you want to use, click **Other** in the **Select a location** list, enter the SharePoint site address in the **Other Workspace Server** dialog box that opens, and then click **OK**.

3. In the **Select a workspace** area, select the template language and meeting workspace template you want to use, and then click **OK**. Or if you want to link to an existing meeting workspace, select that option, click the **Select the workspace** arrow, and then in the list, click the existing workspace.

4. In the **Meeting Workspace** pane, click **OK**.

Attendees can link to the meeting workspace from the meeting request or from the meeting item on their calendars.

See Also For more information about using Outlook with SharePoint products and technologies, see Chapter 10, "Collaborating with Other People."

Meeting
response
options

Display your calendar
for the proposed
meeting date

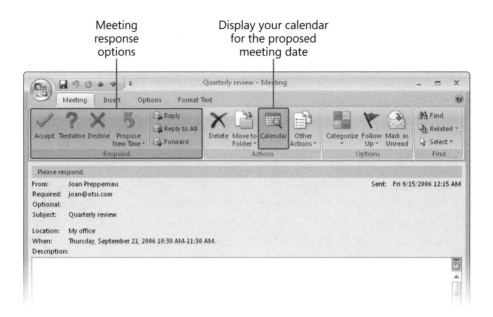

If you don't respond to a meeting request, the meeting remains on your calendar, with your time shown as tentatively scheduled.

If you're unsure whether a meeting time works for you, you can click the Calendar button within the meeting request window to open your Outlook calendar for the suggested meeting day in a separate window, so you can view any conflicting appointments.

When accepting or declining a meeting, you can choose whether to send a response to the meeting organizer. If you don't send a response, your acceptance will not be tallied in the Meeting form, and the organizer and other attendees will not know whether you are planning to attend the meeting. If you do send a response, you can add information to the response before sending it, if you want to convey a message to the meeting organizer.

To manually respond to a meeting request:

1. In the meeting request window, in the Reading Pane, or on the shortcut menu that appears when you right-click the meeting request, click **Accept**, **Tentative**, or **Decline**.

2. Choose whether to send a standard response, a personalized response, or no response at all.

To propose a new time for a meeting:

1. In the meeting request window, in the Reading Pane, or on the shortcut menu that appears when you right-click the meeting request, click **Propose New Time**.

2. In the schedule area of the **Propose New Time** dialog box, similar to the Scheduling page of the meeting request window shown earlier, change the meeting start and end times to the times you want to propose, and then click the **Propose Time** button.

3. In the meeting response window that opens, enter a message to the meeting organizer if you want to, and then click **Send**.

   Outlook sends your response and adds the meeting to your calendar as tentatively scheduled for the original meeting time. After the meeting organizer approves the meeting time change, you and other attendees will receive updated meeting requests.

You can also choose to respond to meeting requests automatically. If you do, Outlook will process meeting requests and cancellations in accordance with your instructions.

To instruct Outlook to automatically respond to meeting requests:

1. On the **Tools** menu, click **Options**.

2. On the **Preferences** tab of the **Options** dialog box, click the **Calendar Options** button.

3. In the **Calendar Options** dialog box, click the **Resource Scheduling** button.

4. In the **Resource Scheduling** dialog box, select the **Automatically accept meeting requests and process cancellations** check box.

5. Select the **Automatically decline conflicting meeting requests** and/or the **Automatically decline recurring meeting requests** check boxes if you want Outlook to do this.

6. Click **OK** in each of the open dialog boxes.

Key Points

- You can create and manage appointments and all-day events in your calendar.

- You can use Outlook to set up meetings, invite participants, and track their responses. Outlook can help you choose a meeting time based on participants' schedules.

- Other people in your organization can see your free, busy, and out-of-office time that you indicate in your calendar. You can personalize the display of your available working hours, and mark appointments as private to hide the details from other people.

- If your organization has a SharePoint collaboration site, you can create a meeting workspace to accompany a meeting request. Meeting workspaces provide a central location for sharing information and files among meeting attendees.

- If you organization is running Exchange Server 2007, you can use the Smart Scheduling feature to quickly identify meeting times of a specific duration during which your planned attendees are available.

Chapter at a Glance

Print a calendar, **page 207**

Link to an Internet calendar, **page 216**

Work with multiple calendars, **page 218**

Send calendar information in an e-mail message, **page 213**

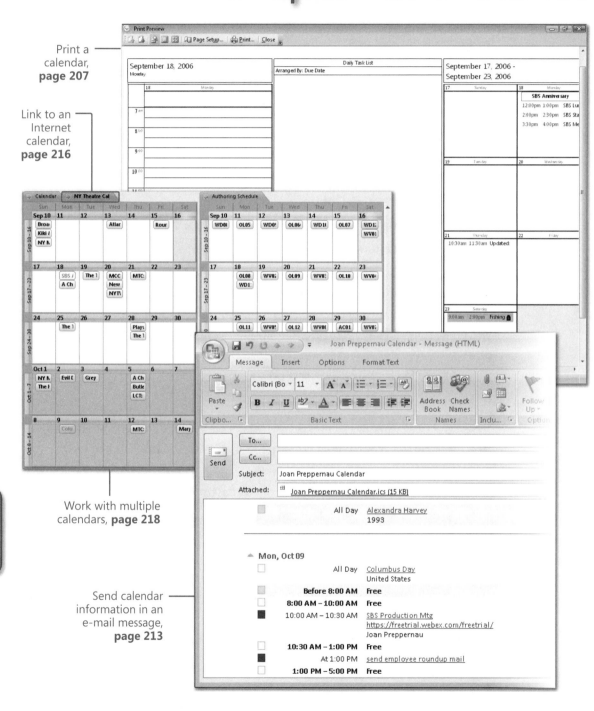

7 Managing Your Calendar

In this chapter, you will learn to:

✔ Display different views of a calendar.

✔ Define your available time.

✔ Configure Outlook for multiple time zones.

✔ Print a calendar.

✔ Send calendar information in an e-mail message.

✔ Link to an Internet calendar.

✔ Work with multiple calendars.

Using the Microsoft Office Outlook 2007 Calendar is a big step toward efficient time management. Earlier in this book, you learned how to enter and update various types of appointments in your calendar. To make your calendar work more effectively for you, and to simplify the process of finding the information you need, you can refine the default calendar settings.

In this chapter, you will learn about the different ways you can display calendar information. Then you will print daily and monthly calendars and attach calendar information to an e-mail message. Finally, you will link to a public calendar on the Internet and experiment with the different ways you can display and move between calendars. You also learn how to add region-specific holidays to your calendar, configure Outlook for use in multiple time zones, save information from your Calendar as a Web page, and create a OneNote page linked to a Calendar item, as well as ways in which you can delegate control of your calendar to another person or manage a calendar on behalf of another person.

See Also Do you need only a quick refresher on the topics in this chapter? See the Quick Reference entries on pages xxxvii–lxv.

> **Important** No practice files are required to complete the exercises in this chapter. For more information about practice files, see "Using the Book's CD" on page xxv.

> **Troubleshooting** Graphics and operating system–related instructions in this book reflect the Windows Vista user interface. If your computer is running Microsoft Windows XP and you experience trouble following the instructions as written, please refer to the "Information for Readers Running Windows XP" section at the beginning of this book.

See Also For information about working with Microsoft SharePoint calendars, sharing your calendar with other Outlook users, or viewing a shared calendar, see Chapter 10, "Collaborating with Other People."

Displaying Different Views of a Calendar

In the Calendar module, the Navigation Pane includes the *Date Navigator*, lists of calendars you can connect to, and links to open, search, share, send, and publish calendars. To help you stay on top of your schedule, you can view your calendar in a variety of ways:

- **Day/Week/Month view.** A calendar view displaying one of the following:

  - Day view, displaying one day at a time separated into half-hour increments.

  - Work Week view, displaying your work week, which by default is defined as Monday through Friday from 8:00 A.M. to 5:00 P.M. You can define your work week as whatever days and hours you want.

    See Also For information about modifying the work week shown in Outlook, see "Defining Your Available Time" later in this chapter.

  - Week view, displaying one week (Sunday through Saturday) at a time.

  - Month view, displaying five weeks at a time.

  You switch among time periods by clicking the buttons at the top of the Calendar pane. In Month view, you can click the week tab at the left edge of a week to display only that week. In Week view, you can display the work week or the full seven-day week. In either view, you can double-click a day to display only that day.

- **All Appointments view.** A list view displaying all appointments (but not events) grouped by frequency of recurrence (none, Daily, Weekly, Monthly, or Yearly).

- **Active Appointments view.** A list view displaying all appointments starting on or after the current day, grouped by frequency of recurrence.

- **Events view.** A list view displaying only day-long events, grouped by frequency of recurrence.

- **Annual Events view.** A list view displaying only events that recur yearly.

- **Recurring Appointments view.** A list view displaying only recurring appointments and events, grouped by frequency of recurrence.

- **By Category view.** A list view displaying all calendar items grouped by Color Category. Items assigned to multiple categories appear in each of the assigned category groups.
- **Outlook Data Files view.** A list view displaying all calendar items grouped by Outlook Data File and then by frequency of recurrence.

By default, Outlook displays your calendar in Day view. To change the view, select the view option you want in the Current View list in the Navigation Pane, or click the view you want on the View menu. To return to the current Day view from any other view, click the Today button on the Standard toolbar.

You can display the previous or next time periods by clicking the Back or Forward button next to the date or date range, or you can display a specific day, week, or month by selecting it in the Date Navigator.

- To display a month, click the current month name and then in the list, click the month you want to display. To scroll beyond the seven-month range displayed by default, point to the top or bottom of the month list.
- To display a week, click the margin to the left of that week. Or, if you display week numbers in the Date Navigator and Calendar, click the week number to display that week.

> **Tip** Week numbers are used in some countries to reference events, vacations, and the like. Week 1 is the calendar week (Sunday through Saturday) in which January 1st falls, Week 2 is the following week, and so on through to the end of the year. Because of the way the weeks are numbered, a year can comprise Weeks 1 through 53. To display week numbers, click Tools on the Options menu, click the Calendar Options button, and then select the Show Week Numbers In The Month View And Date Navigator check box. Then click OK in the open dialog boxes.

- To display a day, click that day.

> **Tip** If you've made changes to any view (such as the order in which information appears) and want to return to the default settings, point to Current View on the View menu, click Customize Current View, and then in the Customize View dialog box, click Reset Current View. If the Reset Current View button is unavailable, the view already displays the default settings.

In calendar views that include the Date Navigator, increasing the width of the Navigation Pane also increases the number of months shown in the Data Navigator. You can allocate up to 50 percent of the program window to the Navigation Pane.

You can use the Outlook 2007 Instant Search feature to quickly locate appointments, events, meetings, or holidays by searching on any text within the calendar item.

See Also For more information about Instant Search, see "Quickly Locating Contact Information" in Chapter 2, "Managing Contact Information" and "Quickly Locating Messages" in Chapter 5, "Managing Your Inbox."

In this exercise, you will display different periods of time in the Date Navigator and in your calendar, and display different views of your schedule.

> **USE** the calendar items you created in Chapter 6, "Managing Appointments, Events, and Meetings." If you did not complete the exercises in that chapter, you can complete them now, or use any appointments, meetings, or events in your own calendar.
>
> **BE SURE TO** start Outlook before beginning this exercise.

1. In the **Navigation** pane, click the **Calendar** button to display the Calendar module.

   By default, Outlook displays your calendar for the current day, which is indicated in the Date Navigator by a red outline. Tasks due today are listed in the Tasks area at the bottom of the Calendar pane.

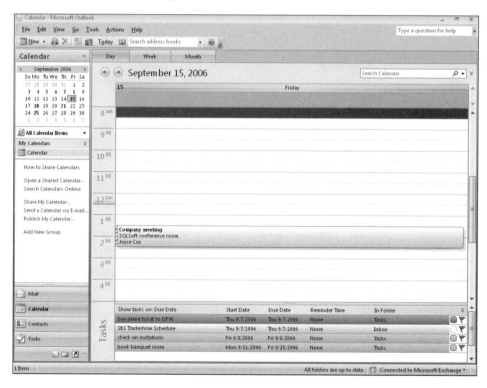

> **Tip** To reset your calendar to the default display settings, point to Current View on the View menu, click Customize Current View, and then in the Customize View dialog box, click Reset Current View. Then click OK in the message box requesting confirmation, and in the open dialog box.

2. In the **Date Navigator**, click a bold date to display your calendar for a day on which you have scheduled appointments or meetings.

Dates with scheduled events (but no appointments or meetings) do not appear bold.

3. At the top of the Calendar pane, click **Week**.

Outlook displays your calendar for the work week of the selected date, and highlights the corresponding days in the Date Navigator. The Tasks area displays tasks due each day.

4. At the top of the Calendar pane, select the **Show full week** option.

Outlook displays the full seven-day week. Time that falls outside of your defined work week appears shaded.

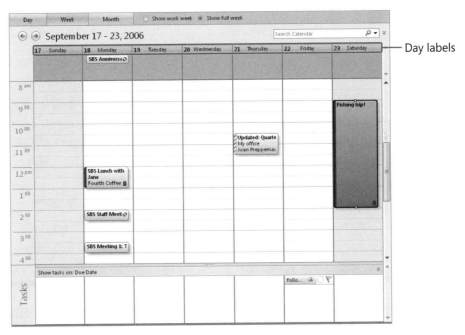

Day labels

5. At the top of the Calendar pane, click **Month**.

Outlook displays your calendar for the month. Alternating months are shaded to provide an obvious visual indicator of the change. The Tasks area is not available in Month view.

Week labels

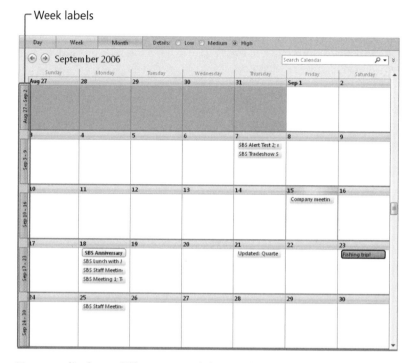

You can display a different month by scrolling the Calendar pane or by clicking the month you want to view, in the Date Navigator.

6. At the top of the Calendar pane, to the right of **Details**, select the **Medium** option.

   The calendar changes to display only events as readable items; appointments and meetings appear as horizontal lines, with the width of the line indicating the amount of time scheduled for that item. The lines representing items assigned to color categories appear in the assigned color.

7. Select the **Low** option to hide appointments and meetings entirely.

8. Click one of the week labels that appears along the left edge of the Calendar pane.

   Outlook displays the selected week in the most recent week view (Work Week or Full Week) you selected. No detail level is available in Day or Week view; Outlook shows all the calendar items.

Forward

9. To the left of the date range in the calendar header, click the **Forward** button.

   The calendar moves forward one week.

10. Click one of the day labels that appears in the calendar header.

    Outlook displays the selected day in Day View.

11. On the Standard toolbar, click **Today** to return to the default view.

Adding and Removing Local Holidays

You can add the national holidays of any country to your Outlook calendar, as follows:

1. On the **Tools** menu, click **Options**. Then on the **Preferences** tab of the **Options** dialog box, click **Calendar Options**.

2. In the **Calendar Options** dialog box, click **Add Holidays**.

3. In the **Add Holidays to Calendar** dialog box, select the check boxes of the countries whose holidays you want to add to your calendar, and then click **OK**.

4. After Outlook adds the selected country's holidays to your calendar, click **OK** in each of the open dialog boxes.

Outlook 2007 assigns a color category named *Holiday* to all holidays in your calendar. If the only holidays in your calendar were added in Outlook 2007, you can view a list of holidays by displaying the calendar in By Category view and then scrolling to the Holiday category. You can then remove all holidays from your calendar by selecting the Categories: Holiday group header and pressing the Delete key.

To remove holidays created in a previous version of Outlook, or if you want to remove only the holidays of a specific country, follow these steps:

1. Display the Calendar in **All Appointments** view.

2. On the **View** menu, point to **Current View**, and click **Customize Current View**.

3. In the **Customize View** dialog box, click the **Group By** button.

4. In the **Group By** dialog box, clear the **Automatically group according to arrangement** check box if it is selected. Then click the **Group items by** arrow, and in the list, click **Location**.

5. Ensure that all the **Then by** lists display **(none)**, and then click **OK** in each of the open dialog boxes.

6. In the **Calendar** pane, collapse the displayed groups or scroll the pane until the **Location** group of the holidays you want to remove (for example, Location: Sweden) is visible.

7. To remove all the holidays of the displayed country, click the **Location** group header, and then press the [Del] key. If a Outlook displays a message box warns you that this action will apply to all items in the selected group, click **OK**.

8. To remove selected holidays, click the holiday(s) you want to delete (hold the [Ctrl] key to select multiple holidays), and then press [Del].

Defining Your Available Time

You can tell Outlook what your work schedule is so that other people can make appointments with you only during the times that you plan to be available. This defined time is called your *work week*.

By default, Outlook defines the work week as Monday through Friday from 8:00 A.M. to 5:00 P.M. You can change this to suit your needs—for instance, if you work a late shift or on weekends. Your work week is colored differently in your calendar and by default is the only time displayed to other people on your network who look at your calendar.

See Also For more information about looking at other people's calendars, see "Accessing Other People's Folders" in Chapter 10, "Collaborating with Other People."

In this exercise, you will view and change your work week. There are no practice files for this exercise.

 BE SURE TO display your calendar in Week view before beginning this exercise.

1. At the top of the **Calendar** pane, select the **Show work week** option.

> **Troubleshooting** If your work week does not match the default days and times described here, work through this exercise using your own settings.

2. Scroll the calendar page so that you can see the beginning or end of the work day.

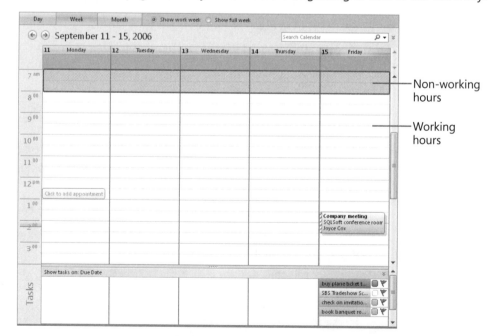

3. On the **Tools** menu, click **Options**.

4. On the **Preferences** tab of the **Options** dialog box, click **Calendar Options**.

   The Calendar Options dialog box opens.

5. In the **Calendar work week** area, select the **Sun** and **Sat** check boxes, and clear the **Tue**, **Wed**, and **Thu** check boxes.

   The work week is now set to Friday through Monday.

6. Click the **Start time** arrow, and in the list, click **3:00 PM**. Then click the **End time** arrow, and in the list, click **11:00 PM**.

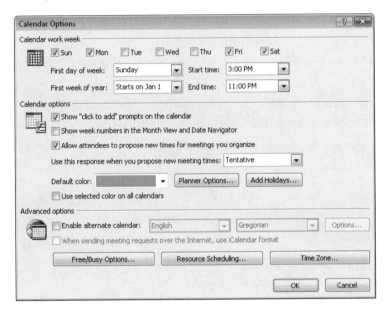

> **Troubleshooting** Outlook doesn't allow you to define a workday that crosses midnight, or to define different start and end times for different days.

7. Click **OK** in each of the open dialog boxes.

   Your calendar displays your new work week settings.

 BE SURE TO set up your work week the way you want it before continuing.

Configuring Outlook for Multiple Time Zones

If you frequently travel to locations outside of your usual time zone, you will find it helpful to change the time zone on your computer. You can do this from Microsoft Windows or from Outlook. When you change the time zone, information such as the receipt time of e-mail messages and appointment times changes to match the new time zone, and if you display the clock in the Windows taskbar notification area, the time shown there also changes.

To change the time zone:

1. On the **Tools** menu, click **Options**. Then on the **Preferences** tab of the **Options** dialog box, click the **Calendar Options** button.

2. In the **Advanced Options** area of the **Calendar Options** dialog box, click the **Time Zone** button.

3. In the **Time Zone** dialog box, click the **Time zone** arrow, and in the list, click the time zone you want. Then click **OK** in each of the open dialog boxes.

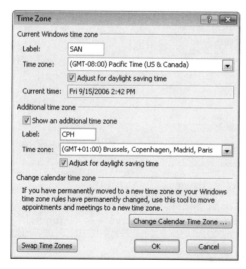

When preparing to travel, or if you schedule meetings involving participants in different time zones, you might want to configure Outlook to display two time zones in your calendar. Outlook then displays the time zones in Day view in two columns to the left of the Calendar pane.

To simultaneously display two time zones in your calendar:

1. On the **Tools** menu, click **Options**.

2. In the **Options** dialog box, on the **Preferences** tab, click the **Calendar Options** button.

3. In the **Calendar Options** dialog box, click the **Time Zone** button.

4. In the **Time Zone** dialog box, select the **Show an additional time zone** check box. Then in the second **Time zone** list, click the time zone you want to display.

5. Type a label for each time zone (such as *San Diego* and *Copenhagen*) in the corresponding **Label** box.

6. Click **OK** in each of the open dialog boxes.

If you set up two time zones in your Outlook calendar, you can quickly switch between them by clicking the Swap Time Zones button in the Time Zone dialog box.

Printing a Calendar

From time to time, you might find it convenient to print a day, week, month, or other period of your calendar; for instance, if you're traveling without a laptop or want to have your weekly schedule quickly available in your briefcase. You can easily print any time period of your calendar. The amount of detail that appears depends on the period you print.

Outlook offers several built-in print styles, and you can create others if you want. The available print styles vary based on what view you're in when you choose the Print command. The default print styles include:

- **Daily Style.** Prints the selected date range with one day per page. Printed elements include the date, day, TaskPad, reference month calendar, and an area for notes.

- **Weekly Style.** Prints the selected date range with one calendar week per page, including reference calendars for the selected and following months.

- **Monthly Style.** Prints a page for each month in the selected date range. Each page includes the six-week range surrounding the month, along with reference calendars for the selected and following months.

- **Tri-fold Style.** Prints a page for each day in the selected date range. Each page includes the daily schedule, weekly schedule, and TaskPad.

- **Calendar Details Style.** Lists your appointments for the selected date range, as well as the accompanying appointment details.

You can select the date or range of dates to be printed and modify the page setup options to fit your needs.

In this exercise, you will learn two ways of selecting print styles as you preview and optionally print your calendar in the Daily and Tri-fold styles. There are no practice files for this exercise.

> **Important** To complete this exercise, you must have a printer installed. If you don't have a printer installed, you can preview the various print options, but not print. To install a printer, click the Start button and then click Control Panel. In Control Panel, under Hardware And Sound, click Printers, and then click Add A Printer. If you are working on a network, your administrator can provide the information you need to install a printer.

> **BE SURE TO** display your calendar in Day view before beginning this exercise. For best results, display a day on which one or more appointments, meetings, or events appear on the calendar.

Print

1. On the Standard toolbar, click the **Print** button.

The Print dialog box opens, with the Daily Style format and today's date selected.

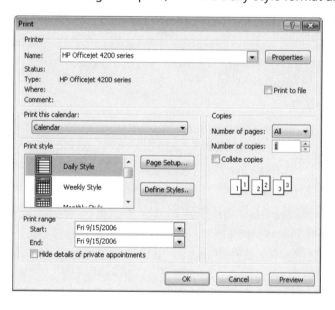

2. In the **Print** dialog box, click **Preview**.

Outlook displays a Print Preview window depicting how your calendar will appear when printed.

3. On the Print Preview window toolbar, click the **Actual Size** button to magnify the calendar page so it is legible.

Actual Size

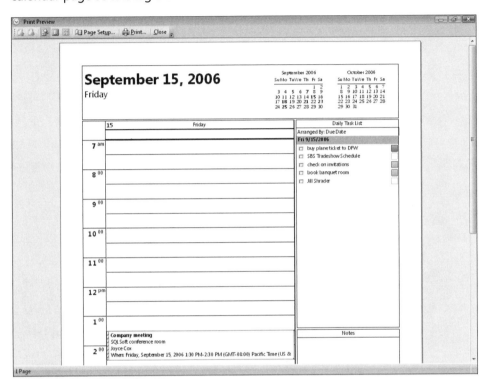

4. On the Print Preview toolbar, click **Print**.

5. In the **Print** dialog box, ensure that the printer you want to use is selected in the **Printer** area, and then click **OK**.

Outlook prints today's schedule in the Daily Style format, which approximates the calendar Day view.

6. On the **File** menu, point to **Page Setup**, and then click **Tri-fold Style**.

The Page Setup dialog box opens, displaying a preview of the Tri-fold print style. In the Options area, you can select the calendar elements you want to print in each of the three panes.

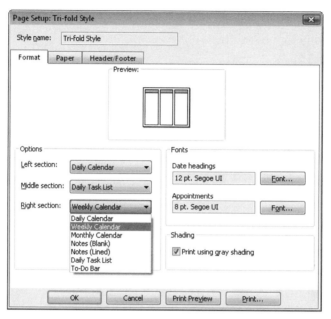

7. In the **Page Setup** dialog box, click **Print**.

Note that Outlook doesn't retain your settings from one print session to the next.

8. In the **Print range** area of the **Print** dialog box, click the **End** arrow, and then in the list, click the date two days from today. Then click **Preview**.

The Print Preview window displays the tri-fold calendar as it will appear when printed. The insertion point changes to a magnifying glass.

9. Click once near the center of the previewed page to magnify the calendar page.

In the lower-left corner of the Print Preview window, the status bar indicates that you are viewing the first of three pages, to match the date range you selected.

With the default options, each page displays the daily calendar on the left, your task list for that day in the center, and the weekly calendar on the right. You can preview the second and third pages by scrolling the document.

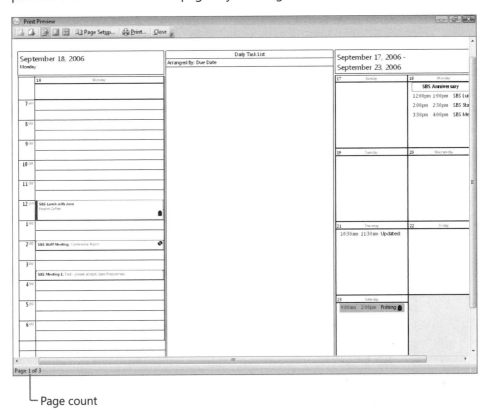

Page count

10. On the Print Preview toolbar, click **Print**, and then in the **Print** dialog box, click **OK**.

    Outlook prints three pages (one page for each day of the selected date range), and then closes the Print Preview window.

11. Experiment with different print styles and date ranges, previewing the results of each.

Saving Calendar Information as a Web Page

You can share your schedule with co-workers by publishing it as a Web page on an intranet site, or with a larger group of people by publishing it as a Web page on an Internet site. Outlook provides a simple method of saving selected calendar information as a static HTML page.

To save calendar information as a Web page:

1. Display your calendar. Then on the **File** menu, click **Save as Web Page**.

    The Save As Web Page dialog box opens.

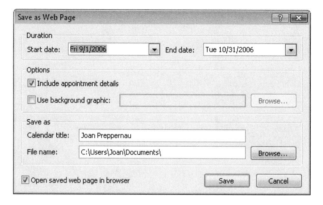

2. Enter the start and end dates for which you want to publish your calendar information.

3. In the **Options** area, select whether to include appointment details or a background graphic.

4. In the **Save as** area, append a file name (the extension is unnecessary) at the end of the path shown in the **File name** box. You can change the title that will be displayed on the Web page, and change the location where Outlook saves it.

    By default, Outlook saves calendar Web pages in your Documents folder.

5. With the **Open saved web page in browser** check box selected, click **Save**.

6. If Outlook displays a security notice asking you to confirm that you trust the link to the Web page you just created, click **Yes**.

7. If Outlook displays a message box asking you whether to open or save the Web page, click **Open**.

    The page opens in your default Web browser. (The browser loads the file from your computer, not from the Internet—you haven't yet published the schedule to the Internet.)

8. Review the calendar. If an Information Bar appears at the top of the window, click it, click **Allow Blocked Content**, and then in the **Security Warning** message box, click **Yes** to allow Windows to run an ActiveX control in order to display nicely formatted content.

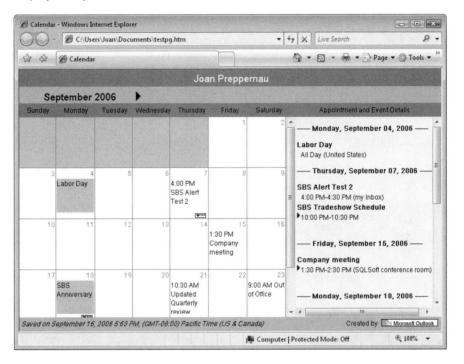

You can publish the calendar Web page to any intranet or Internet site that you have authoring permissions on.

Sending Calendar Information in an E-Mail Message

You might frequently find it necessary to share information about your schedule with colleagues, friends, or family members. With Outlook 2007, you can easily embed selected calendar information as a static image in an e-mail message that you can send to any person who uses an HTML-capable e-mail program (not only people who use Outlook).

You can choose the period of time for which you want to share information (Today, Tomorrow, Next 7 Days, Next 30 Days, or Whole Calendar, or you can specify a custom date range) and the level of detail you want to share:

- **Availability only.** Includes only your availability (Free, Busy, Tentative, or Out Of Office) during scheduled time periods.
- **Limited details.** Includes only your availability and the subjects of calendar items.
- **Full details.** Includes your availability and the full details of calendar items.

The details of calendar items marked as Private will not be shown unless you specifically choose to do so.

See Also For information about private appointments, see "Scheduling and Changing Appointments" in Chapter 6, "Managing Appointments, Events, and Meetings."

In this exercise, you will embed information about your schedule in an e-mail message. There are no practice files for this exercise.

BE SURE TO display your calendar before beginning this exercise.

1. In the **Navigation Pane**, click **Send a Calendar via E-mail**.

   Outlook opens a new message window and the Send A Calendar Via E-mail dialog box.

2. In the **Advanced** area, click **Show** to display all the options.

If you have multiple calendar folders in Outlook, you can choose which calendar you want to send information from.

3. Click the **Date Range** arrow, and then in the list, click **Next 7 days**.

4. Click the **Detail** arrow, and then in the list, click **Full details**.

You can choose whether to include private appointment details and attachments, and whether to present schedule information as a daily schedule or only a list of events.

5. With **Daily schedule** selected in the **E-mail Layout** list, click **OK**.

Outlook embeds the selected calendar information in the e-mail message window and also attaches the same information as an *.ics* file. You can send the e-mail message to any recipient. A recipient using an e-mail program that supports *.ics* files can add your calendar information to his or her calendar list.

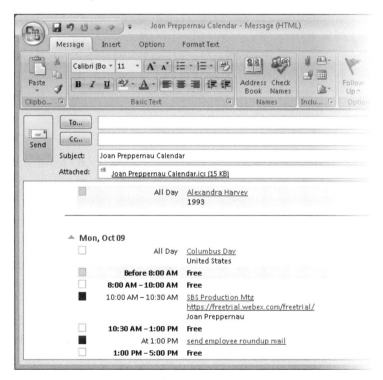

6. Scroll the e-mail to view its contents. Then experiment with other time periods, details, and layout options on your own.

 CLOSE or send the e-mail message.

> ### Creating a OneNote Page Linked to an Appointment, an Event, or a Meeting
>
> If your 2007 Office system installation includes Microsoft Office OneNote, you can link calendar entries from Outlook to your OneNote notebook.
>
> To link one or more calendar entries to OneNote:
>
> 1. Display the Calendar, and select the item (or items) you want to link.
>
> 2. On the Standard toolbar, click the **Notes About This Item** button.
>
>   OneNote starts (if it isn't already running) and, in its Unfiled Notes section, creates a page for each of the selected calendar items. Each page contains the appointment, event, or meeting information and a link that opens the original Outlook calendar item from within OneNote.
>
> You can move pages from the Unfiled Notes section to a notebook section by dragging or by right-clicking the page tab, pointing to Move Page To, and then clicking Another Section. In the Move Or Copy Pages dialog box, click the target notebook section, and then click Move.

Notes About
This Item

Linking to an Internet Calendar

A variety of specialized calendars tracking professional sports schedules, holidays, entertainment, scientific data, and so on are available from the Microsoft Office Online Web site. You can link to these Internet calendars from the Calendar module so that you have up-to-date information conveniently available, in the same place as your own scheduling information.

After you link to an Internet calendar, you can display or hide the linked calendar at any time by selecting or clearing its check box in the Other Calendars section of the All Calendar Items list. You can display Internet calendars within the Calendar module as you would any other, viewing them independently or next to another calendar, or displaying a combined view of information from multiple calendars. You can remove the linked calendar from your list of available calendars by right-clicking the calendar's tab and then clicking Delete.

In this exercise, you will link to an Internet calendar. There are no practice files for this exercise.

> **BE SURE TO** display your calendar before beginning this exercise.

1. At the bottom of the **Navigation Pane**, click **Search Calendars Online**.

   The Internet Calendars page of the Office Online Web site opens in your default Internet browser.

2. Scroll the page to display the **Subscribe to a Free Internet Calendar** section.

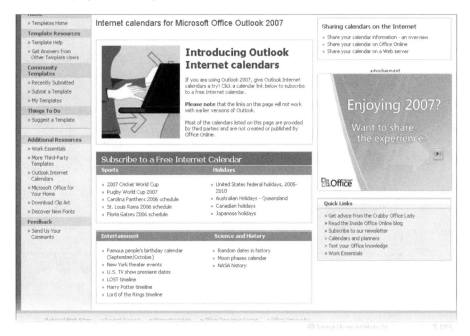

3. In the **Entertainment** list, click **New York theater events** (or click any other Internet calendar that interests you).

4. If an **Internet Explorer Security** message box appears prompting you to allow Outlook to open Web content, click the **Allow** button.

5. In the **Microsoft Office Outlook** message box asking whether you want to add the calendar to Outlook and subscribe to updates, click **Yes**.

   Outlook adds the selected Internet calendar to your Other Calendars list, and displays it in the Calendar pane, side by side with your own calendar.

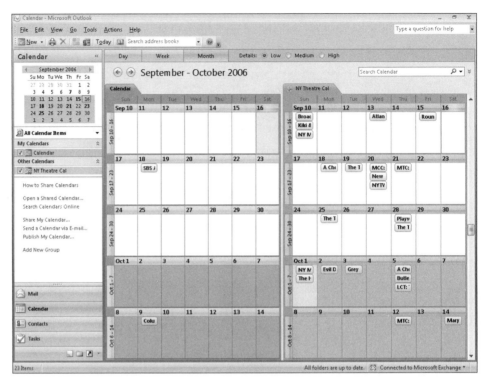

The linked calendar also appears (as *NY Theatre*) in the Other Calendars list in the Navigation Pane. Any calendars you link to that aren't your own—for example, SharePoint calendars, calendars of co-workers, and so on, appear in this list.

 BE SURE TO retain the linked Internet calendar for use in the next exercise.

Working with Multiple Calendars

It is often useful to have more than one Outlook calendar. The process of creating a secondary calendar is the same as that of creating an address book or mail folder—you simply create a folder designated to hold calendar items.

You can display calendars individually, or you can display more than one calendar at a time. For instance, you might have separate business and personal calendars and want to view them together.

You can view multiple calendars next to each other, or you can overlay them to display a composite view of the separate calendars. When you view and scroll multiple calendars, they all display the same date or time period.

You can drag items from one calendar to another, and copy items between calendars by dragging with the right mouse button and then clicking Copy on the context menu.

In this exercise, you will view multiple calendars next to each other and then as a composite. There are no practice files for this exercise.

> **BE SURE TO** display your calendar and complete the previous exercise, "Linking to an Internet Calendar," before beginning this exercise.

1. In the **Navigation Pane**, in the **My Calendars** or **Other Calendars** list, select the check box for at least one other calendar.

   > **Tip** If you just completed the previous exercise, a second calendar is already visible.

   By default, Outlook displays the calendars side by side and in different colors.

   View in Overlay Mode buttons

   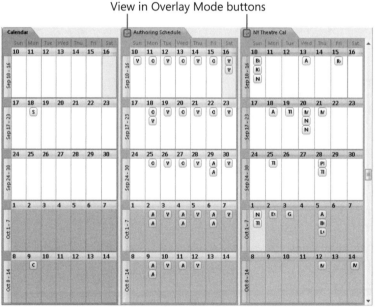

   In Side-By-Side mode, the title bar tab of each calendar other than your own displays a View In Overlay Mode button.

View in
Overlay Mode

2. On the title bar tab of the **NY Theatre** calendar (or any other secondary calendar), click the **View in Overlay Mode** button.

   The secondary calendar overlaps your own calendar (or whichever calendar is active). Appointments on the overlapped calendar appear in a muted font.

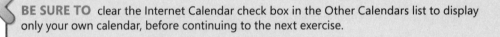

3. Click the **Calendar** tab to display your calendar on top of the Internet calendar.

View in Side-By-Side Mode

4. On either of the overlaid calendars, click the **View in Side-By-Side Mode** button to return to the standard display.

BE SURE TO clear the Internet Calendar check box in the Other Calendars list to display only your own calendar, before continuing to the next exercise.

Delegating Control of Your Calendar

You can delegate control of any Outlook module to a co-worker so that he or she can create and respond to meeting requests on your behalf. Then meeting requests sent to you are delivered to your delegate rather than to you. You receive copies of the meeting requests and copies of your delegate's responses, but you don't have to respond. Your delegate can create meeting requests on your behalf (that is, they appear to come from you)

To delegate control:

1. On the **Tools** menu, click **Options**.

2. On the **Delegates** tab of the **Options** dialog box, click **Add**.

3. In the **Add Users** dialog box, click the person you want to delegate control to, click **Add**, and then click **OK**.

4. In the **Delegate Permissions** dialog box, click the **Calendar** arrow, and then in the list, click the level of permission you want to delegate.

5. Select any other permissions you want to delegate.

6. Select the **Automatically send a message to delegate summarizing these permissions** check box, and then click **OK**.

7. In the **Options** dialog box, select whether you would like to receive copies of meeting requests and responses. Then click **OK**.

Key Points

- You can display a traditional calendar view of your schedule by the day, work week, full week, or month. You can display multiple list views of calendar items.

- You can display multiple time zones, change your calendar as you travel between time zones, and schedule appointments or meetings that start and end in different time zones.

- You can print selected schedule information in a number of different layout styles.

- You can share schedule information by sending it in an e-mail message or by publishing it to a Web site.

- You can subscribe to many types of calendars available from the Internet. Internet calendar information is automatically updated.

- You can view two or more calendars next to each other or as a composite. Outlook displays each calendar in a different color so you can easily tell them apart.

Chapter at a Glance

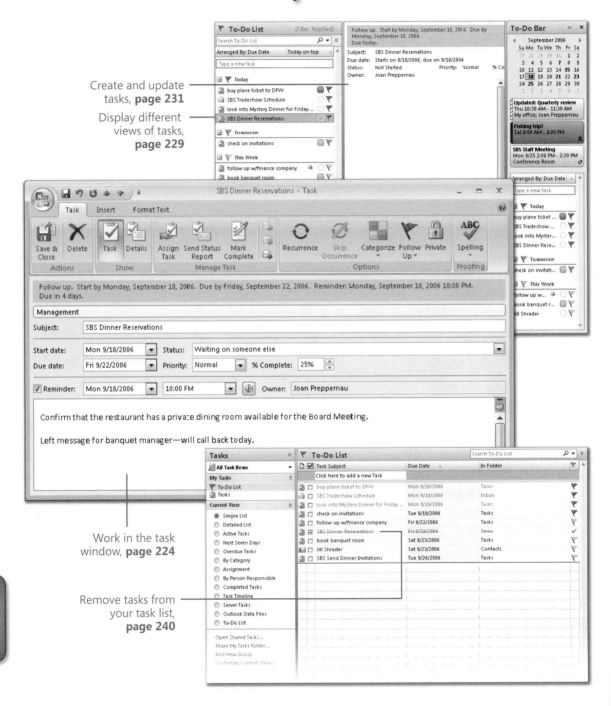

Create and update tasks, **page 231**

Display different views of tasks, **page 229**

Work in the task window, **page 224**

Remove tasks from your task list, **page 240**

8 Tracking Tasks

In this chapter, you will learn to:

✔ Work in the task window.

✔ Display different views of tasks.

✔ Create and update tasks.

✔ Manage task assignments.

✔ Remove tasks from your task list.

Many people keep one or more to-do lists going at all times, listing tasks to complete, things to buy, people to call, and so on. You might cross off tasks as you complete them, transfer unfinished tasks to other lists, create multiple lists for multiple purposes, or follow a specialized system designed by an efficiency expert. You probably write your lists on pieces of paper, even though you've undoubtedly experienced the pitfalls of that age-old system. Paper crumples, tears, and frequently ends up in the lint tray of the clothes dryer (even when you are sure you checked all the pockets before you put your pants in the laundry).

If you use Microsoft Office Outlook on a daily basis, you might find it far easier to use its built-in *task list*, called the *To-Do List*. You can add tasks, assign due dates, receive reminders, and mark tasks as complete when you finish them. You can even assign tasks to other people, and if those people use Outlook, you can view their progress on assigned tasks as they track progress milestones.

These basic functions are very useful, but Outlook 2007 has taken task management one step further, by linking the To-Do List to the Outlook Calendar. When you view your calendar in Day or Week view, tasks with assigned due dates appear on the days they are due. You can schedule a specific block of time to complete a task by dragging it to your calendar, and when you finish the task and mark it complete, Outlook removes it from your calendar. (Completed tasks are always available in your task list if you want to view them.)

But that's not all: Outlook 2007 introduces the To-Do Bar, a vertical pane on the right side of the program window, in which you can display your entire task list arranged in whatever order you want (by due date, by category, by importance, and so on) along with the Date Navigator and your upcoming appointments. You can modify the Date Navigator to display more or fewer of each of these items.

In this chapter, you will look at features of the new Office 2007 Ribbon that are unique to the task window, review different ways of arranging, organizing, and locating tasks, create tasks from scratch, and remove tasks from your list by marking them as complete or deleting them. You'll also learn how to delegate tasks and manage task assignments. If you're running Microsoft Office OneNote, you'll find information about linking tasks and notes in the sidebar "Tracking and Updating Tasks Created in OneNote" later in this chapter.

See Also Do you need only a quick refresher on the topics in this chapter? See the Quick Reference entries on pages xxxvii–lxv.

> **Important** The exercises in this chapter require only practice files created in earlier chapters; none are supplied on the book's CD. For more information about practice files, see "Using the Book's CD" on page xxv.

> **Troubleshooting** Graphics and operating system–related instructions in this book reflect the Windows Vista user interface. If your computer is running Microsoft Windows XP and you experience trouble following the instructions as written, please refer to the "Information for Readers Running Windows XP" section at the beginning of this book.

Working in the Task Window

We refer to the window in which you create or manage a task as the *task window*. Like the contact, message, and calendar item windows, the task window contains its own commands, arranged on the Ribbon instead of on menus and toolbars.

See Also For more information about the user interface for Outlook 2007 item windows, see "Working in the Contact Window" in Chapter 2, "Managing Contact Information."

In this exercise, you will take a tour of the task window elements that differ from the contact, message, and calendar item window elements discussed in earlier chapters. There are no practice files for this exercise.

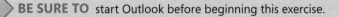

BE SURE TO start Outlook before beginning this exercise.

Tasks

1. In the **Navigation Pane**, click the **Tasks** button to display the Tasks module.

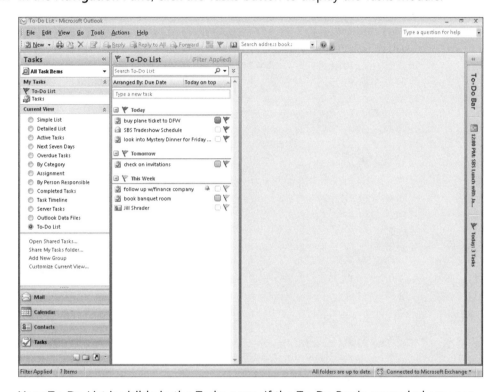

Your To-Do List is visible in the Tasks pane. If the To-Do Bar is expanded, you can see the contents of your task list in both places. If the To-Do Bar is hidden, the number of active tasks due today appears at its bottom end.

New Task

Microsoft Office
Button

2. On the Standard toolbar, click the **New Task** button.

An untitled task window opens.

3. In the upper-left corner of the appointment window, click the **Microsoft Office Button**.

Commands related to managing tasks (such as creating, saving, deleting, and printing) are available from the Office menu that appears.

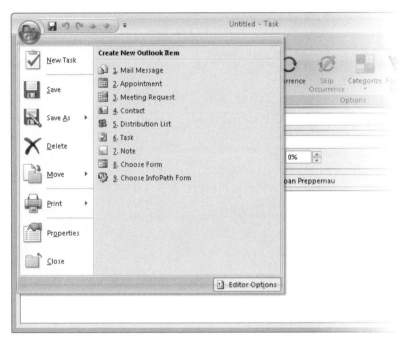

See Also For information about the Print commands, see "Printing Messages" in Chapter 4, "Handling E-Mail Messages." For information about the commands available in the Editor Options dialog box, see "Personalizing Your Office and Outlook Settings" in Chapter 12, "Customizing and Configuring Outlook."

4. Press the [Esc] key to close the Office menu without making a selection.

> **Tip** Depending on what programs you have installed on your computer, tabs and groups other than those described here might also appear on the Ribbon. For example, if Microsoft Office OneNote is installed on your computer, a OneNote group appears on the Appointment tab.

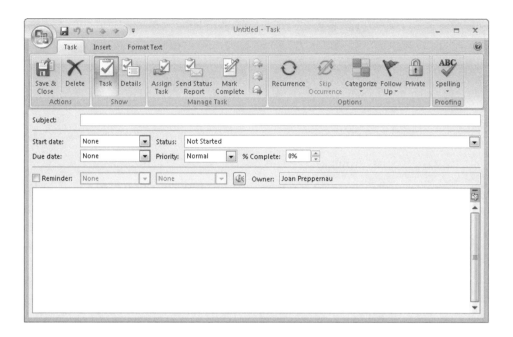

> **Important** Depending on your screen resolution and the size of the task window
> that opens, you might see more or fewer buttons in each of the groups, or the buttons
> you see might be represented by larger or smaller icons than those shown in this book.
> Experiment with the size of the task window to understand the effect on the appear-
> ance of the Ribbon.

The traditional menus and toolbars have been replaced by the following three tabs,
each of which contains groups of commands organized by purpose:

- Task
- Insert
- Format Text

See Also For more information about tabs, see "Working in the Contact Window" in
Chapter 2, "Managing Contact Information."

The Task tab is active by default. Buttons representing commands related to creating tasks are organized on this tab in five groups:

- Actions
- Show
- Manage Task
- Options
- Proofing

You can create and manage most tasks by using only the commands available on this tab.

5. Click the **Insert** tab.

Buttons representing commands related to items you can insert are organized on this tab in six groups:

- Include
- Tables
- Illustrations
- Links
- Text
- Symbols

6. Click the **Format Text** tab.

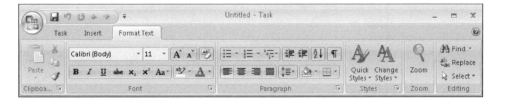

Buttons representing commands related to the appearance of the content in the large task content pane are organized on this tab in six groups:

- Clipboard
- Font
- Paragraph
- Styles
- Zoom
- Editing

 CLOSE the task window.

Displaying Different Views of Tasks

The creators of Outlook 2007 must have had a lot to do—they seem to have been somewhat obsessed with task management. You can view and manage your tasks from more places than ever before. Whereas in previous versions of Outlook, your tasks were available only from certain pages, you can now view your task list from anywhere in Outlook on the new To-Do Bar, as well as in the Tasks module, in the Calendar module, and on the Outlook Today page.

See Also For information about Outlook Today, see "Exploring the Advanced Toolbar" in Chapter 1, "Getting Started with Outlook 2007."

In the Tasks module, the available views of your task list include:

- Simple List
- Detailed List
- Active Tasks
- Next Seven Days
- Overdue Tasks
- By Category
- Assignment

- By Person Responsible
- Completed Tasks
- Task Timeline
- Server Tasks
- Outlook Data Files
- To-Do List

Other than Task Timeline, all of these views are list views. In views displaying only selected tasks, the words *(Filter Applied)* appear on the folder banner at the top of the Tasks pane. You can reorder the tasks in any list view by clicking the heading of the field you want to sort on, and you can display the Reading Pane in any view by pointing to Reading Pane on the View menu and then clicking Right or Bottom.

You can quickly switch between views by selecting the view option you want in the Current View list in the Navigation Pane or on the Advanced toolbar. The Current View list is displayed by default in the Tasks module. You can hide or display it by pointing to Navigation Pane on the View menu, and then clicking Current View Pane.

> **Tip** If you prefer, you can switch views from the Ways To Organize pane. To display this pane, click Organize on the Tools menu, and then click Using Views. This pane is a holdover from previous versions of Outlook, and its usefulness has long been outpaced by other tools.

You can keep your task list close at hand by displaying it on the To-Do Bar. The To-Do Bar Task List displays tasks grouped and sorted by due date (although you can also sort it by category, start date, folder, type, or importance, or create a custom arrangement). You can scroll the list to display all your tasks, or collapse the groups you don't want to view. To increase the space available for your task list, you can close the Date Navigator or show fewer or no appointments.

You can minimize the To-Do Bar so that it displays only your next appointment (if you choose to display appointments) and the number of open tasks due today (if you choose to display tasks). You can switch between views of the To-Do Bar by clicking the Minimize or Maximize button on its header.

See Also For information about the To-Do Bar, including changing the type and amount of content displayed, see "Personalizing Your Outlook Workspace" in Chapter 1, "Getting Started with Outlook 2007."

When you view your calendar in Day view or Week view, the Daily Task List at the bottom of the program window displays the tasks due each day, including the category and task type. In Day view, the start date, due date, and reminder time also appear. If you don't see the Daily Task List under the Calendar pane in one of these views, point to Daily Task List on the View menu, and then click Normal. Like the Navigation Pane and the To-Do Bar, you can minimize the Daily Task List so that it displays only the number of active and completed tasks and provides more space for you to work. You can switch between views of the Daily Task List by clicking the Minimize or Maximize button on its header.

Finding and Organizing Tasks

You can use the Outlook 2007 Instant Search functionality to quickly locate tasks by searching on any text in the task or in a file attached to the task. Type the word or other information you want to find in the Search box in the Tasks pane header. Outlook filters the tasks as you type, displaying only those containing the search criteria you enter, and highlighting your search criteria in the task list and in the Reading Pane (if it is open).

See Also For more information about Instant Search, see "Quickly Locating Contact Information" in Chapter 2, "Managing Contact Information" and "Quickly Locating Messages" in Chapter 5, "Managing Your Inbox."

To help you organize your tasks, you can assign them to Color Categories in the same way that you do any other Outlook item.

See Also For more information about Color Categories, see "Organizing Contacts by Using Color Categories" in Chapter 2, "Managing Contact Information," and "Organizing Messages by Using Color Categories" in Chapter 5, "Managing Your Inbox."

If your task list gets too big, or if you want to maintain separate task lists for different purposes, you can organize tasks into separate folders. To create a folder that can contain tasks:

1. On the Standard toolbar, in the **New** list, click **Folder**.
2. In the **Create New Folder** dialog box, enter the name and select the location of the folder.
3. In the **Folder contains** list, click **Task Items**, and then click **OK**.

If you try to move a task into a Mail, Calendar, Contact, or Note Items folder, a message, meeting, contact, or note window opens with the task's subject entered in the form.

Creating and Updating Tasks

If you use your task list diligently, you will frequently add tasks to it. You can create one-time or recurring tasks from scratch in different ways, or add an existing Outlook item (such as a message) to the task list by flagging it for follow-up. Regardless of how or where you create a task, all tasks are available in the Tasks module and the To-Do Bar Task List.

See Also Another way to add a task to your list is by accepting an assigned task. For more information, see "Managing Task Assignments" later in this chapter.

The only information you must include when creating a task is the subject. You can also specify the following:

- Start date
- Due date
- Status (Not Started, In Progress, Completed, Waiting On Someone, or Deferred)
- Priority (Normal, Low, or High)
- Reminder (date and time)
- Recurrence (Daily, Weekly, Monthly, Yearly, how soon the next recurrence should appear in your task list, and for how long)
- Category

You can attach files to tasks, and you can include text, tables, charts, illustrations, hyperlinks, and other content in the task window content pane by using the same commands you use in other Outlook item windows and in other 2007 Office system programs, such as Microsoft Office Word.

To quickly create a new task, you can type the task subject in the *Type A New Task* box at the top of either the To-Do Bar Task List or the To-Do List in the Tasks module, and then press Enter. Outlook adds the new task to the list of tasks due today. From any view of the task list, you can assign the task to a category, change the due date, add a reminder, mark the task as complete, or delete the task entirely. To access these commands, right-click the task name, category, or flag, and then click the option you want.

To create a task with more detail, on the Standard toolbar, click Task in the New list (or if you're in the Tasks module, click the New Task button) to open a task window. There you can specify the start date, due date, status, and priority of the task, set a reminder, add billing information, or assign the task to someone else.

Outlook doesn't automatically set a reminder for tasks as it does for calendar items. To automatically set reminders for time-limited tasks, click Options on the Tools menu, click Task Options, select the Set Reminders On Tasks With Due Dates check box, and click OK. Set the default reminder time in the Tasks area of the Options dialog box, and then click OK.

In the Task Options dialog box, you can also change the color in which Outlook displays overdue and completed tasks.

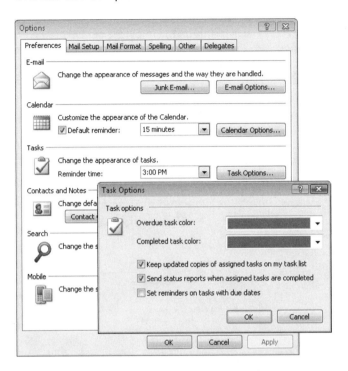

When the reminder date and time arrive, a reminder window opens on your screen. If you have completed the task, click Dismiss to reset the reminder to None. If you haven't yet completed the task and would like to be reminded again at a later time, click the reminder time you want in the Snooze list, and then click Snooze . You can also open the task window directly from the reminder window by clicking Open Item. You can make changes of any type as though you had opened the task from the Tasks pane, and then close the task window to effect those changes.

Sometimes you might want to include information from an e-mail message, appointment, or other item on your task list, to ensure that you complete any necessary follow-up work by a certain date. In Outlook 2007, you can create a task from almost any item by dragging it to the Tasks button in the Navigation Pane.

See Also For more information about creating tasks from e-mail messages, see "Creating a Task or an Appointment from a Message" in Chapter 4, "Handling E-Mail Messages."

In this exercise, you will create and update tasks from the To-Do Bar Task List and from the Tasks pane. There are no practice files for this exercise.

> **BE SURE TO** display the Tasks pane and the To-Do Bar before beginning this exercise.

1. On the **To-Do Bar**, click the **Type a new task** box, type SBS Dinner Reservations, and then press Enter.

Outlook adds the task to your task list, and it appears as a task due today in both the To-Do Bar Task List and the To-Do List.

2. In the **To-Do List**, click the new task.

The task details appear in the Reading Pane. The information available for a task varies depending on the type of task (created from scratch or converted from another Outlook item) and the detail entered in the task window.

Task list   To-Do Bar Task List

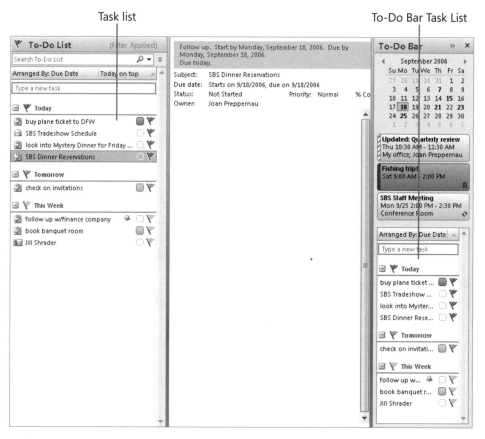

3. In the **To-Do Bar Task List**, right-click the flag following the **SBS Dinner Reservations** task, and then click **This Week**.

In both task lists, the task moves to the This Week group. In the Reading Pane, the due date changes to Friday of the current week.

> **Troubleshooting** Flagging a task for completion This Week sets the start date to the first working day of the week and the due date to the last working day of the week. If your work week is set to something other than Monday through Friday, the start and due dates will reflect that.

4. Right-click the **Category** bar following the **SBS Dinner Reservations** task, and then in the list, click **Management**.

The Category bar in both task lists, changes to yellow to indicate that the task is business management-related, and the yellow Management color category bar appears at the top of the task in the Reading Pane.

> **Troubleshooting** If you did not create the Management category in an earlier exercise, click any color category.

5. Double-click the **SBS Dinner Reservations** task to open it in a task window.

6. In the task content pane, type Confirm that the restaurant has a private dining room available for the Board Meeting.

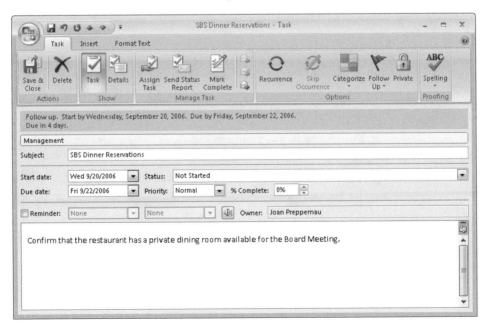

Details

7. On the **Task** tab, in the **Show** group, click the **Details** button.

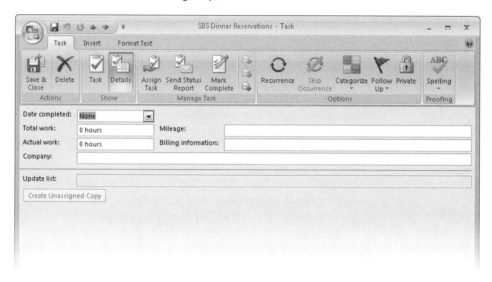

Notice the type of information you can track on the Details page. This could be useful when tracking billable tasks for clients.

8. In the **Actions** group, click the **Save & Close** button.

Save & Close

The task window closes.

9. On the Standard toolbar, click the **New Task** button.

New Task

An untitled task window opens.

10. In the **Subject** box, type SBS Send Dinner Invitations.

11. Click the **Due date** arrow, and then on the calendar, click the **Tuesday** of the next week (not of the current week).

On the calendar, a red outline indicates the current date, and a yellow square indicates the current due date.

> **Tip** You can't assign a task a due date that has already passed.

12. Select the **Reminder** check box.

13. In the content pane, type Invite all Board members, including spouses. Then in the **Actions** group, click the **Save & Close** button.

Outlook adds the task to your task list, and it appears in the Next Week group in both the To-Do Bar Task List and the To-Do List. The bell in the task header indicates that a reminder is set for the task.

14. In the **Tasks** pane, double-click the **SBS Dinner Reservations** task.

For the purposes of this exercise, assume that you are waiting for the banquet manager to confirm whether a private dining room is available. You want to update the task to reflect your progress, and also remind yourself to call again if you don't hear from her by the end of the day.

15. Click the **Status** arrow, and then in the list, click **Waiting on someone else**.

16. In the **% Complete** box, type or select (by clicking the arrows) 25%.

17. In the task content pane, on a new line, type

Left message for banquet manager—will call back today.

18. Select the **Reminder** check box. Click the first **Reminder** arrow, and then on the calendar, click **Today**.

19. Click the second **Reminder** arrow, and then in the list, click **5:00 PM** (or if it's already after 5:00 P.M., click a later time).

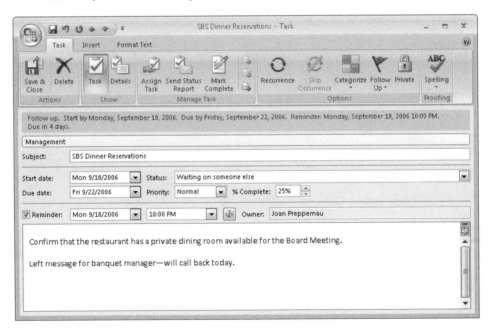

CLOSE the task, saving your work for use in a later exercise.

Managing Task Assignments

You can assign tasks from your Outlook task list to other people within your organization (and other people can assign tasks to you). When you assign a task, Outlook sends a task request, similar to a meeting request, to the person you designated. He or she can accept or decline the task assignment by clicking the corresponding button in the Reading Pane or in the task window header. You can't assign tasks you have created from other Outlook items; you can assign only those you create as tasks.

> **Tip** You can assign a task to a person using Outlook on a Microsoft Exchange Server domain other than yours or using other e-mail programs. When you assign the task, the designated person receives a message that they can respond to manually. Until you change the task status, it is Waiting For Response From Recipient, rather than Assigned.

When you assign a task, you can choose whether to keep a copy of the task on your own task list or transfer it entirely to the assignee's task list. Either way, the task remains on your own task list until accepted, so you won't lose track of it. (If the recipient declines the task, you can return it to your task list or reassign it.)

Assigned Task

Outlook indicates assigned tasks in your task list by an outstretched hand on the task icon, similar to that of a shared folder in Windows Explorer.

After you assign a task to someone else, ownership of the task transfers to that person, and you can no longer update the information in the task window. (The assignee becomes the *task owner* and you become the *task originator*.) If you keep a copy of the task on your task list, you can follow the progress as the assignee updates the task status and details, and you can communicate information about the task to the owner by sending status reports. Unless you choose otherwise, Outlook automatically sends you a status report on an assigned task when the assignee marks the task as complete.

To delegate a task to another Outlook user:

1. Create the task you want to delegate.

Assign
Task

2. In the task window, on the **Task** tab, in the **Manage Task** group, click the **Assign Task** button.

3. In the **To** box that appears, type the e-mail address of the person you want to assign the task to.

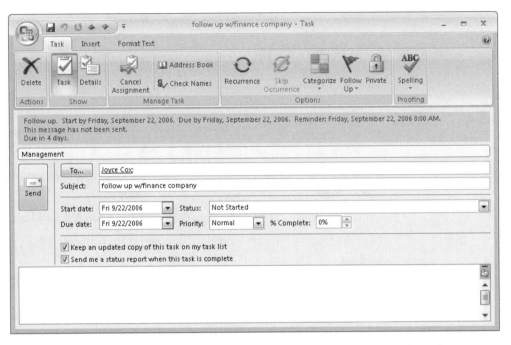

Note that the Keep An Updated Copy Of This Task On My Task List and Send Me A Status Report When This Task Is Complete check boxes are selected by default.

Follow Up ▼

4. If you want Outlook to display a reminder for the task, in the **Options** group, click the **Follow Up** button.

   You can designate when you want to be reminded by clicking an option in the list that appears.

Send

5. In the task header, click the **Send** button. If a message box notifies you that the task reminder has been turned off, click **OK**.

   Outlook sends the task request, and notifies you when the assignee accepts or declines the task.

To reclaim a declined task:

1. Open the *Task Declined* message.

Return to Task List

2. In the message window, in the **Manage Task** group, click the **Return to Task List** button.

You can view the status of tasks you have assigned to other people by displaying your task list in Assignment view.

To update the status of tasks assigned to you by other people:

1. Open the task window.

2. In the **% Complete** list, type or select (by clicking the arrows) the percentage of the project you estimate as complete.

   Outlook changes the Status to reflect your selection. Tasks that are 0% complete are Not Started, tasks that are 1% to 99% complete are In Progress, and tasks that are 100% complete are Completed.

3. If you want to manually change the task status, for example to **Waiting on someone else** or **Deferred**, click that option in the **Status** list.

4. On the **Task** tab, in the **Actions** group, click the **Save & Close** button.

   Outlook updates the task both in your own task list and in the task originator's task list.

To send a status report about a task:

1. Open the task window.

2. On the **Task** tab, in the **Manage Task** group, click the **Send Status Report** button.

   Outlook generates an e-mail message with the task information in the Subject field and message body.

3. Address the message to the people you want to send the report to, and then send the message.

Removing Tasks from Your Task List

When you complete a task, you can remove it from your task list by deleting it or by marking it as complete. When you delete a task, it moves first to the Deleted Items folder, and is permanently deleted when you empty that folder. No record of it remains on your task list. If you want to retain a record of your completed tasks, mark the task as complete by clicking the flag in the To-Do Bar Task List, clicking the flag column so that a selected check box appears in the Tasks pane, or changing the % Complete setting to 100%.

After you mark an instance of a recurring task as complete, Outlook generates a new instance of the task at whatever interval you specified when creating the task.

If a task has a reminder and you'd like to keep the task on your task list but stop the reminder from appearing, you can change or remove the reminder by right-clicking the task, clicking Add Reminder, and then selecting the reminder options you want.

In this exercise, you will mark a task as complete, stop a reminder from appearing, and then delete a task.

USE the *SBS Dinner Reservations* and *SBS Send Dinner Invitations* tasks you created in "Creating and Updating Tasks" earlier in this chapter. If you did not complete that exercise you can do so at this time or use any tasks in your task list.

BE SURE TO display the Tasks pane and the To-Do Bar before beginning this exercise.

1. In the **Navigation Pane**, in the **Current View** list, select the **Active Tasks** option.

   Outlook displays only the tasks that you haven't yet marked as complete.

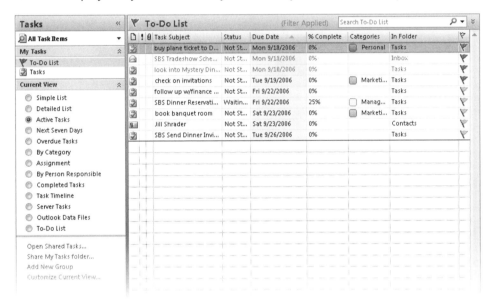

Mark
Complete

2. In the **Tasks** pane, double-click the **SBS Dinner Reservations** task.

3. On the **Task** tab, in the **Manage Task** group, click the **Mark Complete** button.

   Outlook marks the task as complete and closes the task window. Because your task list is displaying only active (incomplete) tasks, the completed task no longer appears in the list.

4. In the **Current View** list, select the **Completed Tasks** option.

   The SBS Dinner Reservations task appears in the list of completed tasks.

5. In the **Current View** list, select the **Simple List** option.

The Simple List view displays all your tasks. Completed tasks are crossed out.

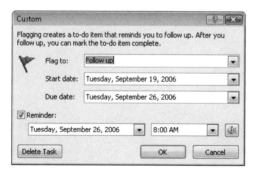

6. In the **To-Do Bar Task List**, right-click the **SBS Send Dinner Invitations** task, point to **Follow Up**, and then click **Add Reminder**.

   The Custom dialog box opens.

7. Click the **Flag to** arrow, and in the list, notice the types of follow-up you can set reminders for. Then click away from the list to close it.

8. Clear the **Reminder** check box, and then click **OK**.

   The bell icon no longer appears next to the task name, indicating that no reminder is set for this task.

9. In the **To-Do Bar Task List**, click the **SBS Send Dinner Invitations** task, and then press the ⌈Del⌋ key.

   Outlook removes the task from your task list.

> **Tracking and Updating Tasks Created in OneNote**
>
> If you use OneNote 2007 to keep track of information, you can convert notes recorded in your OneNote notebook into Outlook tasks.
>
> To link a note to a task, select the note in OneNote, and then on the Insert menu, point to Outlook Task, and click Today. A Task flag appears next to the note, and the task appears on your Outlook task list.
>
> The Outlook task maintains a link to the OneNote note, so marking the task as complete in either program updates both versions of the task.

Key Points

- You can create tasks for yourself and assign tasks to other people.
- Outlook displays tasks in the Tasks pane, in the Daily Task List in the Calendar pane, and on the To-Do Bar, which is available from any Outlook pane.
- You can organize tasks by grouping them in additional task folders or by assigning tasks to categories.
- When you assign tasks, Outlook sends a task request to the designated person, who can accept or decline the task. If you keep a copy of the assigned task, it is automatically updated when the person you assigned the task to updates the original.
- You can update tasks assigned to you and send status reports to the person who assigned the task. A task can have a status of Not Started, Deferred, Waiting, Complete, or the percentage completed.
- You can create one-time or recurring tasks. Outlook creates a new occurrence of a recurring task every time you complete the current occurrence.
- You can set a reminder to display a message at a designated time before a task is due.

Chapter at a Glance

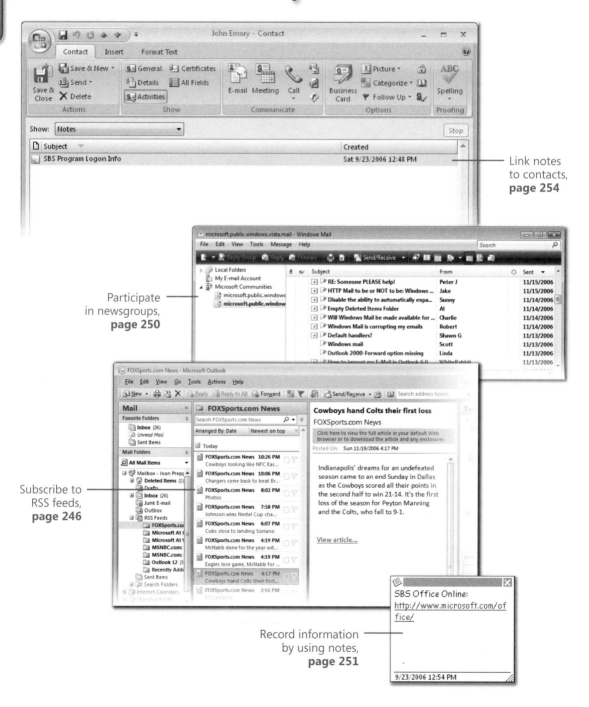

Link notes to contacts, **page 254**

Participate in newsgroups, **page 250**

Subscribe to RSS feeds, **page 246**

Record information by using notes, **page 251**

9 Gathering Information

In this chapter, you will learn to:
- ✔ Subscribe to RSS feeds.
- ✔ Participate in newsgroups.
- ✔ Record information by using notes.
- ✔ Link notes to contacts.
- ✔ Share notes.

In addition to the information you collect and store in Microsoft Office Outlook 2007 as e-mail messages, contact records, task lists, and calendar items, you can collect news and articles from Web sites that interest you and record general notes, so that all the information you need is in one place. You can also share information with other people about a particular topic by participating in newsgroup discussions.

In this chapter, you will subscribe to a news feed and learn how to participate in a newsgroup from Outlook. Then you will create, update, organize, and share electronic notes by using the Outlook Notes component.

See Also Do you need only a quick refresher on the topics in this chapter? See the Quick Reference entries on pages xxxvii–lxv.

> **Important** The exercises in this chapter require only practice files created in earlier chapters; none are supplied on the book's CD. For more information about practice files, see "Using the Book's CD" on page xxv.

> **Troubleshooting** Graphics and operating system–related instructions in this book reflect the Windows Vista user interface. If your computer is running Microsoft Windows XP and you experience trouble following the instructions as written, please refer to the "Information for Readers Running Windows XP" section at the beginning of this book.

Subscribing to RSS Feeds

Many commercial Web sites offer the option of subscribing to a news feed so that you can receive information from the site without actually visiting it. This option is also increasingly offered by personal Web logs. (Commonly referred to as *blogs*, these are personal online journals through which people share information, thoughts, and opinions with the general public.) The technology behind the news feeds is called *Really Simple Syndication (RSS)*.

To receive RSS feeds, you need an RSS reader (a program that receives and processes the information), and until now, that meant that you needed to install one of the many standalone RSS readers that are available. However, you can now use a convenient RSS reader that is included in Outlook 2007.

You can subscribe to a site's RSS feeds from within Outlook or from the site itself. You don't need to provide any personal information when you subscribe to an RSS feed; all you are doing is creating a connection between Outlook and the news server.

Outlook creates a folder for each RSS feed you subscribe to. The folder displays an article item (similar to a message) containing the headline and some text from each article the site feeds to you. You can:

- Display the article on the originating Web site by clicking a link in the article window.
- Download the entire article to Outlook by right-clicking the article item and then clicking Download.
- Use the Instant Search feature to locate relevant content within a feed.
- Add articles to your task list.
- Forward articles to other people.

> **Tip** You can't respond to blog discussions from within your Outlook RSS Subscriptions folder.

Outlook includes RSS subscriptions in your Send/Receive group and updates them with your e-mail accounts, within the limits set by the content provider. If you prefer to update RSS feeds less frequently than the default—for example, if you subscribe to a large number of RSS feeds and are concerned that the download time will interfere with other Outlook activities—you can create a separate Send/Receive group for your RSS feeds.

In this exercise, you will subscribe to an RSS feed from within Outlook and then cancel the subscription. There are no practice files for this exercise.

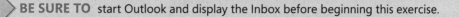

BE SURE TO start Outlook and display the Inbox before beginning this exercise.

1. In the **Navigation Pane**, under your primary mailbox, click the **RSS Subscriptions** folder or **RSS Feeds** folder.

> **Troubleshooting** Depending on the operating system running on your mail server, the folder name might be *RSS Feeds* rather than *RSS Subscriptions*.

The RSS Subscriptions folder is at the same hierarchical level within your mailbox as your Inbox.

2. Scroll the **Outlook Syndicated Content (RSS) Directory** page to the **Partner Feeds** section.

Notice the many types of RSS feeds available from this central location.

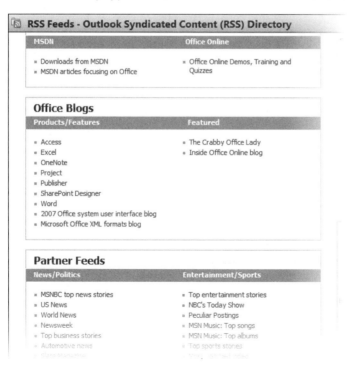

3. In the **Entertainment/Sports** list under **Partner Feeds**, click **Top sports stories**.

   Outlook asks for confirmation that you want to configure the selected RSS feed.

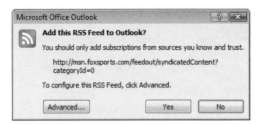

4. In the **Microsoft Office Outlook** message box, click **Yes**.

   A *FOXSports.com News* subfolder containing recent news feeds appears within the RSS Subscriptions folder.

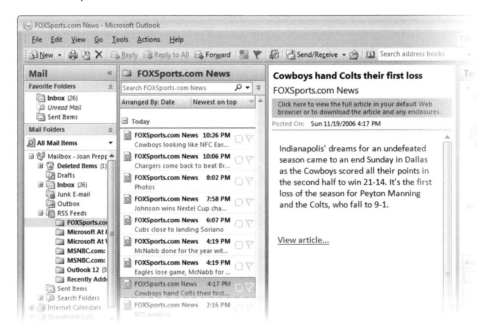

5. On the **Tools** menu, click **Account Settings**.
6. In the **Account Settings** dialog box, click the **RSS Feeds** tab.

On this tab, you can select a feed in the Feed Name list and then click Change to make changes to the display name, delivery folder, download settings, and update limit.

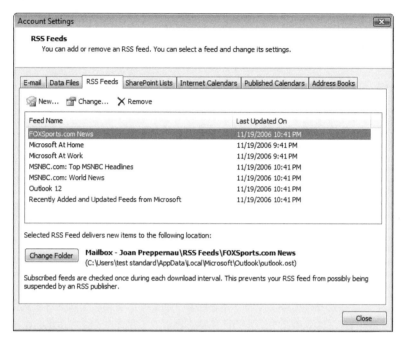

7. In the **Feed Name** list, click **FOXSports.com News**, and then click **Remove**.

8. In the **Microsoft Office Outlook** message box that asks whether to remove the RSS feed from Outlook, click **Yes**.

   Outlook removes the selected feed from the Feed Name list, but leaves the corresponding folder in the RSS Subscriptions folder in case you want to retain the news items it currently contains.

CLOSE the Account Settings dialog box.

BE SURE TO delete the FOXSports.com News folder if you don't want to keep it.

Participating in Newsgroups

A *newsgroup* (also known as a *forum*) is an online discussion group focused on a specific topic. Thousands of newsgroups exist, covering such diverse topics as software programs, technologies, medical conditions, parenting, dieting, and personal service referrals. Some newsgroups are publicly available to anyone wanting to participate, and others are private. Most are moderated on some level to ensure that people don't post inappropriate content, or if they do, that it doesn't remain available for long.

To participate in a newsgroup, you need a *newsreader*, a program that interfaces with the news server hosting the newsgroup. Outlook doesn't provide its own newsreader technology. Instead, it uses the newsreader built into Windows Mail (or if your computer is running Windows XP, Outlook Express). You can subscribe to a newsgroup directly from Windows Mail, or if you prefer, you can connect to the newsreader from within Outlook. To do so, you need to add the News command to the Go menu.

To add the News command to the Go menu:

Toolbar Options

1. On the Standard toolbar, click the **Toolbar Options** button, point to **Add or Remove Buttons**, and then click **Customize**.

2. On the **Commands** tab of the **Customize** dialog box, in the **Categories** list, click **Go**.

3. Drag the **News** command from the **Commands** list to the **Go** menu.

4. Close the **Customize** dialog box.

To start the newsreader, click News on the Go menu. The first time you start the newsreader, Windows Mail leads you through the process of subscribing to a newsgroup.

See Also For more information about Windows Mail, refer to *Windows Vista Step by Step* (ISBN 0-7356-2269-8) by Joan Preppernau and Joyce Cox (Microsoft Press, 2007). For information about Outlook Express, refer to *Microsoft Windows XP Step by Step*, 2nd ed. (ISBN 0-7356-2114-1) by Online Training Solutions, Inc. (Microsoft Press, 2004).

After you subscribe to a newsgroup, you can read messages posted to the newsgroup, respond to existing messages either through the newsgroup or directly to the person who posted the message, and post new messages, by clicking the buttons at the top of the newsgroup window.

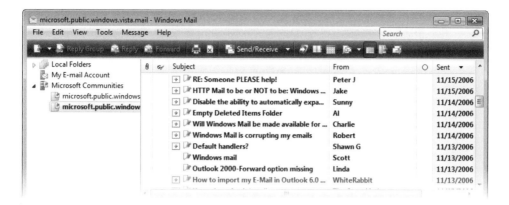

To connect to additional newsgroups, click Accounts on the Tools menu, and in the Internet Accounts dialog box, click the News heading. Click the Add button, click News, and then complete the steps in the wizard to set up a new Newsgroup Account.

Recording Information by Using Notes

You can store miscellaneous information such as reminders, passwords, account numbers, and processes by recording them as electronic *notes*. Because your notes are available to you from wherever you access Outlook, this can be a very convenient way of retaining information you might need later. And because you're less likely to accidentally delete a note than a message, it is safer than sending information to yourself in an e-mail message.

Although notes are a type of Outlook item, they don't appear in the same type of windows as messages, appointments, contact records, and tasks. Instead, they appear in the form of "sticky notes" resembling the popular 3M-brand Post-It notes. You can view, sort, and organize notes in the same way you do other Outlook items. The standard views include:

- Icons
- Notes List
- Last Seven Days
- By Category
- Outlook Data Files
- By Color

You switch the view by selecting the option you want in the Current View list in the Navigation Pane, or by pointing to Current View on the View menu and then clicking the View you want. If you're looking for a specific piece of information in a note, you can quickly locate it by typing a search word or phrase in the Search Notes box above the content pane.

By default, the Reading Pane is hidden in the Notes pane, but if you prefer, you can display the Reading Pane and view the content of notes without opening them. To do so, point to Reading Pane on the View menu, and then click Right or Bottom to display the Reading Pane in that location.

To help you organize your notes, previous versions of Outlook supported five note colors, as well as named categories. The Color Category function in Outlook 2007 serves a similar purpose. You can still create notes in five different colors (blue, green, pink, yellow, and white) but only by changing the default note color.

You can change the default note color, size, or font by clicking Options on the Tools menu, and then clicking Note Options. You can then adjust the settings and click OK to close the open dialog boxes.

In this exercise, you will create two notes. There are no practice files for this exercise.

BE SURE TO start Outlook before beginning this exercise.

Notes

1. In the **Navigation Pane**, click the **Notes** button.

   Outlook displays the Notes pane.

New Note

2. On the Standard toolbar, click the **New Note** button.

Outlook displays a new note. The current date and time appear at the bottom.

3. Type SBS Program Logon Info, and then press the Enter key twice.

The first line of the note appears as its subject or title.

4. Type User name: Administrator, press Enter, and then type Password: Tru$tNo1.

Close

5. To save and close the note, click the **Close** button in the upper-right corner.

The note appears in the Notes pane. Notice that only the subject is visible. You can access the note's information by opening the note (or by displaying the Reading Pane).

6. On the Standard toolbar, click the **New Note** button.

7. Type SBS Office Online: http://www.microsoft.com/office/, and then press Enter.

Outlook formats the URL as a hyperlink. You can click a hyperlink in a note to open the specified site in your default Internet browser.

8. Close the note.

The note appears in the Notes pane. Because the URL is part of the first line of the note, it appears as part of the subject. After you close the note, the hyperlink is available directly from the Notes pane.

BE SURE TO retain the notes for use in other exercises later in this chapter.

Linking Notes to Contacts

If you save information that pertains to a person in your contact list in an electronic note, you can link the note to the contact record so that you can easily retrieve the information later. Linked notes appear on the Activities page of a contact record.

In this exercise, you will link a note to a contact and then access the note from the contact record.

> **USE** the *SBS Program Logon Info* note you created in "Recording Information by Using Notes" earlier in this chapter, and the *John Emory* contact record you created in "Saving and Updating Contact Information" in Chapter 2, "Managing Contact Information." If you didn't complete those exercises, you can do so now, or you can substitute any other note and contact record.
>
> **BE SURE TO** display the Notes pane before beginning this exercise.
>
> **OPEN** the *SBS Program Logon Info* note.

1. In the upper-left corner of the note, click the **Note** icon, and then click **Contacts**.

2. In the **Contacts for Note** dialog box, click **Contacts**.

   The Select Contacts dialog box opens.

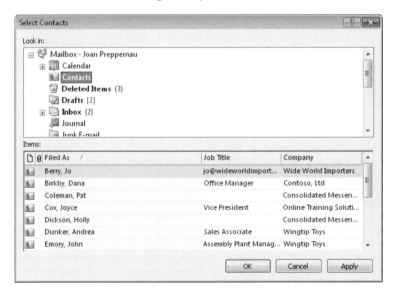

3. With **Contacts** selected in the **Look in** list, click **Emory, John** in the **Items** list. Then click **OK**.

4. Close the **Contacts for Note** dialog box and the note.

5. In the **Navigation Pane**, click the **Contacts** button.

Contacts

Outlook displays the Contacts pane.

6. Locate and open the contact record for **John Emory**.

7. On the **Contact** tab, in the **Show** group, click the **Activities** button.

Outlook generates a list of items linked to the selected contact. While Outlook searches for items, an animated icon of a magnifying glass moving around a piece of paper appears above the list.

8. On the **Activities** page of the contact record, click the **Show** arrow, and then in the list, click **Notes**.

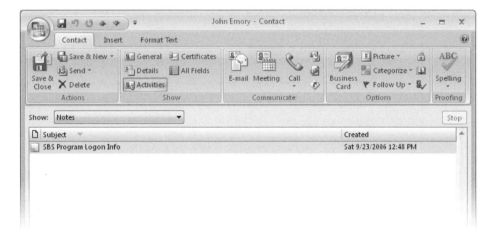

The Activities page displays the *SBS Program Logon Info* note.

CLOSE the John Emory contact record.

Recording Information in the Journal

Outlook can automatically record the details of selected types of activities (including messages, meetings, and tasks) related to specific contacts by using the *Journal* feature. You can view transactions related to a contact on the Activities page of a contact record. Outlook can also record the time you spend working with files created in other Office system programs, including Microsoft Office Access, Microsoft Office Excel, Microsoft Office PowerPoint, Microsoft Office Project, Microsoft Office Visio, and Microsoft Office Word. You can view these records in a timeline or list in the Journal. You can use this feature to help you track the time you spend working on a specific task during the day, or to locate a file you worked on in the past.

To display the Journal, click Journal on the Go menu. If you prefer, you can add the Journal button to the Navigation Pane. To do so, in the lower-right corner of the Navigation Pane, click the Configure Buttons button, point to Add Or Remove Buttons, and then click Journal.

To record activities automatically:

1. On the **Tools** menu, click **Options**.

2. On the **Preferences** tab of the **Options** dialog box, click **Journal Options**.
    The Journal Options dialog box opens.

3. In the **Automatically record these items** box, select the check boxes for the types of activities you want to record.

4. In the **For these contacts** box, select the check boxes for the contacts whose items you want to record.

5. In the **Also record files from** box, select the check boxes for the programs whose files you want to record.

6. Click **OK** in the open dialog boxes.

Saving a Note as a File

If you ever need to work in another program with the information stored in a note, you can save the note as a rich text format (RTF) or plain text file. To save a note as a file:

1. In the open note, click the **Note** icon, and then click **Save As**.

   The Save As dialog box opens.

2. Browse to the folder where you want to save the file.

3. In the **Save as type** list, click the file type you want to create.

4. In the **File name** box, change the file name if you want it to be something other than the current note title.

5. Click **Save**.

Sharing Notes

When you want to send information that is recorded in an electronic note to someone in an e-mail message, you can forward the note instead of retyping or copying the information into the message.

In this exercise, you will forward a note, open the received note, and save a copy with another name.

USE the *SBS Office Online* note you created in "Recording Information by Using Notes" earlier in this chapter. If you did not complete that exercise, you may do so now, or you can use any notes of your own.

BE SURE TO display the Notes pane before beginning this exercise.

1. Right-click the *SBS Office Online* note, and then click **Forward**.

   Outlook opens a message window with the note title as the message subject and the note itself as an attachment. The URL in the Subject box appears as a hyperlink.

2. In the **To** box, type your own e-mail address.

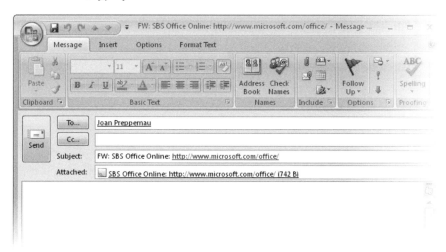

3. In the message header, click the **Send** button.

Outlook sends the message.

4. Display your **Inbox**, and click the URL in the *SBS Office Online* message header.

The Microsoft Office Online Web site opens in your default Internet browser.

5. Return to your Outlook Inbox. In the **Reading Pane**, right-click the attached note, and then click **Open**.

The *SBS Office Online* note opens.

6. Select **Office Online**, type Web Link, and then close the note.

7. In your Inbox, click another message, and then click this one again to see the change.

8. Drag the *SBS Web Link* note from the Reading Pane to the Notes button at the bottom of the Navigation Pane. Then display the **Notes** pane.

The *SBS Office Online* and *SBS Web Link* notes both appear in the notes list.

CLOSE the Internet browser window.

Key Points

- You can receive information from Web sites and blogs that offer RSS feeds by sub-scribing to them. Whether you subscribe to a feed from within Outlook or from the originating site, you can read the content in your Outlook RSS Subscriptions folder.

- Outlook doesn't have a built-in newsreader, but you can access the Windows Mail (or Outlook Express) newsreader from within Outlook.

- You can record miscellaneous information in electronic notes. You can categorize, search, display, and sort notes, and send notes to other people.

Chapter at a Glance

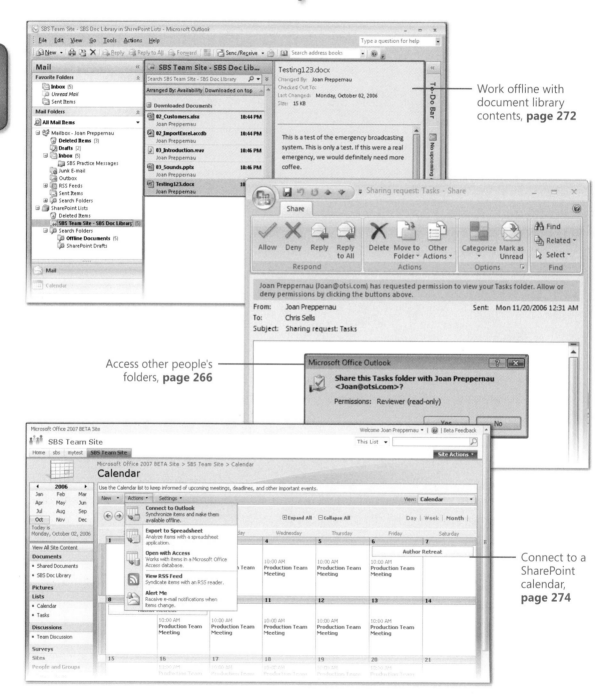

Work offline with document library contents, **page 272**

Access other people's folders, **page 266**

Connect to a SharePoint calendar, **page 274**

10 Collaborating with Other People

In this chapter, you will learn to:

✔ Share your folders with other people.

✔ Access other people's folders.

✔ Create a document workspace from Outlook.

✔ Work offline with document library contents.

✔ Connect to a SharePoint calendar.

Although Microsoft Office Outlook is primarily a personal information management program, it also provides means by which you can share information with other people, whether they are within your organization or external to it. In previous chapters, you learned ways to send finite pieces of information (such as messages, contact cards, and notes) to other people, and ways of incorporating information you receive from other people into your own system. In this chapter, we discuss ways of creating and maintaining real-time connections either to information that is stored in Outlook or to information that is stored on a collaboration site built with Microsoft SharePoint products and technologies.

SharePoint products such as Microsoft Office SharePoint Server 2007, Microsoft Office SharePoint Portal Server, and Microsoft Windows SharePoint Services, provide a simple and effective way for team members to share information and collaborate on projects. It is becoming increasingly common for people in disparate locations to work together, with a collaboration site providing a central location to store and distribute information and to manage team processes.

In this chapter, you will first learn how to share an Outlook folder containing calendar, e-mail, or other items with another person. You will learn how to create a document workspace to share a document with other team members, how to work offline with files that are stored in a document library, and how to view and update a calendar created as part of a collaboration site, all from within Outlook.

See Also Do you need only a quick refresher on the topics in this chapter? See the Quick Reference entries on pages xxxvii–lxv.

> **Important** The exercises in this chapter require only practice files created in earlier chapters; none are supplied on the book's companion CD. For information about practice files, see "Using the Book's CD" on page xxv.

> **Troubleshooting** Graphics and operating system–related instructions in this book reflect the Windows Vista user interface. If your computer is running Microsoft Windows XP and you experience trouble following the instructions as written, please refer to the "Information for Readers Running Windows XP" section at the beginning of this book.

Sharing Your Folders with Other People

Outlook stores your messages, contacts, appointments, and other items in folders. By default, the standard Outlook folders (Calendar, Contacts, Deleted Items, Drafts, Inbox, Journal, Junk E-mail, Notes, Outbox, RSS Feeds, Sent Items, Tasks, and Search Folders) and any folders you create are private, meaning that only you can access them. However, if you are working on a Microsoft Exchange Server network, you can give permission to other people on your network to create and modify items within a folder.

Suppose you have a collection of messages you want to share with a co-worker. You can store those messages in a folder and then give your co-worker permission to access that folder. You can select from eight permission levels controlling whether someone can view, create, edit, and delete items, and whether he or she can share the folder with other people.

For example, you might grant Author permissions to your assistant who will help you manage incoming e-mail. As an Author, your assistant can read items, create items, and edit and delete items that he or she creates on your behalf, but can't edit or delete items other people create, and can't create subfolders. You can define varying levels of permission to each person you share a folder with, and you can grant the same person different permission levels on different folders.

You can share any type of Outlook folder, not only those containing e-mail messages. For example, you can share any of your address books, your calendar or a secondary calendar you create, or even a folder of notes.

You can hand over complete control of one or more of your primary folders (Calendar, Tasks, Inbox, Contacts, Notes, and Journal) to another person on your Exchange Server network by making him or her a *delegate* with permission to control specific items, such as the following:

● An Editor can read, create, and modify items in the folder and send items on your behalf, such as messages, meeting requests, and task assignments.

● An Author can read and create items in the folder, as well as send items on your behalf.

● A Reviewer can read items in the folder.

A delegate can be an Editor in one folder and a Reviewer in another. Recipients of messages sent by a delegate see both your name and the delegate's name in the message header.

> **Tip** Regardless of access level, a delegate cannot create subfolders. To allow someone to create subfolders, you must give him or her permission to share the folder and specifically grant permission to create subfolders.

See Also For more information about delegating control of a folder, see the sidebar "Delegating Control of Your Calendar" in Chapter 7, "Managing Your Calendar."

In this exercise, you will grant a standard level of permission to a folder to another person on your Exchange Server network. You will then modify the level of access granted to that person.

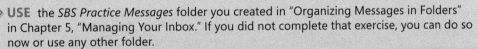

USE the *SBS Practice Messages* folder you created in "Organizing Messages in Folders" in Chapter 5, "Managing Your Inbox." If you did not complete that exercise, you can do so now or use any other folder.

BE SURE TO inform your co-worker that you will be sharing a folder with him or her before beginning this exercise.

1. In the **Navigation Pane**, display the *SBS Practice Messages* folder.

2. Right-click the **SBS Practice Messages** folder, and then click **Change Sharing Permissions**.

The SBS Practice Messages Properties dialog box opens, displaying the Permissions tab.

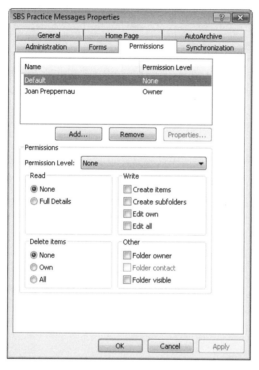

3. In the dialog box, click **Add**.

4. In the **Add Users** dialog box, double-click the name of a co-worker with whom you want to share this folder, and then click **OK**.

5. With your co-worker's name selected on the **Permissions** tab, click the **Permission Level** arrow, and then in the list, click **Editor**.

The selections in the check boxes in the Permissions area change to the default Editor permissions.

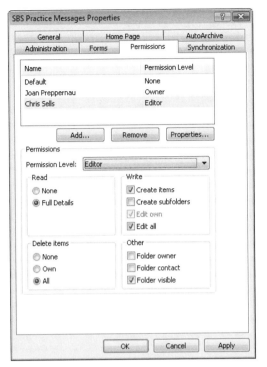

6. In the **SBS Practice Messages Properties** dialog box, click **Apply**.

   Your co-worker can now view the folder by opening it from within Outlook on his or her computer and can create, edit, and delete items within it.

7. In the **Delete items** area, select the **Own** option, and then click **OK**.

   Your co-worker can now create and edit items within the shared folder, but can delete only those items she or he created.

8. If your co-worker is available, ask him or her to connect to your *SBS Practice Messages* folder to verify that the folder is shared as expected.

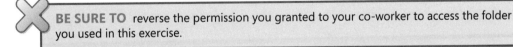

BE SURE TO reverse the permission you granted to your co-worker to access the folder you used in this exercise.

Accessing Other People's Folders

If you would like a co-worker to share one of his her primary mailbox folders with you, you can request access to that folder from within Outlook. Outlook sends a request form to your co-worker, who simply clicks a button to approve the request; then you receive a message from which you can add the shared folder to those that you see in your mailbox.

In this exercise, you will ask another person on your Exchange Server network to share a folder with you. There are no practice files for this exercise.

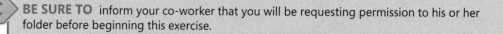

BE SURE TO inform your co-worker that you will be requesting permission to his or her folder before beginning this exercise.

1. On the **File** menu, point to **Open**, and then click **Other User's Folder**.

2. In the **Open Other User's Folder** dialog box, type or select your co-worker's name or e-mail alias.

3. Click the **Folder type** arrow, and in the list, click **Tasks**.

4. In the **Open Other User's Folder** dialog box, click **OK**.

   Assuming your co-worker has not yet granted you permission to his or her Tasks folder, Outlook displays a message asking whether you want to request permission to view the folder.

5. In the **Microsoft Office Outlook** message box, click **Yes**.

   Outlook creates an e-mail message requesting permission to view the selected folder.

   You can give reciprocal permission to your own Tasks folder by selecting the Allow Recipient To View Your Tasks Folder check box.

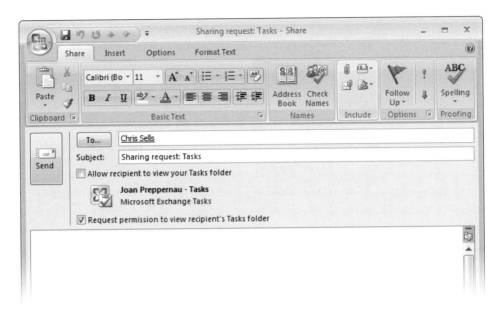

6. In the **Sharing request: Tasks** message header, click the **Send** button.

7. Ask your co-worker to open the sharing request, click the **Allow** button in the **Respond** group on the **Share** tab, and then click **Yes** in the **Microsoft Office Outlook** message box.

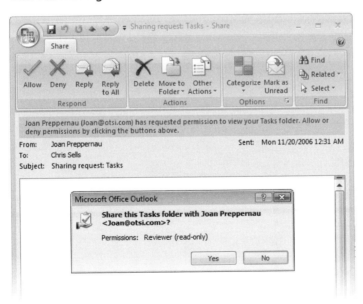

After Outlook shares the folder, a message box appears, informing your co-worker that the folder has been successfully shared. Then you receive a message notifying you that your co-worker has allowed you to view the Tasks folder.

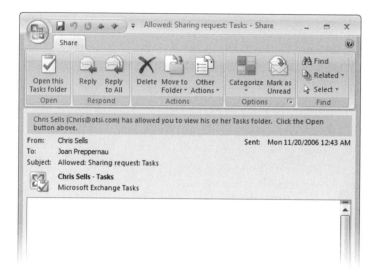

8. In the **Open** group, click the **Open this Tasks folder** button.

> **Tip** If someone shares a folder with you but you don't receive a message containing a link to the folder, point to Open on the File menu, click Other User's Folder, type or select the name of the person who shared the folder with you, select the folder type, and then click OK to link to the shared folder.

Your co-worker's Tasks folder opens in a separate Outlook window; Outlook also adds it to the People's Tasks list in your Tasks module.

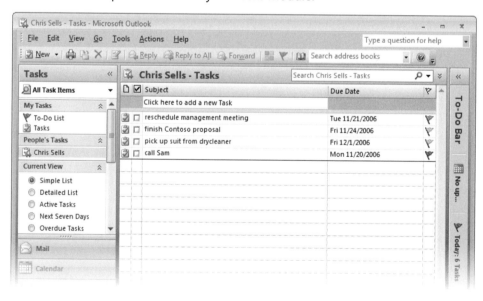

To open the shared Tasks folder at any time, click the Tasks button in the Navigation Pane and then select the shared task list.

BE SURE TO have your co-worker reverse the permission he or she granted to you to access the folder you used in this exercise.

Creating a Document Workspace from Outlook

Frequently, you might want to share useful documents, such as procedural documentation, sales figures, or calendars, with other members of your organization. You can send a document to your co-workers as an attachment to an e-mail message, but if several people return edited versions, you will have to take the time to merge all the changes into one document. If you have permission to add content to your organization's collaboration site, you can add the document to a document library on the site and other people can review and edit the document from there.

You can quickly create a document workspace for one or more files from Outlook instead of from the collaboration site by sending the files as shared attachments to an e-mail message. Shared attachments are made available within a document workspace on a collaboration site, and can be automatically updated with changes that recipients make.

See Also For information about creating workspaces for collaborating on meetings, see the sidebar "Creating a Meeting Workspace" in Chapter 6, "Managing Appointments, Events, and Meetings."

In this topic, we demonstrate the process of creating a document workspace on a collaboration site from Outlook.

Follow these steps:

1. Open a new message window, address the message to the people you want to invite to the document workspace, and insert the message subject.

2. On the **Message** tab, in the **Include** group, click the **Attach File** button.

   The Insert File dialog box opens.

3. Browse to and select the file(s) you want to share through a document library, and then click **Insert**.

Dialog Box
Launcher

4. In the **Include** group, click the **Dialog Box Launcher**.

The Attachment Options task pane opens.

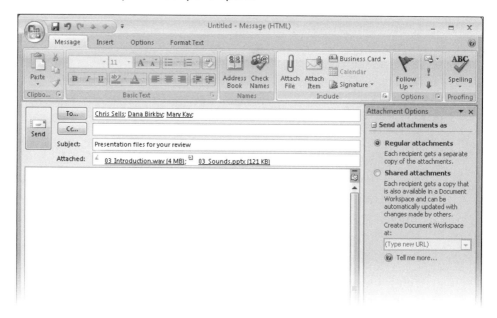

5. Under **Send attachments as**, select the **Shared attachments** option.

6. In the **Create Document Workspace at** box, type the address of your collaboration site (or if the site address appears in the list, click it), and then press the Tab key.

An invitation to the document workspace that will be created when you send the e-mail message appears in the content area.

You have been invited to the 03 Introduction Document Workspace. You can work with either the shared attachment or the workspace copy. Shared attachments opened in the 2003 and later versions of the Microsoft Office programs Word, Excel, PowerPoint, and Visio can be updated automatically with changes made by others.

7. Send the message.

A document workspace containing the file or files you attached to the message is created on the specified collaboration site. The message recipients are added to the workspace as members; you don't need to take any other action to give them permission to edit the document, but you can add other members to the workspace if you want.

You receive a message confirming that the workspace was successfully created, and the message recipients receive the invitation message. Each message contains a link to the document workspace.

Creating Group Schedules

When organizing a meeting, it's helpful to be able to see when attendees are available without having to contact each person individually. With Outlook, you can add them to a meeting request and then view their status on the Scheduling page. If you want to find a time at which several people are all available, and your organization is not running Exchange Server 2007, you can create a *group schedule* that shows the combined schedules of multiple people and resources.

To create a group schedule:

1. Display your calendar, and then on the **Actions** menu, click **View Group Schedules**.

2. In the **Group Schedules** dialog box, click **New**. In the **Create New Group Schedule** dialog box, type the schedule name (for example, Management Team), and then click **OK**.

3. In the scheduling window, add members to the group by clicking in the **Group Members** list and then typing a name or an e-mail alias, or by clicking **Add Others** and then selecting group members from your address book.

   The group schedule immediately displays availability for each group member. You can point to any appointment or meeting to see information about it. Information will not be available if an appointment is marked as private.

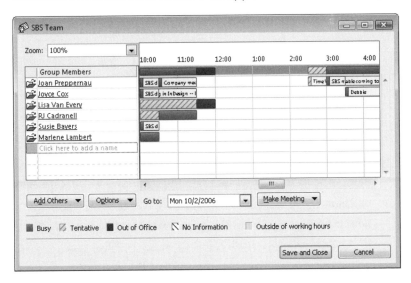

You can view an up-to-date group schedule at any time by clicking View Group Schedules on the Actions menu.

Working Offline with Document Library Contents

You can create a copy of a SharePoint Server 2007 document library as a folder in Outlook 2007. You can then preview in the Outlook message pane any document, workbook, or presentation that is stored in the document library, or you can work with a local copy of the document, workbook, or presentation on your computer.

In this topic, we demonstrate the process of creating local copies of the files stored in a document library in an Outlook folder, and merging changes you make to those files with the original versions.

Follow these steps:

1. On your organization's collaboration site, display the document library you want to work with.

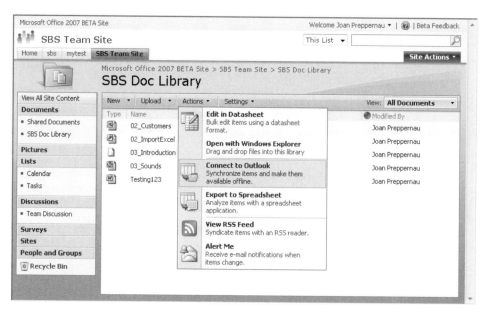

2. On the **Actions** menu, click **Connect to Outlook**. If an **Internet Explorer Security** alert appears (on computers running Windows Vista), click **Allow**.

   Outlook starts, if it isn't already running, and a message box appears asking whether you want to connect the SharePoint document library to Outlook.

3. In the message box, click **Yes**. If a **Connect** dialog box appears, prompting you for your site credentials, enter your user name and password and then click **OK**.

Outlook creates and displays a folder, named for the site and document library, as a subfolder of the SharePoint Lists folder in your mailbox, and downloads a copy of each of the items stored in the document library as an Outlook item within the folder. The icon to the left of the item name indicates the file type (for example, document, workbook, presentation, or database).

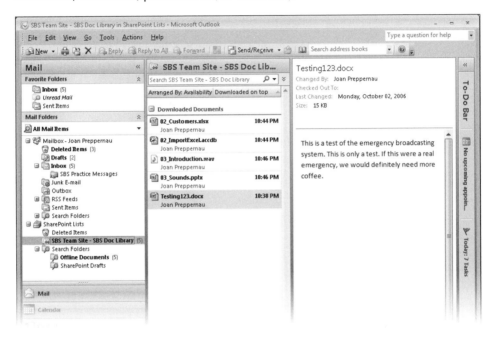

> **Tip** Outlook creates the SharePoint Lists folder the first time you connect a document library or other SharePoint list to Outlook.

You can preview any item by clicking it, or open a read-only version of the item by double-clicking it. When you open an item, a banner at the top informs you that you're working in an Offline Server Document; if you want to make changes and merge them with the document stored in the document library, click Edit Offline.

> **Tip** Opening an offline file does not check out the file to you in the document library.

While you work with an offline copy of a file, a local version is stored in the SharePoint Drafts folder (a subfolder of the SharePoint Lists folder). An icon depicting a red arrow on a page indicates that you are currently editing the item. To transfer changes from the offline file to the document library, save your changes, close the file, and then reopen it. In the Edit Offline message box that appears, click Update.

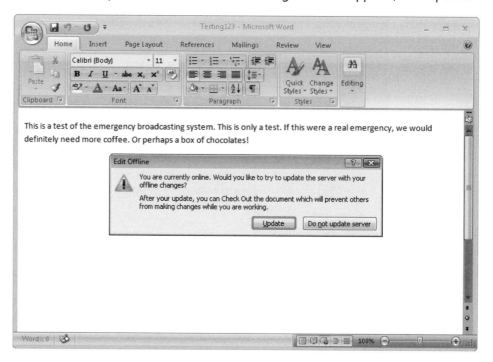

Connecting to a SharePoint Calendar

If your organization maintains team calendars on a collaboration site, you might find it convenient to view the calendar in Outlook rather than on the site. By connecting a SharePoint calendar to Outlook, you can display the SharePoint calendar in the Outlook Calendar pane, either by itself, next to other calendars, or overlaid on other calendars. You can work with the SharePoint calendar as you would with any other calendar. Any changes you make to the SharePoint calendar in Outlook are immediately reflected in the calendar on the collaboration site, and vice versa.

Follow these steps to display a SharePoint calendar in Outlook:

1. On your organization's collaboration site, display the calendar you want to work with.

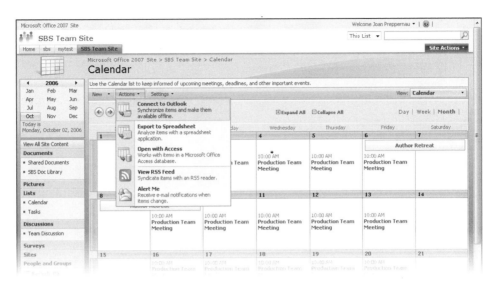

2. On the **Actions** menu, click **Connect to Outlook**. If an **Internet Explorer Security** alert appears, click **Allow**.

   Outlook starts, if it isn't already running.

3. In the **Microsoft Office Outlook** message box asking you to confirm that you want to connect the SharePoint calendar to Outlook, click **Yes**. If a **Connect** dialog box appears, prompting you for your site credentials, enter your user name and password and then click **OK**.

   Outlook displays the SharePoint calendar next to your own.

Key Points

- You can share any type of Outlook folder with other members of your organization. You can grant specific levels of permission to people to create, edit, and delete information within a shared folder.

- You can give full control of all or parts of your mailbox to someone by making him or her a delegate.

- If your organization shares information through a SharePoint collaboration site, you can create document workspaces and assign permissions from within Outlook; maintain a local copy of document library contents in Outlook, work with files, and upload your changes to the SharePoint site; and work with SharePoint calendars within Outlook.

Chapter at a Glance

Work with Outlook items while offline, **page 283**

Automatically respond to messages, **page 287**

11 Working Away from Your Office

In this chapter, you will learn to:

✔ Connect Outlook to your server from a remote location.

✔ Work with Outlook items while offline.

✔ Automatically respond to messages.

In today's workplace, communication, efficiency, and mobility are crucial. Microsoft Office Outlook 2007 can help you improve your performance in all of these areas by providing a means of connecting to your information quickly and securely.

If you have an Internet connection and your organization provides remote connection to its Microsoft Exchange server or is running Microsoft Outlook Web Access (a feature of Exchange), you can access your Exchange account from home, from a client site, from a hotel room, from a tradeshow booth, or even from your local Starbucks. For example, you might need to access your e-mail while working from home, or you might need to set up a meeting with staff at the office while visiting out-of-state clients.

See Also For information about ways to share folders and work with other people, see Chapter 10, "Collaborating with Other People."

Whether or not you have an Internet connection, you will want to use the Out Of Office Assistant to let people know that you are away from your desk and that your ability to respond promptly to messages and requests might be impacted until you return.

In this chapter, you will explore the tools Outlook provides for working remotely. You will examine the ways you can access an Exchange Server account when your computer is not connected directly to your organization's network, and how to ensure that you have up-to-date information when you are working offline. Then you will work with the Out Of Office Assistant, including the new functionality available when your organization is running Microsoft Exchange Server 2007.

See Also Do you need only a quick refresher on the topics in this chapter? See the Quick Reference entries on pages xxxvii–lxv.

> **Important** No practice files are required to complete the exercises in this chapter. For more information about practice files, see "Using the Book's CD" on page xxv.

> **Troubleshooting** Graphics and operating system–related instructions in this book reflect the Windows Vista user interface. If your computer is running Microsoft Windows XP and you experience trouble following the instructions as written, please refer to the "Information for Readers Running Windows XP" section at the beginning of this book.

Connecting Outlook to Your Server from a Remote Location

Wherever you are in the world, if you can connect to the Internet, you can probably work in Outlook from a remote location without much extra effort. In this context, *remote* doesn't mean *far away*; it means *not directly connected*.

> **Tip** The process of connecting your computer to your local area network (LAN) or to the Internet is beyond the scope of this book, but you can read all about it in the *Step by Step* book for the version of Windows running on your computer.

After establishing your connection to the Internet, if you use Outlook to connect to a POP3, IMAP, or HTTP account, you will immediately have access to those resources from wherever you are. If you use Outlook to connect to an Exchange Server account, your options vary depending on the version of Exchange Server your organization is running, and the types of connections allowed. In this topic, we discuss the three most convenient methods.

Connecting over HTTP

Within a network domain, Outlook communicates with your organization's Exchange server by using *remote procedure calls (RPC)*. If your organization is running Microsoft Exchange Server 2003 or later on Microsoft Windows Server 2003, your Exchange administrator can configure the server to permit connections by using the RPC communication path. You can then connect from Outlook to your Exchange account over the Internet by using the *Outlook Anywhere* feature (formerly called simply *RPC over HTTP*). No special connection is required. This is by far the simplest method of remotely accessing Exchange resources.

In this exercise, you will configure Outlook to connect to an Exchange account by using Outlook Anywhere. There are no practice files for this exercise.

> **BE SURE TO** start Outlook and connect your computer to the Internet, but not to your organization's network, before beginning this exercise.

1. On the **Tools** menu, click **Account Settings**.

   The Account Settings dialog box opens, showing the configured e-mail accounts.

2. On the **E-mail** tab of the **Account Settings** dialog box, in the **Name** list, click your **Microsoft Exchange** account, and then click **Change**.

   The Change E-Mail Account dialog box opens, showing the account settings for the Exchange account.

3. In the **Change E-mail Account** dialog box, click **More Settings**.

   The Microsoft Exchange dialog box opens.

4. In the **Microsoft Exchange** dialog box, click the **Connection** tab.

5. In the **Outlook Anywhere** area, select the **Connect to Microsoft Exchange using HTTP** check box.

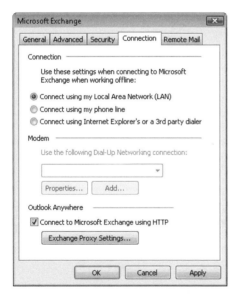

6. Click the **Exchange Proxy Settings** button that becomes active.

   The Microsoft Exchange Proxy Settings dialog box opens, with options for connecting to Exchange over the Internet.

7. In the **Connection settings** area, type your organization's secure Exchange proxy address in the **https://** box.

   You can choose to have Outlook connect first through Outlook Anywhere and then once established, transfer the connection to TCP/IP, by selecting either or both of the check boxes at the bottom of the Connection Settings area. Your specific organization might require an authentication method other than the default; check with your network administrator.

8. In the **Microsoft Exchange Proxy Settings** dialog box, click **OK**.

9. In the **Microsoft Exchange** dialog box, click **OK**. Then in the message box that appears, click **OK** to acknowledge that the change will not take effect until you restart Outlook.

10. In the **Change E-mail Account** dialog box, click **Next**, and then click **Finish**.

11. Close the **Account Settings** dialog box, and then quit and restart Outlook.

    Outlook attempts to connect to your Exchange server, and when it doesn't find a domain connection, switches to Outlook Anywhere. When Outlook Anywhere makes contact with the proxy server, Outlook prompts you to supply your credentials.

12. In the **Connect to** dialog box, enter your user name and password, and then click **OK**.

    Outlook connects to your Exchange account.

BE SURE TO repeat the exercise and turn off Outlook Anywhere if you don't want to use it.

Connecting Through a VPN

A virtual private network (VPN) is, as the name implies, an extension of a network domain through which authorized users can connect securely to network resources. After connecting through a VPN to your network, you have access to all network resources, including servers and printers, and can connect directly to Outlook exactly as you would when sitting in the office with your computer connected to the LAN. Your organization might require that you use a special authentication method, such as a smart card or token, to prove your identity in order to maintain network security.

To support VPN connections to your network, the network administrator must set up a VPN server. Information traveling between your remote computer and the network over the Internet passes through the VPN server.

The process of setting up a VPN connection is relatively simple, but varies depending on the operating system your computer is running.

To set up a VPN connection from a computer running Windows Vista:

1. Click the **Start** button. Then in the right pane of the **Start** menu, click **Connect To**. The Connect To A Network dialog box opens.

2. Click **Set up a connection or network**.

3. Scroll the **Choose a connection option** list, click **Connect to a workplace**, and then click **Next**.

4. Under **Do you want to use a connection that you already have?**, select **No, create a new connection**, and then click **Next**.

5. Under **How do you want to connect?**, click **Use my Internet connection (VPN)** option.

6. Under **Type the Internet address to connect to**, type the Internet address you want to connect to in the **Internet address** box. In the **Destination name** box, type a name for the VPN connection, select any options that you want, and then click **Next**.

7. Under **Type your user name and password**, type your user name and password (the domain name is optional), and then click **Connect**.

To disconnect from a VPN connection on a computer running Windows Vista:

→ Right-click the connection icon, point to **Disconnect from**, and then click the VPN connection name.

To set up a VPN connection from a computer running Windows XP:

1. Display the **Start** menu.

2. If the **Connect To** menu appears on the right side, click **Connect To**, and then click **Show all connections**. Otherwise, open **Control Panel**, switch to Classic view if necessary, and then open **Network and Internet Connections**.

3. In the **Network Connections** window, on the **Network Tasks** menu, click **Create a new connection**.

4. On the first page of the **New Connection** wizard, click **Next**.

5. On the **Network Connection Type** page, select the **Connect to the network at my workplace** option, and then click **Next**.

6. On the **Network Connection** page, select the **Virtual Private Network connection** option, and then click **Next**.

7. In the **Company Name** box, type a name by which you will identify the connection (for example, *Wingtip Toys*). Then click **Next**.

8. If the wizard displays the **Public Network** page, select the **Do not dial the initial connection** option to indicate that you will always connect to the Internet before starting the VPN connection. Then click **Next**.

9. On the **VPN Server Selection** page, type the URL of your organization's VPN server (for example, *mail.wingtiptoys.com*) in the **Host name** box, and then click **Next**.

10. If the wizard displays the **Smart Cards** page, select the **Do not use my smart card** option, and then click **Next**.

11. On the **Connection Availability** page, select **My use only**, and then click **Next**.

12. On the **Completing** page, click **Finish**.

    The Connect dialog box opens.

13. In the **User name** box, type your domain\username (for example, *WINGTIP\chris*).

14. In the **Password** box, type your domain password.

15. Select the **Save this user name** check box and the **Me only** option. Then click **Connect**.

    After your computer connects to the network domain, a connection icon (depicting two computers) appears in the notification area at the right end of the status bar. You can now operate as though you are using the computer at the office.

To disconnect from a VPN connection on a computer running Windows XP:

→ Right-click the connection icon, and then click **Disconnect**.

Connecting Through OWA

Outlook Web Access (OWA) is actually a feature of Exchange, but it deserves special mention here because it will most likely be used by people who regularly use Outlook. If your organization supports OWA, you can access your e-mail, calendar, contacts, automatic response options, and more by connecting from an Internet browser window (not from Outlook) to Exchange.

The OWA interface you see is dependent on the version of Exchange your mailbox is on—OWA for Exchange 2007 has a significantly improved user interface (UI) and more functionality than OWA for Exchange 2003. But they're both a great way to quickly check e-mail, set up meetings, look up a phone number, and so on from someone else's computer.

Working with Outlook Items While Offline

If you use a laptop, you probably do many types of computing without being connected to the Internet. Not having a connection to your mail server doesn't prevent you from using Outlook. You can read and write messages and other items by using the local copy of your mailbox that is stored, by using *Cached Exchange Mode*, on your computer. This makes switching between working online and offline easy.

Cached Exchange Mode was introduced as an option with Outlook 2003 and is turned on by default in Outlook 2007. This feature creates a local copy (a copy that resides on your computer) of the contents of your Exchange mailbox. When you are working online (connected to Exchange) messages, appointments, meetings, tasks, and other Outlook items are kept synchronized between the server and the cache. As a result, when you go offline (disconnect from Exchange, either voluntarily or involuntarily) you can still open and work with all your Outlook items—including attachments—as usual. You can't receive messages while you're offline, but you can send them—at least as far as your Outbox, where they are held until the next time Outlook connects to Exchange. Cached Exchange Mode has greatly streamlined the offline working process, making it simple, for example, to catch up on e-mail on your laptop when you're in an airplane—of the old-fashioned sort, *without* onboard Internet.

Using Cached Exchange Mode in Outlook 2007, you can have available to you while working offline not only the contents of your Exchange account, but also the contents of shared folders and public folders (but only those you add to your Public Folder Favorites list).

> **Tip** If your organization is running Exchange Server 2007, you can take advantage of the Unified Messaging functionality of Exchange Server. For example, rather than checking for voice messages through your telephone system, Exchange Server can send your voice messages to you as audio files attached to e-mail messages. You can also receive faxes by e-mail. This functionality, which is similar to that offered by many Voice over IP (VoIP) companies, enables you to manage all your communications from your Windows desktop, regardless of your location.

Outlook offers these three Cached Exchange Mode download options:

- **Download Full Items.** This option downloads all your messages and their attachments one at a time. If you keep Outlook open and your computer connected to a network, this is the best option because it uses the least bandwidth to download all your messages. If you have a slow connection or receive messages with large attachments, messages might be slow to appear in your Inbox when you reconnect to your server.

- **Download Headers and then Full Items.** This option downloads all the message headers quickly, so that you can be evaluating them while the message bodies and attachments are downloaded.

- **Download Headers.** This option downloads only the message header, and does not download the body of a message or its attachments until you preview or open the message. This is the best option if your connection is very slow or if you are charged for the amount of bandwidth you actually use. You can evaluate messages based on their header information (sender, subject, message size, and so on) and then choose whether to download the message and any attachments.

The above options are available from the File menu. When you're working over a LAN, broadband, or other fast connection, you probably won't notice much difference between the first two options. You will notice obvious differences with the third option, and if you're not accustomed to mentally processing a message based on only a few words, it can be a bit frustrating.

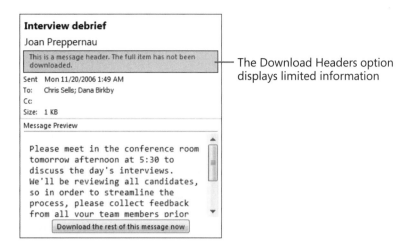

The Download Headers option displays limited information

You also have the option to download only message headers when Outlook detects that its connection to Exchange is slow. To view or change the download options, point to Cached Exchange Mode on the File menu.

If you for some reason choose to disable Cached Exchange Mode, you can still make the contents of selected folders (even your entire Inbox) available when you're working offline. For example, you might create an Action Items folder to which you drag the messages you want to follow up on while traveling. Note that offline folders contain only messages that you received before you started working offline.

To make the contents of a folder available for offline use:

1. In the **Navigation Pane**, select the folder you want to make available offline.

2. On the **Tools** menu, point to **Send/Receive**, point to **Send/Receive Settings**, and then click **Make This Folder Available Offline**.

   A check mark to the left of the menu item indicates that a local copy of the selected folder will be synchronized with each Send/Receive operation.

Viewing Contacts While Offline

When Cached Exchange Mode is enabled, as it is by default, Outlook downloads a copy of the Global Address List along with your mailbox. This *offline address book* provides access to your co-workers' contact information regardless of whether you are online. If your network connection is slow and the address book is large, this download might take a long time. If you prefer, you can disable the automatic download of the address book, or reduce the amount of information transferred, and then manually update your offline address book at your convenience.

To reduce the transfer of address book information during send/receive operations:

1. On the **Tools** menu, point to **Send/Receive**, point to **Send/Receive Settings**, and then click **Define Send/Receive Groups**.

2. In the **Send/Receive Groups** dialog box, click the group you want to change, and then click **Edit**.

3. In the **Send/Receive Settings** dialog box, with the **Download offline address book** check box selected, click **Address Book Settings**.

   You can turn off the automatic address book update entirely by clearing the Download Offline Address Book check box.

   > **Troubleshooting** If the Download Offline Address Book option is unavailable (gray), select the Include The Selected Account In This Group check box.

4. In the **Offline Address Book** dialog box, select the **No Details** option, and click **OK**. Then click **OK** in the **Send/Receive Settings** dialog box, and **Close** in the **Send/Receive Groups** dialog box.

To manually update your offline address book:

1. On the **Tools** menu, point to **Send/Receive**, and then click **Download Address Book**.

2. In the **Offline Address Book** dialog box, with the **Download changes since last Send/Receive** check box selected, select the **Full Details** option, and then click **OK**.

   You can download an entirely new copy of the address book by clearing the Download Changes Since Last Send/Receive check box before clicking OK.

Automatically Responding to Messages

If your organization is running Exchange, you can use the Out Of Office Assistant to inform people who send you e-mail messages of your availability. Turning on the Out Of Office Assistant causes replies to be automatically sent in response to messages received from other people (but only to the first message from each person). You can provide whatever (textual) information you want within the body of the auto-reply message.

Outlook 2007 acts as a front end to the out of office (OOO) functionality provided by Exchange Server, so the interface and experience are different depending on what version of Exchange Server your organization is running. When interfacing with Exchange Server 2007, you have more control over the content and distribution of auto-replies than when interfacing with Exchange Server 2003. Regardless of which Exchange Server environment you're working in, this is a very useful feature.

The purpose of the OOO function is to help you set expectations for response time or give people other information you want them to have. You don't have to be physically out of the office to use this feature; some people use it to let other people know when responses will be delayed for other reasons, such as when they are working on a project that will prevent them from responding promptly to messages, or to let customers who might be in different time zones know when they have left the office for the evening.

In addition to sending auto-replies, you can have Outlook process messages that arrive while you are OOO by using *rules* that are in effect only when the OOO function is on.

See Also For information about using rules to automatically forward, reply to, delete, alert you to, or otherwise process incoming messages, see "Creating Rules to Process Messages" in Chapter 12, "Customizing and Configuring Outlook."

Until you tell it otherwise, the Out Of Office Assistant assumes you are in the office. It does not coordinate with the availability you display when setting up meetings and appointments.

Configuring Auto-Replies for Exchange Server 2003 Accounts

Features of the Out Of Office Assistant that are specific to an Exchange Server 2003 environment include:

- You create one auto-reply message, which Outlook sends in response to the first message received from each person who sends you mail.
- You cannot format the text of the autoreply message.
- The Out Of Office Assistant is active from the time you turn it on until the time you turn it off.

In this exercise, you will configure Outlook to automatically reply to all incoming messages, and then you will create a rule to forward urgent messages to a co-worker. There are no practice files for this exercise.

> **Important** This exercise is specific to Exchange Server 2003 accounts.

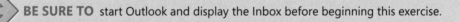

BE SURE TO start Outlook and display the Inbox before beginning this exercise.

1. On the **Tools** menu, click **Out of Office Assistant**.

   The Out Of Office Assistant dialog box opens.

   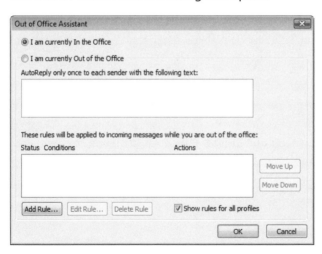

   In an Exchange Server 2003 environment, this is a single-screen dialog box.

2. Select the **I am currently Out of the Office** option.

3. In the **AutoReply only once to each sender with the following text** box, type

I am out of the office today, with limited access to e-mail and voicemail. I will respond to your message within one business day.

Please direct urgent issues to mary@contoso.com.

If you're concerned that the message will be sent to people while you're testing this function, you can substitute other text, such as *I am testing my OOO function*, for the above.

4. In the **Out of Office Assistant** dialog box, click **OK**.

The Out Of Office menu and a corresponding notification appear at the right end of the status bar.

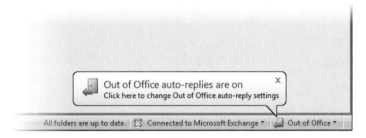

5. Click the notification to close it, or wait until it closes itself. Then on the status bar, click **Out of Office**.

From the Out Of Office menu that opens, you can open the Out Of Office Assistant dialog box or turn off the AutoReply function.

6. On the **Out of Office** menu, click **Out of Office Assistant**.

7. In the **Out of Office Assistant** dialog box, click **Add Rule**.

The Edit Rule dialog box opens. Its interface for creating rules is simpler than the Rules And Alerts interface you work in when creating rules for all of Outlook, but the Edit Rule dialog box still provides a lot of choices.

8. In the **Edit Rule** dialog box, click **Advanced**.

The Advanced dialog box opens.

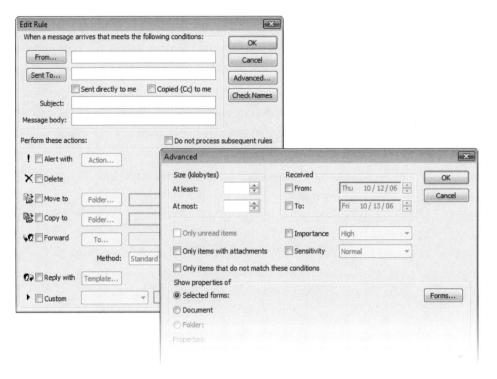

9. In the **Received** area, select the **From** and **To** check boxes.

   This sets the forwarding rule to occur on the current day only. You can specify only a start date or end date, or any date range you want. For example, if you will be out of the office for one week, but be completely without e-mail access for only two days of that time, you might forward urgent messages only on those days. To specify a non-consecutive date span, create a rule for each consecutive date span.

10. Select the **Importance** check box. Then with **High** selected in the **Importance** list, click **OK**.

   > **Troubleshooting** The specifications you entered in the Advanced dialog box are not reflected in the Edit Rule dialog box; in fact, there is no indication that any parameters have been set for this rule.

11. In the **Edit Rule** dialog box, under **Perform these actions**, select the **Forward** check box. Then in the **To** box, type mary@contoso.com.

   > **Tip** If you have access to another e-mail account, either your own or one belonging to a friend or co-worker who is willing to help you, enter his or her e-mail address instead.

12. Click the **Method** arrow to display the forwarding options:

- *Standard* forwards the message content as an inclusion in a message from you, and retains the Importance indicator.
- *Leave message intact* delivers the original message, so that it appears to have been sent directly from the original sender to your designated backup.
- *Insert message as an attachment* forwards the message item as an attachment to a message from you, and does not retain the Importance indicator.

In all cases, the message header includes the information *This message was AutoForwarded*.

13. In the **Method** list, click **Standard**. Then click **OK**.

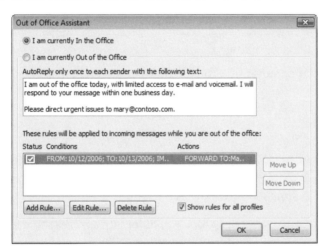

14. In the **Out of Office Assistant** dialog box, click **OK**.

15. If you inserted an actual e-mail address as the forwarding recipient, send two messages to yourself: the first a standard or Low Importance message, and the second a High Importance message.

You will receive an *Out of Office AutoReply* message in response to your first message, but none to your second message. The other e-mail account will receive a High Importance message forwarded from you.

16. On the **Out of Office** menu, click **Turn off Out of Office auto-replies**.

If you open the Out Of Office Assistant dialog box, you will see that your message and rule are intact, but the I Am In The Office option is selected, so no auto-replies will be sent.

Configuring Auto-Replies for Exchange Server 2007 Accounts

Features of the Out Of Office Assistant that are specific to an Exchange Server 2007 environment include:

- You can create two auto-reply messages—one that Outlook sends only to people in your organization (on the same domain) and another sent either to everyone else, or to only the people in your primary address book.

  This allows you to separately control the information made available to co-workers, to friends and business contacts, and to the general public (including senders of spam). For example, you might include your itinerary and mobile phone number in only an internal OOO reply, include your return date in a reply to your contacts, and not send any reply to other people.

- You can specify the font, size, and color of OOO message text and apply bold, italic, or underline formatting.

- You can format paragraphs as bulleted or numbered lists and control the indent level.

- You can specify start and end dates and times for your OOO message so that you don't have to remember to turn off the Out Of Office Assistant.

Refer to the previous exercise for information about features and processes that are not dependent on the Exchange Server version, including creating rules and using the Out Of Office menu that appears on the status bar.

In this exercise, you will configure Outlook to automatically reply to messages during a future time period, and to send different auto-replies to co-workers than to the general public. There are no practice files for this exercise.

> **Important** This exercise is specific to Exchange Server 2007 accounts.

 BE SURE TO start Outlook and display the Inbox before beginning this exercise.

1. On the **Tools** menu, click **Out of Office Assistant**.

   The Out Of Office Assistant dialog box opens.

   In an Exchange 2007 environment, this dialog box includes two tabs: Inside My Organization and Outside My Organization. The Outside My Organization tab includes the notation (On).

2. Select the **Send Out of Office auto-replies** option to activate the dialog box contents.

3. Select the **Only send during this time range** check box. Then set the **Start time** to 5:00 P.M. on the next Friday, and the **End time** to 5:00 P.M. on the following Friday.

By using this schedule, anyone sending mail to you from the time you leave the office on Friday until the end of the day the following Friday will receive an automatic reply to the first message he or she sends. (You could also set this up for Monday through Friday, but the people sending messages on Friday evening or the weekend wouldn't receive an auto-reply.)

4. On the **Inside My Organization** tab, in the message box, type

I'm on vacation! Call my mobile at (858) 555-0123 if anything urgent comes up.

If you're concerned that the message will be sent to people while you're testing this function, you can substitute other text, such as *I am testing my internal OOO function*, for the above.

5. Select the sentence *I'm on vacation!* On the toolbar at the top of the tab, click the **Font Color** button, and then in the gallery, click the **Purple** square.

The buttons representing text and paragraph formatting commands are the same in the Out Of Office Assistant as they are in an e-mail message, or in any 2007 Microsoft Office system product.

6. Click the **Outside My Organization** tab.

   Notice that if you simply turn on the Out Of Office Assistant, auto-replies are sent only to people in your primary Outlook address book. You can prevent auto-replies from going to anyone other than a person within your own e-mail domain by clearing the Auto-reply To People Outside My Organization check box.

7. Select the **Anyone outside my organization** option. Then in the message box, type

   I am out of the office this week and will respond to your message as soon as possible. For more information about Contoso products and services, please visit our Web site at www.contoso.com.

   When you type the final period, the URL becomes a hyperlink.

8. In the **Out of Office Assistant** dialog box, click **OK**.

   The Out Of Office menu does *not* appear on the status bar, because you specified that your Out Of Office period does not begin until 5:00 P.M. next Friday. There isn't any indicator that you've set the Out Of Office Assistant to start at a future time. (This feature might be included in future versions of Outlook.) At the specified start time, the Out Of Office menu will appear at the right end of the status bar to indicate that Out Of Office auto-replies are turned on. At the specified end time, the Out Of Office Assistant will turn itself off, and the menu will disappear.

9. On the **Tools** menu, click **Out of Office Assistant**. Select the **Do not send Out of Office auto-replies** option, and then click **OK**.

> **Tip** If you make changes to one of the OOO messages but not the other, when you close the Out Of Office Assistant dialog box, Outlook displays a message box asking whether you want to change the other. This useful reminder helps ensure that you keep both versions up to date.

Key Points

- Working away from your network or without an Internet connection doesn't mean that you can't use Outlook. If your organization uses Exchange, you have many options for accessing your e-mail messages and other information you manage within Outlook.

- Cached Exchange Mode keeps a copy of your mailbox on your computer so you can keep working even when you are away from your network.

- Cached Exchange Mode handles connecting and synchronizing your local mailbox for you. You can set it to cache all messages or just headers, to save bandwidth.

- When you will be away from your computer for a while, Outlook can send an auto-reply message once to each person from whom you receive a message. This is a convenient way of letting people know when to expect a response from you.

Chapter at a Glance

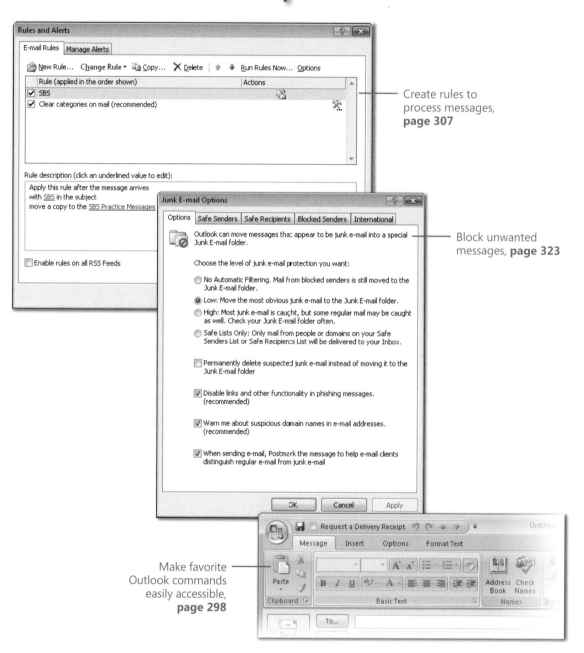

Create rules to
process messages,
page 307

Block unwanted
messages, **page 323**

Make favorite
Outlook commands
easily accessible,
page 298

12 Customizing and Configuring Outlook

In this chapter, you will learn to:

- ✔ Make favorite Outlook commands easily accessible.
- ✔ Personalize your Office and Outlook settings.
- ✔ Create rules to process messages.
- ✔ Store e-mail messages on your computer.
- ✔ Secure your e-mail.
- ✔ Block unwanted messages.
- ✔ Specify advanced e-mail options.

A host of configuration and customization options are available to help you take advantage of everything that Microsoft Office Outlook 2007 has to offer. In addition to customizing the program's interface to your personal working style (which we discussed in "Personalizing Your Outlook Workspace" in Chapter 1, "Getting Started with Outlook 2007"), you can put frequently used commands at your fingertips by adding them to the Quick Access Toolbar. To more easily manage the information you receive through e-mail, you can specify how messages are processed and where they are stored. Most importantly, you can take advantage of the many security features built into Outlook 2007 to keep your outgoing communications secure and to protect your computer system from spam, viruses, Web beacons, and other modern electronic threats.

In this chapter, you will learn how to maintain your information in Outlook in a secure and organized fashion. First you will learn where to find commands that aren't available on the Outlook 2007 item window Ribbon, and how to make those (or other favorite commands) conveniently available by adding them to the Quick Access Toolbar, either for one document or all documents. Then you will learn ways of controlling incoming messages by using rules and by properly managing junk messages, as well as ways of ensuring that your e-mail communications are secure. You will create personal folders and address books to store and transport information, and finally, take a quick look at the additional ways you can configure Outlook to handle messages that you create, send, and receive.

See Also Do you need only a quick refresher on the topics in this chapter? See the Quick Reference entries on pages xxxvii–lxv.

Important No practice files are required to complete the exercises in this chapter. For more information about practice files, see "Using the Book's CD" on page xxv.

Troubleshooting Graphics and operating system–related instructions in this book reflect the Windows Vista user interface. If your computer is running Microsoft Windows XP and you experience trouble following the instructions as written, please refer to the "Information for Readers Running Windows XP" section at the beginning of this book.

Making Favorite Outlook Commands Easily Accessible

The commands you use to control Outlook are available from menus and toolbars within the program window. The basic command structure hasn't changed substantially from that in previous versions of Outlook: Buttons representing common commands are located on the Standard and Advanced toolbars, and other commands that you probably use less frequently can be found on the File, Edit, View, Go, Tools, Actions, and Help menus. You can also invoke many commands by using *keyboard shortcuts*.

Tip To see a list of the available keyboard shortcuts, click the Microsoft Office Outlook Help button, type keyboard shortcuts in the Search box, and press Enter. Then click the Keyboard Shortcuts For Outlook topic.

As we first discussed in Chapter 2, "Managing Contact Information," big changes have been made to the way commands are presented within the Outlook item windows (messages, appointments, contacts, tasks, and so on). Buttons representing commonly used commands are grouped on *tabs* to make them easily accessible in the specific context in which you're working. This new design makes all the commands you need at any given time available with only one click. However, you might find that the buttons you use frequently are scattered on different tabs. To give you more control over the way you work in the 2007 Microsoft Office system, Microsoft has provided the *Quick Access Toolbar*, the Office equivalent of the Quick Launch bar available in Microsoft

Windows. The Quick Access Toolbar is located to the right of the Microsoft Office Button in Outlook item windows, as well as in the Microsoft Office Word 2007, Microsoft Office Excel 2007, and Microsoft Office PowerPoint 2007 program windows. You can add a button for any command to the Quick Access Toolbar so that it is always available no matter which tab is currently active.

In this exercise, you will add a button to the Quick Access Toolbar. There are no practice files for this exercise.

BE SURE TO start Outlook and display the Inbox before beginning this exercise.

OPEN a message window.

Customize Quick
Access Toolbar

1. At the right end of the **Quick Access Toolbar**, click the **Customize Quick Access Toolbar** button.

   The Customize Quick Access Toolbar menu opens, displaying a short list of frequently used commands that you can click to add to the toolbar.

2. Near the bottom of the menu, click **More Commands**.

   The Editor Options window opens, displaying the Customize page. The commands currently appearing on the Quick Access Toolbar are listed (in order of appearance) in the right pane.

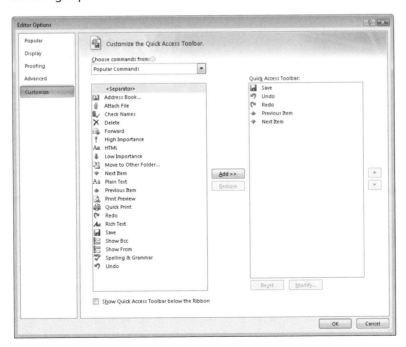

3. Click the **Choose commands from** arrow, and then in the list, click **Options Tab**.

   The list displays all the commands available from the Options tab.

Tip You can display an alphabetical list of all Outlook commands by clicking All Commands in the Choose Commands From list. In some cases, multiple instances of a command appear in the list—these correspond to the locations in which the command appears within the program. Pointing to a command displays the command location in a ScreenTip. Commands that appear on contextual tabs and commands that don't appear on any tab are also available from this list.

---

4. In the **Options Tab** list, point to the first command, **Browse for Themes**.

   A ScreenTip displays the tab and group where you can locate this command. Point to a few other commands to view their ScreenTips and gain a better understanding of how commands are grouped and where you can find them.

5. In the **Options Tab** list, click **Request a Delivery Receipt**. Then between the two command lists, click **Add**.

   Outlook adds the Request A Delivery Receipt command to the end of the list of commands available from the Quick Access Toolbar.

Move Up

6. In the right pane, click **Request a Delivery Receipt**, and then click the **Move Up** button four times to move the selected command to the second position in the list.

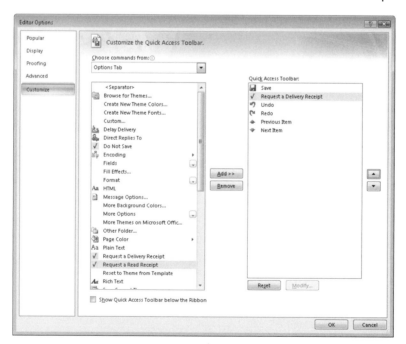

7. At the bottom of the **Customize** page, click **OK**.

The Request A Delivery Receipt check box now appears on the Quick Access Toolbar so that you can conveniently select it before sending a message.

You can remove the button from the Quick Access Toolbar by repeating Steps 1 and 2, selecting the command in the right pane, and then clicking Remove and OK.

BE SURE TO remove the command from the Quick Access Toolbar if you don't want to keep it there.

CLOSE the open message window. If Outlook prompts you to keep a saved draft of the blank message, click No.

Personalizing Your Office and Outlook Settings

While you are still becoming familiar with the 2007 Office system programs, and in particular with Outlook, you might be quite content to work with the default settings. But as you become more experienced, you might want to adjust some of the settings to tailor the Office environment to the way you work.

In this exercise, you will explore the ways in which you can customize Outlook. There are no practice files for this exercise.

BE SURE TO start Outlook before beginning this exercise.

OPEN a message window.

Microsoft Office Button

1. Click the **Microsoft Office Button**, and then in the lower-right corner of the **Office** menu, click **Editor Options**.

The Editor Options window opens, displaying the Popular page.

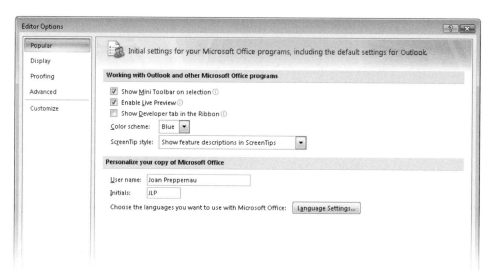

The settings on the Popular page apply to all 2007 Office system programs, not only to Outlook. These settings include showing the Mini toolbar when you select text, enabling live previews of gallery options, showing the Developer tab on the Ribbon, changing the color scheme, and setting the ScreenTip style. In addition, you can specify your user information (name and initials) on this page.

2. In the page list in the left pane, click **Display**.

The settings on the Display page control whether Outlook displays various types of formatting marks within message windows.

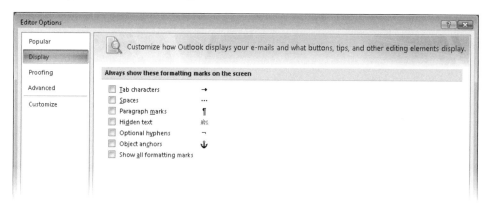

3. In the page list, click **Proofing**.

From the Proofing page, you can set AutoCorrect options to specify how Outlook will correct and format the content of your messages as you type them, and customize the spelling and grammar checking settings.

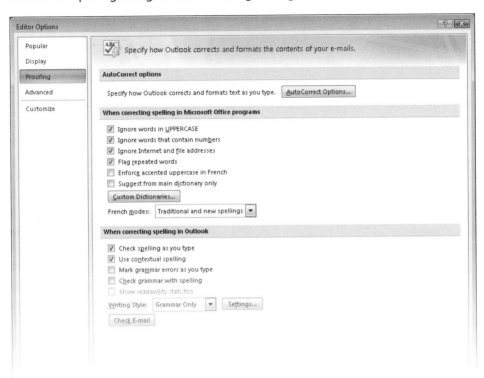

4. In the page list, click **Advanced**.

   This page contains settings for many features you might want to customize to suit the way you work.

   In the Editing Options area of this page, you can turn on or off advanced editing features, such as how Outlook selects and moves text, whether to track formatting changes, and whether Overtype mode is available.

   In the Cut, Copy, And Paste area, you can specify whether Outlook will apply source or destination formatting to text copied within a message, between messages, and from other programs. You can also set options for smart cut and paste (whether to automatically add and remove spaces as needed) and the Paste Options button (whether it appears after a past operation).

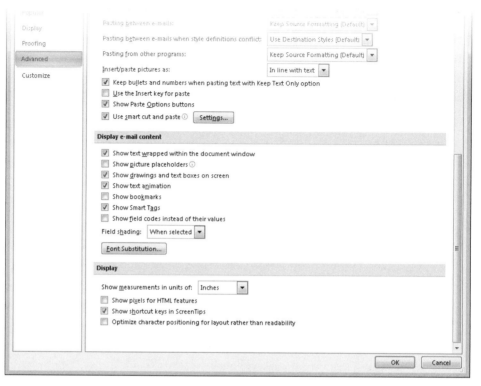

In the Display E-mail Content area, you can specify how Outlook displays your message content on screen. You can turn on or off text wrapping, picture place-holders, Smart Tags, field codes, and text animation.

In the Display area, you can set whether measurements are shown in inches, centimeters, millimeters, points, or picas; whether pixels are shown for HTML features; whether ScreenTips display keyboard shortcuts; and whether character positioning is optimized for layout rather than readability.

5. In the page list, click **Customize**.

As discussed in "Making Favorite Outlook Commands Easily Accessible" earlier in this chapter, from the Customize page, you can add frequently used commands to the Quick Access Toolbar.

6. Make any changes that you want to the default Office settings, to the way Outlook displays, corrects, and formats message and other items, and to the way Outlook functions. Then at the bottom of the **Editor Options** window, click **OK** (or click **Cancel** to close the window without implementing changes).

Creating Outlook Forms

Every Outlook item you create is based on a *form*—you create a message by entering information in a message form that is hosted in a message window; the appointment form consists of the Appointment page and the Scheduling page that you display in an appointment window; you store contact information in a five-page form (General, Details, Activities, Certificates, and All Fields) displayed in a contact window, and so on. The controls you use to interact with the form and its content are part of the item window.

The Outlook 2007 Standard Forms Library includes 11 forms: Appointment, Contact, Distribution List, Journal Entry, Meeting Request, Message, Note, Post, Standard Default, Task, and Task Request. Additional forms might be installed by other programs that interface with Outlook. To access the forms libraries, point to Forms on the Tools menu, and then click Choose Form.

You can create your own form from scratch, or modify an existing form to fit your needs. For example, if you frequently send detailed messages that follow a standard format, want to limit or increase the fields available within a contact record, or want to control the actions a recipient can take with an e-mail message, you can create a custom form containing the specific fields or information you want to have available when you create an item based on that form. Forms can have multiple pages, and can include a variety of information including static content, fields, scripts, and macros. You can specify form properties, including the icon that represents items based on the form; actions that item recipients can perform; and the prefix added to the item subject when they perform those actions.

You can save a custom form in your Personal Forms Library so that it is available to you from any Outlook folder. If your organization is running Microsoft Exchange Server, you can make a form available to anyone within your organization by publishing it to the Organizational Forms Library. Your network administrator can grant you permission to publish to this library.

See Also For a detailed explanation of Outlook forms, refer to *Microsoft Office Outlook 2007 Inside Out* (ISBN 0-7356-2328-7) by Jim Boyce (Microsoft Press, 2007).

Adding and Removing Toolbar Commands

You can personalize the commands shown on the Outlook program window menu bar and toolbars by adding, removing, or rearranging buttons.

To add a button to a toolbar:

1. Click the **Toolbar Options** button at the right end of any toolbar, point to **Add or Remove Buttons**, and then click **Customize**.

2. In the **Customize** dialog box, click the **Commands** tab. In the **Categories** list, click the category containing the command you want to add.

3. In the **Commands** list, locate the command you want to add. Then drag the command from the list to the position where you want it to appear on the toolbar.

To rearrange the commands on a toolbar:

1. Click the **Toolbar Options** button, point to **Add or Remove Buttons**, and then click **Customize**.

2. In the **Customize** dialog box, on the **Commands** tab, click **Rearrange Commands**.

3. In the **Rearrange Commands** dialog box, under **Choose a menu or toolbar to rearrange**, select the **Toolbar** option.

4. Click the **Toolbar** arrow, and then in the list, select the toolbar or menu bar you want to rearrange.

5. In the **Controls** list, click the command you want to reposition, click **Move Up** or **Move Down** as many times as necessary to position the command where you want it, and then click **Close**.

To remove a default button from a toolbar:

→ Click the **Toolbar Options** button at the right end of the toolbar, point to **Add or Remove Buttons**, point to the toolbar name, and then in the list, click the button you want to remove.

To remove a custom button from a toolbar:

1. Click the **Toolbar Options** button, point to **Add or Remove Buttons**, and then click **Customize**.

2. In the **Customize** dialog box, on the **Commands** tab, click **Rearrange Commands**.

3. In the **Rearrange Commands** dialog box, under **Choose a menu or toolbar to rearrange**, select the **Toolbar** option, and then in the list, click the toolbar containing the button you want to remove.

4. In the **Controls** list, click the button you want to remove. Click **Delete**, and then click **Close**.

To reset a toolbar to its default state:

1. Click the **Toolbar Options** button, point to **Add or Remove Buttons**, and then click **Customize**.

2. In the **Customize** dialog box, on the **Toolbars** tab, click the toolbar you want to restore to its default settings, and then click **Reset**.

Creating Rules to Process Messages

You can have Outlook evaluate your incoming or outgoing e-mail messages and make decisions about what to do with them based on instructions called *rules*. You can create rules based on senders, recipients, words, attachments, categories, or other message criteria, and have Outlook automatically move, copy, delete, forward, redirect, reply to, or otherwise process messages based on those criteria.

You can choose from a collection of standard rules or create your own from scratch. All the rules you specify are summarized in a list and are differentiated by icons that indicate what they do.

If you have a Microsoft Exchange Server account, you can set up *server rules* that are applied to messages as they are received or processed by your Exchange server. Whether or not you have an Exchange Server account, you can set up *client rules* that are applied to messages stored on your computer.

Tip You cannot use Outlook rules to filter messages sent to an HTTP e-mail account.

In this exercise, you will create a rule to process incoming messages that meet specific criteria.

USE the *SBS Practice Messages* folder and the messages you created in earlier exercises. If you did not create the folder or messages, you can complete the exercise by specifying your own criteria.

BE SURE TO start Outlook, connect to your mail server, and display the Inbox before beginning this exercise.

1. On the **Tools** menu, click **Rules and Alerts**.

> **Troubleshooting** The Rules And Alerts command does not appear on the Tools menu when you display it from a non-mail folder.

The Rules And Alerts window opens.

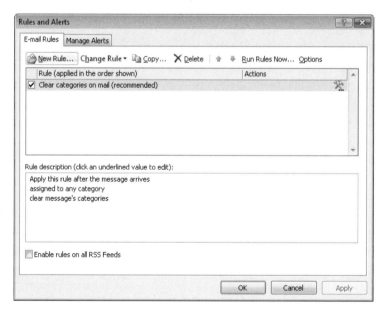

2. On the **E-mail Rules** tab, click **New Rule**.

The Rules wizard starts.

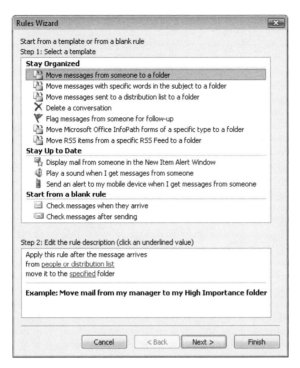

You can base a rule on one of the 10 rule templates provided by Outlook, or you can start from a blank rule. Take a moment to look over the available templates; clicking a template displays an example in the Edit The Rule Description box.

3. In the **Select a template** list, under **Start from a blank rule**, click **Check messages when they arrive**.

   Outlook updates the Edit The Rule Description box to reflect your choice.

4. In the **Rules** wizard, click **Next**.

5. Scroll the **Select condition(s)** list to see the conditions you can apply, and then select the **with specific word(s) in the subject** check box.

   Outlook updates the Edit The Rule Description box to include the selected criterion. You can specify as many criteria as you want.

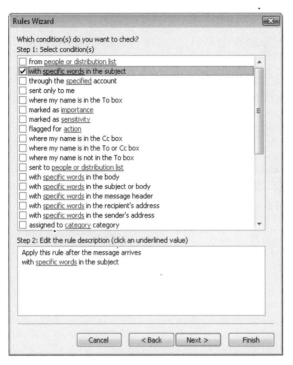

6. In the **Edit the rule description** box, click the underlined term **specific words**.

   The Search Text dialog box opens.

7. In the **Specify words or phrases to search for in the subject** box, type SBS, click **Add**, and click **OK**. Then in the **Rules** wizard, click **Next**.

8. Scroll the **Select action(s)** list to review the actions Outlook can perform on incoming items meeting the criteria you specify. Then select the **move a copy to the specified folder** check box, and in the **Edit the rule description box**, click the underlined word **specified**.

   The Rules And Alerts dialog box opens, displaying the folders in your mailbox.

9. Expand the **Inbox**, click the *SBS Practice Messages* folder, and then click **OK**.

> **Troubleshooting** If you didn't create the SBS Practice Messages folder in an earlier exercise, click Inbox in the Choose A Folder list, click New, type the folder name in the Create New Folder dialog box, and then click OK.

10. In the **Rules** wizard, click **Next**.

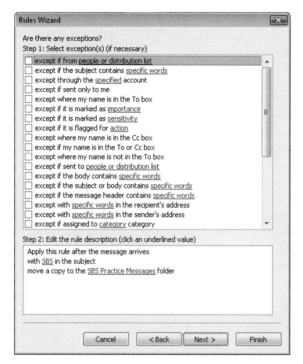

Conditions you specify on this page overrule the original selection criteria.

11. Without selecting an exception, click **Next**.

The final page of the Rules wizard summarizes the parameters of the SBS rule.

12. Select the **Run this rule now on messages already in "Inbox"** check box, and then click **Finish**.

Outlook saves the rule to the Rules And Alerts dialog box and runs it on the contents of your Inbox.

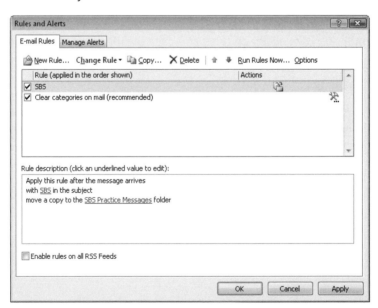

The selected check box to the left of the rule name indicates that this rule is active and Outlook will apply it to all incoming messages.

13. In the **Rules and Alerts** dialog box, click **OK**.

14. In the **All Mail Folders** list in the **Navigation Pane**, expand the **Inbox** if necessary, and then click the *SBS Practice Messages* folder.

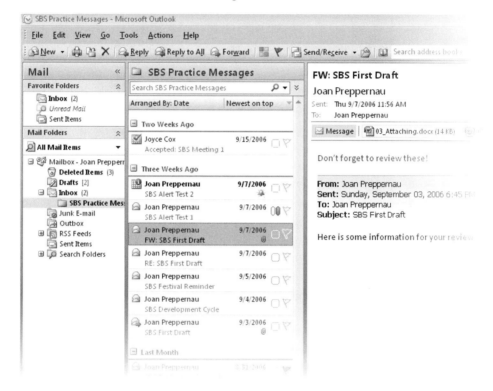

The folder contains copies of any practice messages you created in earlier chapters of this book.

Tip If you are using Exchange Server, you can create rules to filter messages differently when you are away from the office by using the *Out of Office Assistant*. To find out how, click Out Of Office Assistant on the Tools menu.

Storing E-Mail Messages on Your Computer

The items you create and receive in Outlook—including messages, appointments, contacts, tasks, notes, and journal entries—are kept in a *data file* in one of the following locations:

- **On a network server.** If your Outlook items are stored on a server, which is usually the case when you are working on a network that uses Exchange Server, they are stored in a data file called a *private store*. You can access this store only when you are connected to your server. This is the most common storage configuration.

- **On your computer.** If your Outlook items are stored on your computer, they are stored in a data file called a *Personal Folders file*, which has a *.pst* file extension.

> **Important** If your Outlook items are kept on your computer, take care to back up the *.pst* file on a regular basis, because that is the only copy of your data.

Whether your Outlook items are stored on a server or on your computer, you can create Personal Folders files at any time. If your items are server-based, you might want to keep specific items in a Personal Folders file so that they are available whether or not you are connected to the server—for example, if you work on a laptop that you use both in the office and at home—or you might choose to store personal or confidential information in a *.pst* file so that it is not available to other people on your network, or if you want or need to keep your server file small (many companies limit the amount of data employees can store on servers). If you already store your Outlook items in a Personal Folders file, you might want to keep items related to a particular project in a different Personal Folders file—for example, so that you can back up those items separately from your other Outlook items or so that you can copy the file containing those items to a different computer.

In this exercise, you will create a Personal Folders file, move messages and folders to it, and learn how to open and close data files from within Outlook.

> **USE** the *SBS Practice Messages* folder you created in an earlier exercise.

1. On the **File** menu, point to **New**, and then click **Outlook Data File**.

   The New Outlook Data File dialog box opens.

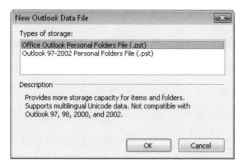

2. If you run Microsoft Outlook 2002 or an earlier version on a different computer and you might want to open this Personal Folders file in that version, click **Outlook 97-2002 Personal Folders File**, and then click **OK**. Otherwise, with **Office Outlook Personal Folders File** selected, click **OK**.

> **Troubleshooting** The Personal Folders file format used by Outlook 2003 and Outlook 2007 supports international *Unicode character sets* and large items. If you want to export a Personal Folders file to a computer that uses an older version of Outlook, you must export the file in the older Personal Folders file format. Both file formats have the same extension (*.pst*).

The Create Or Open Outlook Data File dialog box opens. The default Personal Folders file location is within your Outlook profile folder, but you can save the file anywhere you want.

3. In the **Favorite Links** list, click **Documents**.

4. In the **File name** box, type SBSFolder, and then click **OK**.

The Create Microsoft Personal Folders dialog box opens.

5. Replace the suggested name in the **Name** box with SBS Practice.

If you want, you can assign a password to the file to keep it secure. For the purposes of this exercise, you will not assign a password.

6. In the **Create Microsoft Personal Folders** dialog box, click **OK**.

   Outlook creates the new SBS Practice personal folder, which appears in the All Mail Items list in the Navigation Pane at the same level as your primary mailbox.

7. Click the plus sign to the left of the *SBS Practice* folder to expand it.

   By default, a newly created Personal Folders file contains only a Deleted Items folder and a Search Folders folder. You can create other folders within the Personal Folders file in the same way you would within your Inbox.

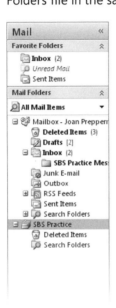

8. Hold down the right mouse button and drag the *SBS Practice Messages* folder from your Inbox to the *SBS Practice* personal folder. When you release the mouse button, click **Copy**.

   Outlook copies the selected folder and its contents into the personal folder.

9. Click the *SBS Practice Messages* folder that now appears in the *SBS Practice* folder. Verify that the contents are identical to the original folder.

10. Right-click the *SBS Practice* folder, and then click **Close "SBS Practice"**.

    The Personal Folders file no longer appears in the All Mail Items list.

11. On the **File** menu, point to **Open**, and then click **Outlook Data File**.

12. In the **Open Outlook Data File** dialog box, browse to your **Documents** folder, and then double-click the *SBSFolder* data file.

The SBS Practice folder re-opens in Outlook. In this way, you can access the contents of any data file from within Outlook.

 CLOSE the SBS Practice folder.

Securing Your E-Mail

As your e-mail messages travel from server to server en route to you or your recipients, they are vulnerable to interception by hackers and others who are intent on viewing them. With Outlook 2007, you can safeguard your messages in several ways, including implementing *digital signatures, encryption, plain text messages,* and *Information Rights Management (IRM).* Only you can decide which of these strategies is most appropriate for your individual situation.

Digital Signatures

When sending messages, you can reassure message recipients that they are receiving valid messages from you by using a digital signature—a piece of code that validates the identity of a message sender (not the actual person, but the e-mail account and computer from which the message originates).

To digitally sign all outgoing messages:

1. On the **Tools** menu, click **Trust Center**, and then in the page list, click **E-mail Security**.

2. On the **E-mail Security** page, select the **Add digital signature to outgoing messages** check box.

3. If all your message recipients don't have *Secure Multipurpose Internet Mail Extensions (S/MIME)* security (for instance, if you're sending messages to people who you know aren't using Outlook), select the **Send clear text signed message when sending signed messages** check box.

4. Click **OK**.

Obtaining a Digital ID

To send digitally signed or encrypted messages over the Internet, you must obtain a digital ID from an independent certification authority. The first time you try to digitally sign or encrypt a message without having a valid digital ID installed on your computer, Outlook prompts you to obtain one. If you prefer, you can obtain one before you need it.

> **Tip** If your organization is running Microsoft Exchange Server 2000 or earlier, you can obtain an Exchange Digital ID from the server itself. Your Exchange Server administrator can provide the information you need.

Obtaining some types of digital IDs, such as those used to certify the source of software programs, involves a stringent application process that can take weeks to complete. However, applying for a digital ID to certify documents and e-mail messages is a relatively simple process. You can have more than one digital ID on your computer, and you can select which one to use for each document or message. For example, you might have one ID for business use and one for personal use.

To obtain a digital ID to sign or encrypt documents and messages:

1. On the **Tools** menu, click **Trust Center**, and then in the page list, click **E-mail Security**.

2. On the **E-mail Security** page, click **Get a Digital ID**.

   The Microsoft Office Marketplace Web page opens in your default Web browser, listing a number of providers from whom you can obtain a digital ID to certify documents and e-mail messages.

> **Tip** If you want to evaluate certification authorities other than those recommended by Microsoft, search the Web for "digital ID" or "certification authority," and you'll find a number of options. You can apply for a digital ID from any certification authority through its Web site. Digital IDs from one non-Marketplace provider we tested have a known compatibility issue with Windows Internet Explorer, so if you use Internet Explorer and you want to be certain you won't run into problems, you might feel safer sticking with the recommended providers.

3. Click the link at the end of a provider's description to display the provider's Web site.

4. Follow the instructions on the Web site to register for a digital ID.

   Some certifying authorities charge a small fee, but most offer free digital IDs or a free trial period. As part of the process, you will likely be required to respond to an e-mail message from your computer.

Your digital ID will be installed on the computer on which you complete the application process; if you need to use it on another computer, you can re-install it from the provider's site, or you can export the digital ID files from the original computer and import them on the other computer.

To export or import a digital ID:

1. On the **Tools** menu, click **Trust Center**, and then in the page list, click **E-mail Security**.

2. On the **E-mail Security** page, click **Import/Export**.

3. In the **Import/Export Digital ID** dialog box, select whether you want to import or export your digital ID, fill in the information, and then click **OK**.

Many US and international certification companies offer digital IDs to certify e-mail. You will probably be most comfortable purchasing a certificate in your native currency. Regardless of where you obtain it, your digital ID is valid worldwide.

To digitally sign an individual e-mail message:

Digitally Sign
Message

→ On the **Message** tab, in the **Options** group, click the **Digitally Sign Message** button.

> **Troubleshooting** If you haven't previously used the Digital Signature feature in Outlook 2007, the Digitally Sign Message button might not be visible. In this case, click the Options Dialog Box Launcher, and then in the Message Options dialog box, click Security Settings. In the Security Settings dialog box, select the Add Digital Signature To This Message check box, and click OK. Then close the Message Options dialog box.

Digital
Signature

A message with a valid digital signature has a red ribbon on its message icon and a digital signature icon (also a red ribbon) in its message header. When you receive a digitally signed message, you can click the digital signature icon to view information about the signature.

Encryption

You can secure the contents of outgoing messages by using encryption. Encryption ensures that only the intended recipients can read the messages you send. The message recipient's e-mail program must have corresponding decryption capabilities in order to read the message.

To encrypt all outgoing messages:

1. On the **Tools** menu, click **Trust Center**, and then in the page list, click **E-mail Security**.

2. On the **E-mail Security** page, select the **Encrypt contents and attachments for outgoing messages** check box.

3. To receive verification that a message recipient received an encrypted message in its encrypted format, select the **Request S/MIME receipt for all S/MIME signed messages** check box.

4. Click **OK**.

To encrypt an individual message:

Encrypt Message
Contents and
Attachments

→ On the **Message** tab, in the **Options** group, click the **Encrypt Message Contents and Attachments** button.

> **Troubleshooting** If you haven't previously used the Encryption feature in Outlook 2007, the Encrypt Message Contents And Attachments button might not be visible. In this case, click the Options Dialog Box Launcher, and then in the Message Options dialog box, click Security Settings. In the Security Settings dialog box, select the Encrypt Message Contents And Attachments check box, and click OK. Then close the Message Options dialog box.

Encryption

An encrypted message has a blue lock on its message icon and an encryption icon (also a blue lock) in its message header. When you receive an encrypted message, you can click the encryption icon to view the layers of security in the message.

> **Tip** If you try to send an encrypted message from Outlook to a recipient whose setup doesn't support encryption, Outlook notifies you and gives you the option of sending the message in an unencrypted format.

Plain Text Messages

These days, viruses and other harmful programs can easily be spread from computer to computer in e-mail messages. To ensure that the e-mail messages you receive won't harm your computer, you might want to display them in plain text, rather than in Rich Text Format or HTML. Links, scripts, and other active content are disabled in plain text messages.

To receive all messages in plain text format:

1. On the **Tools** menu, click **Trust Center**, and then in the page list, click **E-mail Security**.

2. On the **E-mail Security** page, select the **Read all standard mail in plain text** check box, and then click **OK**.

Information Rights Management

If you don't want a message recipient to forward, copy, or print your message, you can send it with restricted *permissions*. You use IRM to set these permissions, which control who can read your messages and what they can do with them. If the restricted message includes an attachment, such as a Word document, an Excel workbook, or a PowerPoint presentation, the recipient can't edit, copy, or print the attachment (unless you have set individual permissions within the document).

To use IRM, you need access to an IRM server. If your organization has its own IRM server, your administrator can advise you how to set restricted permissions. If you don't have access to an IRM server when you first try to set permissions for a message, Outlook prompts you to sign up for a free trial on an IRM server provided by Microsoft. To take advantage of this free trial, you select the Yes option in the Service Sign-Up dialog box and then sign up for a Rights Management (RM) account certificate for your outgoing e-mail address (which must be registered as a Microsoft .NET Passport or Microsoft Windows Live ID). After finishing the process, you can restrict permissions for outgoing messages sent from the computer on which the certificate is installed.

See Also For more information about Passport and Windows Live credentials, refer to *Windows Vista Step by Step* (ISBN 0-7356-2269-8), by Joan Preppernau and Joyce Cox (Microsoft Press, 2007).

To prevent message recipients from forwarding, printing, or copying a message:

Permissions

→ On the **Message** tab, in the **Options** group, click the **Permissions** arrow, and then in the list, click **Do Not Forward**.

The message header in the outgoing and received messages indicates what recipients can and can't do with the message.

> Do Not Forward - Recipients can read this message, but cannot forward, print, or copy content. The conversation owner has full permission to their message and all replies.
> Permission granted by: joan@otsi.com(Passport)

To read a message sent with restricted permissions, recipients must have Outlook 2003 or later.

Protecting Your Privacy

E-mail is increasingly being used as a means of delivering marketing information to customers and potential customers. Many companies include pictures in their marketing messages to help explain their product or to make the message more attractive and noticeable, but these pictures can make e-mail messages large. To avoid this problem, some companies include links to pictures that are hosted on their server. When you preview or open the message, you can see the pictures, but they aren't actually part of the message.

Some junk mail senders are using this technology to include *Web beacons* in their messages. Web beacons are small programs that notify the sender when you read or preview the e-mail message. The notification confirms that your e-mail address is valid, and might result in more junk e-mail being sent to you.

To help protect your privacy, Outlook includes features that block external content such as pictures, sounds, and Web beacons. In addition to helping ensure your privacy, this blocking technique can save bandwidth resources, because you choose whether to download images and sounds, rather than downloading them automatically when you click on a message.

By default, Outlook 2007 blocks external content to and from all sources except those defined in the Safe Senders List and Safe Recipients List. When you open or preview a message that contains blocked content, an InfoBar in the message header provides options for handling the blocked content.

To view the blocked content in an individual e-mail message:

→ In the message header, click the **InfoBar**, and then click **Download Pictures**.

To change the way Outlook handles external content:

1. On the **Tools** menu, click **Trust Center**, and then in the page list, click **Automatic Download**.

2. Select the check boxes for the options you want, which include:

   ● Don't download pictures automatically in HTML e-mail messages or RSS items.

   ● Permit downloads in messages to and from contacts listed in the Safe Senders List or Safe Recipients List.

   ● Permit downloads from Web sites in the Trusted Zone.

   ● Permit downloads in RSS items.

   ● Permit downloads in SharePoint Discussion Boards.

   ● Warn before downloading content when editing, forwarding, or replying to e-mail messages.

3. Click **OK** to save your settings.

Under most circumstances, the security provided by the default settings far outweighs the slight inconvenience of manually downloading content you want to see or hear. You will probably find that many of the messages with blocked pictures are not of interest to you anyway, particularly those you receive through your work e-mail account.

Blocking Unwanted Messages

Outlook offers levels of protection for managing *junk e-mail* messages (also called *spam*)—the unsolicited advertisements, sometimes containing dangerous attachments, that can swamp your Inbox if your e-mail address finds its way into the hands of unscrupulous mailing list vendors. When enabled, the Junk E-Mail Filter either moves messages that appear to be junk e-mail to a special folder or deletes them. You can specify a list of e-mail addresses or domains whose messages should always be treated as junk; you can also specify a list that should never be treated as junk.

Outlook 2007 also offers protection from *phishing messages*—a dangerous and widespread identity theft scam. Phishing messages contain links to *phishing sites* purporting to represent trusted, known entities, such as banks or e-commerce sites that would likely have your personal information on file. The messages request that you "update" your personal information through the link provided. If you do so, you inadvertently provide the requested information (which might include your social security number, bank account number, passwords, and other confidential information) to scam artists, who then sell or otherwise use the information for their own financial gain. In the past, you were in danger only if you submitted your information through the phishing site, but these sites are becoming increasingly sophisticated, with many now hosting malicious keystroke-logging software. You can infect your computer just by visiting the site, which makes it vital that you protect yourself from these threats.

See Also Windows Internet Explorer 7 provides built-in protection against phishing sites. For more information, refer to *Windows Vista Step by Step* (ISBN 0-7356-2269-8), by Joan Preppernau and Joyce Cox (Microsoft Press, 2007).

In this exercise, you will review the spam filtering options provided by the Junk E-Mail Filter. There are no practice files for this exercise.

BE SURE TO display the Inbox before beginning this exercise.

1. On the **Actions** menu, point to **Junk E-mail**, and then click **Junk E-mail Options**.

   The Junk E-Mail Options dialog box opens.

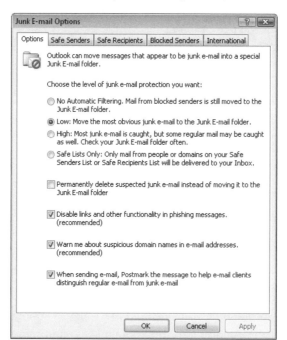

2. On the **Options** tab, select a level of protection.

   If you don't have additional filters in place, such as those that might be supplied by your organization, you might prefer to select the **High** option. Otherwise, select **Low**.

3. If you want Outlook to automatically delete suspected junk e-mail, select the **Permanently delete suspected Junk E-mail instead of moving it to the Junk E-mail folder** check box.

    Do not select this check box if you set the protection level to High or to Safe Lists Only. With these settings, it is likely that the Junk E-Mail Filter will catch quite a few valid messages that you don't want deleted.

    Note that the Disable Links And Other Functionality In Phishing Messages check box is selected by default. Unless you are very confident that you have another protective system in place, leave this option selected.

4. Click the **Safe Senders** tab.

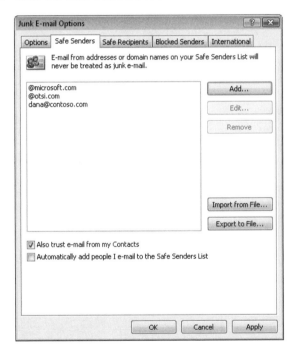

    You can add a specific person's e-mail address to the Safe Senders List (for instance, *tom@contoso.com*), or specify that e-mail received from any sender at a particular domain is safe by adding only the domain (for instance, *@contoso.com*—you don't need to specify a wildcard symbol). To ensure that messages from your legitimate contacts aren't held by the Junk E-Mail Filter, select the Also Trust E-mail From My Contacts and Automatically Add People I E-mail To The Safe Senders List check boxes.

5. Click the **Safe Recipients** tab.

    You can add addresses or domains to your Safe Recipients List to ensure that messages you send to them will never be treated as junk e-mail.

6. Click the **Blocked Senders** tab.

   You can manually add e-mail addresses and domain names to the Blocked Senders List, or Outlook will add them for you whenever you identify a received message as junk e-mail.

   > **Tip** To add the sender or recipient of a message to one of your Junk E-Mail lists, right-click the message in your Inbox or other mail folder, point to Junk E-Mail, and then click Add Sender To Blocked Senders List, Add Sender To Safe Senders List, Add Sender's Domain To Safe Senders List, or Add Recipient To Safe Recipients List.

7. Click the **International** tab.

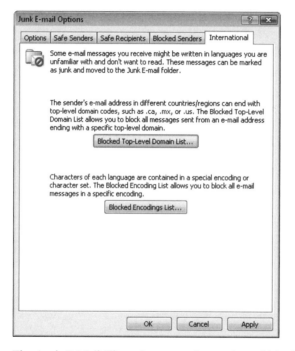

   The Junk E-Mail Filter gives you the option of blocking all messages from a country-specific, top-level domain (click Blocked Top-Level Domain List to see them all), or all messages containing specific non-English text encoding (click Blocked Encodings List to see them all).

8. If you want to keep any changes you've made to the Junk E-Mail Filter options, click **OK**; otherwise, click **Cancel** to close the **Junk E-mail Options** dialog box without saving your changes.

Specifying Advanced E-Mail Options

Outlook includes a selection of advanced options so that you can manage your e-mail most effectively. To avoid losing your work, you can choose to have Outlook automatically save messages you have created but not yet sent. When new messages arrive, you can choose to have Outlook alert you by playing a sound, briefly changing the mouse pointer to an envelope icon, showing an envelope icon in the notification area, or any combination of these effects. You can also set default options for sending a message. For example, if you are concerned about privacy, you might choose to set the sensitivity of all new messages to Private.

In this exercise, you will review the types of settings you can control, save message drafts more frequently, specify how Outlook saves messages, what happens when new messages arrive, and which options are used when sending messages. There are no practice files for this exercise.

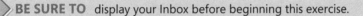

BE SURE TO display your Inbox before beginning this exercise.

1. On the **Tools** menu, click **Options**.

    The Options dialog box opens.

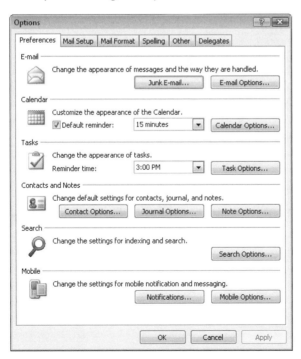

From this dialog box, you can control the settings and appearance of many Outlook features, including the following:

- E-mail accounts, functionality, and formatting
- Editorial and archive functions
- The Outlook Panes (Navigation Pane, Reading Pane, and the To-Do Bar)
- Your calendar, tasks list, contact list, and notes
- The Journal
- The indexing and search functions
- The new telephone and voice mail functions

2. On the **Preferences** tab, click **E-mail Options**, and then in the **E-mail Options** dialog box, click **Advanced E-mail Options**.

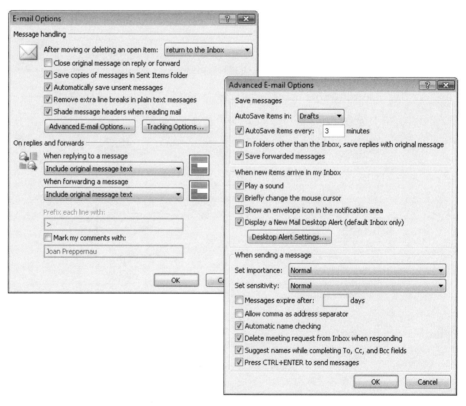

3. In the **Save messages** area, with the **AutoSave items every** check box selected, replace the number in the **minutes** box with 1.

Every minute, Outlook will save any message that you are composing but have not yet sent in your Drafts folder. In the event of a computer crash—for example, if you experience a power failure, or your toddler turns off your computer—you won't lose more than one minute's worth of work.

4. In the **When new items arrive in my Inbox** area, clear the **Briefly change the mouse cursor** check box.

Outlook will alert you to the arrival of new messages by sounding a chime and displaying a desktop alert. If you haven't activated a message since the most recent message was received, an envelope icon appears in the notification area at the right end of the Windows taskbar.

See Also For more information about desktop alerts, see "Working with New Mail Notifications" in Chapter 4, "Handling E-Mail Messages."

5. In the **When sending a message** area, click the **Set importance** arrow, and then in the list, click **High**.

You'll see the effect of this setting later in this exercise.

6. Select the **Allow comma as address separator** check box.

Enabling this option allows Outlook to recognize commas as well as semicolons as separators between names or addresses in the To, Cc, or Bcc boxes. This very convenient option should (in this author's opinion) be set by default! For some reason, this has not been the case in any version of Outlook to date.

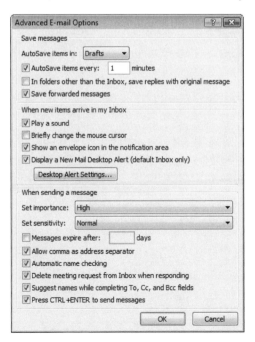

7. Take note of the other available options (and make any changes you want). Then click **OK** in each of the open dialog boxes to close them and save your changes.

New Mail Message

8. On the Standard toolbar, click the **New Mail Message** button.

A new message window opens. On the Message tab, in the Options group, the High Importance button is active, indicating that the message will be flagged as high priority. This probably isn't a setting you want to keep, but it's a good visible indication of the changes you made to the e-mail options.

High importance

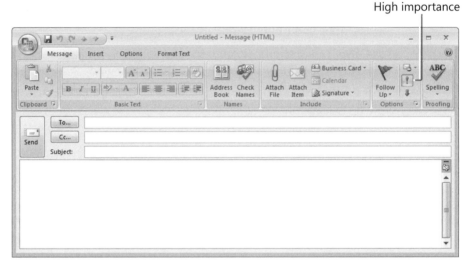

9. Close the message window. If prompted to save it, click **No**.

10. On the **Tools** menu, click **Options**. Click **E-mail Options**, and then click **Advanced E-mail Options**.

11. In the **Advanced E-mail Options** dialog box, in the **Set importance** list, click **Normal**.

By default, new messages will now be normal priority. You can set an individual message to high or low priority by clicking the High Importance or Low Importance button in the Options group on the Message tab of the message window.

12. Select or clear any other options you want, and then click **OK** in each of the open dialog boxes to close them and save your changes.

Key Points

- Need one-click access to commands that are scattered in different places? Simply add a button for that command to the Quick Access Toolbar.

- You can adjust many aspects of the Outlook environment to tailor it to the way you work.

- It's worth taking the time to set up a few rules so that Outlook can evaluate and process messages depending on the sender, subject, contents, time, or almost any other criteria you care to set. You can create a different set of rules to be applied when you are out of the office.

- You can store e-mail messages and other Outlook items on your organization's server or locally, on your own computer.

- You can digitally sign your messages so that recipients will know the messages haven't been tampered with; encrypt them so that only intended recipients can read them; and set restricted permissions so that recipients can't forward, print, or copy them. You can also display messages in plain text to disable any active content.

- Built-in filters block annoying or hazardous messages that conform to spam patterns or that contain active content. You determine the level of protection, and specify trusted (and untrusted) message senders.

- Advanced e-mail option settings give you control over the way Outlook handles the messages you write. If you frequently send messages with the same settings, you can save time by setting the defaults to your liking.

Glossary

appointment A block of time you schedule on your calendar that has a defined start time and end time, and to which you do not invite other attendees.

appointment window The program window displaying the form in which you enter information about an appointment.

archiving Moving older or unused items to a secondary location for the purpose of backing up or long-term storage.

arrangement The order in which Microsoft Office Outlook displays messages or other items.

AutoArchive An Outlook feature that automatically archives items meeting specific age and location criteria at regular intervals.

blog A personal journal posted online to share information, thoughts, and opinions with the general public.

Cached Exchange Mode A feature of Outlook that creates local copies of your mailbox and address book on your computer and keeps them synchronized. Cached Exchange Mode monitors your connection status and speed and optimizes data transfer accordingly.

calendar item windows Collectively refers to the program windows displaying the forms in which you enter information about appointments, meetings, and events.

category A group to which you can assign Outlook items for the purpose of sorting or filtering related items together.

client rule Or *client-side rule*. Rules that Outlook applies to messages after they arrive on your computer (as opposed to server rules).

color category An Outlook feature in which category names are linked to color icons to provide a quick visual representation of information.

contact A person whose contact information you record in your address book.

contact record A body of information you collect about a contact and store as an Outlook item.

contact window The program window displaying the form in which you enter information about a contact to create a contact record.

contacts folder Or *address book*. A storage folder within your mailbox, containing contact records and distribution lists.

Contacts module The framework providing the functionality to display and manage address books.

data file A file consisting of data in the form of text, numbers, or graphics, from a program file of commands and instructions.

Date Navigator The small calendar that appears next to the appointment area in the Outlook Calendar. The Date Navigator provides a quick and easy way to change and view dates.

delegate A person given permission to read, reply to, and delete your messages in one or more folders.

desktop alert A notification that appears on your desktop when a new e-mail message, meeting request, or task request appears in your Inbox.

dial-up networking A component of Windows with which you can connect your computer to a network server through a modem using a phone line.

Dialog Box Launcher A button found in the lower-right corner of a group of commands on the Ribbon when an associated dialog box or task pane is available. Clicking the Dialog Box Launcher opens the dialog box or task pane.

digital signature A security mechanism used on the Internet that relies on two keys, one public and one private, which are used to encrypt messages before transmission and to decrypt them on receipt.

document workspace A temporary space, usually on a Microsoft SharePoint site, dedicated to a single document. It provides a forum where everyone can work from a single location.

draft A temporary copy of a message that has not yet been sent, located in the Drafts folder.

e-mail Short for *electronic mail*; messages sent between defined entities over the Internet.

e-mail server A network computer running Microsoft Exchange Server or another mail server program, responsible for the routing and storage of e-mail messages and other information.

e-mail signature A block of text that is appended to the end of a message you send.

e-mail trail An e-mail message and all responses to that message. When an individual message receives multiple responses, the e-mail trail can branch into multiple trails. You can view all the branches of an e-mail trail in Conversation view.

encryption The process of converting content based on code stored in a private key for the purpose of preventing unauthorized access. After validating his or her identity, the intended recipient can decrypt the content by using a public key.

event A block of time you schedule on your calendar that does not have a defined start time and end time.

event window The program window displaying the form in which you enter information about an event.

floating toolbar A toolbar that is not docked on any side of the program window. You can move a floating toolbar to any location on your screen, within or outside of the program window.

form The framework within which you enter information into an Outlook item. Standard forms include those for contacts, messages, and appointments. You can design custom forms of one or more pages, containing the specific fields, buttons, and commands you want.

forum A meeting place for public discussion, often moderated.

Global Address List (GAL) A central address book created and maintained through Exchange Server, containing information about people and managed resources within the organization. The Exchange administrator creates and maintains this address book.

global formatting A theme or style applied to an entire document.

group In an Outlook 2007 item window, a set of buttons on the Ribbon representing commands related to a common task or feature.

group schedule A view of the free/busy information for multiple people and resources within a domain.

HTML See *Hypertext Markup Language (HTML)*.

HTTP See *Hypertext Transfer Protocol (HTTP)*.

Hypertext Markup Language (HTML) In Outlook, an e-mail message format that supports paragraph styles, character styles, and backgrounds. Most e-mail programs support the HTML format.

Hypertext Transfer Protocol (HTTP) A protocol used to access Web pages from the Internet.

IMAP See *Internet Message Access Protocol.*

importance The property defining the urgency of a message or other Outlook item. The default setting is Normal; you can optionally change the setting for an individual item or for all items to High or Low.

Information Rights Management (IRM) A functionality that helps users have greater control over who can open, copy, print, or forward information created in many Microsoft Office products. Users must validate their identity against a server-based system.

Internet Message Access Protocol (IMAP) An e-mail–handling protocol that organizes messages on the server, and you choose messages to download by viewing their headers.

Journal An Outlook module containing journal entries of activities that you choose to have Outlook track.

junk e-mail Unsolicited advertisements, sometimes containing dangerous attachments.

keyboard shortcut A key or combination of keys that when pressed perform an action within an application that would normally require several user actions, such as menu selections.

local formatting Formatting applied at the text or paragraph level.

meeting request A message generated by Outlook to invite people to attend a meeting.

meeting window The program window displaying the form in which you enter information to place a meeting on your calendar.

meeting workspace A shared site for planning a meeting and tracking related tasks and results.

message header Basic information identifying an e-mail message, such as the date, time, sender, subject, and size. When working on a slow connection, you can download message headers and, based on the header information, decide whether to download the entire message.

message window The program window displaying the form in which you create or respond to an e-mail message.

Microsoft Exchange Server The messaging and collaboration server system from Microsoft.

Microsoft Office Button A button that displays a menu listing commands related to managing Outlook settings and items (rather than managing the content of those items).

Mini toolbar A toolbar of formatting commands that appears when you select text.

Mobile Address Book An address book containing contact records that include mobile phone numbers, which is automatically created if you have an Outlook Mobile Service account.

module Areas of Outlook in which you can work with specific functions, such as the Calendar module, the Contacts module, and the Mail module. Modules are represented as folders in the Navigation Pane.

newsgroup A topic-specific online discussion forum consisting of messages and replies posted by newsgroup users.

newsreader A program or Web-based interface to a newsgroup.

notes Unstructured information you store in the Outlook Notes module. You can categorize and organize notes as you can other Outlook items.

Office menu The menu displayed when you click the Microsoft Office Button. The Office menu includes commands for working with Outlook and with Outlook items, rather than with the item content.

offline address book A local copy of an address book, usually a Global Address List, stored on your computer.

Out of Office Assistant An Outlook feature through which you can automatically reply to messages from specified groups of senders while you are away from your desk. Available functions vary based on the version of Exchange.

Outlook Address Books System-level address books created by Outlook.

Outlook Anywhere A way to connect from Outlook to Exchange Server over the Internet. Formerly referred to as *RPC over HTTP*.

Outlook Rich Text Format (RTF) An e-mail message format that supports paragraph styles, character styles, backgrounds, borders, and shading, but is compatible with only Outlook and Exchange Server. Outlook converts RTF messages to HTML when sending them outside of your Exchange network.

permissions Restrictions set on user accounts, networks, or information that control what other users can do.

Personal Folders file A data file stored locally on your computer. You can open one or more data files within Outlook in addition to your usual mailbox; each appears in the Navigation Pane as a root-level folder.

phishing message E-mails falsely claiming to be from a legitimate enterprise in an attempt to scam the recipient into surrendering private information that will be used for identity theft.

phishing site Web sites where users are asked to update personal information, such as bank accounts and passwords, which will be used for identity theft.

Plain Text An e-mail message format that does not support character or paragraph formatting. All e-mail programs support Plain Text.

plain text message See *Plain Text*.

Post Office Protocol 3 (POP3) A common protocol used to retrieve e-mail messages from an Internet e-mail server.

print style The options governing the look of a document when printed. Outlook includes several item-specific print styles, and you can create custom print styles to save frequently used print settings.

private store A database for storing public folders in an Exchange server.

Quick Access Toolbar A customizable toolbar that appears in Outlook item windows. The default toolbar displays the Save, Undo, Repeat, and Print buttons, but you can customize it to include any command, even a legacy command not available from the Ribbon.

Quick Styles Formatting options that you can apply to individual elements of a message.

Really Simple Syndication (RSS) A subscription news feed that you can receive news from without visiting the site.

recall Instructing Outlook to delete or replace any unread copies of a message already sent.

recurring Repeating on a regular basis. You can specify an appointment, meeting, or event as recurring, and specify the frequency of recurrence. Outlook then creates a series of items based on your specifications.

reminder An optional message displayed by Outlook a specific amount of time prior to an appointment, meeting, event, or task milestone. You can dismiss the reminder, reset it for a later time, or open the item from the reminder window.

remote procedure calls (RPC) The method by which Outlook communicates with your organization's Exchange server.

resend Creating a new version of an original message with none of the extra information that might be attached to a forwarded message.

resolving The process of matching a user name to the information on a network server, resulting in the user name being replaced by a display name and the name underlined.

Ribbon An area at the top of an individual item window from which you can access commands pertaining to that item and to Outlook as a whole. The Ribbon includes the Microsoft Office button, the Quick Access Toolbar, and the Microsoft Office Outlook Help button, as well as multiple function-specific tabs organized into action-specific groups of buttons.

Rich Text Format (RTF) See *Outlook Rich Text Format (RTF)*.

RPC See *Remote Procedure Call (RPC)*.

RSS See *Really Simple Syndication (RSS)*.

rules A set of conditions, actions, and exceptions that process and organize messages.

sans serif A style of typeface with no ornamentation on the upper or lower end of the character.

ScreenTip A small text box that appears when you point to an icon, button, or other user interface element. A ScreenTip might display information such as the item's name or a description of its function.

Secure Multipurpose Internet Mail Extensions (S/MIME) A standard specification for authenticating and encrypting e-mail.

sensitivity An optional setting that indicates, by icons or words, that an item is Personal, Private, or Confidential.

server rule Or *server-side rule*. A rule that Exchange applies when receiving or processing a message, before delivering it.

shared attachments Attachments saved on a SharePoint document workspace Web site, where a group can collaborate to work on files and discuss a project.

signature See *e-mail signature*.

SmartArt A technology first introduced by Microsoft with the 2007 Office system, with which you can easily create professional business graphics within documents, spreadsheets, presentations, and messages.

S/MIME See *Secure Multipurpose Internet Mail Extensions (S/MIME)*.

spam Electronic junk mail. Unsolicited messages, usually containing advertising but often containing malicious content masquerading as advertising.

synchronizing Copying changed items between a mailbox or address book on a server and its corresponding offline folder so that both are up to date.

tabs An area below the title bar of the program window that displays buttons related to working with presentation content.

task list A representation of the items stored in the Outlook Tasks module, available from the Tasks module, the To-Do Bar, and Outlook Today.

task originator The person who creates a task, specifically when assigning the task to someone else.

task owner The person to whom a task is currently assigned. After a task has been assigned, the task originator can no longer update the information in the task window.

task window The program window displaying the form in which you enter information to create or manage a task.

third-party add-ins A software program that extends the capabilities of a larger program created by another company.

threaded A series of messages that have been sent as replies to each other.

title bar The area at the top of a program window or item window containing the name of the file or application. You can often move a window by dragging the title bar.

To-Do List The built-in task list of Outlook where you can add tasks, assign due dates, receive reminders, and mark tasks as complete.

Unicode character sets An industry standard designed to allow text and symbols from all of the writing systems of the world to be consistently represented and manipulated by computers.

URL Represents the address of Web pages and other resources available on the Internet.

views Different ways in which the Outlook window can be arranged for viewing messages.

virtual folder Folder that looks like and links to an original folder.

voting buttons Used in conjunction with an Exchange Server account, this feature enables recipients to respond to a poll by clicking a button corresponding to a specific response option. Responses return to the sender in a format that allows easy collating and tabulation.

Web beacons A link to a graphic image, placed on a Web site or in an e-mail message, that is used to monitor the behavior of the user visiting the site or sending the e-mail.

work week The days and times you define within Outlook as available for work-related activities.

Index

A

accepting meeting requests
  automatically, 195
  tentatively, 192
account profiles
  adding, 15
  adding e-mail accounts to, 9–10
  choosing, when prompted, 16
  creating, xxxviii
  displaying current, 14
  multiple, 12
  naming, 15
  prompting for on startup, xxxviii, 16
  renaming, 15
  setting as default, 12, 17
  storage location of, 12
  switching between, 14
Account Settings dialog box, 248
accounts, e-mail
  adding to profiles, 9–10
  connecting, xxxvii
  different signatures for, 109
  grouping messages by, 150
  Outlook support for different types, 2
  switching between, 10
Active Appointments view, 198
Activities button, 255
Actual Size button, 209
Add Card Picture dialog box, 51
Add Holidays To Calendar dialog box, 203
Add New button, 48
Add New Category dialog box, 163
Add New E-mail Account wizard, xxxvii, 10, 15
Add New Member dialog box, 48
Add Shape button, 94
address books
  creating, 52
  exporting, xl, 56
  offline, 286, 336
  searching, xlii
  sharing, xl, 53
address cards, xli
Address Cards view, 57

address lists
  contacts in (see contacts)
  for Exchange Server, 37, 334
  global, 37, 334
  viewing, 38
addresses, e-mail
  commas, separating with, 329
  validating, xli, 9, 82
addressing messages
  checking addresses before, 82
  commas as separators when, 81
  from contact records, 44
  to contacts, 38
  as courtesy copies, 82
  to internal addresses, 81
  to multiple people, 81
Adobe Acrobat, e-mail message problems and, 83
advanced e-mail options, 327
Advanced toolbar
  in Calendar module, 26
  in Contacts module, 26
  displaying, 25
  in Mail module, 25
alerts. See also reminders
  for appointments, 182, 184
  customizing, xliii
  defined, 333
  deleting messages with, xliv, 130
  for e-mail messages, 126
  location, customizing, xliii
  managing, 26
  marking messages as read with, xliv, 130
  moving, 129
  setting length of time visible for, 129
  transparency, setting, 129
  turning off, xliv, 128
All Appointments view, 198
All Attendees list, 191
alphabets, 58
animation, 304
Annual Events view, 198
Appointment Recurrence dialog box, 185, 187
Appointment tab, 179

appointment window
  defined, 176, 333
  opening, 177, 184
  Ribbon in, 178
  switching to event window, 180
  switching to meeting window, 181
appointments. See also events
  adding, 184
  adding directly to calendar, 183
  calendars, viewing grouped by, 198
  changing number shown in To-Do Bar, 22
  creating, xlv, 134, 177
  creating, from e-mail messages,
  defined, 182, 333
  hiding, 184
  moving, xlix, 183
  opening, 184
  Out of Office, showing time as, 184
  Private, marking as, 184
  recurring, 182, 185, 188
  reminders for, 182, 184
  scheduling, xlviii
  showing availability during, 182
  time, changing, 184
  time zone, setting, 180–81
Archive dialog box, 172
archiving, 333
archiving messages, 169
  automatically (see AutoArchive)
  cancelling while in progress, 172
  folder options, xlviii, 172
  manually, xlviii
arrangement, 333
arranging e-mail messages, 148, 151
art in e-mail messages. See SmartArt
Assign Task button, 238
Assigned Task icon, 238
assigning tasks, liii. See also task requests
  from contact records, 26, 44
  following progress after, 238
  outside organization, 238
  status reports on, 238
  with reminders set, 239
Attach File button, 89, 269
attaching files to messages. See attachments
Attachment Options task pane, 270
attachments, 90
  attaching, xlii
  encrypting, 320 (see also digital IDs)
  grouping messages by, 149
  notes, forwarding as, 257
  opening, xliv, 117, 120

  previewing, xliv
  previewing in Reading Pane, 117, 119
  when replying to messages, 124
  restricting permissions for, 321
  saving to hard disk, 117
  searching, 144
  shared (see shared attachments)
  switching between messages and, 120
  viewing details about, 119
attendees. See events; meetings
Author role for delegating, 263
auto-reply messages. See also Out Of Office
    Assistant
  configuring, lix, 290
  creating, lix, 289
  restricting recipients, lx, 294
  scheduling, lx, 293
  turning off, 291
AutoArchive, 169
  declining, 171
  defined, 333
  options, 172
  settings, xlviii, 171
AutoArchive dialog box, 170
AutoCorrect options, 302
automatic search filtering, xlvi, 62, 144. See also
    searching
  contacts, finding with, xl
  implementing, 145
automatic setup
  defined, 3
  troubleshooting, 7
AutoPick Next button, 192
AutoPreview, 26, 116–17, 153
AutoSave, 329
availability, sharing, 213

B

Background Color button, 51
background color of messages, 104
backing up Personal Folder files, 314
Bcc field, xlii
BE SURE TO paragraphs, xxiv
birthdays, entering in contact records, 42
blind carbon copies, xlii
blocked content, viewing, lxiii, 322
Blocked Senders List, 326
blocking
  e-mail, 326
  external content, 322

blogs, 246, 333. See also RSS feeds
bulleted lists
    changing level in, 85
    creating, 84
    promoting/demoting list items in, 85
Bullets button, 84
Bullets gallery, 85
Business Card button, 51
business cards, 49
    background color, applying, 51
    e-mailing, xlii, 91
    editing, 51, 52
    graphics, adding, 51
    sending to other people, 50
    as signatures, 109
Business Contact Manager, 13
Business Tools tab, 35
buttons, toolbar, 298. See also specific button
        names; tabs
    adding, 299, 306
    arrows on, 32
    margin icons for, xxiv
    moving, 300, 306
    removing, 301, 306
By Category view, 199

C

Cached Exchange mode
    defined, 283, 333
    download options, 284
calendar bar. See To-Do Bar
Calendar button, 134, 200
calendar item windows
    defined, 176, 333
    tabs, 179–181
Calendar Options button, 206
Calendar Options dialog box, 195, 203, 205–06
calendars
    Active Appointments view, 198
    All Appointments view, 198
    Annual Events view, 198
    available time, 201, 204–205
    By Category view, 199
    copying items between, 219
    Day view, 199Day/Week/Month view, 198
    default display, 200–201
    delegating control of, liii, 220
    displaying multiple, 219
    e-mail messages, creating items from, 131, 134
    e-mailing (see sharing calendars)

Events view, 198
    holidays, l, 203
    Internet, 216
    items, creating from e-mail messages, 131, 134
    items, moving between calendars, 219
    level of detail, setting, 202
    Month view, 201
    multiple, 218–19
    navigating, 199, 202
    OneNote, linking to, lii, 216
    Outlook Data Files view, 199
    permissions, granting to other users, liii, 220
    printing, li (see printing calendars)
    publishing on the Web, 212
    Recurring Appointments view, 198
    resetting, 201
    saving as Web pages, lii, 212
    SharePoint, 274
    sharing, li, 212–14
    Side-By-Side mode, 219
    switching to other calendar from, 216
    time periods, switching between, 198
    views, 198–99
    week numbers, displaying, 199
    work week, 201, 204–205
    Work Week view, 198
canceling messages, xlii, 88
categories, 44, 161
    adding, 163
    applying, 161
    calendars, viewing grouped by, 199
    colors, changing, xlvii, 163
    contacts, assigning to, xxxix, 45
    creating, xlvii
    default, setting, 161
    defined, 333
    displaying current, 162
    displaying default, xlvii
    e-mail messages, assigning to, 99
    grouping contacts by, 60
    grouping messages by, 149, 161, 164
    for holidays, adding, 203
    as Quick Click categories, 161
    renaming, xlvii, 162
    shortcut keys, assigning to, 163
    sorting Inbox by, xlvii
    standard, 44
    for tasks, changing, 235
    viewing messages in, 161
Categorize button, 45, 161–62
Categorized Mail folder, 160
Category bar, 161

category views, 148
CCing messages, xlii, 82
CD, companion to book
   how to use, xxiii
   practice files on, xxv
   resources available on, xxvi
CD icon, xxiv
Certificate Import Wizard, 7
certificates, 7
certification authorities, 318. See also
   digital IDs
Change Colors button, 96
Change E-Mail Account dialog box, 279
changes, tracking, 304
chapter thumb tabs, xxiii
character positioning options, 304
Check Address dialog box, 41
checking e-mail addresses, xli, 9, 82
checking spelling as you type, 302
Choose A SmartArt Graphic dialog box, 92
Choose Profile dialog box, 16
Clear Search button, 64, 148
clearing searches, 64, 148
client rules, 307, 333
Clipboard task pane, 36
Close button, 31, 253
CLOSE paragraphs, xxiv
closing
   data files, lxiii
   e-mail messages, after replying, xlv, 123
   menus, 35
   notes, 253
   Reading Pane, 23
   To-Do Bar, 22
collaboration sites
   calendars, 274
   connecting to Outlook from, lvii, 272
Collapse button, 61, 155
collapsing
   e-mail messages, 61
   groups, xlvi, 155
   menus, 178
color
   background, 51, 104
   business cards, applying to, 51
   font, 103
   of notes, changing, 252
   in tasks, changing, 232
color categories
   adding, 163
   applying, 161
   calendars, viewing grouped by, 199

colors, changing, xlvii, 163
contacts, assigning to, xxxix, 45
creating, xlvii
default, setting, 161
defined, 333
dialog box, 46, 162
displaying current, 162
displaying default, xlvii
e-mail messages, assigning to, 99
grouping by, 60, 149, 161, 164
for holidays, adding, 203
as Quick Click categories, 161
renaming, xlvii, 162
shortcut keys, assigning to, 163
sorting Inbox by, xlvii
standard, 44
for tasks, changing, 235
viewing messages in, 161
color-coding message headers, 161
Colors gallery, 96
columns
   deleting from Inbox, 158
   reordering, xlvi, 157
commands, 298
   displaying list of, 300
   new organization of, xii
   on Quick Access Toolbar (see Quick Access
     Toolbar)
commas as separators when addressing
   messages, 81, 329
companion CD
   how to use, xxiii
   practice files on, xxv
   resources available on, xxvi
conference rooms, requesting, 190. See also
   meetings
Confidential, marking messages as, 98
Configure Buttons button, 256
configuring
   Exchange Server, as IMAP account, 7
   server settings, manually, 5, 8
Connect dialog box, 282
Connect To A Network dialog box, 281
connecting Outlook over HTTP, lvii, 279
connection speed minimum for Office 2007,
   xxvii
contact records
   as address cards, 57
   addressing messages from, 44
   assigning tasks from, 44
   Business Card area (see electronic business
     cards)

as business cards (see electronic business cards)
color categories, xxxix, 45, 60
creating, xxxviii, 33
defined, 333
Display As box, 40
displaying, 33, 56, 255
File As field, 40
grouping by color category, 60
items linked to, displaying, 255
maps of contact addresses, displaying, 44
meeting requests, creating from, 44
navigating, 57
notes, adding to, lv, 254
OneNote, linking to, xli, 71
as phone list, 57
placing Internet calls from, 44
printing selected, 67, 70
sorting, xl, 59
views, xl, 57
Web sites, displaying from, 44
Contact tab, 35
contact window
defined, 333
Quick Access Toolbar in, adding items to, 31
tabs in, 35
contacts
additional details, displaying, 42
addressing Outlook items to, 26, 38
birthdays, entering, 42
default mailing address, displaying, 41
defined, 333
distribution lists of, 46, 48
e-mail addresses, entering, 40
e-mailing, 91
editing, xxxviii–xxxix
folders (see contacts folders)
information stored for, 39
Journal, recording activities in, 256
names, entering, 40
opening records for, 42
phone numbers, entering, 40
searching, xl, 63
street addresses, 40–41
Web page associated with, viewing, 26
window for entering information about, 31, 35
Contacts button, 33
contacts folders
creating, xxxix, 53
defined, 38, 333
sharing, 53
storage location, selecting, 54

Contacts For Note dialog box, 254
Contacts list, 47
Contacts module, defined
Contacts pane, 33, 255
context toolbar, 102, 302
Contextual tabs, 86
Control Panel, 14
conversations, 149
converting text to bulleted list, 84
copying
calendar items, between calendars, 219
e-mail messages, preventing, 99
formatting, 103
text, 304
courtesy copies, xlii, 82
Create Microsoft Personal Folders dialog box, 315
Create New Folder dialog box, 53, 166, 231, 311
Create Or Open Outlook Data File dialog box, 315
Custom dialog box, 242
Custom View Organizer dialog box, 159
Customize dialog box, 306
Customize Quick Access Toolbar button, 76
Customize View dialog box, 156, 201
customizing
forms, 305
Outlook, lxi, 301
Quick Access Toolbar, 76, 299
Search Folders, xlvii, 160
To-Do Bar, 22
cutting and pasting, 304

D

Daily Style for printed calendars, 207
Daily Task List, 230
dashboard, Business Contact Manager, 13
data files
closing, lxiii
creating, 314
defined, 333
on network server, 314
opening, lxiii, 316
on personal computer (see Personal Folders files)
date, grouping messages by, 149
date bar. See To-Do Bar

Date Navigator
   appointments, adding in, 183
   customizing number of months displayed in, 22
   default display of, 183
   defined, 333
   displaying different date in, 183
   months shown in, increasing, 199
Day view, 199
Day/Week/Month view, 198
deadlines. See due dates
declined tasks, reclaiming, 239
declining meeting requests, 192, 195
Delegate Permissions dialog box, 221
delegates
   defined, 333
   roles for, 263
delegating
   calendar control, liii, 220
   folders, 263
   subfolder permission, 263
   tasks (see assigning tasks)
Delete Item button, 130
Deleted Items folder, 125
deleting
   e-mail messages, 125
   e-mail messages, with desktop alerts, xliv, 130
   holidays, 203
   Inbox columns, 158
   Internet calendars, 216
   junk e-mail, automatically, 325
   permanently, 125
   RSS feeds, 248
   signatures, 110
   task reminders, 240
   tasks, liv, 240, 242
delivery receipts, 99
demoting bulleted list items, 85
Desktop Alert Settings dialog box, xliv, 128–29
desktop alerts. See also reminders
   for appointments, 182, 184
   customizing, xliii
   defined, 333
   deleting messages with, xliv, 130
   for e-mail messages, 126
   managing, 26
   marking messages as read with, xliv, 130
   moving, xliii, 129
   setting length of time visible for, 129
   transparency, setting, 129
   turning off, xliv, 128
Desktop Search Engine. See Instant Search
Detailed Address Cards view, 57

Details button, 42, 236
Developer tab on Ribbon, 302
diagrams in e-mail messages. See SmartArt
dial-up networking, 334
Dialog Box Launcher, 32, 36, 99, 334
dialog boxes
   Account Settings, 12, 248
   Add Card Picture, 51
   Add Holidays To Calendar, 203
   Add New Category, 163
   Add New Member, 48
   Appointment Recurrence, 185, 187
   Archive, 172
   AutoArchive, 170
   Calendar Options, 195, 203, 205–206
   Change E-Mail Account, 279
   Check Address, 41
   Choose A SmartArt Graphic, 92
   Choose Profile, 16
   Color Categories, 46, 162
   Connect, 282
   Connect To A Network, 281
   Contacts For Note, 254
   Create Microsoft Personal Folders, 315
   Create New Folder, 53, 166, 231, 311
   Create Or Open Outlook Data File, 315
   Custom, 242
   Customize, 306
   Customize View, 156, 201
   Custom View Organizer, 159
   Delegate Permissions, 221
   Desktop Alert Settings, xliv, 128
   Edit Business Card, 51
   Edit Rule, 289
   Folder Properties, 264
   Font, 37
   Group Schedules, 271
   Import/Export Digital ID, 319
   Inbox Properties, 171
   Insert Business Card, 91
   Insert File, 89
   Internet Accounts, 251
   Journal Options, 256
   Junk E-mail Options, 324
   Location Information, 40
   Mail, 15–16
   Mail Setup, 14
   Microsoft Exchange, 279
   Microsoft Exchange Proxy Settings, 279
   Move Items, 167
   Move Or Copy Pages, 216
   New Outlook Data File, 314

New Profile, 15
New Signature, 108
Open Other User's Folder, 266
Options, 107, 127, 169, 327
Other Settings, 158
Out Of Office Assistant, 288, 292
Page Setup, 138, 209
Plan A Meeting, 26
Print, 66, 137, 208
Propose New Time, 195
Rearrange Commands, 306
Recall This Message, 88
Rename Category, 45
Rules And Alerts, 26, 310, 312
Save As, 257
Save As Web Page, 212
Search Options, 64
Search Text, 310
Select Contacts, 254
Select Members, 47
Send A Calendar Via E-mail, 214
Service Sign-Up, 321
Set Quick Click, 131
Show Fields, 151, 157
Signatures And Stationery, 107
Task Options, 232
Time Zone, 206
To-Do Bar Options, 22
digital certificates, 7
digital IDs
    exporting/importing, lxiv, 319
    multiple, 318
    obtaining, lxiv
digital signatures
    attaching, lxiii, 319
    as default, 317
    defined, 334
    icons for, 319
    viewing information on, 319
Digitally Sign Message button, 319
discussion groups, 250–51
Display As box, in contact records, 40
display name, replacing user name with, 9
displaying
    Contacts pane, 255
    Field Chooser window, 26
    Journal, 256
    Reading Pane, 25
distribution lists, 46, 48. See also contacts
docking menu bar, 23
document libraries, 272–73

document workspaces
    creating from Outlook, lvii, 269
    defined, 334
documents
    sharing, lvii, 269–70, 272–73
    title bar, 31
Documents folder in Windows XP, xv
domains, blocking e-mail from, 326
double-clicking tabs, 78
downloading
    blocked pictures, 322
    Internet calendars, 217
drafts
    defined, 334
    saving, 82
    settings, lxiv
dragging menu bar, 23
due dates, task
    changing, 234
    grouping messages by, 150
    setting for This Week, 235
    specifying, xlv

E

e-mail. See also e-mail accounts; e-mail
        messages
    attachments (see e-mail attachments)
    defined, 334
    digital signatures, 317, 319
    junk (see junk e-mail)
    options, 327
    securing, 317
    signing digitally, 317, 319
e-mail accounts
    adding to profiles, 9–10
    connecting, xxxvii
    different signatures for, 109
    grouping messages by, 150
    Outlook support for different types, 2
    switching between, 10
e-mail addresses
    commas, separating with, 329
    validating, xli, 9, 82
e-mail attachments, 90
    attaching, xlii
    encrypting, 320 (see also digital IDs)
    grouping messages by, 149
    notes, forwarding as, 257
    opening, xliv, 117, 120

e-mail attachments (continued)
  previewing, xliv, 117, 119
  when replying to messages, 124
  restricting permissions for, 321
  saving to hard disk, 117
  searching, 144
  shared (see shared attachments)
  switching between messages and, 120
  viewing details about, 119
e-mail message window, 75-80
e-mail messages
  addressing (see addressing messages)
  appointments, creating from, xlv, 134
  archiving, xlviii, 169, 172 (see also AutoArchive)
  arranging, 148, 151
  attaching files to (see attachments)
  auto-reply (see auto-reply messages)
  autosave settings, 329
  background color, 104
  blocked content, viewing, 322
  business cards (see business cards)
  Calendar items, creating from, 131, 134
  cancelling, xlii, 88
  closing after replying, xlv, 123
  collapsing, 61
  color categories for (see color categories)
  commas as address separators in, 329
  courtesy copies, xlii, 82
  creating, xli
  default appearance of, 100
  deleting, xiiv, 125, 130
  diagrams in (see SmartArt)
  displaying in Reading Pane, 115
  drafts, saving, 82
  encrypting, lxiii, 320
  etiquette, 122
  expanding, 61
  files, attaching (see attachments)
  filtering (see rules)
  flagging, 131–32
  folders (see folders)
  font color, 103
  font size, 103
  formatting text of, xliii
  forwarding (see forwarding e-mail messages)
  graphics in (see SmartArt)
  grouping (see grouping messages)
  headers, 161
  importance of (see importance)
  marking as read, xliv, 116, 130
  marking as unread, 152
  meeting attendees, sending to, 192
  moving into folders, 167

  new, getting notifications for, 126–27
  old, storing, xlviii, 169, 172 (see also AutoArchive)
  opening in own window, 115, 120
  organizing, xlvi (see also folders)
  paging through, with Spacebar, 115
  plain text, 321
  predefined text blocks in (see signatures)
  preventing from being forwarded or copied, 99, 322
  previewing, 26, 116–18, 153
  printing, xlv
  read status, xliv, 116, 130, 152
  recalling, xlii, 88
  receipts, requesting, 99
  replacing, after sending, 88
  replying to (see replying to e-mail messages)
  restricting permissions for, 99
  saving, changing automatic settings for, 329
  schedule information in, li
  sending (see sending messages)
  sensitivity of, 98
  setup, configuring, lxv
  signatures in (see signatures)
  size, grouping by, 150
  SmartArt diagrams in (see SmartArt)
  sorting, 151
  starting, 75
  styles, 101
  tables in, 85–86
  tasks, creating from, xlv, 131
  text, formatting, xliii
  themes, applying, xliii
  tracking, 99
  unread (see unread messages)
  viewing in Reading Pane, consecutively, 115
  voting buttons, 99, 122
E-mail Options button, 81
e-mail pane. See Reading Pane
e-mail server, 334
e-mail signatures, 334
e-mail trails, 334
e-mailing
  business cards, xlii, 91
  calendars (see sharing calendars)
  contacts, 91
Edit Business Card dialog box, 51
Edit Rule dialog box, 289
editing
  business cards, 51, 52
  contacts, xxxviii–xxxix
  tasks, 237
Editor Options window, 299, 301

Editor role for delegating, 263
electronic business cards, 49
  background color, applying, 51
  e-mailing, xlii, 91
  editing, 51–52
  graphics, adding, 51
  sending to other people, 50
  as signatures, 109
electronic notes. See notes; OneNote
emptying Deleted Items folder, 125
Encrypt Message Contents And Attachments
    button, 320
encrypted connection not available message, 7
encryption
  defined, 334
  for individual messages, 320
  for recipients without encryption support, 320
  icon indicating, 320
  S/MIME receipts, requesting for, 320
  setting as default, 320
  with digital IDs, lxiv, 318–19
environment, 30
equipment, requesting for meetings, 190
Event tab, 181
event windows
  defined, 176, 334
  opening, 187
  switching between, 180–81
events. See also appointments
  calendars, viewing grouped by, 198
  creating, 180, 187
  defined, 186, 334
  meetings, converting to, 190
  opening, 187
  recurring, xlix, 187–88
  scheduling, xlix
Events view, 198
Exchange Server, 189
  address list, 37, 334
  connecting to, troubleshooting, 7
  e-mail accounts, ability to configure only
      one, 11
  e-mail accounts, multiple profiles for, 12
  as IMAP account, 7
  Outlook support for, 2
  settings, xxxvii
  sharing folders over, lvi, 262, 268
exercises in book, system requirements for,
    xxvii
Expand button, 61, 155
Expand The Query Builder button, 146

expanding
  e-mail messages, 61
  groups, xlvi
  Navigation Pane, 21
exporting
  address books, xl, 56
  digital IDs, lxiv, 319
external content, blocked, 322

F

Field Chooser window, 26
field codes, 304
fields
  adding/removing, xlvi
  in Inbox, adding/deleting, 157–58
  organizing, 151
  reordering, 157
File As field, in contact records, 40
file attachments, 90
  attaching, xlii
  encrypting, 320 (see also digital IDs)
  grouping messages by, 149
  notes, forwarding as, 257
  opening, xliv, 117, 120
  previewing, xliv, 117, 119
  when replying to messages, 124
  restricting permissions for, 321
  saving to hard disk, 117
  searching, 144
  share (see shared attachments)
  switching between messages and, 120
  viewing details about, 119
File menu. See Office menu
file name extensions, 90
file types, 90
files, attaching to messages. See attachments
filing messages. See archiving messages
filtering
  e-mail messages (see rules)
  Inbox, xlvi, 145
  tasks, as you type, 231
flagging messages
  creating tasks with, 132
  setting task due dates when, 131
floating menu bars/toolbars, 24, 334
folders
  archive settings, 172
  available views, displaying, 26
  bold names, 160
  for contact information, xxxix, 38, 53–54

folders (continued)
  creating, xlviii, 53, 166
  delegating control of, 263
  displaying, 168
  marking for offline use, lix
  moving, 316
  moving messages into, 167
  names, bold, 160
  navigating, 25
  offline availability, 285
  opening, from other user, 266
  organizing messages in, 165
  permissions, changing, 264
  permission to view, requesting, 266
  for RSS feeds, 246–47
  shared, linking to, 268
  SharePoint document libraries as, 272
  sharing, lvi, 262
  structuring, 165
  for tasks, liii, 231
Font button, 102
font color, 103
Font Color button, 103
Font Color gallery, 103
Font dialog box, 37
font size, 103
Font Size button, 103
fonts
  applying to text, 103
  default, 100
foreign alphabets, 58
Format Painter button, 103
Format Text tab, 36, 80, 179, 228
formatting
  collections of (see themes)
  copying, 103
  default, 100
  options for, 100
  Quick Styles, 100–101
  themes (see themes)
formatting marks, 302
forms
  creating, 305
  customizing, 305
  defined, 334
  included with Outlook, 305
  installed, accessing, 305
  libraries, accessing, 305
  Organizational Forms Library, publishing
    to, 305
  properties, 305
  publishing, 305
  saving, 305

forums, 334. See also newsgroups
Forward button, 124, 202
forwarding e-mail messages, xliv, 121, 124
  automatically, when out of the office, lix, 290
    (see also auto-reply messages; Out Of Office
    Assistant)
  preventing, lxiii, 99, 322
  specifying signature for, 122
forwarding notes, lvi, 257
free/busy information, 191
freezing menu bar, 23

G

GAL (Global Address List), 37, 334
galleries
  Bullets, 85
  Colors, 96
  Font Color, 103
  Layouts, 96
  Page Color, 104
  Quick Styles, 101
  SmartArt Styles, 96
  Themes, 105
getting help
  with book/companion CD, xxxi
  on the Internet, xxxv
  with Outlook, xxxi
  ScreenTips and, 302, 304
Global Address List (GAL), 37, 334
global formatting
  defined, 334
  options, 100
glossary terms, formatting of, xxiv
graphics
  blocked, downloading, 322
  in business cards, 51 (see also business cards)
  in e-mail messages (see SmartArt)
  placeholders, turning on/off, 304
gridlines, 158
Group By box, 26
group schedules
  creating, lvi, 271
  defined, 334
  viewing, 271
Group Schedules dialog box, 271
grouping messages, 149
  by color categories, 161, 164
  by sender, 154
groups
  collapsing, 155

defined, 334
Dialog Box Launcher, 32, 36, 99
expanding/collapsing, xlvi

H

hard disk requirements for Office 2007, xxvii
headers
  adding, 140
  color-coding, 161
help
  with book/companion CD, xxxi
  on the Internet, xxxv
  with Outlook, xxxi
  ScreenTips and, 302, 304
hiding
  appointments, 184
  Field Chooser window, 26
  Navigation Pane, 21
  Reading Pane, 25
  Ribbon, 79
  tabs, 79
High importance, 98
holidays, l, 203
HTML message format, 80, 335
HTTP
  connecting Outlook over, lvii, 279
  defined, 335
  e-mail accounts, 307
hyperlinks in notes, 253
Hypertext Markup Language (HTML) message
      format, 80, 335
Hypertext Transfer Protocol (HTTP)
  connecting Outlook over, lvii, 279
  defined, 335
  e-mail accounts, 307

I

icons
  for digital signatures, 319
  for encrypted messages, 320
  for new mail, 126
  for recurring events, 188
  for toolbar buttons, xxiv
.ics files, 213–14
images
  blocked, downloading, 322
  in business cards, 51 (see also business cards)

in e-mail messages (see SmartArt)
  placeholders, turning on/off, 304
IMAP message format, 80, 335
Import And Export Wizard, 56
Import/Export Digital ID dialog box, 319
importance, 98
  default, changing, 329
  defined, 335
  grouping messages by, 150
Important paragraphs, xxiv
importing
  digital certificates, 7
  digital IDs, lxiv, 319
  SharePoint Contacts List, xli, 31
Inactive Message flag, 132
Inbox
  conversations in, 149
  default settings, restoring, xlvi
  fields in, 157–58
  filtering, xlvi
  filtering to display search results, 145
  grid lines, customizing, 158
  searching in, 145
  sorting, by category, xlvii
  threaded conversations in, 149
Inbox Properties dialog box, 171
incomplete tasks, 241
index of book, how to use, xxiii
Information Rights Management (IRM), 321.
      See also permissions
Insert Business Card button, 91
Insert Business Card dialog box, 91
Insert File dialog box, 89
Insert SmartArt button, 92
Insert tab, 35, 79, 179, 228
inserting
  business cards, in messages, 91
  files, in e-mail messages (see attachments)
  signatures, xliii
  SmartArt, in messages, 92
  tables, 85
Install Certificate button, 7
installing
  digital certificates, 7
  practice files, xxviii
  printers, 140, 208
Instant Search, xlvi, 62, 144. See also searching
  contacts, finding with, xl
  implementing, 145
interface elements in exercises, formatting of,
      xxiv
internal addresses, addressing messages to, 81

Internet Accounts dialog box, 251
Internet calendars, 216
Internet calls, 44
Internet Message Access Protocol (IMAP),
     80, 335
Invite Attendees button, 181
inviting meeting attendees, 182. See also
     meetings
IRM (Information Rights Management), 321.
     See also permissions

J

Journal
   activating, 256
   defined, 335
   displaying, lv, 256
   recording activities with, lv
Journal button, lv, 256
Journal Options dialog box, 256
junk e-mail, 323
   defined, 335
   deleting automatically, 325
   level of protection, selecting, 324
   notifications of receipt, 322
   Web beacons, 322
Junk E-Mail Filter, lxiv, 323
Junk E-Mail Options dialog box, 324

K

keyboard shortcuts
   assigning to color categories, 163
   available, 298
   defined, 335
   in ScreenTips, turning on/off, 304

L

languages, displaying additional, 58
Large Mail folder, 160
Layouts gallery, 96
libraries, document, 272–73. See also document
     workspaces
linking
   calendars, to OneNote, 216
   contacts, to notes, 254
   OneNote notes, to Outlook, 243
   to shared folders, 268

lists
   changing level in, 85
   creating, 84
   promoting/demoting list items in, 85
local formatting, 335
Location Information dialog box, 40
logos on business cards, 51. See also business
     cards
Low detail level, setting in calendar, 202

M

Mail dialog box, 15, 16
Mail module, 74
Mail Setup dialog box, 14
mailbox, viewing size of, 169
Mailbox Cleanup, 169
mailing address, specifying default for
     contacts, 41
maps of contact addresses, displaying, 44
Mark Complete button, 241
marketing communications, distributing with
     Business Contact Manager, 13
marking e-mail messages as read, 116
   manually, xliv
   with desktop alerts, xliv, 130
marking tasks as complete, liv, 241
Medium detail level, setting in calendar, 202
meeting requests
   accepting, 192, 195
   attendee status, 191
   creating, 44, 190
   declining, 192, 195
   defined, 188, 335
   delivering to delegate, liii, 220
   Optional Attendee status, 191
   Required Attendee status, 191
   for resources, 190
   responding to, xlix, l, 192, 194–195
   scheduling, 191
   sending, xlix
   status, of attendees, 191
   tentative bookings, 191
Meeting tab, 181
meeting window, 176, 182, 335
Meeting Workspace button, 193
meeting workspaces, 193, 335
meetings
   addressing to currently selected contact, 26
   attendees, adding, 191
   conflicting appointments, viewing, 194

creating, 181
events, converting to, 190
Exchange Server 2007 and, 189
inviting attendees, 182
modifying, 192
proposing new time for, l, 192, 194
requesting (see meeting requests)
rescheduling, 190
scheduling, 188
time, changing, 191
updating, 190
memory requirement for Office 2007, xxvii
menu bar
docking, 23
dragging, 23
floating, 24
moving, 23
menus
closing, 35
collapsing, 178
new organization of, xii
Message button, 118
message headers
adding, 140
color-coding, 161
defined, 335
message importance, 98
default, changing, 329
defined, 335
grouping messages by, 150
Message tab, 78
message window
defined, 74, 335
opening, 75
Ribbon (see Ribbon)
messages, e-mail
addressing (see addressing messages)
appointments, creating from, xlv, 134
archiving, xlviii, 169, 172 (see also AutoArchive)
arranging, 148, 151
attaching files to (see attachments)
auto-reply (see auto-reply messages)
autosave settings, 329
background color, 104
blocked content, viewing, 322
business cards (see business cards)
Calendar items, creating from, 131, 134
cancelling, xlii, 88
closing after replying, xlv, 123
collapsing, 61
color categories for (see color categories)
commas as address separators in, 329

courtesy copies, xlii, 82
creating, xli
default appearance of, 100
deleting, xliv, 125, 130
diagrams in (see SmartArt)
displaying in Reading Pane, 115
drafts, saving, 82
encrypting, lxiii, 320
etiquette, 122
expanding, 61
files, attaching (see attachments)
filtering (see rules)
flagging, 131–32
folders (see folders)
font color, 103
font size, 103
formatting text of, xliii
forwarding (see forwarding e-mail messages)
graphics in (see SmartArt)
grouping (see grouping messages)
headers, 161
importance of (see importance)
marking as read, xliv, 116, 130
marking as unread, 152
meeting attendees, sending to, 192
moving into folders, 167
new, getting notifications for, 126–27
old, storing, xlviii, 169, 172 (see also AutoArchive)
opening in own window, 115, 120
organizing, xlvi (see also folders)
paging through, with Spacebar, 115
plain text, 321
predefined text blocks in (see signatures)
preventing from being forwarded or copied, 99, 322
previewing, 26, 116–18, 153
printing, xlv
recalling, xlii, 88
receipts, requesting, 99
replacing, after sending, 88
replying to (see replying to e-mail messages)
restricting permissions for, 99
saving, changing automatic settings for, 329
schedule information in, li
sending (see sending messages)
sensitivity of, 98
setup, configuring, lxv
signatures in (see signatures)
size, grouping by, 150
SmartArt diagrams in (see SmartArt)
starting, 75

messages, e-mail (continued)
   styles, 101
   tables in, 85–86
   tasks, creating from, xlv, 131
   text, formatting, xliii
   themes, applying, xliii
   tracking, 99
   unread (see unread messages)
   viewing in Reading Pane, consecutively, 115
   voting buttons, 99, 122
Microsoft Exchange dialog box, 279
Microsoft Exchange Proxy Settings dialog
      box, 279
Microsoft Exchange Server, 189
   address list, 37, 334
   connecting to, troubleshooting, 7
   defined, 335
   e-mail accounts, ability to configure only
      one, 11
   e-mail accounts, multiple profiles for, 12
   as IMAP account, 7
   Outlook support for, 2
   settings, xxxvii
   sharing folders over, lvi, 262, 268
Microsoft Knowledge Base, xxxv
Microsoft Office 2007, xxvi
Microsoft Office Button, 30, 335
Microsoft Office OneNote
   calendars, linking to, lii, 216
   contacts, linking to, xli, 71
   moving pages in, 168
   notes in, linking to Outlook, 243
   notes in, moving, 216
   sending e-mail messages to, xlviii, 168
Microsoft Office SharePoint Server 2007
      document libraries, lvii, 272-73
Microsoft Office Outlook
   automatic setup, 3
   customizing, lxi, 301
   e-mail accounts supported by, 2
   Inbox (see Inbox)
   left pane, 21, 199
   Navigation Pane, 21, 199
   profiles (see profiles)
   setting up, 3, 7
   starting, 3
   uses for, xi
Microsoft Press Knowledge Base, xxxi
Microsoft Product Support Services, xxxv
Microsoft Windows SharePoint site, 193
Microsoft Windows XP
   dialog boxes in, navigating, xvii

   practice files, managing, xv
   Start menu, xvi
   starting Outlook on, xvi
   virtual private network (VPN) connection,
      setting up under, lviii, 282
Mini toolbar, 102, 302, 335
Minimize button, 31
minimizing
   Daily Task List, 230
   Navigation Pane, 21
   To-Do Bar, 21, 230
Mobile Address Book, 38, 335
modules, defined, 335
monitor requirements for Office 2007, xxvii
Monthly Style for printed calendars, 207
Move Items dialog box, 167
Move Or Copy Pages dialog box, 216
Move Up button, 300
moving
   appointments, 183
   desktop alert location, 129
   menu bar, 23
   messages, into folders, 167
   Quick Access Toolbar, 76
   Reading Pane, 22
   Ribbon, 77

N

name bar, 31
names, contact. See contacts
naming profiles, 15
navigating
   calendars, 199, 202
   contacts, 57
   folders, 25
Navigation Pane
   expanding, 21
   minimizing, 21
   widening, 199
networking. See sharing
New Appointment button, 177, 190
New Contact button, 33, 40, 47
New Mail Message button, 75, 83, 89, 129, 329
New Mail Message icon, 126
new mail notifications, 126–27
new messages. See unread messages
New Note button, 253
New Outlook Data File dialog box, 314
New Profile dialog box, 15
New Signature dialog box, 108

New Task button, 226, 236
News command on toolbar, 250
news feeds
  deleting, 248
  folders for, 246–47
  readers for, 246
  removing, liv
  subscribing to, liv, 248
  updating, 246
  viewing available, 247
newsgroups
  accessing, 250
  adding, 251
  defined, 335
  reading, 250
newsreaders, defined, 250
notes, 251. See also OneNote
  closing, 253
  color, 252
  contacts, adding to, lv, 254
  creating, lv, 253
  default settings, 252
  defined, 335
  displaying, 252
  files, saving as, 257
  formatting, lv
  forwarding, lvi, 257
  hyperlinks in, 253
  opening, lvi
  Reading Pane and, 252
  saving, 253
  saving, as files, lvi
  searching in, 252
  sharing, 257
  text, adding, 253
  views for, 251
Notes About This Item button, 216
Notes button, 252
notification of new e-mail messages, 126–27
notification windows. See desktop alerts
numbered steps, formatting conventions used
    in, xxiv

O

Office 2007 system requirements, xxvi
Office Button, 30, 335
Office menu, 30, 178
Office Online Web site, 217
offline address books, 286, 336
offline content

defined, 283
download options, 284
files in document libraries, 273
Offline Server Documents, 273
OneNote. See also notes
  calendars, linking to, lii, 216
  contacts, linking to, xli, 71
  moving pages in, 168
  notes in, linking to Outlook, 243
  notes in, moving, 216
  sending e-mail messages to, xlviii, 168
opening
  appointment window, 177, 184
  attachments, xliv, 117, 120
  contact records, 42
  Control Panel, 14
  data files, lxiii, 316
  e-mail messages, in own window, 115, 120
  events, 187
  folders, from other user, 266
  message window, 75
  notes, lvi
  Outlook, 3
  Personal Folders files, 316
  Print Preview, 137
  task window, 235
Open Other User's Folder dialog box, 266
OPEN paragraphs, xxiv
operating system version required for Office
    2007, xxvii
Optional Attendee status, 191
Options dialog box, 107, 127, 169, 327
Options tab, 79
Organizational Forms Library, 305
organizations, addressing messages within, 81
Other Actions button, 88
Other Settings dialog box, 158
Out Of Office Assistant. See also auto-reply
    messages
  defined, 336
  Exchange Server 2003 features, 288
  Exchange Server 2007 features, 292
  using to set time as, 158
Out Of Office Assistant dialog box, 288, 292
Outlook
  automatic setup, 3
  with Business Contact Manager, 13
  customizing, lxi, 301
  e-mail accounts supported by, 2
  Inbox (see Inbox)
  Navigation Pane, 21, 199
  profiles (see profiles)

Outlook (continued)
  setting up, 3, 7
  starting, 3
  uses for, xi
Outlook 2007 Standard Forms Library, 305
Outlook 2007 Startup wizard, xxxvii, 3
Outlook 2007 with Business Contact
    Manager, 13
Outlook Address Books, defined, page 336
Outlook Anywhere, lvii, 279, 336
Outlook Data Files view, 199
Outlook forms
  creating, 305
  customizing, 305
  included with Outlook, 305
  installed, accessing, 305
  libraries, accessing, 305
  Organizational Forms Library, publishing
    to, 305
  properties, 305
  publishing, 305
  saving, 305
Outlook Today page, 25
Outlook Web Access (OWA), 283
Outlook with Business Contact Manager, 13
Outlook Rich Text Format (RTF), defined, 336
Overlay mode, viewing multiple calendars
    in, 219
Overtype mode, 304
overview page, 25
OWA (Outlook Web Access), 283

P

page color, 104
Page Color button, 104
Page Color gallery, 104
Page Setup button, 138
Page Setup dialog box, 138, 209
Paste Options button, 304
people. See contacts
permissions. See also Information Rights
    Management (IRM)
  for calendars, delegating, liii, 20
  defined, 336
  restricting, 99
  for sharing folders, 262
  for subfolder creation, granting, 263
  to view folders, requesting, 266
Personal, setting messages as, 98

Personal Folders files
  backing up, 314
  creating, lxii, 56, 314
  defined, 336
  expanding, 316
  exporting to older version of Outlook, 315
  folders, moving to, 316
  folders in, default, 316
  moving messages to, lxii
  opening, 316
personalizing. See customizing
phishing messages, 323, 336. See also junk
    e-mail
Phone List view, 57
phone lists, xl. See also contacts
phone numbers, 40
pictures
  blocked, downloading, 322
  in business cards, 51 (see also business cards)
  in e-mail messages (see SmartArt)
  placeholders, turning on/off, 304
plain text messages, lxiii, 80, 321, 336
Plan A Meeting dialog box, 26
pop-up toolbars, 102, 302
pop-up windows for alerts. See desktop alerts
POP3, 336
populating distribution lists, 46, 48. See also
    contacts
Post-It Notes. See notes
Post Office Protocol 3 (POP3), 336
practice files, xxv
  installing, xxviii
  in Windows XP, location of, xv
Preview button, 208
previewing
  attachments, xliv, 117, 119
  e-mail messages, 26, 116–17, 153
  as printed (see Print Preview)
Print button, 66, 208
Print dialog box, 66, 137, 208
Print Preview
  opening, 25, 67, 137, 208
  scrolling, 210
Print Preview button, 67
print styles, 137, 210, 336
printer installation, 140, 208
printing
  address cards, xli
  calendars, li
  contacts, selected, 70
  e-mail messages, xlv
  phone lists, xl

printing calendars, 207
  date range, selecting, 210
  default styles for, 207
  previewing (see Print Preview)
  print styles, 210
  printer, selecting, 209
printing e-mail messages
  with default options, 137
  headers for, 140
  paper options, 139
  print styles, 137
printing range, selecting, 67
priority. See importance
privacy, 322
Private, marking items as, 98, 184
Private button, 184
private stores, 314, 336
process diagrams. See SmartArt
processor requirement for Office 2007, xxvii
profiles
  adding, 15
  adding e-mail accounts to, 9–10
  choosing, when prompted, 16
  creating, xxxviii
  displaying current, 14
  multiple, 12
  naming, 15
  prompting for on startup, xxxviii, 16
  renaming, 15
  setting as default, 12, 17
  storage location of, 12
  switching between, 14
program interface elements in exercises,
    formatting of, xxiv
projects, organizing with Business Contact
    Manager, 13
promoting bulleted list items, 85
Propose New Time dialog box, 195
Propose Time button, 195
proposing new meeting time, 192, 194
protecting e-mail, 317. See also digital
    signatures; encryption; plain text messages;
    Information Rights Management (IRM)
protecting privacy, 322
.pst files
  backing up, 314
  creating, lxii, 56, 314
  expanding, 316
  exporting to older version of Outlook, 315
  folders, moving to, 316
  folders in, default, 316
  moving messages to, lxii
  opening, 316

publishing
  calendars, 212
  forms, 305

Q

Quick Access Toolbar, 30, 298
  adding items to, in contact window, 31
  buttons, adding, lx, 299
  buttons, moving, 300
  buttons, removing, 301
  commands on, 31
  commands on, adding, 77
  customizing, 76, 299
  defined, 336
  moving, 76–77
Quick Click categories, 161
Quick Launch bar. See Quick Access Toolbar
Quick Print, 137
Quick Reference, how to use, xxiii
Quick Styles, 100, 336
Quick Styles gallery, 101

R

RAM requirement for Office 2007, xxvii
reading newsgroups, 250
Reading Pane
  closing, 23
  displaying, 230
  displaying messages in, 115
  moving, 22
  notes and, 252
  position of, 115
  previewing attachments in, 117, 119
  previewing e-mail messages in, 118
  task details in, 234
  turning on/off, 25
  viewing consecutive messages in, 115
Really Simple Syndication (RSS) feeds
  defined, 336
  deleting, 248
  folders for, 246–47
  readers for, 246
  removing, liv
  subscribing to, liv, 248
  updating, 246
  viewing available, 247
Rearrange Commands dialog box, 306
rearranging. See sorting

Recall This Message dialog box, 88
recalling messages, xlii, 88, 336
receipts for delivery, 99
recent searches, viewing, 64
recipients, grouping messages by, 150
reclaiming declined tasks, 239
recording activities. See Journal
records, contact. See also contacts
  addressing messages from, 44
  assigning tasks from, 44
  Business Card area (see electronic business
    cards)
  Display As box, 40
  File As field, 40
  maps of contact addresses, displaying, 44
  meeting requests, creating from, 44
  placing Internet calls from, 44
  Web sites, displaying from, 44
Recurrence button, 185, 187
recurring, defined, 336
recurring appointments, 182, 185, 188
Recurring Appointments view, 198
recurring events
  creating, xlix, 187
  default settings, 187
  icon indicating, 188
refining searches, 146. See also searching
relocating the Ribbon, 77
Reminder button, 184
reminders
  for appointments, 182, 184
  defined, 336
  deleting, 240
  dismissing, 233
  setting, 232, 236
  setting snooze for, 233
  for tasks, 239
  turning off, liv
remote connections, 278
remote procedure calls (RPC), defined, 336
Rename Category dialog box, 45
renaming
  color categories, xlvii, 162
  profiles, 15
  Search Folders, xlvii
reordering
  columns, 157
  contacts, xl
  contacts, by column, 59
  e-mail messages, 151
  task lists, 230
repeating appointments, 182, 185, 188

replacing messages after sending, 88
Reply button, 123
replying to e-mail messages, xliv
  all recipients included, 121
  attachments and, 124 (see also attachments)
  automatically (see auto-reply messages; Out Of
    Office Assistant)
  closing message after, xlv, 123
  preventing, lxiii
  Reply To All function, disabling for
    recipients, 122
  specifying signature for, 122
Request A Delivery Receipt command, 300
requesting meetings. See meeting requests
Required Attendee status, 191
resending messages, 88, 337
Reset Current View button, 157
resetting
  calendars, to default display, 201
  toolbars, to default, 307
  views, to original settings, 159
resolving, defined, 337
resolving e-mail addresses, xli, 9, 82
resources, requesting for meetings, 190
responding to e-mail messages, xliv
  all recipients included, 121
  attachments and, 124 (see also attachments)
  automatically (see auto-reply messages; Out Of
    Office Assistant)
  closing message after, xlv, 123
  preventing, lxiii
  Reply To All function, disabling for
    recipients, 122
  specifying signature for, 122
Restore Down/Maximize button, 31
restoring Inbox to default settings, xlvi
restricting message permissions, 99
retention policies, 169
Return To Task List button, 239
Reviewer role for delegating, 263
Ribbon, xii, 32, 78. See also tabs
  in calendar item windows, 179–181
  in contact window, 35–37
  defined, 337
  hiding, 79
  in message window, 76–80
  moving, 77
  in task window, 228
Rich Text Format (RTF) files, 80
  defined, 337
  saving notes as, 257
RPC (remote procedure calls), defined, 336

RPC over HTTP. See Outlook Anywhere
RSS feeds
  deleting, 248
  folders for, 246–47
  readers for, 246
  removing, liv
  subscribing to, liv, 248
  updating, 246
  viewing available, 247
RSS Feeds folder, 247
RSS Subscriptions folder, 247
RTF files, 80
  defined, 337
  saving notes as, 257
rules, 307
  actions, specifying, 310
  client, 307
  creating, lxii, 308
  criteria, specifying, 309
  defined, 337
  HTTP e-mail accounts and, 307
  managing, 26
  running, 312
  saving, 312
  server, 307
  templates for, 309
Rules And Alerts dialog box, 26, 310, 312
Rules And Alerts window, 308
Rules wizard, 308

S

safeguarding e-mail, 317. See also digital
    signatures; encryption; plain text messages;
    Information Rights Management (IRM)
Safe Recipients List, 322, 325
Safe Senders List, 322, 325
sales metrics, reviewing with Business Contact
    Manager, 13
sans serif, 337
Save & Close button, 41, 46, 184, 188, 236
Save As dialog box, 257
Save As Web Page dialog box, 212
saved addresses. See contacts
saving
  attachments, to hard disk, 117
  calendars, as Web pages, lii, 212
  drafts, lxiv
  e-mail messages, 82, 329
  forms, 305

notes, lvi, 253, 257
rules, 312
scams. See junk e-mail; phishing messages
schedules, group
  creating, lvi, 271
  defined, 334
  viewing, 271
scheduling
  appointments, xlviii
  auto-reply messages, lx
  events, xlix
Scheduling button, 191
scheduling events and appointments. See
    appointments; events
screen resolution minimum for Office 2007,
    xxvii
ScreenTips
  defined, 337
  keyboard shortcuts displayed in, turning
    on/off, 304
  style, setting, 302
Search Folders
  creating, 160
  custom, xlvii
  customizing, xlvii, 160
  displaying, 160
  modifying messages in, 160
  renaming, xlvii
  updating, 160
Search Options dialog box, 64
Search Text dialog box, 310
searches
  clearing, 148
  criteria, adding, 146
  folders for (see Search Folders)
  messages no longer appearing in, 148
  refining, 146
  results, displaying in folder (see Search Folders)
searching. See also Instant Search
  address books, xlii
  attachments, 144
  clearing results of, 64
  contacts, xl, 63
  folders, all, 148
  Inbox, 145
  narrowing results of, 145
  notes, 252
  recent searches, 64
  setting options for, 64
  for tasks, 231
Secure Multipurpose Internet Mail extensions
    (S/MIME), 317, 337

securing e-mail, 317. See also digital signatures; encryption; plain text messages; Information Rights Management (IRM)
Security Alert message box, 7
security certificates, 7
See Also paragraphs, xxiv
Select Contacts dialog box, 254
Select Members button, 47
Select Members dialog box, 47
Send A Calendar Via E-mail dialog box, 214
Send button, 53, 87, 90, 192, 239, 258, 267
Send Status Report button, 240
Send To OneNote button, 168
senders, grouping messages by, 150, 154
sending address books, xl, 56
sending calendars as e-mail, li
    customizing level of detail for, 213
    date range, selecting, 214
    on the Web, 212
sending messages, xli, 87. See also e-mail messages
    configuring, lxv
    courtesy copies, xlii, 82
    to meeting attendees, 192
    from multiple accounts, 10
    to OneNote, xlviii, 168
    from Sent Items folder, 88
sensitivity, 98, 337
Sent Items folder, 88
server certificates, 7
server configuration, 5, 8
server rules, 307, 337
Service Sign-Up dialog box, 321
Set Quick Click dialog box, 131
setting up
    Outlook, 3, 7
    server settings, 5, 8
shared attachments, 87
    creating document workspaces with, 269
    defined, 337
    sending, lvii, 270
shared meeting sites, 193
shared resources, 190
SharePoint calendars, 274
SharePoint Contacts List, xli, 31
SharePoint document libraries
    connecting to Outlook, lvii, 273
    editing offline, 273
    as folders, 272
    offline files, editing, 273
    previewing items in, 273
    read-only items in, 273
SharePoint Lists folder, 273

SharePoint meeting workspaces, 193
SharePoint sites, connecting to, lvii, 272
sharing
    address books, xl, 53
    contacts folders, 53
    documents, lvii, 269–70, 272–73
    folders, lvi, 262
    notes, 257
    permissions for, changing, 264
sharing calendars, li
    customizing level of detail for, 213
    date range, selecting, 214
    on the Web, 212
Show As button, 184
Show Bcc button, 82
Show Fields dialog box, 151, 157
showing. See displaying
signatures
    associating with accounts, 109
    business cards as, 109
    creating, xliii, 106–107
    default, setting, 109
    defined, 337
    deleting from messages, 110
    formatting, 108
    including by default, 109
    inserting, xliii
    multiple, for different accounts, 109
    specifying different for replies and forwards, 122
Signatures And Stationery dialog box, 107
Signatures button, 107
signing e-mail digitally. See digital IDs; digital signatures
Single Key Reading Using Space Bar option, 115
size, grouping messages by, 150
smart cut and paste, 304
Smart Tags, 304
SmartArt
    defined, 337
    inserting in messages, xlii–xliii, 92
    shapes, adding, 94
    text, adding, 94
    Text Pane, displaying, 93
SmartArt Styles gallery, 96
S/MIME (Secure Multipurpose Internet Mail extensions), 317, 337
sorting
    columns, 157
    contacts, xl, 59
    e-mail messages, 151
    task lists, 230
sounds for new mail notifications, 127

spam, 323
  defined, 337
  deleting automatically, 325
  level of protection, selecting, 324
  notifications of receipt, 322
  Web beacons, 322
standard color categories, 44
Standard Forms Library, 305
start dates, grouping messages by, 150
starting
  e-mail messages, 75
  Outlook, on Windows Vista, 3
  Outlook, on Windows XP, xvi
Startup wizard, xxxvii, 3
status, task, 237. See also tasks
Step by Step series conventions, xxiii
sticky notes. See notes
storing old messages. See archiving messages
street addresses
  checking validity of, 41
  displaying maps of, 44
  entering, for contacts, 40
structuring folders, 165
Style Sets, 101
styles, changing all, 101
subfolders, creating, 263
subjects, grouping messages by, 150
subscribing
  to Internet calendars, 217
  to newsgroups, 250–51
  to RSS feeds (see RSS feeds)
suppressing. See hiding
Swap Time Zones button, 207
switching
  between e-mail accounts, 10
  between profiles, 14
synchronizing, 337
system requirements for Office 2007, xxvi

T

Table button, 85
table of contents, how to use, xxiii
tables
  entering information in, 86
  inserting, 85
tabs, 32, 298. See also Ribbon
  Appointment, 179
  Business Tools, 35
  Contact, 35
  contextual, 86

  defined, 337
  double-clicking, 78
  Event, 181
  Format Text, 36, 80, 179, 228
  hiding, 79
  hiding commands on, 78
  Insert, 35, 79, 179, 228
  Meeting, 181
  Message, 78
  Options, 79
  Task, 228
task creation, liii, 226, 232, 234–36
  from e-mail messages, xlv, 131
  by flagging messages, 132
task list, 337. See also To-Do List
Task Options dialog box, 232
task originator, defined, 337
task owner, defnined, 337
task reminders
  deleting, 240
  setting, 232, 236
  setting snooze for, 233
task requests, 238–39. See also assigning tasks
task status
  changing, 237
  reports, sending, liv, 240
  updating, liv
Task tab, 228
task window, 224, 235, 337
tasks
  assigning to others (see assigning tasks; task
    requests)
  availability of, 231
  categories, changing, 235
  color, changing default settings for, 232
  completed, displaying, 241
  declined, reclaiming, 239
  delegating, liii
  deleting, liv, 240, 242
  details, displaying, 236
  due dates, changing, 231, 234
  due dates, setting, xlv, 131, 236
  due each day, displaying, 230
  filtering as you type, 231
  flagging for completion This Week, 235
  folders, creating for, liii, 231
  incomplete, displaying, 241
  information for inclusion in, 232
  marking as complete, liv, 240–41
  modifying, 232
  percentage complete, changing, 237
  Reading Pane details, 234

tasks (continued)
  reordering, 230
  searching for, 231
  status of, 237
  To-Do List, removing from, 240
  updating, liii, 237
  viewing, 229
  views, 229–30
Tasks button, 133, 225
team calendars, 274
templates
  for message formatting (see themes)
  for rules, 309
text
  converting to bulleted list, 84
  copied, choosing source or destination
    formatting for, 304
  copying formatting of, 103
  fonts for, 100, 103
text animation, 304
text files, notes as, 257
text messages, lxiii, 80, 321
Text Pane button, 93
text wrapping, 304
themes
  applying, xliii, 104
  modifying, 105
Themes button, 104
Themes gallery, 105
third-party add-ins, defined, 337
threaded conversations, 149, ee7
thumb tabs in book, how to use, xxiii
time periods in Calendar, switching between, 198
time slots, appointment, 183. See also
    appointments
Time Zone dialog box, 206
time zones
  appointments, scheduling across, 180
  changing, li, 206
  displaying multiple, li, 206
  setting, 181
  switching between, 207
Time Zones button, 180
timelines, creating. See Journal
Tip paragraphs, xxiv
title bar, 31, 337
To-Do Bar, 224
  closing, 22
  customizing, 22
  minimizing, 21, 230
  tasks on, 225
  To-Do List, displaying on, 230

To-Do Bar Options dialog box, 22
To-Do List
  defined, 338
  increasing space allotted to, 230
  link with Calendar, 223
  tasks, removing from, 240
  To-Do Bar, displaying on, 230
Toolbar Options button, 250, 306
toolbars
  buttons on, lxi, 306
  commands, rearranging, lxi
  displaying, 24
  floating, 24
  Mini, 102, 302
  new organization of, xii
  primary (see Ribbon)
  Quick Access (see Quick Access Toolbar)
  resetting to default, lxi, 307
tracking
  activities (see Journal)
  changes, 304
  messages, 99
Tri-fold Style for printed calendars, 207
troubleshooting setup, 7
Trust Center, 317–21, 323
turning off
  AutoPreview, 26
  desktop alerts, xliv, 128
  reminders, liv
turning on AutoPreview, 117, 153
type, grouping messages by, 150

U

Undo button, 26
undoing, 26
Unicode character sets, defined, 338
Unified Messaging, 284
Uniform Resource Locators (URLs), 338
units of measurement, 304
Unread Mail folder, 160
unread messages
  appearance of, 115, 153
  cursor changing to indicate, 329
  displaying only, 155
  marking messages as, 152
updating
  meetings, 190
  RSS feeds, 246
  Search Folders, 160
  tasks, liii, liv, 237

URLs (Uniform Resource Locators), 338
USE paragraphs, xxiv
Usenet. See newsgroups
user environment, 30
user folder access, lvi, 262
user input in exercises, formatting of, xxiv
user name
  replacing with display name, xli, 9, 82
  setting, 302

V

validating e-mail addresses, xli, 9, 82
verifying digital certificates, 7
View Certificate button, 7
View In Overlay Mode button, 219
View In Side-By-Side Mode button, 220
views, 148. See also specific views
  calendar, 198–99
  Current View list, 26
  customizing, 156
  for Daily Task List, toggling, 230
  default settings, returning to, 199
  defined, 338
  for notes, 251
  resetting to original settings, 159
  switching, 148–49, 230
  for tasks, 229
  for To-Do Bar, switching between, 230
virtual folders, 160, 338
virtual private network (VPN)
  connecting to, 281
  disconnecting from, 281
  setting up connection to, lviii, 281–82
voting buttons, 99, 122, 338
VPN (virtual private network)
  connecting to, 281
  disconnecting from, 281
  setting up connection to, lviii, 281–82

W

warnings for appointments, 182, 184
Ways To Organize pane, 230
Web beacons, 322, 338
Web logs, 246, 333. See also RSS feeds
Web pages
  publishing calendars as, lii, 212
  viewing, from contact records, 26
Web sites
  blogs, 246, 333 (see also RSS feeds)
  displaying from contact records, 44
Web toolbar, 25
week numbers, displaying in calendar, 199
Weekly Style for printed calendars, 207
weeks. See work week
Windows XP
  dialog boxes in, navigating, xvii
  practice files, managing, xv
  Start menu, xvi
  starting Outlook on, xvi
  virtual private network (VPN) connection,
    setting up under, lviii, 282
wizards
  Rules, 308
  Startup, 3
work day, setting, 205
work week
  default, 204
  defined, 338
  displaying, 201, 204
  setting, li, 205
Work Week view, 198
working offline, 283–84
workspaces, document, lvii, 269–70, 272–73
wrapping text, 304

X

XP. See Windows XP

What do you think of this book?

We want to hear from you!

Do you have a few minutes to participate in a brief online survey?

Microsoft is interested in hearing your feedback so we can continually improve our books and learning resources for you.

To participate in our survey, please visit:

www.microsoft.com/learning/booksurvey/

...and enter this book's ISBN-10 number (appears above barcode on back cover*). As a thank-you to survey participants in the United States and Canada, each month we'll randomly select five respondents to win one of five $100 gift certificates from a leading online merchant. At the conclusion of the survey, you can enter the drawing by providing your e-mail address, which will be used for prize notification only.

Thanks in advance for your input. Your opinion counts!

* Where to find the ISBN-10 on back cover

ISBN-13: 000-0-0000-0000-0
ISBN-10: 0-0000-00000

0 0 0 0 0

0 000000 000000

Example only. Each book has unique ISBN.

Microsoft Press